THE TATTOOED GIRL

ALSO BY DAN BURSTEIN AND ARNE DE KEIJZER

The Secrets Series
Secrets of the Code
Secrets of Angels & Demons
Secrets of the Widow's Son (by David A. Shugarts)
Secrets of Mary Magdalene
Secrets of 24
Secrets of the Lost Symbol

Big Dragon: The Future of China:
What It Means for Business, the Economy, and the Global Order

The Best Things Ever Said About the
Rise, Fall, and Future of the Internet Economy

PREVIOUS TITLES BY DAN BURSTEIN
Blog!
Road Warriors
Turning the Tables
Euroquake
Yen!

ALSO BY JOHN-HENRI HOLMBERG
Drömmar om evigheten: science fictions historia
Kvinnor i science fiction (with Per W. Insulander)
Fantasy
Dunkla drifter och mörka motiv: om psykologiska och romantiska thrillers
Inre landskap och yttre rymd: science fictions historia I–II
Filmtema

AS EDITOR
Framtiden inför rätta
Den fantastiska julen
Cyberpunk
Första stora science fiction-boken
När allt förändrades

THE TATTOOED GIRL

The Enigma of Stieg Larsson and the Secrets Behind the Most Compelling Thrillers of Our Time

DAN BURSTEIN,

ARNE DE KEIJZER, *and*

JOHN-HENRI HOLMBERG

St. Martin's Griffin ⚜ New York

www.stmartins.com

Map by Paul J. Pugliese

Book design by Rich Arnold

Library of Congress Cataloging-in-Publication Data

Burstein, Daniel.
     The tattooed girl : the enigma of Stieg Larsson and the secrets behind the
most compelling thrillers of our time / Dan Burstein, Arne de Keijzer, and
John-Henri Holmberg.—1st ed.
         p. cm.
     ISBN 978-0-312-61056-2
     1. Larsson, Stieg, 1954–2004.   I. De Keijzer, Arne J.   II. Holmberg,
John-Henri, 1949–   III. Title.
PT9876.22 A6933Z79 2011
839.73'8—dc22

                                                                    2011008086

First Edition: May 2011

10   9   8   7   6   5   4   3   2   1

For Julie, in celebration of our two Stockholm adventures forty years apart,
and all the love in between.
For David, with pride and happiness born of the experience of
running our book marathons together.

—Dan Burstein

For Helen and Hannah, who make my heart sing.
Thank you for everything, always.
For Steven, and Bob, with love and admiration. And Brian and the
rest of my extended family, whose friendship means so much.

—Arne de Keijzer

My part of this book is to the memory of Stieg,
hoping that I've managed to do him justice,
and to Eva, hoping that she will think so.

—John-Henri Holmberg

Contents

STOCKHOLM

0   1 mile

0   1 kilometer

SOLNA

VASASTADEN

GÄRDET

ÖSTERMALM

Lake Mälaren

KUNGSHOLMEN

NORRMALM

Riddarfjärden

DJURGÅRDEN

Saltsjön

LILJEHOLMEN

SÖDERMALM

Årstaviken

HAMMARBY SJÖSTAD

NORRMALM

Riddarfjärden

Monteliusvagen: Sit on the benches to enjoy the beautiful view over the water, including the Stockholm Court House where Mikael's and Lisbeth's trials take place.

Lunda Bridge (Lundabron): The bridge leads to Lundagatan and the apartment where Lisbeth grew up.

SÖDER MÅLARSTRAND

Mellqvist Kaffebar: Called just Kaffebar in Larsson's books, it was renamed in 2008.

TAVASTGATAN

LUNDAGATAN

HORNSGATAN

Restaurant Tabbouli: Thought to be the model for Samir's Cauldron.

Lundagatan: Location of apartment where Lisbeth was raised.

Mariatorget Square: Larsson observed right-wing extremist rallies here.

Hotel Rival: A 1937 treasure, restored in 2003 by its current owner, ABBA's Benny Andersson.

N W E S

0   300 yards

0   300 meters

SÖDERMALM

Map by Paul J. Pugliese

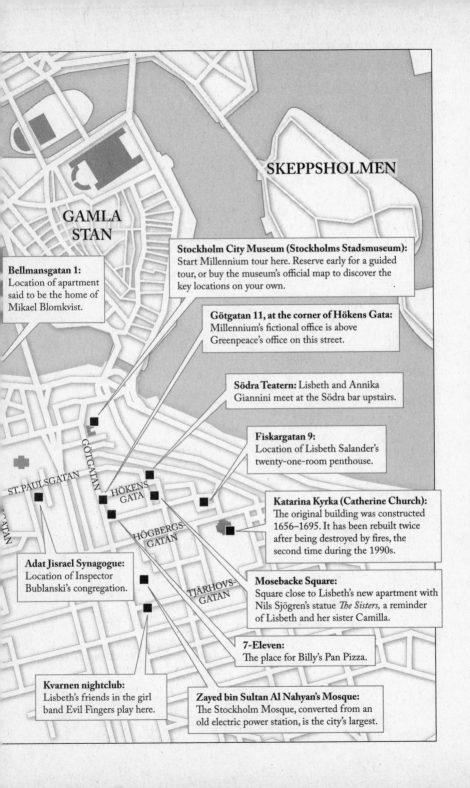

SKEPPSHOLMEN

GAMLA STAN

Bellmansgatan 1:
Location of apartment said to be the home of Mikael Blomkvist.

Stockholm City Museum (Stockholms Stadsmuseum):
Start Millennium tour here. Reserve early for a guided tour, or buy the museum's official map to discover the key locations on your own.

Götgatan 11, at the corner of Hökens Gata:
Millennium's fictional office is above Greenpeace's office on this street.

Södra Teatern: Lisbeth and Annika Giannini meet at the Södra bar upstairs.

Fiskargatan 9:
Location of Lisbeth Salander's twenty-one-room penthouse.

Katarina Kyrka (Catherine Church):
The original building was constructed 1656–1695. It has been rebuilt twice after being destroyed by fires, the second time during the 1990s.

Mosebacke Square:
Square close to Lisbeth's new apartment with Nils Sjögren's statue *The Sisters,* a reminder of Lisbeth and her sister Camilla.

Adat Jisrael Synagogue:
Location of Inspector Bublanski's congregation.

7-Eleven:
The place for Billy's Pan Pizza.

Kvarnen nightclub:
Lisbeth's friends in the girl band Evil Fingers play here.

Zayed bin Sultan Al Nahyan's Mosque:
The Stockholm Mosque, converted from an old electric power station, is the city's largest.

ST. PAULSGATAN

GÖTGATAN

HÖKENS GATA

HÖGBERGS-GATAN

TJÄRHOVS-GATAN

INTRODUCTION

As soon as the *The Girl with the Dragon Tattoo* was published in the United States in September 2008, the book's memorable title and cover design seemed to pop up everywhere, calling out to me from bookstore shelves, movie marquees, and excited online buzz from Web sites and blogs. I had a vague impression that it was some sort of coming-of-age story about a girl with tattoos, and I had heard it had a lot of explicit sexual detail and violence. I wasn't interested.

Then something happened to change my thinking. It was May 2010. *The Girl with the Dragon Tattoo* was still on the top of the best-seller list and the electronic version had started outstripping the sales of the physical ones, already demonstrating that it would become the best-selling e-book of all time. On *The New York Times* best-seller list it had been followed closely by its successor, *The Girl Who Played with Fire.* The third volume, *The Girl Who Kicked the Hornet's Nest,* was about to be published in the United States and would also rocket to the top of the best-seller list.

An old friend was visiting New York from California—MeraLee Goldman, whose own essay about how she first encountered *The Girl with the Dragon Tattoo* can be found in chapter 8. My wife, Julie, and I were going to meet her for dinner and see a Broadway show together. I have known MeraLee for fifty years, since I was a small child. She was one of my mother's best friends and they had been in the same book groups throughout the 1960s and '70s and up until my mother's death in 1983. My mother was one of the best read and most deep-thinking readers I have ever known, and the book groups she and MeraLee participated in over the years usually focused on the most important and intellectually challenging books of their day.

Over drinks after the play, MeraLee surprised us by asking if we had read *The Girl with the Dragon Tattoo.* Given the book's reputation for sexual violence and vengeance, the question was unexpected. Still caught up in Lisbeth Salander's spell, MeraLee told us that if we read the book we would encounter a heroine like none other she had ever known in literature. She promised us a powerful reading experience.

Knowing that I had created the Secrets series of best-selling books that served as reader's guides to *The Da Vinci Code* and numerous other recent culture phenomena, MeraLee mentioned that there were a lot of unanswered questions about Stieg Larsson himself and that it might be a good idea to create a similar book to examine the compelling world of Stieg Larsson.

I went home and downloaded *The Girl with the Dragon Tattoo* to my Kindle. Forty-eight hours later, I had finished *Tattoo* and started on the just-published *The Girl Who Kicked the Hornet's Nest* (yes, I read them out of order the first time around).

A few days later, I was in Cambridge to give a talk at an event at Harvard. I stopped in to the Harvard Coop to pick up the physical Larsson books to go along with the e-books I had downloaded. In the Coop, I found myself in a state of amazement. Arguably the most intellectually intense bookstore in America, it sported nine separate displays of Larsson books encompassing every area of the store. Already sensing we might be going to Stockholm soon, Julie suggested we pick out a variety of books about Sweden as well.

Over the next few weeks I read and reread the three books that compose the Millennium trilogy and listened to them on audio as well. I began to understand Larsson's architecture and his desire to tell an epochal tale on a grand and complex scale about the pervasiveness of violence and abuse against women, especially young and vulnerable women.

I thought a lot about Lisbeth Salander and why she captivated reader attention and seemed to enter not just our heads or our hearts, but to get into our very bloodstreams. I was developing a sense of how huge the global phenomenon around Salander was, and how people old, young, and middle-aged, men and women, and those reading in forty or more languages had gravitated toward Lisbeth, these towering tales, and the urgent call to action Larsson had issued in the form of a series of "crime novels."

I began to feel that Lisbeth resonated with twenty-first-century audiences the way only a few characters in literary history had resonated in their own times. The comparables seemed to me to be Holden Caulfield in mid-twentieth century or Huck Finn in the late nineteenth century. And Mikael Blomkvist was no slouch of a character, either. I thought of Flaubert confessing, *"Madame Bovary c'est moi,"* and realized that Larsson had gone the great French novelist one better: Larsson was himself part Lisbeth and part Blomkvist. Different as they are, they represent the yin and yang of the author's own male and female sides.

I came across a commentary by Mario Vargas Llosa, who would win the Nobel Prize for literature a few months later, likening the experience of reading Larsson to the excitement of his youth in reading Charles Dickens, Victor Hugo, and Alexandre Dumas. Vargas Llosa was not the only notable to compare Larsson to Dickens: Charles McGrath, the former editor of *The New York Times Book Review,* spoke of American readers who had completed the first two Larsson books waiting for the publication of *Hornet's Nest* the way they had once lined the docks in the nineteenth century awaiting the next installment of Dickens, or, in more recent times, the way they had lined up for each new Harry Potter book.

I found crusading *New York Times* op-ed columnist Nicholas Kristof analogizing Larsson and the Millennium trilogy to Harriet Beecher Stowe and *Uncle Tom's Cabin.* Just as *Uncle Tom* had awakened the world to the moral repugnance of slavery, Kristof said, perhaps the Larsson trilogy will awaken the world to the moral repugnance of sex trafficking.

Despite the weight of Larsson's "message," I discovered his cliffhangers were more than good enough for Stephen King, the ultimate master of plot, who called his books "unputdownable." And Larsson's characters were memorable enough to elicit this comment from a critic for *USA Today*: "Then there's Lisbeth, the digital age's first true heroine. This 92-pound outcast with the social skills of a feral cat, the computer savvy of a WikiLeaker and the vengeful ferocity of a Norse goddess has hacked her way into the world's psyche."

I mapped out the way Larsson used all sorts of techniques, tools, and genres to tell his story: The "locked room" mystery of Agatha Christie . . . the financial thriller . . . the police procedural . . . the noir crime novel of a Raymond Chandler or a Dashiell Hammett . . . the international espionage tale of John le Carré . . . courtroom drama . . . action plots out of Ludlum . . . the new tough female lead of a Sara Paretsky novel . . . the investigative reporter diligently working away to crack his story . . . the murderous and dysfunctional family . . . the super heroine of anime and fanzines . . . the frightening bureaucracy of the state as in Kafka.

Although Larsson's writing is clearly something new and different and can be identified more with U.S. and U.K. English-language female crime writers than with his Swedish predecessors and contemporaries, he is also not completely disconnected from the grit of the Nordic sociological crime novel that I myself had been reading in English translation most of my adult life. Indeed, it was easy to see elements in Larsson's books of Maj Sjöwall and Per Wahlöö, whose *Laughing Policeman* and other Martin Beck novels I read in the early 1970s, or Peter Høeg's *Smilla's Sense of Snow* from the early '90s, or Henning Mankell's Wallander series, or his American breakout best seller, *The Man from Beijing,* which I had read just prior to encountering Larsson.

Larsson marshaled all these genres, techniques, and source material for a grand purpose: to make his case that violence against women is the elephant in the room of our dysfunctional modern societies. Because we never treat violence against women and children as the overarching political or social issue that it should be (the way we treat unemployment, immigration, or civil rights as issues), he dedicated his fiction to forcing us, as readers, to confront the nightmarish status quo that we otherwise accept all too easily.

The last twenty years of Larsson's life were spent primarily focused on his highly engaged political and investigative journalism, exposing neo-Nazis in Sweden and the danger to democracy from the extreme right. He did this primarily through *Expo,* the crusading magazine of which he was a founder. He wrote only a few articles that specifically focused on violence and abuse against women and edited one book. But when he began to write fiction right after the turn of the millennium, he used what would become the Millennium trilogy as his outlet for exploring the big political and social issue that was not his main focus in *Expo*: the treatment of women in the modern world.

While I think Larsson's literary achievement is remarkable, I am not oblivious to how brilliant and simultaneously flawed his writing is—just like his lead characters. There are plenty of clunky scenes, trite dialogue, erroneous facts, and overused phrases. Some worry that Larsson walks too fine a line between exposing the sexual abuse of women and describing it so graphically as to be voyeuristic and exploitive. Others wonder whether the personal morality of Lisbeth is really an excuse for amorality, or whether she is interested in revenge to the exclusion of justice.

Nora Ephron had a point when she parodied Larsson's writing style with a withering satire in *The New Yorker* that depicted Blomkvist at Lisbeth's door, beseeching her for help in restoring his umlaut key to his computer keyboard:

> "'I need my umlaut," Blomkvist said. "What if I want to go to Svavelsjö? Or Strängnäs? Or Södertälje? What if I want to write to Wadensjö? Or Ekström or Nyström?"
>
> It was a compelling argument.
>
> She opened the door.

But even Ephron's deft parody mainly serves to point up another example of the compelling power of Larsson's fiction, especially with regard to American audiences. Neither the unpronounceable words, nor the unknown incidents in Swedish history, nor even those Swedish umlauts and other symbols could stop normally impatient-with-things-foreign Americans from buying millions upon millions of Larsson's books and making his novels simultaneously nos. 1, 2, and 3 on the best-seller list. Indeed, Larsson sales are so brisk that workers at America's rapidly vanishing physical bookstores have taken to calling the books "The Girl Who's Paying Our Salaries for the Next Few Months."

By the end of June 2010, a strong visceral feeling came over me as I was reading and thinking about all of this. I was growing more committed to writing this book. And that was before I had spent much time looking into the intriguing facts about Larsson himself. When I did so, I became even more convinced that I was going to enjoy spending the next few months caught up in the issues Larsson's work touches upon—from women's rights to privacy, hacking, and technology; from the life of the outcasts on the margins of society to the efforts to define new personal and social morality in a postmodern world. Most of all, I wanted to dig into the mysteries of Stieg Larsson's life and death.

I wanted to know more about his sudden death of a heart attack at age fifty, just after he had signed his three-book publishing deal and before the books had actually appeared in print.

I wanted to learn everything I could about the "coincidences" surrounding November 9, 2004, when Larsson, the out-of-shape neo-Nazi hunter who had faced numerous death threats in his journalistic career, reportedly discovered the elevator at his *Expo* magazine office not working, climbed seven flights of stairs, collapsed, and ultimately died way too young—on a day when he was supposed to be speaking at a Kristallnacht anniversary seminar.

I wanted to understand how the legacy of this champion of women's rights could end up becoming ensnared in an unending battle between the moral rights of Eva Gabrielsson, the woman he had lived with for thirty-two years and had been his life partner, and the legal rights of his brother and father who have ended up inheriting everything.

And I wanted to know what happened to the mysterious "fourth book," of which somewhere between 160 to 200 pages, or maybe more, were said to be on Stieg Larsson's laptop at the time of his death. Does Eva have it?

Does *Expo* have it, since the laptop itself was apparently *Expo* property? Do Erland and Joakim (the father and brother) have it? Is there a fifth manuscript as well? Do notes and plots exist for up to ten books, as Stieg hinted before his death?

The mysteries about Stieg Larsson are legion. Every day for the last many months I have learned tantalizing bits of new information in answer to all of the above questions, and many more.

Now it is time to share what we have learned about the phenomenon of Stieg Larsson, his ideas, his fiction, and his world. And that's the ultimate point of this book.

Arne de Keijzer and I have published six prior books in the Secrets series. In all of these works, we have endeavored to bring many voices, many experts in different disciplines, and many new and fresh ideas to the discussion. We have taken the same approach in assembling *The Tattooed Girl: The Enigma of Stieg Larsson and the Secrets Behind the Most Compelling Thrillers of Our Time*. We are, of course, responsible for all the content in the book, but this is an anthology and there is a wide diversity of opinion reflected in these pages. Each writer and contributor speaks to our readers with their own voice and their own point of view.

Our partner in *The Tattooed Girl* is Swedish writer, editor, publisher, and translator John-Henri Holmberg, who first met Stieg Larsson at a science fiction fanzine convention in the early 1970s when Stieg was still a teenager, and remained friends with him until Larsson's unfortunate and untimely death in 2004. I commend John-Henri's many special contributions to this book, including his groundbreaking, three-part biography of Larsson in chapter 10 and his fascinating reportage on Stieg's early interest in science fiction and crime writing and how it influenced his crime novels, which can be found in chapter 4.

In chapter 9, John-Henri tells us about the mysterious "fourth book," which he perhaps knows more about than anyone other than Eva Gabrielsson. In chapter 2, he tells us that in some important ways, the books we read in English are not exactly the ones Larsson wrote, summarizing a variety of problems with the editing and translation of Larsson's work that occurred after his death. A notable example is the difference between the original Swedish description of Lisbeth's dragon tattoo and the completely different way her tattoo is described in the English translation. (Hint: It's much larger in Swedish.)

Throughout the book we bring you a series of provocative commentators and essayists, from Christopher Hitchens to Laura Miller, Jenny McPhee, and Lizzie Skurnick, all with their own unique take on Stieg Larsson's life and the rich themes of his books. Key people who worked with Larsson, including Daniel Poohl, Stieg's successor at *Expo,* tell their favorite Stieg stories and recount a variety of their experiences with him in chapter 3.

Chapter 3 also features two essays that capture Eva Gabrielsson in her own words through the interviews she has given and the memoir she has written that details her life with Stieg, the great emotional toll his death took on her life, and the intense anger she feels toward those who, in her mind, want to steal his legacy and commercialize it. (Published in France as *Millénium, Stieg et Moi,* Actes Sud, January 2011, and soon to be published in the U.S. as *"There Are Things I Want You to Know" About Stieg Larsson and Me,* Seven Stories Press, June 2011.)

In chapter 5, experts tell us about the Sweden that has lost its utopian veneer of "Swedishness." The Sweden that appears in the novels of Larsson and other contemporary crime writers is one of a bleak, corrupt, violent, and crime-ravaged country.

American publishers are now on a quest to find the "next Stieg Larsson." While unlikely, since Larsson was such a unique person and such an unusual voice, there are a number of great new crime writers coming out of Scandinavia today. In chapter 6, we feature interviews with and essays by several of these writers, including Anders Roslund and Börge Hellström, whose newest book is on the *New York Times* best-seller list as I write this. And coming soon to our shores are Alexander and Alexandra Ahndoril who write together as "Lars Kepler," as well as Karin Alfredsson, Veronica von Schenck, and Katarina Wennstam, all three of whom have created powerful female characters and socially significant plots in their crime novels.

In chapter 8, Laura Gordon Kutnick provides a haunting perspective on the trilogy that brings together all the many questions still lingering about Larsson's death and legacy. She also provides an amazing and surprising inventory of prescient allusions in the Millennium trilogy to events that only came into view after Larsson's death, from sudden heart attacks to issues with estate and inheritance law.

Other unique insights and thought-provoking sidelights await you, from commentaries about the efforts to turn *The Girl with the Dragon Tattoo* into a Hollywood film (premiering in December 2011), to an interview with the U.S. ambassador to Sweden, to a talk with the real-life champion boxer, Paolo Roberto, who, after Larsson's death, suddenly discovered himself a character in the novels.

Much additional food for thought lies ahead in these pages. I hope you will find in them a fascinating and thought-provoking book that will help keep the discussion of Stieg Larsson and his world alive, even all these years after his death.

—Dan Burstein, March 2011

PART ONE

THE MAN WHO CONQUERED THE WORLD

With all my defenses as a reader and critic leveled by the hurricane force of his story, I just spent a few weeks reading Stieg Larsson's Millennium trilogy. It left me with the happiness and excitement of febrile children and adolescents who read the series on the Musketeers by Dumas or the novels of Dickens and Victor Hugo, wondering at every turn of the page "What now, what will happen?" and the foreboding anguish of knowing that the story was going to end soon.

—Mario Vargas Llosa, 2010 Nobel Prize winner for literature

Like everyone, I'm reading the Stieg Larsson trilogy. I'm addicted. We're in glorious Santa Barbara, but I don't want to leave the house, or fall asleep at night so caught up in the web of books am I. —Lesley Stahl, *60 Minutes*

The political honesty, the rage at sexism, the suspense, the overpowering narrative, the focus on modern sexual mores, the sexual tension between Mikael and Lisbeth have made the Millennium trilogy not only a runaway commercial success but perhaps the best, most broadly focused examination of modern politics in popular fiction. To have written these three novels may have killed Larsson, but he left a monument behind, a modern masterpiece. —Patrick Anderson, *The Washington Post*

1. THE AUTHOR WHO KICKED THE HORNET'S NEST

THE PROFOUND PRESCIENCE OF STIEG LARSSON
by Dan Burstein

Most recent crime novels don't call out to be read a second time for at least a few years, if ever. But in the case of the Millennium trilogy, I couldn't wait. There's so much in Stieg Larsson's books that, like a good film you immediately want to see again, and in which you "see so much more" the second time around, they proved even more interesting to me on the second read than they were when I rushed through them the first time, compelled along by the plot, the perils, and the cliffhangers. Taking *The Girl with the Dragon Tattoo, The Girl Who Played with Fire,* and *The Girl Who Kicked the Hornet's Nest* together as the single whole trilogy that they compose, you can see that just below the surface of potboiler action there lie deep veins of Stieg Larsson's cosmology. Lisbeth and Blomkvist walk the streets of Stockholm engaged in the plot of the book, while just beneath them, like the city's vast *tunnelbana* metro system, Larsson elaborates, argues, and explores his social, political, moral, technological, economic, and psychological themes. His early-twenty-first-century critique of the world as we know it, as well as his vision for changing it, is interlaced with his plot. His worldview is there to reflect on, debate, and learn from—or not—at the reader's discretion (although it occasionally surfaces in the reader's face with a little too much didacticism).

The best reviews of the Millennium trilogy highlight the breadth of Larsson's vision. Writing in the *Washington Post* in May 2010, just after the publication of *Hornet's Nest,* Patrick Anderson wondered out loud how these books, by an obscure and now deceased Swedish writer, who had never published much fiction before, came to capture the attention of the world. Arguing that, "The trilogy ranks among those novels that expand the horizons of popular fiction," Anderson offered several reasons for the author's posthumous success:

The most obvious is the brilliance of Larsson's narrative. It's a rich, exciting, suspenseful story, with a huge cast, and involves us deeply in Lisbeth's fate, even as it carries us into all levels of Swedish society.

Another reason for the trilogy's success is its political message. There are neo-Nazis, criminals and corporate villains in these books, but finally the enemy is corrupt government officials who wage war not only on individuals but on democracy itself. Readers throughout the world have recognized that rogue elements of government do operate in secret. To some degree, Larsson based his plot on real scandals in his own country, but the dangers he exposes are universal. . . .

The third reason, Anderson hypothesized, is the passionate attack on sexism.

All this—the political honesty, the rage at sexism, the suspense, the overpowering narrative, the focus on modern sexual mores, the sexual tension between Mikael and Lisbeth—has made the Millennium trilogy . . . not only a runaway commercial success but perhaps the *best, most broadly focused examination of modern politics in popular fiction* (emphasis added). . . . To have written these three novels may have killed Larsson, but he left a monument behind, *a modern masterpiece.*

Like a twenty-first-century version of the best Norse sagas, Larsson's tales are infinitely complex and feature a multiplicity of characters, plots, and subplots. Indeed, a family tree of the fictional Vanger family (worthy of a reader's guide to a Tolstoy novel) is depicted in *Tattoo* to help keep all the players straight. But in addition to their plots, subplots, and clever mixture of crime and thriller genres, the books also tackle many real-world themes. Here are some of the most important ones.

Men Who Hate Women

Stieg Larsson's stated intention was to call all three books *Men Who Hate Women* and then give each volume of the trilogy a relevant subtitle. As we know from published correspondence, Norstedts, the Swedish publisher, lobbied him to change this title, but he was insistent on it. In fact, he told his editors in essence that they could change many things about the books in editing, but not the title. The first book was published in Sweden accordingly. But the U.K. publisher who acquired the English-language publication rights after Larsson's death (MacLehose/Quercus) changed the title to *The Girl with the Dragon Tattoo*. In doing so, they made a brilliant commercial decision. But at the same time undercut the key statement the author was trying to make.

Larsson is often described as a feminist; Eva Gabrielsson, his partner in life, said he described himself that way ever since she first met him as a teenager in the early 1970s. But his feminism was a different, more political, and more passionate feminism than what most readers would think of as a modern male who calls himself a feminist. In the first place, he dared to paint a detailed, thorough, and hyperrealistic picture of the pervasiveness of violence, abuse, rape, and murder of women. He attacked Sweden's sacred cow of its self-image and its complacent pride in its gender-equalizing achievements. Yes, almost half the Parliament is female and yes, huge progress has been made in empowering women over the last several decades. But Larsson refused to accept the general progress in society as a reason not to excoriate that society's deficiencies. He tracked numerous cases of women beaten, brutalized, raped, murdered, and systematically denied their rights and the protection of the state even in genteel Sweden. Several well-known real-life cases are mirrored in the plots of his books.

We don't know what Stieg Larsson would have thought if he had lived to learn about Göran Lindberg, but let's just say when I read about this case in the summer of 2010, I thought I had fallen headfirst into a Larsson novel. Tragically, it was a true story. A former police chief and director of the Swedish National Police Academy, Lindberg presented himself as the consummate supporter of female members of the police force. He lectured and convened workshops designed to raise male policemen's consciousness about working with their female partners, prevent sexual harassment, and make it easier for women to progress through police ranks. But when he was arrested in 2010, it was reported that even while he had been acting as such an enlightened figure, he had been a serial rapist (including raping a seventeen-year-old girl) and had been involved in procuring, prostitution, and various kinds of dehumanizing sexual acts with numerous women.

Larsson wanted us to "get it" that people like Lindberg are not all that unusual in our cultures. The amount of abuse and violence that takes place is much greater than what is reported; the conviction percentages for the crimes that are reported are way too low; and the jail sentences are way too short and trivial. There was no condescension or do-gooding in Larsson's approach to feminism. He wanted readers to be uncomfortable. He wanted us to experience, even for just a brief moment, the brutalization and suffering faced by women who are violated and abused.

Stieg Larsson wanted to challenge us: how often do we see a horrific, gruesome story on TV about a serial rapist or killer, about a girl held hostage for years, about the operations of a sex-trafficking ring? Why don't we connect the dots? Our culture becomes fascinated with tawdry tabloid stories about famous and powerful men who become involved with prostitutes and seamy relationships, or who abuse the women they live with. Whether it's Elliot Spitzer, Tiger Woods, Mel Gibson, Senator David Vitter, Italian Prime Minister Silvio Berlusconi, or O. J. Simpson, we profess shock and decry the specific incidents, but we don't face up to the pattern.

While I was researching this book, I came across a *New York Times* report on sex trafficking in the middle of Manhattan. "Americans tend to associate 'modern slavery' with illiterate girls in India or Cambodia. Yet there I was the other day, interviewing a college graduate who says she spent three years terrorized by pimps in a brothel in Midtown Manhattan," wrote Nicholas Kristof in 2010, who proceeded to recount the story of Yumi Li (a nickname) who grew up in northeastern China but dreamed of going abroad. After university graduation in China, she became an accountant. Eventually she accepted an offer from an employment agent to be smuggled to New York, where she was supposed to be hired for a position using her accounting skills and paid $5,000 a month. Her relatives had to pledge their homes as collateral for her, in case she did not pay back the $50,000 smugglers' fee from her earnings. But on arrival in New York, it turned out that Yumi was ordered to work in a brothel.

According to Kristof, "She says that the four men who ran the smuggling operation—all Chinese or South Koreans—took her into their office on 36th Street in Midtown Manhattan. They beat her with their fists (but did not hit her in the face, for that might damage her commercial value), gang-raped her and videotaped her naked in humiliating poses. For extra intimidation, they held a gun to her head."

This is the kind of real-life story that occurs all too frequently in our world. Larsson is asking us: when are we going to stop treating these cases as despicable crimes at the margins of society, and face up to the fact that abuse of women is an epidemic at the heart of many advanced, Western countries—even those that have made great progress on jobs, rights, and economic opportunity for women?

Taking Responsibility, Refusing to Be the Victim

For Larsson, a conviction of a criminal in the courts or the passage of a new piece of crimes-against-women legislation is not enough. Lisbeth Salander is there to illustrate the alternative option. She makes it a rule not even to talk to the police. She solves problems her own way. She strikes such a nerve with so many at least in part because she takes the delivery of a severe Old Testament, eye-for-an-eye-type process of vengeance, retribution, and justice into her own hands.

She famously responds to Bjurman's brutal rape not by going to the police and hoping to get him arrested, convicted, and sent to jail, but by carefully planning to turn his existence into a permanent living hell. She punishes him with more than a taste of his own painful and humiliating medicine and forces him to watch the replay of his own evil deeds and accept responsibility for them. She traumatizes and ruins him forever by branding him with the tattoo that will remind him and anyone else who ever gets close to him of exactly who and what he is every day for the rest of his life. For good measure, Bjurman, who once took for granted his power and control over her, is turned into her vassal doing her bidding and reporting regularly to the authorities on her good behavior.

Lisbeth is an avenging angel with the requisite combination of martial arts, computer hacking, and strategic thinking skills to seek and find just the right punishment for any man who harms her. In a few cases, such as Dr. Forbes in *Fire,* she even metes out justice to a man she doesn't know who is about to do harm to a woman she doesn't know.

A 92-pound misfit and outcast, she will not allow herself to be a victim. She does not want Blomkvist's sympathy or pity—or anyone else's, including yours. As Christopher Marcus, the creator of one of the first Larsson fan sites, says on the home page of SallysFriends.net (with Sally referring obviously to Salander):

> [It is not easy to be] . . . friendly towards a troubled punk-hacker-girl, who all too often ends up getting in the way of serial killers, corrupt politicians or just get shot by Soviet ex-spies. . . . Idiots . . . have found out—the hard way—that being friends with a girl who plays with fire is perhaps a bit more than they bargained for. . . !
>
> Lisbeth Salander is not easy to befriend, and I don't think any of us ever really will be able to. But we might do our best, again and again, to lend her a hand when she's gotten herself into new trouble, treating her with dignity and respect. And even if we never get anything in return . . . well, maybe it will still be worth it. Maybe. With Lisbeth you never quite know for sure.

Larsson knows every woman can't nor should be Lisbeth Salander. But in every chapter he finds ways to promote independent, powerful, morally centered women. Almost all the leading female characters in the book (Erika Berger, Monica Figuerola, Sonja Modig, Annika Giannini, Malin Eriksson, Miriam Wu, and Harriet Vanger) are generally strong, independent, professional, and righteous. Many of them also appear to be capable of defining and enjoying their own sexuality without becoming anyone's possession. Larsson has sprinkled bits of history into the text designed to teach us about women warriors like Boudicca, the Celtic Queen who organized one of the bloodiest rebellions against the Roman Empire two thousand years ago, or even stories of women disguising themselves as men to fight in the Civil War, a true part of American history that very few Americans have ever heard about.

Larsson drew pieces of Lisbeth's character from intriguing, innovative, and powerful female figures in popular culture. Pippi Longstocking is one such role model—physically strong, strong-willed, completely independent, nonconformist, always ready for adventure, defining her own sense of right and wrong, not accepting society's standard parameters of normal behavior, and making no effort to play up to boys. Red-haired like Lisbeth, and living in a big house with an endowed budget provided by a fortune of somewhat mysterious origin (similar to Lisbeth in her apartment on Fiskargatan), Pippi is a clear inspiration to Larsson, as he himself highlighted in discussing the birth of the Lisbeth character in his own mind.

Another major influence on Lisbeth is Modesty Blaise. (I have Stieg Larsson to thank for my introduction to Modesty, whom I had never heard of prior to the research for this book.) Although never catching a huge cultural wave in the United States, the Modesty Blaise comic strips, novels, and films were very popular in the U.K. and Scandinavia in the 1960s. And Stieg Larsson, as a teenager, was very fond of this character who is sometimes described as a female James Bond. But there's much more to Modesty's story than this. Created by Peter O'Donnell, Modesty first appears in a post–World War II refugee camp as a young girl with no memory of her past. She survives difficult experiences and privations, attaching herself to Lob, a wandering refugee /scholar who is the equivalent of Palmgren in the Millennium trilogy. She learns to fight and live by her wits, but she also learns great knowledge and life lessons from Lob. In Tangier she takes over a criminal network and becomes rich as a result. Like Lisbeth with Blomkvist, Modesty connects with a somewhat older man (Willie Garvin) who is comfortable in his role as her junior partner. She's always the star of the show.

Armed with her wealth from her days in The Network in Tangier (think: Hacker Republic), Modesty retires but is always willing to be called back into action, along with Willie, for a matter of particular interest. Modesty faces plenty of evildoers and is not afraid to kill, but like Lisbeth, she prefers not to. Instead, she fights her way out of situations with strategy, cunning, and skill.

Yet another female character Stieg drew on was the eponymous heroine from Robert A. Heinlein's 1982 novel, *Friday*. Heinlein was Larsson's favorite sf author, and in Friday, we find a character who has superhuman abilities (like Lisbeth) but faces prejudice from the human community (like Lisbeth).

Larsson promotes female authors of crime fiction, science fiction, and children's books whenever he can. Like a well-constructed product placement, there are several scenes in which Blomkvist is relaxing by reading a crime novel that just happens to be written by a female crime writer. Among those specifically mentioned are Sara Paretsky, Dorothy Sayers, Val McDermid, Elizabeth George, Sue Grafton, Agatha Christie, Astrid Lindgren, and Enid Blyton.

Hacking, Privacy, and WikiLeaks

Just after I started to conceive of this book in June 2010, I read a lengthy *New Yorker* profile of Julian Assange, the founder of WikiLeaks. His was basically an unknown name to me then, although he was about to burst onto the world stage with a vengeance. Reading the profile of Assange, I thought: here is a real-world character who seems to be made out of equal parts Mikael Blomkvist and Lisbeth Salander. Like Blomkvist, Assange thinks of himself as a crusading journalist. He is (or at least claims to be) dedicated to openness, transparency, and cracking the codes of official secrets, cabals, and conspiracies set up to hide the truth from the people in the name of state security. Like Lisbeth, Assange is a consummate hacker. Like her, he grew up as an odd child, on the run from an abusive stepfather, moving all the time, and without the traditional stabilizing influences of home, school, and family. Early personal computers, and early networks of teenage hackers, became his friends, just as Lisbeth is most socially comfortable when she is electronically connected to her Hacker Republic friends. Like Blomkvist to a degree, and like Lisbeth to an even greater degree, Assange developed his own moral code about whose secrets to hack and whose secrets to publish. The fact that Assange was recently conducting much of his activity from bases in Scandinavia made the parallelism even more compelling. When he later ended up on the run in London trying to escape extradition to Sweden over allegations involving rape, failure to use a condom, and nonconsensual sex, he seemed like even more of a Larsson creation.

The technology in the Millennium trilogy is old, because seven to nine years have passed since Stieg Larsson wrote his novels. The PowerBook and the Palm Tungsten that figure so prominently in the novels are ancient artifacts today. But Larsson envisioned all the key issues of contemporary cyberculture. He understood how easily networks could be compromised. He imagined a world in which someone like Lisbeth could know the inner thoughts, sexual perversions, bank account data, and travel plans of friend and foe alike.

The trilogy creates a culture in which traditional investigative reporting must be married up with cybersleuthing to find the truth. Larsson already knew that there really is no such thing as privacy anymore, despite the efforts of governments to continue to legislate it. When loose networks of real-life hackers decided in 2010 to attack credit card companies and others who had cooperated with government efforts to squelch WikiLeaks, they were mirroring a scene of Larsson's creation at least seven years earlier where Lisbeth's friends in the Hacker Republic offer to "shut down Stockholm" electronically if Swedish authorities continue to try to convict her for crimes she didn't commit.

Larsson was reportedly not much of a technologist, other than being nearly attached at the fingertips to his laptop, the same way he was with the typewriter he received as a birthday gift when he was twelve. But he understood we are moving into a murky world where the same technology that can compromise our privacy also makes it possible to patrol and intervene in the activities of the dark forces of governments, corporations, and financial criminals. And from his voracious reading of science fiction, he could imagine both the powerful potential, as well as the dangers, of all the technology we have at our disposal today.

The Rise of the Extreme Right

Much of Stieg Larsson's time, energy, and intellectual passion from the 1980s until his death in 2004 was spent documenting the rise of the extreme right in Sweden and warning about its threat to democracy. Not long before he died, he reiterated his longstanding concerns about the Sweden Democrats, a pleasant enough sounding name for a group that has historic ties to neo-Nazis and seems to believe that the solution to all social problems is to severely limit or totally prohibit immigration. Larsson expected the SDs might get enough votes to win seats in Parliament by the time of the 2006 election. He didn't live to see that election, and the SD party did not get enough votes to qualify for Parliament then. But his forecast was prescient just the same: by September 2010, the SD party got enough votes to occupy twenty seats in the Swedish Parliament today.

Ruthless in his exposure of Nazis, neo-Nazis, and extremists of all kinds, Larsson is one of a small handful of Swedish writers to crack open the myth of Swedish World War II–era "neutrality." As Blomkvist listens to Henrik Vanger tell the history of his dysfunctional family empire in *Tattoo,* the list of family members who are Nazis, Nazi sympathizers, and anti-Semites—not just during World War II but even today—continues to grow. Larsson is using his fiction to enter into the Swedish political debate: Swedes may believe in the idea of an open, tolerant, egalitarian, social democratic state, but it is an illusion, a "castle made of air," as the Swedish title for the third book implies. The ugly (and generally undiscussed) role of Swedish Hitler supporters in World War II, plus the growth of the white power movement, various anti-immigrant movements, and actual neo-Nazi parties in contemporary Sweden—not to mention the periodic waves of anti-immigrant violence and attacks—are all realities that Larsson believed should be confronted, not swept under the rug.

A significant subplot of *Hornet's Nest* revolves around the inadequacies of the Swedish constitution. While there are unique flaws and unexplained contradictions in the Swedish system, Larsson's point is a broader one (and could well be applied to the United States and other countries): on the one hand we love our constitution and we know it is the bedrock of our freedoms and our system of laws. But many of us also know that, however well it has done in regenerating its relevance for more than two centuries, we now face issues and problems where the constitution provides little guidance. How can societies move forward on the road of expanding economic opportunity and promoting tolerance and personal freedom when the machinery of the state is increasingly bureaucratic, if not completely polarized, and the treatment of women, immigrants, and minorities is increasingly barbaric? Can we continue to progress as a society—with all the dehumanizing and decivilizing forces all around us—without a willingness to consider overhauling the way our institutions and social systems actually work?

Of Millennials in Their Twenties and Boomers Facing their Fifties

One of Larsson's themes I find most intriguing is the relationship between the middle-aged Blomkvist and the young Lisbeth. This relationship mirrors the one between the Western world's aging Baby Boomer generation—which in

Sweden, as in America and elsewhere, was the generation that was committed to "changing the world" in the 1960s and '70s—and the rising younger generation of Boomer offspring, known in the U.S. as the Millennials.

Stieg Larsson was part of the Swedish 1960s generation that assumed that bringing about huge transformations in society was their role in life. By the turn of the millennium, it's my guess that Larsson looked back with nostalgia on the great political and social upheavals of those days. The ideals, the comradeship, the energizing sense of meaning that the 1960s and '70s had imbued in him were now memories more than realities. And he also knew that the world is a different place today, and that increasingly, its future depends not on the Blomkvists, but on the Lisbeths, who don't see themselves on a generational mission to "change the world," yet are more than ready to jump in to solve specific problems and right specific wrongs.

Stieg Larsson was passionate about his political causes. He had been an activist in the anti-Vietnam war movement, a Maoist, and a Trotskyist, all while still in his teenage years. As you can see in our photo section, even when his classmates went for a ski weekend, he stayed inside with his typewriter to write a commentary on the French student movement of 1968. In the late 1970s he would go to Eritrea, in the early '80s to Grenada. He stayed involved with the Trotskyist group he had joined in his youth probably longer than he wanted to, because he was a person who took movements and parties and loyalties seriously, even while critiquing their rigidity or intolerance. But by the mid to late 1980s, the causes of the political left had hit a low tide in terms of popular support, or even interest. The Berlin Wall would fall, and there would be a rush of people all over the world toward Western-style capitalism, materialism, freedom, and democracy. Russia, China, and most other socialist countries, whatever different directions they had evolved in during the twentieth century, were almost all shifting gears and heading into various forms of capitalism. It was not a great time to be a leftist intellectual.

But then the waves of anti-immigrant violence hit Sweden and the neo-Nazis began their marginal but frightening ascendancy. By the mid '90s, Stieg Larsson was reenergized around the causes of antiracism and antifascism and hard at work on *Expo* magazine. While *Expo*'s circulation was limited, its finances troubled, and its existence always threatened by right-wing attacks (Blomkvist's *Millennium* is depicted in the books as far more influential than *Expo* ever was), my guess is that *Expo* was still an important, virtuous, and satisfying commitment for Larsson.

Eventually, however, the neo-Nazi movement peaked and quieted down.

Expo, even after finding its voice and institutionalizing itself as the leading authority on the extreme right-wing danger, had trouble remaining self-supporting.

That he was concerned about his approaching fiftieth birthday well before the actual date in 2004 is obvious from many indicators in the books. He was in his late forties when he started writing his novels. With *Expo* facing constant financial problems, with the neo-Nazis not quite as visible as they had been a few years before, and with decades of evidence confirming that no revolution was going to happen in Sweden (and with so many of the revolutions elsewhere that held such promise for a romantic like Larsson having demonstrably failed), Stieg turned back the clock of his onrushing half-century mark by looking to his younger years. It was then that he had written all manner of stories and sketches in his childhood notebooks and in the fanzines he and his friends dreamed up in the 1970s.

In talking with Robert Aschberg, I discovered that around this time (late 1990s, early 2000s), Stieg started sending Aschberg and a few other people short stories, dialogues, humor pieces, and a host of other extracts and commentaries, usually without explanation. These were his warm-up exercises for sitting down to write the Millennium trilogy, which he believed, from the moment he started, would be commercially successful and would lead to a "pension" plan for Eva and him.

All of this is guesswork on my part, but I imagine this scene: laptop on the table, cigarettes and coffee at hand, nostalgic pop music (Elvis, jazz, Debbie Harry, David Bowie) playing, Stieg Larsson sat back and reflected on his life experiences, including all he had lived through intellectually and politically, and in more than three decades of love and intimacy with Eva. He thought about the sordid news events of our world and the strengths and weaknesses of individual moral codes in an era where there often seems to be no properly understood norms of right and wrong, and where many of the institutions of society have become severely corrupted. He sat back and let his storytelling gifts take over. Soon he realized that writing crime novels was one of the most enjoyable experiences he had ever had. He was in the flow and it was coming to him fast and furiously. He brought his incredible characters to life and set them off down their own roads into his plots, allowing him to burrow into the story and create his layers of meaning and political and social substance beneath the surface.

There was no revolution in sight. But Stieg Larsson had the next best thing as he approached his fiftieth birthday—a three-book publishing contract that was going to allow him to reach more readers with his ideas than he ever could through *Expo* or any other kind of political journalism. News that his books had sold in the big German market, and that there was interest in a movie deal as well, also meant he could become his own benefactor. He and Eva were going to build a writer's cottage of their own design and live together and write. He had finished the first three books and had already started on the fourth and fifth. He had ideas, notes, and plots for many, many more. In November 2004, he was thinking actively about Blomkvist and Salander in the arctic north of Canada's Banks Island, where he had implied in correspondence the fourth book would be set.

He had discovered something even more exciting than a revolutionary movement: the unfettered power of his own imagination.

2. WHY WE CAN'T GET ENOUGH OF THE TATTOOED GIRL

THE AUTHOR WHO PLAYED WITH FIRE
by Christopher Hitchens

One of the first big American media stories to recount the nonfiction drama of Stieg Larsson's life and death was a 2009 report by Christopher Hitchens in Vanity Fair. The Girl with the Dragon Tattoo *and* The Girl Who Played with Fire *had both become American best sellers;* The Girl Who Kicked the Hornet's Nest *was still to come in the U.S. market, as were the three Swedish movies. But with "Tattooed Girl"-mania beginning to move out of the bookstore and into the popular culture,* Vanity Fair *published this intriguing article, teasing the story to their readers by saying:*

"Just when Stieg Larsson was about to make his fortune with the mega-selling thriller The Girl with the Dragon Tattoo, *the crusading journalist dropped dead. Now some are asking how much of his fiction—which exposes Sweden's dark currents of Fascism and sexual predation—is fact." On his way toward an answer, Hitchens shares his insights into all things Larsson with his usual panache.*

In addition to his role as a contributing editor to Vanity Fair, *Hitchens is a visiting professor at The New School and a widely published columnist and essayist. His book* God Is Not Great *was a National Book Award nominee. Hitchens's most recent book is a memoir,* Hitch-22.

I suppose it's justifiable to describe "best-selling" in quasi-tsunami terms because when it happens it's partly a wall and partly a tide: first you see a towering, glistening rampart of books in Costco and the nation's airports and then you are hit by a series of succeeding waves that deposit individual

---

Originally published in *Vanity Fair* (December 2009) and reprinted with permission of the author.

copies in the hands of people sitting right next to you. I was slightly wondering what might come crashing in after Hurricane Khaled. I didn't guess that the next great inundation would originate not in the exotic kite-running spaces at the roof of the world but from an epicenter made almost banal for us by Volvo, Absolut, Saab, and Ikea.

Yet it is from this society, of reassuring brand names and womb-to-tomb national health care, that Stieg Larsson conjured a detective double act so incongruous that it makes Holmes and Watson seem like siblings. I say "conjured" because Mr. Larsson also drew upon the bloody, haunted old Sweden of trolls and elves and ogres, and I put it in the past tense because, just as the first book in his "Millennium" trilogy, *The Girl with the Dragon Tattoo,* was about to make his fortune, he very suddenly became a dead person. In the Larsson universe the nasty trolls and hulking ogres are bent Swedish capitalists, cold-faced Baltic sex traffickers, blue-eyed Viking Aryan Nazis, and other Nordic riffraff who might have had their reasons to whack him. But if he now dwells in that Valhalla of the hack writer who posthumously beat all the odds, it's surely because of his elf. Picture a feral waif. All right, picture a four-foot-eleven-inch "doll" with Asperger's syndrome and generous breast implants. This is not Pippi Longstocking (to whom a few gestures are made in the narrative). This is Miss Goth, intermittently disguised as *la gamine.*

Forget Miss Smilla's sense of the snow and check out Lisbeth Salander's taste in pussy rings, tattoos, girls, boys, motorcycles, and, above all, computer keyboards. (Once you accept that George MacDonald Fraser's Flashman can pick up any known language in a few days, you have suspended enough disbelief to settle down and enjoy his adventures.) Miss Salander is so well accoutred with special features that she's almost over-equipped. She is awarded a photographic memory, a chess mind to rival Bobby Fischer's, a mathematical capacity that toys with Fermat's last theorem as a cat bats a mouse, and the ability to "hack"—I apologize for the repetition of that word—into the deep intestinal computers of all banks and police departments. At the end of *The Girl Who Played with Fire,* she is for good measure granted the ability to return from the grave.

With all these superheroine advantages, one wonders why she and her on-and-off sidekick, the lumbering but unstoppable reporter Mikael Blomkvist, don't defeat the forces of Swedish Fascism and imperialism more effortlessly. But the other reason that Lisbeth Salander is such a source of fascination is this: the pint-size minxoid with the dragon tattoo is also a traumatized victim and doesn't work or play well with others. She has been raped and tortured and otherwise abused ever since she could think, and her private phrase for her coming-of-age is "All the Evil": words that go unelucidated until near the end of *The Girl Who Played with Fire*. The actress Noomi Rapace has already played Salander in a Swedish film of the first novel, which enjoyed a worldwide release. (When Hollywood gets to the casting stage, I suppose Philip Seymour Hoffman will be offered the ursine Blomkvist role, and though the coloring is wrong I keep thinking of Winona Ryder for Lisbeth.) According to Larsson's father, the sympathy with which "the girl" is evoked is derived partly from the author's own beloved niece, Therese, who is tattooed and has suffered from anorexia and dyslexia but can fix your computer problems.

In life, Stieg Larsson described himself as, among other things, "a feminist," and his character surrogate, Mikael Blomkvist, takes an ostentatiously severe line against the male domination of society and indeed of his own profession. (The original grim and Swedish title of *The Girl with the Dragon Tattoo* is *Men Who Hate Women,* while the trilogy's third book bore the more fairy-tale-like name *The Castle in the Air That Blew Up:* the clever rebranding of the series with the word "girl" on every cover was obviously critical.) Blomkvist's moral righteousness comes in very useful for the action of the novels, because it allows the depiction of a great deal of cruelty to women, smuggled through customs under the disguise of a strong disapproval. Sweden used to be notorious, in the late 1960s, as the homeland of the film *I Am Curious (Yellow),* which went all the way to the Supreme Court when distributed in the United States and gave Sweden a world reputation as a place of smiling nudity and guilt-free sex. What a world of nursery innocence that was, compared with the child slavery and exploitation that are evoked with perhaps slightly too much relish by the crusading Blomkvist.

His best excuse for his own prurience is that these serial killers and torture fanciers are practicing a form of capitalism and that their racket is protected by a pornographic alliance with a form of Fascism, its lower ranks made up of hideous bikers and meth runners. This is not just sex or crime—it's politics! Most of the time, Larsson hauls himself along with writing such as this:

> The murder investigation was like a broken mosaic in which he could make out some pieces while others were simply missing. Somewhere there was a pattern. He could sense it, but he could not figure it out. Too many pieces were missing.

No doubt they were, or there would be no book. (The plot of the first story is so heavily convoluted that it requires a page reproducing the Vanger dynasty's family tree—the first time I can remember encountering such a dramatis personae since I read *War and Peace.*) But when he comes to the villain of *The Girl with the Dragon Tattoo,* a many-tentacled tycoon named Wennerström, Larsson's prose is suddenly much more spirited. Wennerström had consecrated himself to "fraud that was so extensive it was no longer merely criminal—it was business." That's actually one of the best-turned lines in the whole thousand pages. If it sounds a bit like Bertolt Brecht on an average day, it's because Larsson's own views were old-shoe Communist.

His background involved the unique bonding that comes from tough Red families and solid class loyalties. The hard-labor and factory and mining sector of Sweden is in the far and arduous North—this is also the home territory of most of the country's storytellers—and Grandpa was a proletarian Communist up toward the Arctic. This during the Second World War, when quite a few Swedes were volunteering to serve Hitler's New Order and join the SS. In a note the 23-year-old Larsson wrote before setting out for Africa, he bequeathed everything to the Communist party of his hometown, Umeå. The ownership of the immense later fortune that he never saw went by law to his father and brother, leaving his partner of 30 years, Eva Gabrielsson, with no legal claim, only a moral one that asserts she alone is fit to manage Larsson's very lucrative legacy. And this is not the only murk that hangs around his death, at the age of 50, in 2004.

To be exact, Stieg Larsson died on November 9, 2004, which I can't help noticing was the anniversary of Kristallnacht. Is it plausible that Sweden's most public anti-Nazi just chanced to expire from natural causes on such a date? Larsson's magazine, *Expo,* which has a fairly clear fictional cousinhood with "Millennium," was an unceasing annoyance to the extreme right. He himself was the public figure most identified with the unmasking of white-supremacist and neo-Nazi organizations, many of them with a hard-earned reputation for homicidal violence. The Swedes are not the pacific herbivores that many people imagine: in the footnotes to his second novel Larsson reminds us that Prime Minister Olof Palme was gunned down in the street in 1986 and that the foreign minister Anna Lindh was stabbed to death (in a Stockholm department store) in 2003. The first crime is still unsolved, and the verdict in the second case has by no means satisfied everybody.

A report in the mainstream newspaper *Aftonbladet* describes the findings of another anti-Nazi researcher, named Bosse Schön, who unraveled a plot to murder Stieg Larsson that included a Swedish SS veteran. Another scheme misfired because on the night in question, 20 years ago, he saw skinheads with bats waiting outside his office and left by the rear exit. Web sites are devoted to further speculation: one blog is preoccupied with the theory that Prime Minister Palme's uncaught assassin was behind the death of Larsson too. Larsson's name and other details were found when the Swedish police searched the apartment of a Fascist arrested for a political murder. Larsson's address, telephone number, and photograph, along with threats to people identified as "enemies of the white race," were published in a neo-Nazi magazine: the authorities took it seriously enough to prosecute the editor.

But Larsson died of an apparent coronary thrombosis, not from any mayhem. So he would have had to be poisoned, say, or somehow medically murdered. Such a hypothesis would point to some involvement "high up," and anyone who has read the novels will know that in Larsson's world the forces of law and order in Sweden are fetidly complicit with organized crime. So did he wind up, in effect, a character in one of his own tales? The people who might have the most interest in keeping the speculation alive—his publishers and publicists—choose not to believe it. "Sixty cigarettes a day, plus tremendous amounts of junk food and coffee and an enormous workload," said Christopher MacLehose, Larsson's literary discoverer in English and by a nice coincidence a publisher of *Flashman*, "would be the culprit. I gather he'd even had a warning heart murmur. Still, I have attended demonstrations by these Swedish right-wing thugs, and they are truly frightening. I also know someone with excellent contacts in the Swedish police and security world who assures me that everything described in the 'Millennium' novels *actually took place.* And, apparently, Larsson planned to write as many as 10 in all. So you can see how people could think that he might not have died but been 'stopped.'"

He left behind him enough manuscript pages for three books, the last of which—due out in the U.S. next summer—is entitled *The Girl Who Kicked the Hornet's Nest,* and the outlines and initial scribblings of a fourth. The market and appetite for them seems to be unappeasable, as does the demand for Henning Mankell's "Detective Wallander" thrillers, the work of Peter (*Smilla's Sense of Snow*) Høeg, and the stories of Arnaldur Indridason. These writers come from countries as diverse as Denmark and Iceland, but in Germany the genre already has a name: *Schwedenkrimi,* or "Swedish crime writing." Christopher MacLehose told me that he knows of bookstores that now have special sections for the Scandinavian phenomenon. "When Roger Straus and I first published Peter Høeg," he said, "we thought we were doing something of a favor for Danish literature, and then 'Miss Smilla' abruptly sold a million copies in both England and America. Look, in almost everyone there is a memory of the sagas and the Norse myths. A lot of our storytelling got started in those long, cold, dark nights."

Perhaps. But Larsson is very much of our own time, setting himself to confront questions such as immigration, "gender," white-collar crime, and, above all, the Internet. The plot of his first volume does involve a sort of excursion into antiquity—into the book of Leviticus, to be exact—but this is only for the purpose of encrypting a "Bible code." And he is quite deliberately unromantic, giving us shopping lists, street directions, menus, and other details—often with their Swedish names—in full. The villains are evil, all right, but very stupid and self-thwartingly prone to spend more time (this always irritates me) telling their victims what they will do to them than actually doing it. There is much sex but absolutely no love, a great deal of violence but zero heroism. Reciprocal gestures are generally indicated by cliché: if a Larsson character wants to show assent he or she will "nod"; if he or she wants to manifest distress, then it will usually be by biting the lower lip. The passionate world of the sagas and the myths is a very long way away. Bleakness is all. That could even be the secret—the emotionless efficiency of Swedish technology, paradoxically combined with the wicked allure of the pitiless elfin avenger, plus a dash of paranoia surrounding the author's demise. If Larsson had died as a brave martyr to a cause, it would have been strangely out of keeping; it's actually more satisfying that he succumbed to the natural causes that are symptoms of modern life.

THE GIRL WHO CONQUERED THE WORLD: WHY WE CAN'T GET ENOUGH OF STIEG LARSSON'S HACKER HEROINE
by Laura Miller

Laura Miller, co-founder and a senior writer at Salon.com, finds Larsson's prose "as featureless as the Scandinavian landscape." Yet his novels clearly enthrall readers. Why? It is the "unedited-documentary-footage texture" of the narrative, she says, and the "integration of the mundane and the mythic." The trilogy, particularly through the character of Lisbeth Salander, also resonates with the warring impulses we find within ourselves, Miller says—the struggle to balance the need for the rule of law with the desire to spill the blood of revenge. In this essay, one of her regular "What To Read" columns, Miller uses the publication of The Girl Who Kicked the Hornet's Nest, *the final installment of the Millennium trilogy, as her springboard for a thoughtful review.*

Can anyone be seriously contemplating reading *The Girl Who Kicked the Hornet's Nest* who hasn't already read the two previous novels in Stieg Larsson's bestselling Millennium Trilogy, *The Girl With the Dragon Tattoo* and *The Girl Who Played with Fire*? And can there be a reader of those first two books who hopes to resist the third? Anyone who has succumbed to Larsson fever knows what it is to lavish the waking hours of entire weekends on his weirdly matter-of-fact and even more weirdly addictive fiction, surfacing at the end of the binge, bleary-eyed and underfed, wondering what just happened.

So let this installment of "What to Read" address the Millennium trilogy as a whole and ponder the secret of its appeal. Certainly the charm doesn't lie in Larsson's prose; it's as flat and featureless as the Scandinavian landscape it ought to be evoking (but doesn't). Those who have proved immune to the Larsson virus protest that the books are filled with clichés, but that presumes the author to be reaching for more color than he is. There are not

---

a lot of hearts pounding or chills running down spines in *The Girl Who
Kicked the Hornet's Nest.* As Larsson went along, he almost entirely jettisoned
the dime-store thriller theatrics; a heart does occasionally "sink like a stone"
in the third book, but such moments are few and far between.

Which is not to say that his writing became more terse and economical.
If anything, *Hornet's Nest* luxuriates in even more of the pointlessly meticulous, step-by-step detail that marked the first two novels. Here's how one
character begins her day:

> She blinked a few times and got up to turn on the coffeemaker be-
> fore she took her shower. She dressed in black pants, a white polo
> shirt, and a muted brick-red jacket. She made two slices of toast
> with cheese, orange marmalade and a sliced avocado, and carried her
> breakfast into the living room in time for the 6:30 television news.
> She took a sip of coffee and had just opened her mouth to take a bite
> of toast when she heard the headlines.

I should point out that this is a supporting character briefly introduced in
the earlier books, and while she plays a more significant role in this novel,
there's really no reason to so exhaustively describe her morning. It's the sort
of thing that drives the Larsson naysayers nuts, and even some fans have
been known to complain that certain portions of the books "drag." So let me
now testify: *I love this stuff,* although why, exactly, has long been something
of a mystery to me.

My favorite part of *The Girl with the Dragon Tattoo* (after the scene where
Lisbeth Salander triumphs over the court-appointed guardian who abused
her) is the part where crusading journalist Mikael Blomkvist sets up, box
by box, a research office in a little cabin on a remote Swedish island. My
favorite part of *The Girl Who Played with Fire* (after the chapter where Salander infiltrates the bad guys' security system) is when she goes to Ikea to
furnish her secret hideout and Larsson *lists every last thing she buys there.*

Of course, I couldn't bear to read 500-odd pages of Swedish people
munching on toast and buying reasonably priced plastic wastebaskets if that's
all there was to it—if it weren't for Salander, the titular "girl" and the core of
what a marketing director might (and for all I know already does) refer to as
"the franchise." Larsson begins each of the four parts of *The Girl Who Kicked
the Hornet's Nest* with a few paragraphs of canned factoids about women warriors in ancient and modern history, but Salander is not really a warrior. Like
Larsson, she reserves a special hatred for misogynists (the Swedish title of the

first novel in the trilogy translates literally as *Men Who Hate Women*), but unlike the activist and leftist journalist who created her, she is no crusader or soldier. What motivates Salander is not justice, but revenge.

A folklorist once told me that revenge is the root of all narrative; few stories have more immediate practical utility to the teller than the brutal causality of "That man wronged me, and this is how I punished him for it." You might expect a Nordic writer, someone emerging from a culture whose earliest literature is all about seeking retribution, to be acutely aware of this. For some reason, though, Larsson's examples of fighting females are all taken from the classical world and the American Civil War, instead of the shield-maidens of Scandinavian lore, who (besides Pippi Longstocking) would seem to be Salander's logical precedent.

This is primitive stuff, and by the time you get to the beginning of *The Girl Who Kicked the Hornet's Nest*, with Salander surviving both a bullet wound in the head and being buried alive in a shallow grave, there's a dangerous drift toward Tarantino country. What keeps Salander from turning into a cartoon like the Bride from *Kill Bill* is the unedited-documentary-footage texture of the novel's narration. It's this integration of the mundane and the mythic that enables the trilogy to hold its readers in thrall.

The antagonists in the first novel were corporate; in the second they were organized criminals and their accomplices. *The Girl Who Kicked the Hornet's Nest* beards the ultimate villains in their den: abusers of legitimate state authority, specifically the Swedish Security Service, or Säpo, the national police. "I don't believe in collective guilt," says Blomkvist, that authorial sock puppet, and so Larsson takes great care to illustrate that the "system" isn't inherently to blame, but rather individuals who warp it for their own ends.

The climax of *Hornet's Nest* is, naturally, a trial. Salander, who long ago (and with good cause) lost any faith in institutions or official authority, is vendetta personified, confronting the Enlightenment institution of the rule of law. One side is so satisfying, so charismatic, so immediately appealing to our instinctive sense of right and wrong; the other, as Larsson himself was no doubt aware, is the only thing keeping us from descending back into the bloody world of the Icelandic sagas. It's a contest that still captivates us because we all feel those warring impulses within ourselves. The story may be ancient, but somehow it never gets old.

LISBETH SALANDER, THE MILLENNIUM TRILOGY, AND MY MOTHER

by Jenny McPhee

In producing The Girl with the Dragon Tattoo, The Girl Who Played with Fire, *and* The Girl Who Kicked the Hornet's Nest, *Stieg Larsson has given us "a stunning feminist manifesto," writes Jenny McPhee. "Even though his agenda is both repetitive and emphatic, it is so convincingly integrated into the plot and into the characters' lives that rather than feel harangued, a reader feels refreshingly represented."*

McPhee is the author of the novels A Man of No Moon, No Ordinary Matter, *and* The Center of Things, *as well as a regular contributor to the web magazine Bookslut.*

My mother had been urging me to read Stieg Larsson's Millennium trilogy. Like her, I love a good thriller but a ways into the first book, I had my doubts. There just wasn't much thrill in this thriller. Then, on page 263 of *The Girl with the Dragon Tattoo*, whose original title is *Men Who Hate Women*, protagonist extraordinaire Lisbeth Salander performs an act that made me laugh out loud, shiver with vicarious revenge, and definitively confer upon her Bombshell Status. (She has short black hair but makes ample use throughout the trilogy of a blond wig.) Under five feet and an anorexic-seeming 90 pounds (she eats voraciously), Salander uses a taser to immobilize her evil guardian, who previously had raped her brutally, and straps him to his bed. She then proceeds to tattoo across his belly "I AM A SADISTIC PIG, A PERVERT, AND A RAPIST." I almost stood up and clapped.

Though the Millennium trilogy does not offer up particularly great sentences, it does bestow upon us a truly great character in Lisbeth Salander. She is unpredictable and possessed of an Asperger-type social diffidence and secret genius. She has a photographic memory, is one of the world's most

---

This essay was written for the Bookslut blog (www.bookslut.com) and appears here with permission of the author.

talented hackers, has expert financial savvy, and at one point solves Fermat's Last Theorem. Her petite body is a showcase of piercings and tattoos. She is bisexual, likes to use props during sex, and has a penchant for much older men. An excellent boxer (trained by a champion heavyweight), she is a natural with an array of weaponry. Her fierce protectiveness of her mother is the catalyst for the entire saga. She fits squarely into the tradition of anti-heroes who defy a corrupt authority and answers only to a higher morality: her own. She does not hesitate to use violence to right wrongs—usually injustices against women. She is a feminist version of Dirty Harry.

She is no Lara Croft or Charlie's Angel who must pay the price for her physical prowess by titillating the phantom male reader/viewer with her 36-24-36 scantily clad body. In fact, Lisbeth's breasts are so underdeveloped that in the second book she has them enhanced (begging the question: do women undergo plastic surgery to feel better about their self-image or to change how they imagine they appear to a male gaze? Lisbeth's motivation is clearly the former). The books contain plenty of titillation, including sexual violence towards women. I put such easy manipulation on a par with using terminally-ill children or the Holocaust to raise emotional content. The author, however, balances the sexual violence with other kinds of titillating sexual encounters between consenting adults. The possibilities are infinite for sexual fantasy, Larsson indicates, and need not be limited to the porn industry's paltry choices. Furthermore, Larsson seems to be acutely aware of what will turn on his readership. The ideal reader of these books is a heterosexual woman with a fairly fluid concept of sexual preference. Not a bad strategy given that women make up the vast majority of the fiction reading population.

I fully understand why my mother, a member of NOW since the '70s, had been urging me to read these books. Revenge is sweet; for women it rarely comes in such a guilt-free, hugely entertaining package. Few women have been so violently abused as the twenty-something Lisbeth Salander, but as epigraphs in the first book note, a very high percentage of women in Sweden (and by extrapolation everywhere since Swedish society claims to be the most egalitarian in the world) will encounter some form of sexual harassment during their lifetimes. Many female characters in these books triumph over relentless male aggression in deeply satisfying ways. The Millennium trilogy is one long female revenge fantasy.

Throughout the trilogy an overt feminist consciousness presides. The books take on domestic violence, abuse, rape, torture, the serial murder of women within a wealthy industrial family, sex trafficking and the exploitation of immigrant women, severe sexual harassment within a major newspaper, and entrenched sexism in the police force and criminal justice system. The narrative consistently brings the reader's attention to minor and major instances of sexism. Though this agenda is both repetitive and emphatic, it is so convincingly integrated into the plot and into the characters' lives that rather than feel harangued, a reader feels refreshingly represented.

My mother is convinced that Larsson's girlfriend, Eva Gabrielsson, is the real author of the trilogy, or was assisted by Larsson rather than vice-versa. In any case, the author(s) have produced a stunning feminist manifesto within a series of thrillers that goes down like honey. S(he) has done what no one yet has quite been able to do: formulate a feminism palatable for the masses. The trilogy raises our awareness of sexism and institutionalized unfairness towards women, reminds us of our duty to rectify these injustices legally, and if this becomes impossible, calls us to arms. Indeed, the final book incorporates short essays on the history of women warriors.

The most successful aspect of these books perhaps lies, not in the revenge fantasies, nor in thriller conventions (conspiracies and labyrinthine plotting . . .), but rather in the ultimate female sexual fantasy expressed by the relationship between the other two principle protagonists: Mikael Blomkvist and Erika Berger. Erika, a successful magazine editor, is happily married to a man whom she adores and who adores her. They have a great sex life and thoroughly enjoy each other's company. Erika also has a lover, her colleague, the charming, renowned investigative journalist Blomkvist. Erika's husband knows about the affair and understands his wife's need for periodic outside affirmation of her sexual self. For men the mistress paradigm has been around a long time, but this is a particularly female construction of the age-old triad: no children are involved (the guilt would be overwhelming) and the "betrayed" partner is fully acquiescent with minimal needs of his own.

I'll sign up for that. And my mother will too.

THE NOVELS YOU READ ARE NOT NECESSARILY THE NOVELS STIEG LARSSON WROTE

by John-Henri Holmberg

Decisions made by translators, editors, and publishers after Larsson's death might not have been approved had he lived through the publication process.

Part I: How Have the Millennium Novels Been Edited?

The question is more pertinent in the case of Stieg Larsson's novels than normally. When a novel is bought for publication, an editor will usually read the manuscript pen in hand and suggest changes. The author will then discuss the suggestions with the editor, accept some, discard some, sometimes make alternate changes. But in the end, the author will have decided what changes to make.

With the Millennium novels, this was not the case. According to Eva Gedin, the editor handling the books at Norstedts, Larsson's Swedish publisher, "Stieg often stressed that he hoped I and the copy editor, Elin Sennero, would be harsh on his books. He appreciated editorial input, not least because he had often been on the other side of the process and knew how important it was for his text to be put through the mangle to make it as good as possible." I have no doubt that this is true; Stieg did appreciate input, suggestions, even objections or arguments for drastic changes. He never believed his texts to be impossible to improve. But the problem is that he died before the second and third of his novels had been edited, and so had no chance to approve or reject the changes made to his work.

Stieg Larsson's three novels in their Swedish editions run to 1,902 pages; they will be referred to here as book 1 (*The Girl with the Dragon Tattoo*), book 2 (*The Girl Who Played with Fire*), and book 3 (*The Girl Who Kicked the Hornet's Nest*). A detailed comparison of the manuscripts (which Stieg e-mailed me long before any editorial changes had been made) with the printed text would fill hundreds of pages and not be particularly interesting. Most of the many thousand changes are slight.

But there are also substantive changes. Let us look at a few of them.

Stieg's original idea was to use *Men Who Hate Women* as the overall title for the three books. Each volume had a subtitle: *Millennium*; *The Witch Fantasizing About a Jerry Can and a Match*; *The Queen of the Castle in the Air*. Eva Gedin disliked Stieg's main title:

> I did not think the title *Men Who Hate Women* was good. It sounded too hard. It could sound off-putting. It sounded more like a non-fiction title. . . . He came back after a while and said he was certain that the first book had to be called *Men Who Hate Women*. We were welcome to change other things, but that was something he was not prepared to give way on. An instance of his more uncompromising side perhaps. . . .

At least in Sweden, Stieg's *Men Who Hate Women* title was used for the first novel. I assume that he agreed to the series title "Millennium"; what is not known is whether he also agreed to the title changes for the second and third novel.

At the time of Stieg's death, editing of the first novel in Swedish was basically finished and he had seen the changes suggested. For this reason, I refrain from discussing the first book here.

In books 2 and 3, line editing is sometimes heavy. In the first chapter of book 2, Stieg wrote, "Historically, Grenada was one of many insignificant former British colonies where Captain Blackbeard might or might not have come ashore to bury a treasure." But the as-published sentence is cut off after "colonies," leaving out the reference to Blackbeard. When he writes that Maurice Bishop "was murdered in 1983 by a bunch of crazed Stalinists ever since interred in the local jail," the sentence is cut after "1983." A short paragraph about some of the things Lisbeth Salander did during her seven weeks in Grenada is deleted. In the original manuscript, it goes: "Maybe once a week she had visited the market in St. George's or taken day tours to the extinct Grand Etang volcano. She had taken a three-day tour to the neighboring island Carriacou, including an interesting boat trip crossing *Kick 'em Jenny*, a constantly bubbling subsurface volcano. She liked the name of the volcano." Lisbeth's approval of the name is an example of Stieg's humor; the rest adds a few details about how she spends her time in Grenada. But Norstedts apparently didn't think this important. There are hundreds of similar examples of words or sentences being deleted. Few affect the action.

What is taken out is generally asides that add interesting details, humor, or insight into the characters.

There is also a troubling tendency to tone down Stieg's views on nondemanding sex. (In the examples that follow, the underlined words and sentences are the ones deleted by the publisher.) In chapter 6, book 2, Lisbeth Salander is visiting Miriam Wu. Lisbeth says, "Mimmi, I am as I am. So are you. You're trying to get into the pants of everyone with breasts and even of someone like me almost without. That's why having sex with you was so nice. You didn't care one whit what I was doing, and if I was busy you found someone else. And you don't give a damn about what people think of you." For the deleted part, the noncommittal words, "I've always liked having sex with you" are substituted.

There are other brief cuts in the next pages. And later in the same dialogue:

"You're sexy as hell to me. You give me so many orgasms."
"You too. That's why I return to you."
"Not love?" Mimmi asked in a voice pretending hurt.
Lisbeth shook her head.
"Me neither," Mimmi said seriously. "You know, you hit on people just like a guy at a meat market."
"What?"
"You're so obviously interested only in having sex and walking out in the morning."
Lisbeth didn't know how to respond to that. She knitted her brows.
"Insulted? Don't be. I'm pretty much the same. You know that. And when we hung out or whatever I should call it, you were never whiny or put off if I had sex with someone else."
"Are you seeing someone right now?"

These deletions and substitutions represent a material change to Stieg's depiction of how these characters reason and behave, which is an integrated part of his theme.

In Stieg's view, the basis for all discrimination is the idea of inequality. Those viewing people of another color, sex, or sexuality as inferior also believe themselves to have the right to treat their "inferiors" as they would not treat their equals.

The corollary is that those who believe in the equal rights and value of all individuals must never overstep the boundaries set by each individual's right to integrity, free choice, and personal preference. This demands that all relations between individuals are based on mutual consent, choice, and desire. In such relations, there is no room to express feelings of ownership, control, or jealousy, physically or emotionally. Which means that between free agents who feel that way, sex is a value in itself, to be accepted when mutually desired, but implying no claim on any participant.

To Stieg, this view was basic, and it permeates his writing. Throughout the Millennium books, this is how the "good" characters—Lisbeth Salander, Mikael Blomkvist, Erika Berger and her husband Greger, Miriam Wu, Monica Figuerola, and many others—consistently behave. They have sex freely when they feel like it, but it involves no claims or dependencies. Whereas sex to the "bad" characters always involves submission and degradation; to them, convinced of their inherent superiority, sex is not an act of mutual pleasure, but of violence and domination, and consequently of hatred.

Many passages relevant to this view of sex and relationships have been deleted. One example is around 270 words long, which, in Stieg's manuscript, begins chapter 18 of book 3. Mikael Blomkvist wakes up after spending his first night with Monica Figuerola. He has slept only three hours and aches all over. Monica, on the other hand, is in great shape: "Her body was her temple." Mikael asks her if all muscular women are as dominant. Monica says that she doesn't know, and pays him a compliment: "I might want to do it again one of these days."

Elsewhere, when Figuerola is introduced a few pages into chapter 12, book 3, part of her characterization has also been deleted. The original manuscript tells us that she was, "the prototype of the stereotypical wheat-blonde, athletic Swedish woman any average nutty Nazi would have loved to use as a poster model depicting an Aryan Valkyrie. Unfortunately for them, Monica Figuerola was smart. She hated Nazis and was of the opinion that skinheads might at worst be used as training material in martial arts classes." Whether or not anyone thought her ideal use of Nazis as punching bags was funny, it is typical of the way in which Stieg wanted to editorialize.

One of the longest passages cut from Stieg's manuscripts is the first scene of chapter 1, book 3, close to eight hundred words written from the viewpoint of the helicopter pilot transporting Lisbeth Salander to the hospital in Gothenburg. It's a bridging scene between the end of book 2 and the start of the action in book 3; though not necessary to the action, deleting it to me seems a deplorable instance of someone just unable to let things alone.

Right after this deleted scene, we are introduced, in Stieg's manuscript, to the physician who examines Lisbeth Salander. His name is Dr. Anders Jacobsson. But readers of the published book will know this important character as Dr. Anders Jonasson.

Why this change?

Dr. Anders Jakobsson is a real person. He and Stieg Larsson became friends as gymnasium students in Umeå and remained so until Stieg's death. In the case of Dr. Jakobsson, Stieg obviously wanted a friend to appear as himself. Dr. Jakobsson is an M.D. and chief surgeon living in Gothenburg. He would have been the ideal doctor on call when the critically wounded Salander was brought in.

When visiting Umeå early in 2005, however, Dr. Jakobsson happened to meet Stieg Larsson's father, Erland, in a store. They had words, and Erland Larsson says that Dr. Jakobsson "called me a few names that made me feel very bad." After having discussed the incident with his son Joakim, Erland Larsson asked Norstedts to remove Dr. Jakobsson's name from Stieg's novel. "Small-minded or revengeful, call it what you will, but that was the decision," Erland Larsson later said to a TV journalist.

Dr. Jakobsson responded by publishing an open letter, writing, "As a close friend of Stieg Larsson for more than thirty years I am in a position to state that Stieg would definitely not accept that anyone corrupted his books nor robbed his life partner Eva of his legacy. In fact, Stieg Larsson would have done anything to stop this, had he been alive. Without any limits whatever." But this stand got Dr. Jakobsson thrown out of the book.

Another character who was a real-life friend of Stieg's since their teens is psychiatrist Svante Brandén. He is one of the expert defense witnesses slated to be called in the trial against Lisbeth Salander, and is mentioned in chapter 27, book 3, although he is never put on stage in the novel. In a published letter to Joakim Larsson, he writes that,

> As a specialist in criminal psychiatry, I want my name in some sense to be associated with justice and morality. That Stieg wanted to use my name in his novel was an honor. But after his death, you are profiteering from Stieg's work, and use my name entirely without my consent. . . . I demand that you immediately stop using my name in Stieg's novel. . . . When you try to appear a moral heir by claiming in the media that Stieg willingly refrained from writing a will, in order for you and your father instead of Eva to inherit, you are no longer only pathetic. You are also reviling Stieg, making him out to be a

weird and irresponsible person, totally alien to all of us who knew
him and Eva.

Svante Brandén's name, however, has not been removed, despite his wish.

In summary, a number of changes and deletions have been made that lessen
the presence of Stieg's personal voice and opinions, as well as his ironic humor.
This is a pity; its main effect is to make the novels more bland than in
manuscript.

Additionally, many changes and cuts have been made to passages depicting or arguing for Stieg's views on sex and morality. These changes are as a
whole offensive, as they weaken the theme of the novels and the author's arguments for it.

Part II: The Troubled Translation from Swedish to English

Although Stieg Larsson's novels have now been published in over forty languages, nearly half of their 50 million copies have been sold in English
language editions, principally from MacLehose Press (a division of the
London-based publisher Quercus), and from Knopf (a division of New York–
based Random House). Many other editions have been translated from the
English version, rather than from the original Swedish. Most of Stieg Larsson's readers, in other words, have met him only via the English translation
of his novels. But how well does that translation actually represent his talent? Sadly, a review of the books by someone fluent in English and Swedish
will show that the translations are often disappointingly sloppy and inac-
curate. The English-language version changes descriptions, implications,
emotional sense, and other attributes of the text throughout the novels.

Stieg Larsson himself was not primarily concerned with stylistic elegance. When choosing a specific word he would consider its informational
rather than aesthetic value. His aim was to convey details and implications
of a scene. Typical of the translation of the three Millennium books overall
is that much of the information from the original text has been excluded.
But worse: the English translation of the Millennium books is, in fact, un-
faithful to the originals on the whole, haphazardly edited, and surprisingly
bad. It is impressive that Stieg Larsson's storytelling and characters have

managed to overcome the obstacle of this translation to be loved by millions and millions of readers.

Let me add here that I am unable to place the blame for the translation on any specific culprit. The translator of the novels, Steven T. Murray, was given a commission to translate the novels in a great hurry by Norstedts, Larsson's Swedish publisher, who needed an English version in order to sell international publishing rights. After MacLehose Press made the first deal to acquire the English-language rights, Murray's translation was subjected to extensive editing in-house by the MacLehose team. These editors apparently either did not know Swedish or failed to check their edits against the Swedish original. Instead, they may well have made matters worse by letting translation mistakes lead to further distorting changes.

Although the extent of the changes made by MacLehose—whose definitive edit was the basis for the North American versions published by Knopf/Random House—cannot be determined at this time, it is significant that Steve Murray chose to remove his name from the books. This is why his pen name "Reg Keeland" appears as the translator of the English-language editions. As I have not been able to check Murray's original translation against the published version of the books, I can give no opinion on the relative merits of the unedited versus the published versions of the translation. Murray seems publicly ambivalent. On the one hand, he removed his name as the translator. On the other hand, he now seems to accept bookstore invitations to sign the English version of the novels.

Stieg Larsson was an author very open to editorial suggestions. But there was one documented matter on which he absolutely insisted—maintaining his original title for the first book: *Men Who Hate Women.* Norstedts had no choice but to retain this title in Swedish since Stieg explicitly refused any change. However, after Norstedts sold the foreign rights, publishers in different countries were apparently given free reign to pick their own titles. MacLehose decided on *The Girl with the Dragon Tattoo,* which appears exactly nowhere as a phrase in Stieg's books, in his notes, or in his correspondence.

Now, what about the tattoo?

What does the actual dragon tattoo on Lisbeth Salander's body actually look like—and where does it reside physically? In fact, she sports different dragon tattoos in Swedish and English. In the first two novels, the tattoo is mentioned and described four times. All four descriptions are different in

English than in the Swedish original. We'll compare just two of the English versions to their original counterparts.

The description in the first and second paragraphs of book 1, chapter 23, in English reads:

> *He looked down at the dragon on her shoulder blade.*
>
>   *He counted her tattoos. As well as a wasp on her neck, she had a loop around one ankle, another loop around the biceps of her left arm, a Chinese symbol on her hip, and a rose on one calf.*

The Swedish text reads quite differently. Instead of having a "dragon on her shoulder blade," the Swedish Lisbeth has a dramatic tattoo indeed:

> *He looked down on the dragon stretching across her back, from her right shoulder blade down to her buttock.*
>
>   *He counted her tattoos. Apart from the dragon on her back and the wasp on her neck she had a loop around one ankle, another loop around her left biceps, a Chinese sign on her hip and a rose on her calf. Except for the dragon, her tattoos were small and discrete.*

In other words, the author is stressing that the tattoo is huge. It runs "from her right shoulder blade down to her buttock." Given the size and prominence of this tattoo as described in Stieg Larsson's version, re-titling the book *The Girl with the Dragon Tattoo* might even seem reasonable.

But in English, the dragon has shrunk remarkably. For some reason it is now merely a small tattoo just "on her shoulder blade." A feature so important as to give the book its English title is thus all but obliterated.

Near the end of chapter 5 in *The Girl Who Played with Fire*, we find Stieg's most complete description. In English, the tattoo is described as follows: ". . . the tattoo on her back—it was beautiful, a curving dragon in red, green and black." But the original Swedish refers specifically to the "large" tattoo on Lisbeth's back and then goes on to say: "It was beautiful, a long, slithering dragon in red and green and black that began on her shoulder and whose slim tail continued down over her right buttock to end on her thigh."

Why this change? Did someone feel that Stieg went too far, and had to be curbed? Or is the reason as pedestrian and pathetic as that the novel's British publisher had already commissioned the cover art, discovered that the tattoo on the covers was fairly small, and decided to make the author's text fit the covers?

Sadly, this seems most plausible. The result is that Lisbeth Salander is not the same person in Swedish and English. The dragon tattoo is both important to her self-image and a feature striking to those she allows to get close to her. (Both Blomkvist in *Tattoo* and the doctor in *Hornet's Nest* have scenes where they behold this large, back-covering dragon and reflect on it.) The Swedish Salander really is the "Girl with the Dragon Tattoo." But the English Salander is more demure—with only a small dragon tattooed on her shoulder blade.

But the dragon tattoo is just one striking example of the liberties taken in the English translation. Translation mistakes and confusing changes abound. A few paragraphs after the dragon tattoo quote from book 1, chapter 23, for example, we find another telling case of unprofessional work. In English, the following conversation occurs:

> A *couple of hours later over breakfast Blomkvist said, "How are we going to solve this puzzle?"*
> *"We sum up the facts we have. We try to find more."*
> *"For me, the only question is: why? { . . . }"*

This seems straightforward. Since only two characters are present, who says what is obvious. But how can "the only question is why" be a relevant response to someone suggesting more facts are needed? This is resolved by the original, which reads:

> A *couple of hours later they were having breakfast in the garden. Lisbeth Salander looked at Mikael.*
> *"We have a riddle to solve. How do we do it?"*
> *"Sum up the facts we have. Try to find more."*
> *"One fact is that someone close to us is gunning for you."*
> *"The only question is why? { . . . }"*

The alterations here are of two different kinds. The next to last line of original Swedish text is missing from the English. Since the statement "One fact is that someone close to us is gunning for you" is vital here; I would infer that the translator excluded it by mistake. An editor (whose function is to check and correct spelling, grammar, and breaks in continuity) most probably then read the text and decided that the dialog made no sense; that editor deleted the "Salander looked at Mikael" sentence, a change which makes Blomkvist, not Salander, speak the first sentence. In the English version, the speakers are Blomkvist, Salander, and Blomkvist, which attributes the first two lines to the wrong speakers.

Rather than covering up the error of a line being dropped, the reasonable thing would have been to re-insert the missing line. What we are given is the result of a non-Swedish-reading editor trying to correct what he, or she, mistakenly assumes is an inconsistency in the text. And that is what you end up with when an editor is allowed to treat a translation of a published book as if it were an unpublished work written in English.

The problems with the translation are not always as obvious as the description of the tattoo or the dropping of a critical line and the resulting mix-up of speakers. But the problems are everywhere, even from the first pages of chapter 1, book 1. The translation almost immediately departs from the original courtroom scene. We learn that Blomkvist has been sentenced for a crime, and, while facing the reporters and checking who is present, he notes in Swedish, "oh, *Dagens Industri*. I must have become famous." In English, amazingly, it is an entirely different Swedish newspaper whose reporter he recognizes: "ah yes, *Dagens Nyheter*. I must be a celebrity." But *Dagens Nyheter* is the largest morning paper in Sweden, present at any newsworthy event in Stockholm. The paper Blomkvist notes is a business and economics daily, and would not automatically cover court cases.

Next, in English, we get this:

> *"Give us a sound bite, Kalle Blomkvist." It was a reporter from one of the evening papers.*
>
> *Blomkvist, hearing the nickname, forced himself as always not to roll his eyes.*

But in Swedish, it goes:

> *"Give us a quote, Kalle Blomkvist", the reporter from one of the two afternoon tabloids said.*
>
> *Mikael Blomkvist, whose full name happened to be Carl Mikael Blomkvist, as always when hearing the nickname forced himself not to wince.*

Here, Stieg explains the nickname. In English, Blomkvist's full name was given a page earlier, while by waiting to give Blomkvist's full name until the nickname is used, Stieg makes the connection obvious to readers familiar with the Astrid Lindgren boy detective. In English, the explanation follows more than a page later.

Some mistakes are unfathomable, as when Blomkvist's condominium apartment is described in English as being located "right at the end of Bellmansgatan," when in Swedish he lives "right at the start of Bellmansgatan." Well, is it the Swedish "start" or the English "end"? In the case of Bellmansgatan, which is a real street in Stockholm, the Swedish is correct—it is the start, and the building Blomkvist lives in even has no. 1 as its street address. In book 3, an anonymous email to Erika Berger is translated as saying "You're going to get fucked in the cunt with a screwdriver, whore!" (incidentally an excellent example of how informal Swedish can be turned into absurdly pedantic English) when the original Swedish quotes this abuser as threatening to use the screwdriver in Berger's anus.

The peculiar use of everyday Swedish descriptive titles is worth noting. "Advokat," "Fru," and "Herr" are used as titles. Why these words are not translated is a mystery. "Advokat" is a generic term for "lawyer." "Fru" was once reserved for noble females, but now just means "wife" or "Mrs."; the same goes for "Herr," once a male honorific, now meaning only "Mr."

In chapter 1, book 2, reference is made to a gang of bank robbers wearing Disney character latex masks (in translation claimed to come from Disney World). The police dubs the robbers "the Donald Duck Gang," but journalists rename them "the Bear Gang." This becomes intelligible only if you know that *Donald Duck* is the Swedish name for the Disney comic book, while "the Bear Gang" is the Swedish name for the Beagle Boys, those hapless criminals forever trying to rob Uncle Scrooge.

Idiosyncratic expressions are translated literally—"That ain't cat shit" is, strangely, something Swedes actually say when impressed by something, but is hardly idiomatic in English. When Salander texts online, the query "Is there something on G?" isn't very clear. However, the phrase "på G," as in "på gång," is very common Swedish slang for "going on" or "happening." And, although much harder to show by examples, that is really the main problem with the translation: it sounds like Swedish rendered word by word into English. Most of the words are reasonably translated, but the end result is stilted, quaint and pedantic—everything that Stieg Larsson's quick, journalistic prose isn't.

A good example of this: "Harald Vanger had gone back to his cave by the time Blomkvist came out. When he turned the corner he found some-one quite different sitting on the porch of his cottage reading a newspaper." In Swedish, the sentences read: "When Mikael came back outside, Harald Vanger had disappeared from the road, perhaps back into his hole. As he turned the corner of the cottage, he saw the back of someone sitting on the porch, reading a newspaper."

Sometimes the translation becomes unintelligible because of nuances missed, as when Dragan Armansky "glanced suspiciously at his colleague Lisbeth Salander. . . . His mistrust was both wise and irrational. In Arman-sky's eyes, Salander was beyond doubt the most able investigator he had met." But if she's so good, why suspicion and mistrust? Actually, because both "suspicion" and "mistrust" are used for the single Swedish word "mis-stroget," which in this context means "incredulous." Armansky's problem isn't that he mistrusts Salander, but that her appearance clashes with her talents. There is any number of similarly off-key translations, where the wrong among alternate meanings has been picked.

And a final small, but telling, point. Stieg habitually gives times in words, not digits, since most times are approximate—there is a difference between the original's "Her mobile woke Erika Berger at five past nine," and the translation's "Berger's mobile was ringing. It was 9.05." Even the ex-pressly vague Swedish sentence, "Monica Figuerola woke Mikael Blomkvist around one in the afternoon" becomes the pedantic, "Figuerola woke Blom-kvist at 1.00 in the afternoon." Such nonsense is typical of the translation.

The sad final verdict:

The English translation shows no feeling and no respect for Stieg Lars-son's style or intentions. There are innumerable misinterpretations, wrongly selected words, misunderstandings and textual changes. Surprisingly often, the translation seems smugly to correct the author; clarifications and indica-tions of mood and character are cut or abbreviated. Slang words and phrases and typical Swedish idioms are misinterpreted. Stieg's humor, often ex-pressed by consciously repeating the same word or phrase but inferring slightly different meanings, is often erased since the translation avoids all repetition, obviously never suspecting that it may serve a purpose. In short, the English translation is stilted, reads badly, is full of unwarranted cuts, deletions, changes, and misunderstandings, and gives no true impression of the style, atmosphere, or storytelling "voice" of Stieg Larsson's novels.

A number of the online reviews posted by English-language readers on various book-related websites have noted that there are problems with the translation. Even without any knowledge of Swedish, they have found the translation lacking. And they are right. There is even an essay in this book that accuses Stieg of lacking any sense of humor. I can't argue with that assessment of his translated books. But I can assure you that Stieg is often quite funny in Swedish. In the English book 3, a policeman meeting Salander for the first time reflects: "It was possible that the bit about Satanism was an exaggeration. She did not look the type." But in the Swedish original, he thinks: "Though perhaps that thing about Satanism might be an exaggeration. She didn't look particularly satanic." Sadly, Stieg is humor*less* in English.

Ever since his teens, Stieg read fiction as well as nonfiction primarily in English. He even claimed to read Swedish crime authors in English translation, as English to him was the proper language in which to experience noir crime novels. He would have been appalled at the kind of translation his novels have been subjected to. Whoever is responsible for it obviously did not understand Stieg Larsson. Or, in my opinion, much Swedish.

His death must have been a terrible blow to morale.
We decided very quickly that the shock and grief had to come later and that we had to finish everything that Stieg was involved in. For two weeks after he died I had to work on the magazine and also on a book we had been writing together. Everybody agreed that the best way to handle the situation was to continue the work that Stieg had started.

You said he was welcoming and generous. What other character traits stood out?
He was very loyal and very funny. He wanted to help people. But he also had a problem delegating, which sometimes made him more stressed than he should have been because of the workload he took on. I also think he was quite frustrated at times with *Expo*. He wanted it to grow, to be something that it wasn't at that moment. But, thankfully, he was patient and he stayed when many others left.

I think another thing was that he was not motivated to be a journalist for its own sake. Journalism was the way he could be a crusader for the things most important to him, from feminism to exposing neo-Nazi political groups. He was a dogged researcher but what he did better than anyone else was to analyze these problems in society.

How could someone who was so busy running *Expo* find time to write these three—possibly more—books?
It's astonishing. But I do think there is something of a misperception out there of how burdened he was with work. He usually arrived here at *Expo* after lunch, and then worked for eight to ten hours. Then he went home. When I go home, I usually put on the television, but I guess the first thing he did was to switch on his laptop and start to do the other thing he had loved doing all his life: tell and write stories.

Was he stressed? Yes. But Stieg worked at *Expo* because it was his passion. And he went home and wrote his books because he saw that as fun.

Even so, it's impressive that someone who writes for *Expo* can find the time and energy to do so much writing on the side.
Yes, but he didn't write so much for *Expo*. If you look at the magazine the last two years that Stieg was alive he wasn't doing a lot of reporting. He wrote reports, routine things that he published because he had to. But that was not the same kind of writing. I also think he sometimes wrote his books at work.

Do you think he would have stayed on at *Expo* after he became a literary success?

My sense is that he wanted to move on, that he wanted to write more books. There were meetings where it was quite obvious that he was passing on some of his responsibilities. We never talked about this explicitly. But that is my feeling.

What was your reaction when you read the Millennium books?

It was unmistakably Stieg's storytelling. The subject is very serious, of course, but I felt a sense of humor in the books that I recognized as a kind of "Stiegishness" that is very hard to explain in English. An example is the title of one of his absolutely favorite TV series, *Buffy the Vampire Slayer*. Here you have a sweet name joined with the image of a vampire. It is absurd and intellectually playful at the same time. He loved that approach.

Did Stieg's work for *Expo* ever put him in danger? And do you yourself feel in danger now?

Stieg was one of the first people in Sweden to be an expert on the extreme right, and visibly so. Of course he was targeted. He was seen as a threat to the movement. I don't know if there were plans to kill him or just beat him up. But he had good reason to worry. During the end of the '90s two people who wrote for *Expo* had their car bombed. They survived. And we still don't know who did it. But as far as the police can say, the only possible reason for putting a bomb in their car was because they were writing about the extreme right. I've also been threatened. When I've been reporting on far-right demonstrations, I have been chased. I've been kicked. They don't like us at all.

But currently these groups have been trying to transform themselves into an acceptable political alternative and have united under the banner of the Sweden Democrats, who managed recently to get twenty seats in Parliament this way. They don't bomb cars as a political strategy because they know that's the wrong way to get what you want in Sweden today. However, there are people inside these organizations who get fed up with the idea of having to be patient and they think they have to do something violent. At least every third year or so, we have a group who plans to bomb things and kill people. They put up lists of people they want to get rid of. And, of course, *Expo* is one of the groups they see as their enemy. So of course it's risky.

Has the popularity of Stieg's books raised *Expo*'s profile?

Stieg's books have made *Expo* one of the most famous magazines in the world when you take into account its size. I have people from Japan wanting to friend me on Facebook just because I work for *Expo*. It has enabled us to look at the possibility of cooperating with similar organizations globally, something we are very interested in.

There has been a lot of controversy over Stieg's legacy. Did he leave anything to *Expo*? Has the foundation benefited at all?
We have benefited not because Stieg left anything to us but because his brother and his father have given *Expo* 5.5 million Swedish crowns (US$860,000) in recent years. It's a lot of money for us and it's one reason why we have three rooms and a bigger staff than a couple of years ago.

And how about Eva, who is so at odds with Stieg's family? Do you have a good relationship with her?
I like Eva. As far as I am concerned we have a good relationship. It's been a very complicated situation for us because I have tried to support Eva as well as I can, but we have had to put *Expo* first. I think sometimes I've disappointed her for doing so.

I take it she would rather you weren't taking money from Stieg's father and brother?
Yes, of course. And I guess that she would not have wanted us to cooperate with the publishing house Norstedts in the way that we have. We are participating with them in a jury that has an annual prize in Stieg's name. This year the prize went to a nurse who organizes medical help for illegal immigrants in Sweden. I can understand if Eva sometimes feels disappointed, but there is no big problem as far as I see.

Are there other ways *Expo* could be benefiting financially from its association with Stieg?
Yes. But we haven't gone down that route because we don't want to use Stieg. That's not a good way to honor him. A good way to honor him is to do things as he would have wanted us to, namely continuing to work with *Expo* and trying to make *Expo* grow.

Where do you see *Expo* going in the years ahead?
When I close my eyes and think of *Expo* in fifty years, I see an organization that is spread all over the world. We want more contacts and a bigger network. Intolerance is not just a Swedish problem, it's a global problem.

You have been generous with your time but I noticed that, unlike
Stieg, you don't drink coffee every five minutes.

Yeah, but I've been sitting here for fifty minutes wondering when you
would let me stop talking so I could get a cup.

MY COLLEAGUE, STIEG LARSSON
an interview with Mikael Ekman

Mikael Ekman was an idealistic fifteen-year-old when he first made contact with Stieg Larsson. After reading an issue of Expo, *Ekman volunteered himself as a source for information about the growing influence of the local Nazi party on youth culture in his hometown. Tall and blond, with blue eyes, he quickly befriended the skinheads, infiltrated their group, and even found himself at the local Nazi propaganda chief's birthday party.*

Ekman headed to Stockholm at the age of nineteen, and soon became a key member of the Expo *team. In 2001, he and Larsson co-authored* Sverigedemokraterna, *an influential book about the Sweden Democrats, the extremist right-wing party. Between 1999 and 2005, he specialized in researching Sweden's Nazi scene, traveling across the country on behalf of* Expo, *giving lectures and taking part in seminars about far-right threats for police departments and schools.*

Since then Ekman has carved out a successful career as a television producer and a journalist. But he still spends about twenty hours a week working for Expo, *largely on the foundation's annual report on the Swedish white power movement. In thinking about Larsson again, Ekman told us, "As much as he was fighting against xenophobia and everything else, he never lost his faith in humanity."*

How did you meet Stieg?
I grew up in Karlskrona, a small town in the south of Sweden with a population of about sixty thousand. When I was fourteen, there was a strong youth culture centered around the local Nazi party. I wanted to work against these kinds of groups because even then I believed in democracy and freedom. So I went to the library and ordered three books, one of which was *Extremhögern,* a book about right-wing extremism that Stieg co-wrote with Anna-Lena Lodenius in the early '90s. (See the interview with Lodenius in chapter 3.)

It was around that time, at a Youth Against Racists meeting, that I first saw *Expo* magazine. Afterward, I called *Expo* and asked if I could help. I started to monitor the Nazi movement in Karlskrona. And I had my first contact with Stieg, over the phone, around '95 or '96. He was like a role model for me. I thought it was really cool to talk to the author of a book I had read.

Did you find him an easy person to talk to?
Yes. He was really interested in what I had to say because at that time the Nazi movement in Karlskrona was growing fast. Stieg wanted information and I sent as much as I could. I mailed him Nazi leaflets and articles written by Nazis. I even started going to the local courthouse to see what I could dig up.

Was it dangerous snooping on Nazis, especially considering you were only fifteen or sixteen years old?
It was more like I was debating with them and discussing the issues openly. Of course, I didn't tell people I was working for *Expo*.

So how did you go from researching Nazis to working undercover for Stieg?
One night, around midnight, I started arguing with one of the local leaders of the National Socialist Front. I said, "If you have something to tell me, why don't we go out and have a coffee one Sunday and talk about it." So he took me up on the offer.

I look like a typical Aryan, with blond hair and blue eyes. He and his friends couldn't understand why I wasn't a National Socialist. They asked me: "You read so much about us and what we believe. Why don't you become a National Socialist?"

I told Stieg about this and I suggested that I could become a member and get even more material. Stieg encouraged me to do it. I became a member in early '97. They wanted to believe that I wanted to be a member, so they accepted me. I went to a lot of meetings and got a lot of information.

What kind of information were you passing to Stieg?
It was everything from the weapons I saw them carrying to the private newsletters they sent only to people inside the movement. I also got to talk to higher-ranking people at events such as the propaganda chief's birthday party. I found out how they worked and came to understand their point of view.

Why do you think people were attracted to this ideology?
There are youths who have had a bad childhood and who are trying to find a way to belong. I would say about one-third were like that. Then there were those whose parents were racists and for whom it was only a short step to becoming more radical than their parents. And then there were the people who joined the National Socialists for the same reason that other people become conservatives or socialists. They believed in it.

What united them all were their attitudes toward immigration and race. They believed they were the supreme Aryan race whose power was being eroded. Anti-Semitism was a very strong component as well.

How big is the Nazi movement in Sweden today?
I would say there are between three thousand and five thousand activists who will go out on the streets and demonstrate. But there are a lot more people who like listening to the music or hanging out in Internet forums. The biggest Swedish Nazi forum has about twenty thousand members. But the biggest organized Nazi party, Svenskarnas Parti (Swedish People's Party), had enough support to win a local election, the first time since the Second World War that Nazis became elected in Sweden.

When you finished high school in 1999, you abandoned your undercover work and became a researcher at *Expo*. What was it like to work for *Expo* in those days?
It was a struggle. The last issue of the magazine had been published in '97. By '99, we were just writing short reports for our network of contacts and sometimes being published in a Norwegian newspaper called *The Monitor*. *Expo* paid next to nothing, so I had to work at the post office and as a waiter and a bartender to earn a living. Our office was one room about 150 square feet.

And it was around this time that you wrote a book with Stieg?
In February 2001, I mentioned to Stieg that the Sweden Democrats—a right-wing party that had by then differentiated itself from the Nazis— always said that immigrants were criminals. However, when I looked at court documents it was obvious that many of the cases involved Sweden Democrats themselves. Stieg told me to check it out and within six weeks I found out that about 25 percent of Sweden Democrats running for office had prior criminal convictions. I suggested writing an article about it but Stieg said it was time to write a book. I was twenty-one and I didn't have a

clue how much work it would be. Stieg said it was pretty easy: "We just do it."

So, in May we went to a publishing house, got a book deal, and started writing.

What was it like to work with Stieg on a project like that?
It was fun. I was mainly doing research, checking out our suppositions, and also doing some writing. There was a lot of sitting and writing at the desks, smoking a lot, and drinking coffee a lot. Apart from Stieg taking two weeks out to go sailing, we worked all that summer. I stayed at *Expo* all the time, even overnight, and we had the book done by November third. I lost thirty-five pounds.

Did the book get noticed?
We got a lot of interest from newspapers and TV stations. The publisher thought it would sell around three thousand copies but we sold about fourteen thousand. It started a discussion about the Sweden Democrats and their heritage. It also got us marked as an ideological target by them, accusing us of being terrorists, leftists, and militant antifascists.

And yet the Sweden Democrats are even more popular today than they were when you wrote the book.
Absolutely. In the 2002 election, they got about 1.4 percent of the national vote, not enough to get into parliament, which requires 4.0 percent or more. But in the 2010 election, they received about 5.7 percent of the vote and now have twenty seats. It's a disaster. But it's not a surprise. Even at that time, Stieg was saying that we would have them in government by the election of 2010.

What was his answer to combating them?
He said that you have to give strength to the good side. That's why *Expo*'s work is to gather information rather than join the debate. We exist to help people see through far-right lies and propaganda and to help other political parties fight them.

Sometimes Stieg is portrayed as a political soldier, who only fought on one side. But I don't think that is a true picture of him. During our time at *Expo,* he worked with every political party in Sweden, from the conservative Christian Democrats to the left-wing parties. The most important thing for him was an open society.

Was the book a financial success for you and Stieg?
It was not a huge book deal, but I was only twenty-one so it seemed like a lot of money at the time. When we got our first check we split it in three parts. One went to *Expo,* one to me, and one to Stieg. My part was about thirty thousand kroner (about US$4,000) and I went out and spent it straight away.

After a while, the publishing house called me and asked if I could talk to Stieg. They said that Stieg hadn't cashed his check and that they kept having to send replacements. It wasn't that Stieg was rich. He just wasn't interested in the money. He had enough to pay his bills and to buy cigarettes, coffee, food, and a card for the bus and that was all he needed.

Many people describe Stieg as a good storyteller. Did you find this to be true?
The first time I met Stieg was at his and Eva's place in November 1996. We were drinking wine and eating cheese and he told me these incredible anecdotes about his past. I thought he must be a liar because the stories seemed a little too good to be true. But over the years, I met the people and learned of the events he had told me about. Of course, he had embellished his tales a little, but they were basically true. Over the following years, he told the same stories again and again to anyone who joined *Expo.* He was a pro at it, always knowing the right way to tell it and the place to take breaks to wait for a laugh or reaction.

When was the first time Stieg told you about his Millennium novels?
We were at his place, drinking whisky and discussing the future. I asked him what he would do when he got older because he hadn't saved any money. And he said, "I will write a couple of crime novels and become a multimillionaire." When he got his first check from Norstedts, I think it was around sixty thousand Euros (about US$80,000), he showed it to me and said: "I told you so."

That was the thing with Stieg. He was a visionary. A lot of the stuff he was talking about ten or fifteen years ago—what *Expo* could be, the rise of the Sweden Democrats, his books' success—was really hard to see back then. But when I look back now at what they have all become, I think "he knew it"—and that's pretty cool. Of course, he couldn't have seen how big his own success would be. But he knew it was coming.

If Stieg were alive today, how do you think he would have reacted to becoming a literary celebrity?

He would have hated being a celebrity. But he would have used it in a good way. He would have called the big TV shows, not just in Sweden but also around the world, and he would have used his powerful position to shine a spotlight on far-right groups everywhere. It's really sad that he died because Sweden and the rest of the world needs a voice like his.

"I OFFERED THEM A SHRIMP SANDWICH": HOW ROBERT ASCHBERG GOT A PUBLISHER TO TAKE STIEG LARSSON SERIOUSLY

an interview with Robert Aschberg

Journalist, media executive, and one of Sweden's most popular television personalities, Aschberg has reported, written, and produced every kind of content for the Swedish media, from hard-edged documentaries to his current reality show that tries to settle arguments neighbors have with each other. A Maoist radical in his youth, his politics have moved more to the center over time, but he remains strongly committed to civil liberties and combating the rise of the right wing and neo-Nazi movements in Sweden. In this interview, he tells the story of how he came to be publisher of Expo *magazine and a member of the* Expo *Foundation board, which at the time he joined in the late 1990s was led by Editor in Chief Stieg Larsson.*

Having befriended Larsson through his support of Expo, *Aschberg was one of the people Larsson asked to read the manuscripts for his three Millennium novels. As soon as he read them, Aschberg was convinced that he held a literary hit in his hands. After learning the manuscripts were rejected unread by the first major publisher Larsson had tried, Aschberg picked up the phone and dialed the CEO of Norstedts, Sweden's oldest publishing house, and told him someone there had better take a serious look at the books. Within weeks, Larsson was signed. Although Aschberg here downplays his role in the process, the reality is that his call to Norstedts could have made all the difference in whether Larsson's novels were ever brought into the world.*

Aschberg began his career as a reporter and columnist in the 1970s and then moved to TV3, one of the first nongovernmental television channels, where he hosted a number of popular and award-winning shows. He was also one of the founders, in 1988, of Strix, a television production company and a major international distributor of Survivor *as well as creators of original reality TV programs. In his own words, "I've done all kinds of genres, from war reporting to talk shows to reality programs and*

have been there twenty years and survived thirteen program directors and
thirteen CEOs so far." At times serious, at times full of wry wit and self-
deprecating humor, and always the raconteur, Aschberg told us how he
jumped in to save Expo *at a perilous time and then "kicked Stieg's ass" to*
give the world a colossal "shrimp sandwich."

How did you meet Stieg Larsson?
I got to know Stieg in the mid to late '90s. I was hosting a talk show on
TV3 and a guy on the staff found this magazine called *Expo*. Being an antiracist is one of the few things that remain from my leftist youth, so I found
this magazine pretty interesting. It was not the least flashy; quite dry and
boring really. But it impressed me anyway.

A year or so later I read in the newspapers that the printing house that
published *Expo* had been attacked by right-wing extremists. They smashed
the windows and sprayed the place with Nazi slogans. The printer didn't
dare publish the coming issue and that upset me. So I called *Expo* and asked
if I could make a contribution that would help them pay for a different
printer. They were a bit secretive at the time, so I met this guy on the street.
We sat in my car, and I handed him some money.

Was that Stieg?
No, it was one of his protégés, a very clever and serious guy who worked
with Stieg. A month or so later, the *Expo* guys called and asked if I would
make an official stand as a supporter of *Expo*. They wanted to run my
picture alongside photos of others saying that they too supported *Expo*. I
said, of course.

Then, about half a year later, they asked if I wanted to sit on the Board
and I accepted. At that time, there was an activist feeling at the office and
the Board was filled with leftists and do-gooders. Everybody was chain
smoking, and there were constant arguments. I saw one of my missions as
broadening the composition of the Board to include people from industry
and conservative politicians—those who could see intolerance as an overrid-
ing issue that transcended status or politics. It took some time but I think
Expo has been successful in this effort.

And Stieg was in favor of this?
As you can imagine after reading his books, he was not only a journalist/
crusader, he had a good nose for what was commercial as well.

Are you still a supporter of *Expo*?

Yes, I am. I'm still on the board and I am technically the "publisher"—which means here in Sweden that if one of the reporters at *Expo* does something and gets sued, I go to jail, not the writer. They're more concerned about this than I am. But I do read every issue thoroughly.

As for *Expo*, its finances are healthier than ever. We have a few new advertisers and supporters, including a publishing house, the trade unions, and even a taxpayers' association that we helped out recently after it was almost infiltrated by the right-wing Sweden Democrats.

Stieg was very concerned about the Sweden Democrats even many years ago, right?

He said as far back as the 1990s that they would end up in Parliament—and in the last election they got twenty seats.

What can you tell us about Larsson during the period when he was writing his novels?

He was a workaholic, obviously. He wrote all the time. I have a comfortable house in the archipelago [a set of islands east of Stockholm much favored for summer vacations, especially by more affluent Swedes], and I told him to take some time off and enjoy it for as long as he'd like. Instead, he took some small shack somewhere, and what did he do there? He just typed and wrote and sat at his computer, mailing out stories, mainly short criminal stories and historical curiosities, and many with his trademark puckish humor and wordplay. Sometimes they included some funny historical fact. And there was always a twist, or two stories intertwined. He was very good at writing material that once you started reading, you couldn't stop until you reached the end. I was on a short list of friends he sent these little short stories and commentaries to. In retrospect, it seems, he was warming up for sitting down and writing the novels.

Then at some point he showed you a manuscript . . .

Yes. He said, "I've written a novel. It's kind of a modern Pippi Longstocking," the famous Swedish children's book character known for doing what she likes without regard for society's conventions and who has crazy adventures that often show off her physical strength. I thought, "That's weird, what's he done?" We discussed it, and then he asked if I wanted to read it.

I find that when people ask you to read stuff it's usually a waste of time.

But when I started reading the first book one night I didn't turn off the lights until five or six in the morning. The next night the same thing happened. I gave it to my wife and it was the same with her. I got the second book and it was the same phenomenon again. Stieg told me he was just finishing the third book and I said I could hardly wait.

That is when you urged him to find a publisher.
It wasn't a big thing. Everyone around him had read the books. I said, "Stieg, what are you doing? This is fantastic. This is your pension fund. You're going to be a rich man." But money was not such a driver for Stieg. He was very humble. He always paid his bills from the cash in his wallet and knew what he had to spend each week because that was what was left in it.

I said, "Stieg, you have to send it to a publishing house. I mean, by all means keep on writing, but also publish." First, he sent it to a major publishing house called Piratförlaget [The Pirate Publishing House]. And there it lay for months. But Stieg didn't do anything about it. We had to push him, kick his ass, and say, "What's happening? Aren't they answering you?" After a couple of months, he followed up and then he got one of those standard rejection letters.

They probably didn't even read the stuff, which is pretty normal. One of the biggest publishers in the country said no to Astrid Lindgren, the inventor of Pippi Longstocking and one of the greatest successes in Swedish publishing history.

A few years earlier, I had published a couple of books of newspaper columns with Norstedts. So I called up the CEO, a guy I happened to have met once or twice. I got through to him. And I said to him, "You want a shrimp sandwich?"

A shrimp sandwich?
A shrimp sandwich is a huge sandwich, with a hard-boiled egg, lettuce, mayonnaise, and a lot of boiled and peeled shrimp. And in Swedish slang, it means a big opportunity. I said, "If you want a shrimp sandwich just do me a favor. I'll have some manuscripts delivered to you today if you make me one promise: have somebody read them and give us an answer." Two weeks later, Stieg was signed. It had never happened in Swedish publishing history that a publisher gets three world best sellers on the table just like that. Here you go, here's not just one shrimp sandwich, but three.

I hate these people nowadays, though.

Why is that?

After Norstedts made him a publishing offer, Stieg asked me about movie rights. I said that although I was no expert I would try to help him. So he put it in my hands. At the time I was CEO of Strix, the TV production company that is part of MTG, the big media conglomeration, and I talked to my boss and to the head of the group's movie company. I told them I'd give my left hand or even my right hand to get the movie rights and they gave me carte blanche.

A day or so before he died Stieg and I were at Norstedts together to negotiate for the rights. I knew, and they knew, it was going to be expensive because of its huge potential. I said, "Whatever other bid you may get, I'll go higher." Sure enough, they gave it to another company.

Now I hate to read in the papers about the money the movies are making because I would have wanted that for my company. They have tried to make up with me. They have invited me for lunch. But I don't answer.

Did Stieg talk to you about his future plans?

The only thing he said to me was that he had a plan in his head to write ten books. There's a mystery fourth book out there, I know, and a magic, secret computer with two or three chapters in it. But it would be a shame to try and do something with that. I know people who've read what there is and they say it's not worth it, that it wouldn't be an honorable thing to publish it.

How do you feel knowing that the Millennium trilogy phenomenon was kicked off because of your intervention?

It really was nothing. I made a phone call, that's all. And I tried to kick Stieg's ass, because I realized that there was huge commercial potential.

But I didn't do it just for the money it could bring Stieg. I thought it would be fantastic for people to read. I wanted it published for Stieg's sake and for the story's sake. A good story is a good story. It should be spread. But Stieg wasn't stupid. He would have published it sooner or later.

EXPOSING THE EXTREME RIGHT
an interview with Anna-Lena Lodenius

In the 1980s, Anna-Lena Lodenius was researching and writing about the growth of the extreme right and neo-Nazi groups in Sweden. A mutual friend introduced her to Stieg Larsson, who shared her interests, for the purpose of working on a book together documenting these trends. The result was the Lodenius-Larsson co-authored book Extremhögern *(The Extreme Right), published first in 1991. In this interview, Lodenius talks about her continuing work exposing economic, social, and political injustice. She also talks about her experience working with Larsson two decades ago. Turns out it was not always easy or uncomplicated.*

Tell us about the book *Extremhögern*, which you wrote jointly with Stieg Larsson in the early 1990s. How did you and Stieg Larsson come to know each other and how did you divide up the work on the book? If we were to look back at that book today, how does it hold up in terms of the continuing importance of the issues it addressed twenty years ago?

Extremhögern (The Extreme Right) was a piece of investigative journalism that we published as a book in 1991 (revised edition 1994). We tried to dig into the neo-Nazi world. We wrote about organizations with roots in the 1930s and 1940s, as well as more recent groups. We even investigated what were then the new xenophobic movements, such as Sverigedemokraterna (Sweden Democrats, or SD), founded in 1988, which won seats in the Parliament only recently (September 2010).

The reason for undertaking this book was that this extreme right movement was growing at that time. A series of nasty crimes had taken place particularly in Gothenburg in the middle of the 1980s. We had a feeling the leaders of these neo-Nazi groups were cooperating with movements in other countries. We wanted to show what was happening and trace the organizations and leaders abroad that inspired the Swedish extreme right.

Stieg Larsson and I were introduced to each other by Sven Ove Hansson.

He was active in the Social Democratic Party and had read my articles about the extreme right in a magazine published by the Social Democratic Youth Organization (SSU) in 1986. Sven Ove asked me to help him with a book about the more or less secret political work of the big business/employers' organizations in Sweden. The book was published before the 1988 election by Tiden, a publishing company that was part of the Swedish Workers Movement. Sven Ove then suggested to Tiden that they should ask Stieg and me to write a book together about the extreme right. He promised to help us during the process, since neither of us were very experienced in writing books. *Extremhögern* can still be read as a history book telling about the activities, people, and organizations of the extreme right in that time period.

We did not put so much effort into analyzing the phenomena. Our focus was mainly to expose and describe. But the book provides a good description of the roots of the SD Party, and the people that took the initiative to start that party in 1988.

In the beginning, Stieg and I cooperated well in investigating, organizing interviews, etc. But in the writing process, we worked separately. Stieg was not an easy person to cooperate with. He made his standpoints clear and wanted things to go his way. I wrote the first part about Sweden, he wrote most of the international sections except the chapters about Norway and Denmark. We cooperated more on the third part that involved digging into the reshaping of the Nazi movement and criminal activities with a Nazi connection. I wrote most of the third part in the first edition; he did more of the writing for the second edition.

I regret we did not put each of our names on the chapters we wrote. A couple of years later, Stieg and another researcher wrote a book about Sverigedemokraterna (the SD party) using most of my research and writings for the initial parts of the book without even asking. I was quite upset about it at the time, but I figured it would do more harm to argue about it. Besides, I also wanted to expose SD as much as possible, and I thought that was the main point of the new book. I am not sure if Stieg was disappointed that I did not participate in launching *Expo.* I could not get involved at that time, mainly for personal reasons—I gave birth to my first child the same year as *Expo* started. Maybe Stieg didn't give my contribution to the book much of a thought, since his focus was to expose right-wing parties in any possible way. Since I had already provided him with all the documentation (we made copies of all the materials) from our first project together, maybe he figured he could use whatever he wished without consulting me.

What do you think of Stieg Larsson's novels? How did you find them as literature? There was speculation in the Swedish media from some people who had worked with Stieg as a journalist that he could not have written the Millennium trilogy because he was not a "good enough writer." What's your opinion? Is it true that he told you he was interested in writing crime fiction as early as the 1990s, long before he actually started on the Millennium trilogy?

Of course he wrote the books. I dealt with his texts a lot during the editing work on *Extremhögern,* as I was the more experienced journalist. It took me a while before I was able to read his novels. We didn't have much contact in the years before he died but I still found it difficult to read the books. When I finally did read the novels, I could hear his voice reading the lines for me. I recognized many of his favorite expressions from our work together many years earlier. So no question: he is the author.

I am not a great reader of crime novels. Obviously many people like this genre and you can get easily hooked on a good page-turner. My impression is the political content was of less importance to him than presenting an exciting story.

Soon after I first met him, Stieg talked to me about a desire he had to write true crime books. He wanted to write about the case of the "Laser Man," a serial killer who murdered many immigrants and other people in the early 1990s, at first using a laser scope on his rifle. Stieg never wrote this true crime book; much later another writer, Gellert Tamas, wrote a best seller about the Laser Man. Stieg was reading crime fiction all the time, particularly American female writers such as Sara Paretsky, Sue Grafton, Elizabeth George, and others. But he never talked to me about writing crime fiction.

Stieg Larsson is sometimes described as a feminist. How did you find the experience of actually working with him?

This idea of Stieg as a feminist was a new one to me. He had a fatherly approach to many people, not only women. He liked to educate people. He had a great admiration for certain more mature women, such as Lisbeth Lindeborg, a Swedish journalist based in Germany. But working side by side with others was not all that easy for him. He was a loner. In spite of this, I quite liked to work with him. He had a great sense of humor and was full of stories. He knew a great deal and he was happy to share his knowledge. But he was also quite stubborn. I am not sure he would have respected me more if I had been a man. We didn't actually fight about things; he would rather go away and come back with texts that were written in a totally different way than I thought we agreed on. When I called this to his attention, he wouldn't even know what I was talking about. The experience was extremely frustrating at times, but basically I quite enjoyed working with him.

Tell us about your current work—specifically your most recent book, *Migrantarbetare*. What is this book about?
I have written several books since my book with Stieg Larsson on the extreme right. Last year I wrote a thick book about the SD party (*Slaget om svenskheten,* 2009, with Mats Wingborg). It deals with the politics, how to take the debate. We also published a report last year about right-wing populist parties in Sweden, Norway, and Denmark. These RHP parties, as they are called, are a great threat to democracy all over Europe. Our next project is to expand our research to the rest of Europe. We are not only studying the RHP parties; we are also investigating policies for asylum, refugees, migrant workers, minority rights, etc.

In 2008 Mats and I wrote a book about migrant workers in both a local and international context. It was focused on how to fight for workers' rights in a world where more and more people lack documentation and were born and raised in other countries. We have a growing problem in all European countries with migrant workers earning lower wages and working in particular sectors that are separated from the rest of the market (restaurants, cleaning, transportation, etc.). If the trade unions want to keep the ability to represent all workers, they must include the migrant workers. It is also important that they take up the debate with RHP parties since many of their voters are working-class men.

In 2006 I published a book about right- and left-wing extremism (*Gatans parlament,* which means "The Parliament of the Streets"). This book compared different extremist groups and their way of using political violence. My next book is about how the extreme left took over a certain small trade union.

According to some of those people who have studied Stieg Larsson's life, the book you wrote together, *Extremhögern,* led to a frightening reaction from extreme right groups, with one neo-Nazi newspaper publishing your pictures, addresses, and telephone numbers, and concluding with the provocation as to whether Larsson "should be allowed to continue his work, or if something should be done." Can you tell us more about what happened back then?

The article was published in 1994 in a magazine called *Storm,* connected with the Swedish version of White Aryan Resistance. The words mentioned above were about me, not about Stieg. They wrote about him as well but using different (and not as nasty) words. They actually wrote about many people in this magazine (possibly fifteen to twenty names were mentioned). The threats they made against me became the reason the case was taken to court. Two Nazis were sentenced, one did a few months in jail. As far as I know nobody was sentenced for harassing Stieg, but few such trials were held and hardly anybody was caught by the police, so it doesn't mean he didn't suffer. I think he was quite frightened, as most of us were. Stieg was very cautious; he talked a lot about security. But we all did. That was part of the work.

EVA GABRIELSSON ON THE RECORD
a compilation

Eva Gabrielsson was the love of Stieg Larsson's life. They were a couple for thirty-two of Larsson's fifty years. They exchanged ideas, dreams, and visions. They were also true partners in their intellectual and creative lives.

Stieg Larsson's sudden death in 2004 was shocking in and of itself, an incredible emotional blow to Eva that she recounts in her recent book, Millénium Stieg et Moi *(Actes Sud, 2011). Adding another dimension to her pain has been the fight over Stieg's legacy.*

Grieving and otherwise wanting to stay above the fray, Eva only later started to give interviews to the international press in which she sought to explain the real Stieg and "clear up the misunderstandings" about their life together, the degree of her input into the novels, whether or not there was a fourth book and where it may be, and, of course, the feud with Larsson's father and brother.

What follows is a composite of some of the things she has said on the record. Sources are noted after each quote.

What was Stieg like?

In response to Stieg being labeled a workaholic: "He was so much fun. If you take chores like doing the laundry, we'd wait until it really piled up and do it together. With him around, doing laundry was fun. . . . [We would] crack jokes on our way back and forth to the laundry room. He was fun to be around. He was a very open person. At least, he was open around me." —interview on Swedish television, February 2010

On Stieg's commitment to feminism: "He referred to himself as a feminist as far back as when we first met [1972]. It was fairly unusual back then. . . . It was the age of women's lib, men weren't 'allowed' to be feminists. . . . Stieg didn't care, he defined himself as a feminist. It wasn't just a label, he lived up to it, too." —interview on Swedish television, February 2010

On intolerance: "Stieg thought that racism and sexism were two sides of the same coin." —promotional video for a theatrical production of *Men Who Hate Women,* which premiered in December 2010 at the Nørrebro Theater, Copenhagen

Summing it up:

"He was unique. He was a great guy. Very dedicated and serious but so much fun." —Mirror.co.uk, August 2010

"I had a good life with that man." —*Nightline* interview, August 2010

About why they never married

"In Sweden, public records are easily available. . . . Getting married would have made Stieg more traceable and would have been a huge mistake." —*Daily Mail,* 2010

"He wouldn't have lived to write the books if we had. Someone would have killed him." —*The Observer* (London), July 2009

"Our respective childhoods did not prepare us for starting a family . . . there was always something more pressing to do. We wanted a more stable economic situation, to build something more solid before jumping in. . . . And time passed. . . . In the fall of 2004, we said to each other, we'd put on a big celebration for our fiftieth birthdays and reveal then that, in fact, it was a wedding feast." —in *Millénium Stieg et Moi*

Her hopes for what could have been

"A marvelous period had begun which counts among the happiest of my life." —in *Millénium Stieg et Moi*

"Ten books were planned. The proceeds from the first three were meant for us. For the first time, our needs were top priority. We expected the trilogy to bring in about 3 or 4 million kronor [US$500,000 to $600,000]. And when the film rights were sold a few years later, there might be more. But the proceeds from the rest were meant for charity." —promotional video for a theatrical production of *Men Who Hate Women,* Nørrebro Theater, Copenhagen

"We had also planned where to write the books. We wanted to build a small house in the archipelago. We made the architectural drawings ourselves. . . . We sent the drawings to a craftsman to get a price. Two weeks later, Stieg was dead." —promotional video for *Men Who Hate Women*

On how closely she collaborated with the man whose name is on the cover of the books

[Was Stieg the author?] "I'm not sure you can say that." —*The New York Times Magazine,* May 2010

"Being together with someone for thirty years, large chunks of it becomes ours. He sort of held the pen, but just being able to be an efficient writer doesn't create any books. —*Nightline* interview, August 2010

"The books are the fruit of Stieg's experience, but also of mine." —*The Times* (London), January 2011

"I've been involved in everything Stieg wrote, he liked me to edit his work. But this time around I thought: 'Hang on, . . . This comes from a wellspring. The smallest pebble I drop into it might do some harm. So I don't even want to try.' I was not involved in the writing, the craft itself." —interview on Swedish television, February 2010

"People say both that I contributed nothing [to the Millennium books] and that I was the one who wrote all of them. What I can say simply is that, just as we had a common language, we often wrote as a team." —in *Millénium Stieg et Moi*

The bitter legacy

"I think it's great injustice. It would have been beyond Stieg's worst nightmare to know that someone other than me was handling the rights to his book and to know that the money we planned to invest is gone." —*The Observer* (London), July 2009

"The Millennium books are about moral responsibility and justice. It is interesting that the people who are representing Stieg in financial matters stand for the opposite." —promotional video for *Men Who Hate Women,* Nørrebro Theater, Copenhagen

"What an insult to Stieg, to his life, to our life of 30 years together. I'm torn between anger, indignation, despair, and panic." —*The Times* (London), January 2011, quoting from *Millénium Stieg et Moi*

"It was never about money, but about common sense and upholding the quality of Stieg's work." —*The Guardian* (U.K.), January 2010

"It's as if my identity has been erased. It's like being dispossessed. The Swedish laws are based on medieval German laws. It is all about protecting the bloodlines." —*Globe and Mail* (Canada), October 2010

"It is my brainchild as well. . . . [I]t is like someone selling your children, placing them in any old whorehouse for the rest of their lives." —*Daily Mail,* January 2010

Why the books became so popular

"I think it reflects . . . the joy in seeing people fighting back, like old-time superheroes. There is something universal in this." —CBC interview, October 2010

"People must find something in what is being said: the fight against corruption, the barbarism and discrimination and violence against women, the cowardice of the media, [and] the blindness and corruption of politicians. . . . I interpret [reader interest in Larsson's books] almost as a way of voting. They are voting for Stieg's ideals." —*The Observer* (London), July 2009

On the commercialization of Stieg's ideals

"[Stieg would have been] furious that his legacy is being handled like potatoes, chopped up into chips or anything that's sellable. . . . He would have gone to great extent to get revenge." —ABC News interview with Gloria Riviera, February 2010

"I don't want to . . . expose every detail of our lives. That only provides more grist for the mill for people who want to profit from our lives. . . . My life isn't all about telling people how much milk Stieg had in his coffee, what time he got up in the morning, or what kind of whisky he liked, what brand. It's idiotic, obsessive." —interview on Swedish television, February 2010

"The horrible thing is that [the rights] are being sold like potatoes. There's no respect for content, the labor and thought that went into it—which aren't just Stieg's but mine, too. There's no respect for the original author's but it's got his name on it." —*Mirror* (U.K.), October 2010

"I don't want his name to be an industry or brand. The way things are going, his name could end up on a bottle of beer, a coffee packet, or a car." —*Millénium Stieg et Moi,* quoted in *The Times* (London), January 2011

The future of the Millennium series: is there a fourth book?

"[Can you finish writing Stieg's next book?] It would be as difficult as trying to finish a painting by Picasso." —*The Observer* (London), July 2009

"[Any plans to complete the manuscript?] I'm unable to discuss that." —interview on Swedish television, February 2010

"There probably is the beginning of a fourth book. . . . I know what it is about, but I haven't read it. I probably could do it. I'm sure I could do it." —Nightline interview, August 2010

"The day after Stieg's death my sister Britt went with Erland [Stieg's father] to *Expo* and I asked her to take along my partner's backpack . . . [which] contained *Expo*'s computer. . . . The fourth volume of *Millennium* can be found on it . . . perhaps. It comprises a little more than two hundred pages . . . I could have worked on his texts and finished the fourth volume, which I'm quite capable of doing." —in *Millénium Stieg et Moi*

IN HER OWN WORDS: EVA GABRIELSSON TELLS HER STORY
by Paul De Angelis

What follows is a summary of the French-language edition of Eva Gabri-
elsson's memoir, Millénnium Stieg et Moi *(Actus Sud, January 2011),*
co-written with Marie-Francois Colombani. The American version of this
book is due out from Seven Stories Press in June 2011 under the English-
language title: There Are Things I Want You to Know About Stieg
Larsson and Me. *Paul De Angelis served more than three decades in the*
book publishing business as editor, editorial director, or editor in chief. In
1996 he founded Paul De Angelis Book Development, which assists au-
thors, agents, publishers, and organizations in turning ideas and manu-
scripts into books.

One evening in the fall of 1972, Eva Gabrielsson attended a DFFG (National Liberation Front) rally against the Vietnam War in the small Swedish
town of Umeå. At the door to welcome newcomers was an energetic, engaging, yet vulnerable teenager named Stieg Larsson. Eva and Stieg soon found
out that they had far more in common than their political views: a love of
science fiction; intellectual curiosity; a passion for reading, writing, and lively
discussion; and a drive for fairness and social justice. In 1974 they moved in
together and began a relationship that would turn out to be a lifetime partnership. It is this vibrant relationship so suddenly shattered by Stieg's death
in 2004—and the severe emotional toll that death took on Eva—that is the
subject of Gabrielsson's new memoir.

Along the way she also wants to set the record straight about the real
Stieg, about who wrote the Millennium books, and about the way she has
been treated by the family members she believes have betrayed her and are
profiting from Stieg's legacy. In *Millénium Stieg et Moi,* Eva recounts the
common roots she shared with Stieg in remote northern Sweden. She writes
of her own family trauma—alcoholic father, absent mother, raised by her
paternal grandmother. Between the lines of Eva's reminiscences, one senses
that parental abandonment may have constituted a critical emotional part

of the bond between her and Stieg, and that he was a somewhat lost and lonely boy who found in his relationship with her the warm nest he was lacking at home with his own parents. Their relationship, driven by endless cups of Turkish coffee and marked by real give and take and mutual learning, deepened quickly once they started living together.

Their bond intensified in 1977 when, according to the book, Stieg went to aid the Eritrean rebels in Ethiopia on behalf of the Trotskyist Fourth International. The trip, Gabrielsson suggests, showed both how reckless a young man he could be and how intense a bond he had developed with her. In a letter he wrote from a hospital bed in Addis Ababa after he nearly died from kidney failure associated with contracting malaria, he declared his love for Eva and his commitment to her. Just how seriously he meant this becomes even clearer when Eva discovers, the night before Stieg's memorial service, a small box "not to be opened before my death." In it is a letter drafted by Stieg just before leaving on his Eritrean mission with the message that he loves her "more than he has ever loved anyone."

The pattern of Eva and Stieg's life together reached a kind of climax in 1999, the year "with all the dangers and changes." Eva had lost her regular architect's job in the banking and real estate crisis earlier in the decade. According to her account, Stieg took early retirement from his news agency job at TT to devote full time to his struggling antifascist magazine *Expo* amid increased threats and a dwindling budget. She writes that Stieg was so preoccupied juggling his various commitments during the 1990s that she felt compelled to move out a couple of times during that decade to gain his attention.

Then in the next few years life began to come together. While Gabrielsson had always urged Larsson to write, even when he lacked self-confidence and she was the principal breadwinner, both Eva and Stieg now began to focus on their respective writing projects: she on a book about noted Swedish architect Per Olof Hallman, and he on what would become the Millennium series—started, she says, when he was looking for a writing idea while on summer vacation. Eva says she suggested that Stieg tease out the story he had started some years before about a man who receives a flower every year (which became the prologue to *The Girl with the Dragon Tattoo*). In the meantime, even *Expo* managed to get enough funding from several advocacy organizations to support a couple of salaries.

Once Norstedts (Stieg's Swedish publisher) made a significant offer for the Millennium trilogy in the spring of 2004, a brighter, more secure future seemed assured. "A marvelous period had begun which counts among the happiest of my life," Gabrielsson says in *Millénium Stieg et Moi*. One day Stieg turned to her and said, "What if we were to get married?" She happily agreed, she writes, and the plan was that at Stieg's fiftieth birthday party they would "reveal to our friends it was, in fact, a wedding celebration." With confidence, Eva made sketches for the "writing cottage" she and Stieg would build in the Stockholm archipelago with a view of the water (much like the fictional one in Sandhamn used by Mikael Blomkvist).

Eva's life disintegrated after Stieg's unexpected death just a few months later, about which she writes movingly and in some detail, quoting diary entries such as "Eva feels like an unconscious animal, functioning at a minimal level, just surviving, and barely."

While Eva was trying to cope with the emotional loss of her life partner, there was more bad news, she writes. Under Swedish law, "common law spouses" such as Gabrielsson inherit nothing unless specifically written into the deceased person's will. In the case of someone who dies "intestate" (without a will), their estate goes to their surviving blood relatives—in this case, Stieg's father and brother, with nothing mandated to go to the woman he had loved, lived with, and worked with for three decades. "What an insult to Stieg, his life, to our life of 30 years together," she wrote in her diary. "I'm torn between anger, indignation, despair, and panic."

Also plaguing her were the persistent questions about her role in the writing of the Millennium books and whether or not a fourth book had been written. In answer to the former she tells readers, "I can simply say that we often wrote together." The books, she goes on, are "the fruit of Stieg's experience, but also of mine." She does not go as far as to say, as she did in an interview on the American TV program *Nightline* in 2010, "He sort of held the pen, but just being able to be an efficient writer doesn't create any books."

As for the fourth book, Eva confirms the story that Larsson, typing on a computer whose current location she keeps from the reader, wrote about 160 to 200 pages before his untimely death. The computer, she writes, is owned by the magazine *Expo*. She now says she wants to finish the fourth book, "something I'm quite capable of"—although this is different from what she had said earlier in some of her interviews. She also reveals the fourth book was to be called *God's Vengeance* and that while "it is not my intention to recount here the plot," she does summarize the theme: "I want to say that Lisbeth little by little frees herself from her ghosts and her enemies. . . . [And] each time she manages to take revenge on someone who has hurt her she removes the tattoo that, in her imagination, embodies that person."

Eva's memoir also contains tidbits that will help satisfy the curiosity of those who want to know how closely the Millennium books match Stieg and Eva's real-life world. Among them:

- Lisbeth's superhero traits derive partly from comic books like *Superman* and *Spider-Man*, but also from Stieg's fascination with strong women such as Boudicca (or Boadicea), queen of the Celtic tribe that rose up against the Romans, whose statue in London Stieg particularly liked to visit.
- The chess matches between Holger Palmgren and Lisbeth in *Fire* resemble those between Stieg and Eva's brother Björn, which Stieg almost always lost.
- The description of the architecturally oriented book by Greger Beckman, the artist husband of Erika Berger, actually describes the book Eva was working on about Per Olof Hallman while Stieg was composing Millennium.
- Anita Vanger in *Tattoo* is modeled on Eva's younger sister Britt, who lived for many years in London.
- Svante Brandén, the good psychiatrist in *Hornet's Nest*, is a psychiatrist and longtime friend of Eva's. Stieg and Eva sublet a room from Brandén when they first moved to Stockholm.

One of the most striking features of Gabrielsson's memoir is her emphasis on a kind of Old Norse/Old Testament vengeance. Both she and Stieg, she says, had extremely influential grandparents in their lives, whose older generation values emphasized personal honor and commitment. They believed that individuals, not just societies, have a responsibility for their actions, and that abstract principles can be overridden by personal circumstance. As a boy Stieg sometimes got into fights; he would wait until the right time for the payback moment. Likewise, in the Millennium trilogy, Stieg was able to "pay back" in written caricature many of those who had done him harm over the years, she suggests.

Eva Gabrielsson has adopted this same tradition as the guiding star of her widowhood. On the first New Year's Eve without Stieg, Eva and her friends enacted a purifying ritual. The ceremony involved the composition and oral recitation of a *nid*—a scolding or vilification based on Norse mythology—directed against all of Stieg's enemies. One of the verses calls on two of the Norse god Odin's crows to "peck out your skulls/and open you to common sense." In ancient versions of this ceremony, Viking warriors decapitated a horse; Eva instead used two ceramic horses accidentally joined during firing that were given to her once as a precious gift. She split them and offered up one to Lake Mälaren near Stockholm; the other was kept in the apartment she had bought with Stieg, though it could no longer stand upright by itself.

Eva describes being approached by a crow on one of her walks some months later—a creature that seemed the literal embodiment of the crows she had described in her New Year's vituperation, as if sent by Odin himself. The encounter with the crow made her feel as if Stieg was somehow back, supporting her, and she walked home with a new determination to fight.

Revenge was something Stieg believed in, writes Gabrielsson. "He was generous, faithful, warm, and a deeply good man. But he could also be completely the opposite. When people wronged Stieg . . . it was 'an eye for an eye, a tooth for a tooth.' He never forgave." *Millénium Stieg et Moi* can sometimes feel like a continuance of this drive for vengeance. In her chapter called "My Diary for the Year 2005," she reveals the entries that record, blow by blow, her feelings of a double betrayal: by Stieg's father and brother (for promoting Stieg's name as a "brand") and by the publisher, Norstedts (for not completing an agreement Stieg had asked for that would have paid royalties to a joint company he and Eva would own).

Eva vows in the memoir to fight on to regain control of Stieg's work no matter the cost and to protect his legacy. Gabrielsson wants to do what Larsson would have wanted: support the anti-extremist publication *Expo* to which he gave his heart and talents, and support shelters for battered women in the name of the feminist cause he so deeply believed in. But the "enemies" are hereby put on notice by these comments about the fourth Millennium book from Marie-France Colombani's preface:

All of us who love *Millénnium* . . . can look forward to meeting its heroes again. The enemies of Lisbeth Salander and Mikael Blomkvist should start trembling. The book's title will be *God's Vengeance*. They should know that Eva, the salsa dancer beheld by the Eternal, is prepared to finish the work and lead the dance on their graves.

4. THE WELLSPRINGS OF HIS IMAGINATION

STIEG LARSSON AND SCIENCE FICTION
by John-Henri Holmberg

Part I: Stieg in Fandom: The Life and Times of a Trufan

The Umeå Background

Science fiction fandom, the community of sf readers who start clubs, publish or write for fanzines, attend conventions, and communicate with other fans, was born in the U.S. at the end of the 1920s. It soon spread to Britain and, in the 1950s, to Japan and Europe. Just as all subcultures, science fiction fandom has words of its own, developed during its eighty years of existence. "Trufan" means a "true fan," someone who is an active, driving force, publishing and inspiring others.

For close to ten years, from early 1972, Stieg Larsson was a prominent member of sf fandom and one of its genuine trufans.

In Sweden, the first sf club was founded in 1950, the first fanzines appeared in 1954, and the first sf convention was held in 1956. The first generation of Swedish fans were those active in the 1950s. I belong to the second generation, those who became active in the early 1960s. Stieg Larsson belonged to the third, those appearing from the late 1960s until the mid 1970s.

When Stieg and Rune Forsgren started *Sfären* in early 1972, theirs was the first new Swedish fanzine in more than two years. Stieg was living then in Umeå, four hundred miles north of Stockholm.

According to Rune Forsgren's account:

In 1970 I met Stieg Larsson (then young and quiet) for the first time. Little did I suspect what this indirectly would lead to in the future. . . . We played mini-golf, travelled East, went to Universum [the Umeå university student restaurant and pub] and thought only occasionally about science fiction. . . . In 1971 I discovered the existence of fandom. . . . I received my first issues of a few fanzines. . . . In 1972 the time was ripe. It was time to wake fandom from its slumber, and to that purpose the first issue of *Sfären* was published in January.

After starting *Sfären*, Rune and Stieg attended the 1972 Swedish sf convention in Stockholm. Later, Stieg met Eva Gabrielsson and her brother and sister, who all read science fiction. In 1973, the Umeå fans published ten fanzine issues, and in 1974 twelve, including the first two issues of *Fijagh!*

A fanzine, or even a fan, can be "sercon" or "fannish." "Sercon" is short for the slightly ironic "serious and constructive," which means directly pertaining to science fiction, while "fannish" is that centered on the hobby of fandom itself, usually with a humorous slant. *Fijagh!* was a fannish fanzine.

In the second issue, Stieg writes about liking Western movies while Rune refuses to even watch one. He goes on to tell the story of how the collective acquired a cat and almost became a playground for neighboring children, which he finally manages to obstruct by a brilliant piece of misdirection:

Something really had to be done! I opened the door. The kids were outside. A couple or four of them.

"No," I said (holding the door at a slit), "today you can't come in to play. We're having a meeting."

"A meeting?" they said in chorus. "What kind of meeting?"

"A secret agent meeting," I said in a mysterious tone of voice.

"Oohh . . . A secret agent meeting . . . OOHH. . . ." Their eyes shone.

I closed the door, sat down and felt very satisfied. For almost ten seconds, until the doorbell rang again.

Not again, damn it, I thought, rolling up my sleeves before throwing the door wide.

There was Rune, his attaché case over his head, surrounded by half a dozen kids all talking urgently to each other. I heard Rune say, "No, I said, no, I'm not a secret agent."

I dragged him in and locked the door.

Politics had a prominent place in *Fijagh!* In the second issue a long letter from Malmö fans Folke Andersson and Lars-Göran Hedengård appeared. Hedengård had published a short-lived fanzine but was better known for his political views. He was a staunch defender of Nixon, U.S. involvement in Vietnam, and the military coup in Chile. Stieg was fascinated by

Hedengård and loved baiting him. In a comment on the revelations of Watergate in *Fijagh!* he added, "It would be interesting to hear some reactions. From Lars-Göran Hedengård, for instance . . . Or have you bitten your tongue off after seeing the self-proclaimed policeman and protector of the 'free world' revealed as a simple, corrupt second-rate politician?"

This provoked Hedengård's and Andersson's letter to *Fijagh!* 2. As expected, they were unrepentant: "We claim that Richard Nixon, despite the Watergate affair, was one of the best and greatest of American presidents. That you, Stieg, call Nixon a bastard is mudslinging typical of the undemocratic communist you undeniably are. Dictators in communist dictatorships are many times worse crooks."

Stieg's reply was as long as the letter. "That . . . you are still willing to defend the gravediggers of your bourgeois democracy is almost over the top. Even Nixon's voters and party friends have realized how rotten his actions were . . . Your letter made me wonder what some right-wing extremists are made of."

At this time, Stieg Larsson had just turned twenty while Hedengård was sixteen or seventeen. But in a sense their fanzine exchanges presaged their careers. Stieg kept coming across Hedengård for many years, as Hedengård, in time, became influential in Swedish neo-Nazi groups, including becoming chairman of the Swedish section of the NSDAP-AO, the "official" resurrection of Hitler's party. Fandom, in this way, saw some of Stieg's first clashes with the right-wing extremists he would later devote himself to thwarting.

The cover of the third issue of *Fijagh!* sports a feminist symbol and the legend "Stop exploiting women," making it the most overtly political fanzine cover published in Sweden. In the letters column, Kjell Rynefors takes Stieg to task for opposing nuclear power. This became an ongoing debate between Stieg and Kjell, both privately and in fanzines. In Kjell Rynefors, Stieg found a discussion partner holding opposite views on most issues, but whom he respected and valued highly. His discussions with Rynefors (described in a letter Stieg wrote to me in 1987) exemplify how Stieg throughout life wanted to argue—dispassionately, factually, logically:

Even though I didn't meet Kjell in person more than perhaps a half dozen times . . . I always considered him one of the nicest and most comfortable people I knew during those years. I could add that Kjell and I, in mutual respect, carried on a considerable political debate. . . . Neither of us changed his mind and we both always agreed that the other one was wrong. But in contrast to many other fans who tried discussing politics, there was never any nonsense to Kjell's commitment. He would present weighty and well considered arguments, and you either had to respond in kind or hang up your gloves.

Stieg also published a humorous piece on whether Lars-Göran Hedengård could actually exist. He examined three possibilities: 1) Hedengård is a product of Stieg's own mental disturbances; 2) Hedengård exists, but as one of the wall shadows in Plato's thought experiment, where what we see bears only slight resemblance to the reality, and is created not by a benevolent but by an evil god; or 3) Hedengård is a sadistic joke perpetrated by some other fan. He opts for the last theory, concluding that Hedengård is a practical joke perpetrated by "John-Henri Holmberg," in other words, me. After this, he opens one of his desk drawers, and to his horror, discovers a pile of weird letters typed on his own typewriter. Stieg is forced to realize that he himself is the Jekyll and Hyde of fandom, that in the dark hours of his soul he turns into Lars-Göran Hedengård and, in a savage frenzy, sends off innumerable insane letters.

This, of course, was pure irony. Hedengård was real enough. And although Stieg and I disagreed on most political issues—Stieg was then a Trotskyite communist, while I was an individualist libertarian—we were equally aghast at Hedengård's militantly reactionary views.

In *Fijagh!* 4, Hedengård, undeterred, contributes two pages commenting on my own letter in the previous issue, noting that, "Holmberg's turn to the left is due to the reason that is the basis of all other Marxists and communists: ENVY! . . . Therefore, all Marxists, socialists and communists are urged to seek psychiatric help for their complexes and ailments. . . ."

Stieg's reply is devastating in that he refuses to write a serious response. Instead, he writes a short note in very simple words lamenting the cold winter, saying that he longs for summer when he intends to go bicycling and may visit the outdoor baths, and ending by saying that if the weather is bad the next day, he might go to the cinema. It was the end of the Hedengård exchange, and one of the very few times that Stieg gave up trying to discuss with someone.

In *Fijagh!* 7 a letter from Torbjörn Wärnheim receives a long reply from

Stieg, who discusses censorship and talks about his absolute aversion to the idea of nationalism, patriotism, and borders: "My tolerance for the insincerity called nationalism is equal to my appreciation of rattlesnakes as bedmates."

In *Fijagh!* 8 Eva Gabrielsson contributes an essay on the similarities between the institutionalized discrimination of blacks in South Africa, the illegal but rationalized discrimination of blacks in the U.S., and the discrimination of women in Sweden. *Fijagh!* 8 was published in late 1976. By the time *Fijagh!* 9 was published in early 1978, Umeå fandom was no more. At thirty-two pages, it was both the largest and last issue of *Fijagh!* In feeling and in fact, it was Stieg Larsson's belated farewell to Umeå fandom; he writes about moving to Stockholm and about the fatherly advice Rune gave him the evening before his departure: Stieg must watch out for the Stockholm fans because they were dangerous in their demands for work and internecine intrigue.

But Stieg did not listen. A couple of days before writing this column, he and Eva had been to a crayfish party in my apartment. I had been the president of SFSF (Skandinavisk Förening för Science Fiction, the largest sf fan organization in Sweden) in 1976, was then on the club board and would again be president in 1978. After a sufficient number of drinks, Stieg and Eva had almost been talked into joining the SFSF. At least they'd agreed to go to the inauguration party in the new clubhouse, in just a few days.

The party would be their formal induction into Stockholm fandom, although they had already had an inkling of things to come. Stieg had attended ScanCon, the 1976 Stockholm science fiction convention, and after the final party, he had agreed to get the guest of honor, author Jack Vance, back to his hotel, an experience he later claimed almost cost him his life. "Jack Vance is both large and heavy," he wrote, "and at the time was also drunk as a skunk. At no time during the drive did he even seem to wonder about my suffocated and panicky gasps every time the cab made a left turn and centrifugal forces inexorably pushed Vance on top of me. I have never since been able to read one of his novels without a heavy weight settling on my chest."

Sf in Stockholm

In 1976, Sweden had a science fiction book club with some one thousand five hundred members, but the owner, Askild & Kärnekull publishers, decided to fold it. SFSF negotiated to buy the book club and its stock for slightly above cost. They then offered book club members the opportunity to join the club and continue buying books cheaply by mail. More than half accepted, and so SFSF suddenly grew from approximately two hundred members to nearly one thousand, some three hundred in the Stockholm area. In late 1976, we decided to get a place for the club, and in 1977 we signed a lease for a former shop with a large basement. The basement held three rooms, suitable for a print shop and meeting rooms; the street level had a 550-square-foot shop with display windows plus an office. The idea was to start a science fiction bookstore and hold club meetings in the basement. We spent months cleaning, painting, building, and furnishing. And this was just the moment when Eva and Stieg had the bad fortune to move to Stockholm.

The inauguration party was held September 16, 1977. All was far from finished, but study circles were held Tuesdays and Wednesdays, club meetings Thursdays, and movie evenings Sundays.

In December, SFSF hosted the first of several miniconventions. Stieg and Eva had spent much of the fall being useful at SFSF. At the general meeting on December 8, they were justly punished by being elected to the board and spent the next year working for the club. In 1979, the general meeting chose Stieg and Eva to edit the member fanzine *Fanac* during 1979. They produced issues 97 through 103, while Stieg also agreed to be on the editorial board of the club magazine, *Science Fiction Forum*.

SFSF was facing huge problems, though. The club had little money and the bookstore was underfinanced. Worse, the organization was insufficient. Keeping open fifty hours a week using unpaid board members is difficult, and no easier when the same people simultaneously publish two magazines, run a mail-order business, prepare study circle meetings, and, in their spare time, clean two large clubroom levels.

Meanwhile, the club had become a battlefield. Many new fans turned up in the mid 1970s. There was suddenly a large group of loud, opinionated, and hyperactive teenagers more or less living on the club premises. During 1978, the young activists wanted club facilities to be open more days and longer hours. They wanted the *Fanac* editors replaced. And they wanted the club to deal with fandom instead of sf. Meetings turned into shouting contests, opponents standing on chairs and refusing to yield.

In December 1978, the two most aggressive of the young fans, Ahrvid Engholm and Anders Bellis, started a weekly news fanzine called *Vheckans ävfentyr* ("The Wheek's Adfentures"), which published 47 issues in 1979 and 40 in 1980. Nearly all ninety issues, handed out in the clubrooms, contained attacks on the SFSF board. Some of the most strident related to the organization's approach toward women.

The majority of SFSF members were male. Most female members never showed up, or showed up once and never returned. The board suspected that female members felt shut out by the dominant and always present male fans, and it seemed reasonable to try to remedy this. A page in *Fanac* was baptized "Feminac" and set aside for a women's group started by Lena Jonsson that included Eva Gabrielsson.

Vheckans äventyr quickly attacked, calling this "a vague and pointless page half-heartedly suggesting women fans to become more active." Feminac covered two pages in the next issue with three letters from readers. One from a male asked, "Why should girls in SFSF have their own page of *Fanac?* Guys don't have a page of their own!" The others, from women, applauded the initiative. In a comment, Stieg pointed out that the gender bias of the SFSF membership was so obvious that doing something about it must be considered an important part of the club's agenda.

To that, Ahrvid Engholm responded at length, saying, among other things, "The Feminac column should be abolished. . . . It's as meaningful as a column aimed at, for instance, red-haired fans (who I'm sure are just as neglected in fandom as female fans)," while Anders Bellis called the next Feminac text "worse written, more infantile and less thoughtful even than normal, which must be viewed as an impressive accomplishment. I won't honor the writer by saying more than that the entire message of the story is twisted and untrue."

The reality was that out of the seven hundred SFSF members, approximately a hundred were women. One or two pages of the twenty in the member fanzine had been set aside for women to discuss the club. After this had been condemned and debated for half a year, Stieg vented his anger in print, noting that criticisms of Feminac had been characterized by personal attacks and reflected an insufferable dogmatism and childishness.

As rather naïve male feminists, both Stieg and I were appalled and honestly surprised by the opposition to the Feminac initiative. These were, after all, sf fans, used to thinking about alternatives and change, tolerant and smart. I suspect the experience contributed in many ways to Stieg's understanding of men's opposition to women wanting to be heard. I know it did to mine.

By autumn, the Feminac group had begun work on its own fanzine, with the club sponsoring printing costs. The Feminac group published a total of six issues and they remain among the most interesting fanzines of that time.

Meanwhile, our landlord informed us that rent would be doubling. The club's economy could not cope with this, and so SFSF would need to move. Feelings were running very high, and *Vheckans ävfentyr* featured a front-page heading, "DICTATORSHIP IN SFSF!!!" Slogans like, "This is where the Nazi mob lurks" appeared on the door to the boardroom. When the 1979 general meeting was held in December, the walls were full of handmade posters. The debate ran on for hours with Engholm, Bellis, and others reading manifestos and lists of demands. But virtually none of their demands was accepted. The more rational majority rallied and Stieg Larsson was elected club president for 1980.

It was a depressing year of constant problems and quarrels, and on September 30, the club vacated its premises. Club property was stored in a rented basement impossible to use for meetings. *Vheckans ävfentyr* continued to attack Feminac, the board, and "Chairman Stieg," while Stieg and Eva published two issues of a new member fanzine, *The Magic Fan*, urging members to attend the 1980 general meeting in December. At this meeting, virtually the entire board of SFSF resigned, Stieg, Eva, and myself included. It fell to others to pilot the club through the following period.

Farewell to Fandom

In 1979, Stieg and Eva attended the 37th World SF Convention in Brighton, England, and throughout 1980, Stieg contributed reviews and essays to *Science Fiction Forum* while Eva wrote for *Feminac*. But they became increasingly disenchanted with fandom. Later, Stieg wrote about the SFSF period, saying that, although he had fond memories of many of those he knew during his fan years, he also encountered some of the worst jerks he had ever met. The worst idiots, he noted, were a small minority, but made enough noise to make you tire of it all. During the time when he and Eva were editing *Fanac*, he said that they often wondered how the hundreds of club members outside of Stockholm viewed the incomprehensible quarrels. "To me, all the stupidities entirely spoiled the fun of fandom. I gafiated [a fan acronym meaning "get away from it all"] and since then . . . have had no contact with fandom. It is no secret that on the day I left, I did so full of disgust at having spent the preceding year wasting my time on nonsense."

After publishing more than thirty fanzine issues, contributing to many more, attending numerous conventions, and working for three years on the board of Scandinavia's largest fan organization, Stieg left fandom. But not without many times looking back at his experiences: his discussions with Lars-Göran Hedengård had been his first close encounter with the extreme right he would keep fighting; his support for the Feminac group had honed his understanding of male opposition to women's equality.

Part II: Reading (and Sometimes Writing) Science Fiction

The Books Stieg Read

Stieg Larsson's first real passion in the world of literature was science fiction.

Stieg started school at the age of seven in 1961 and quickly became a voracious reader. We can assume that he read mainly in Swedish until he was at least twelve, when he began learning English, and we know that his favorite author at that time was Robert A. Heinlein, whom Stieg always mentioned as his first literary love. Heinlein was one of the few sf authors extensively translated into Swedish. Eight of his books were available in translation in the early sixties: *Sixth Column, The Man Who Sold the Moon, Starman Jones, Space Cadet, Farmer in the Sky, Have Space Suit—Will Travel, Citizen of the Galaxy,* and *Double Star.*

Heinlein was central to modern science fiction. He introduced greater technical and social realism into sf, preferring to write about the near future. Humanity's first steps into space was a favorite subject. *The Man Who Sold the Moon* collects early stories, one on the invention of cheap, unlimited solar electricity, another about an entrepreneur who finances the first manned trip to the moon. *Starman Jones, Space Cadet, Farmer in the Sky, Have Space Suit—Will Travel,* and *Citizen of the Galaxy* all feature teenage protagonists, though otherwise written in the same style as Heinlein's other work. All are set in space or on other planets; all express the author's conviction that mankind must reach for the stars. Heinlein infused his stories with his fascination for knowledge and technology—and with his commitment to human liberty. Stieg kept reading, and rereading, Heinlein for most of his life, finding in him an irresistible storyteller and a great literary inspiration.

Another notable theme in sf from the mid 1940s and into the 1970s is intellectual and biological evolution. In the work of Arthur C. Clarke, the intellectual transcendence of humanity is central, both in his *Childhood's End* and in his most famous work, his novel and screenplay collaboration with Stanley Kubrick on *2001: A Space Odyssey.* The film premiered in Sweden in late August 1968, when Stieg had just turned fourteen, and for a long time he named it his favorite movie.

Another basic idea expressed in science fiction that drew Stieg was tolerance. In order to conquer space, a species has to have evolved to a high level
of scientific, technological, and social sophistication, and to most sf authors
this implied that ethnocentricity, prejudice, nationalism, and aggression
must be left behind on the scrapheap of history. The author who most consistently advocated tolerance was Clifford D. Simak. One of his best novels,
Time and Again, translated into Swedish in 1959, is in fact all *about* the necessity for tolerance. Virtually all of Simak's work was dedicated to the supreme value of life and intelligence.

Even so, the science fiction that Stieg and I grew up on was in many
ways grounded in mid-twentieth-century traditional, even reactionary social and moral values. The protagonist of virtually every story was male,
white, and heterosexual—the last by implication, since in fact sex in any
form was virtually nonexistent in science fiction. Even by 1965 less than
twenty sf novels had featured female protagonists.

As an adult, Stieg was very much aware of this. In an essay called "But
She Writes Just Like a Real Man" (*Feminac* 5, 1980), he expressed the opinion that few, if any other forms of literature had so consistently expressed
male chauvinism, disdain for women, and reactionary values. He called sf a
fascinating mirror of its present, but noted that this was both interesting
and tragic. While calling sf a "field filled with curiosity and ideas," he also
said it "will always be associated with the contradictory cowardice typical of
its childhood."

Nonwhites were also usually ignored in sf writing. Despite that, the acclaimed science fiction writer Samuel R. Delany said that he began writing
sf partly due to reading Robert A. Heinlein's *Starship Troopers* (1959). At the
end of that novel, in an off-hand aside, readers learn that the hero is "colored." To the young Delany, this meant that science fiction could depict a
world where the color of your skin is so insignificant that nobody mentions
it. Delany, the first major black sf author, was another favorite of Stieg Larsson and Eva Gabrielsson's.

There is no doubt that the science fiction field deserves to be criticized
for some of its values. However, what science fiction emphasizes is that everything is subject to change, including our most cherished "eternal values";
that tolerance and acceptance are fundamental virtues; and that reason and
science are our means to understand and improve the world. Stieg learned
these lessons well. To him, tolerance and the willingness to embrace change
were fundamental values, as was respect for science and reason. When he
began writing feature essays, debunking "new age spiritualism" and other

forms of pseudoscience was a favorite subject. He also retained his fascination with space.

Stieg continued to read sf voraciously. Isaac Asimov's Foundation Trilogy briefly entranced him. The Foundation novels are inspired by Edward Gibbon's *The History of the Decline and Fall of the Roman Empire*. Asimov enlarged the Empire to span the Milky Way and added "psychohistorian" Hari Seldon, who foresees the fall of this empire and, to shorten the period of barbarism before the rise of a new stable order, sets up a secret foundation on a distant planet with the purpose of intervening in history to counteract chaos. It is an absurd story, but intellectually fascinating; Seldon's "psychohistory" is conceived as an exact science, by which the behavior and reactions of humans can be foreseen centuries in advance. This forces Asimov to examine and discuss concepts such as free will, chance, systems of belief and convictions, and the role of individuals in history.

Stieg later read the first volume of Asimov's autobiography, *In Memory Yet Green,* and was flabbergasted. "The man has done absolutely nothing in his entire life except sit behind a typewriter," he said. "Yet he manages to make it fun to read about him writing. How is it possible?"

When Stieg began to read in English, he preferred it to Swedish and claimed to read even Swedish authors in translation. As far as science fiction was concerned, reading in English was virtually a necessity. Though the number of translations increased during the 1970s, few of the interesting new authors were published in Sweden.

The Fiction He Wrote

What kind of short stories did Stieg Larsson write?

I have in my collection six short stories, all published in fanzines from 1972 through 1974 and so written before Stieg was twenty years old. But judging from what he said, these stories represent a very small percentage of what he wrote; he discarded dozens or hundreds of short stories and several attempts at novels. He kept writing science fiction at least until the end of the 1970s; a novel he had worked on for years was discarded at that time.

"The Wax Cabinet"

His first published story is "The Wax Cabinet" ("Vaxkabinettet," around two thousand words), which appeared in the first issue of *Sfären* (January 1972). It is not science fiction, but a horror story. The protagonist, Judy, a decorator at Madame Tussaud's in London, is working late on the Queen Victoria display and falls asleep in the queen's bed. When Judy wakes up, she hears distant voices, and an angry queen upbraids her for daring to sleep in her bed.

Judy is saved from the queen by Napoleon, who introduces her to Lord Nelson, a couple of the Beatles, and numerous other celebrities. She relaxes and begins to enjoy herself, but she makes the fatal mistake of asking the wax figures how they can move and talk. They close in on her, intending to make her into a wax doll so that she won't tell, but she frees herself, grabs a sword, and cuts Napoleon's head off before she is stopped.

In the morning, a caretaker discovers that someone has entered Madame Tussaud's. The police search the exhibits, and in the Chamber of Horrors discover a body by the guillotine. Since Judy had killed Napoleon, the others had apparently decided on a French execution for her.

"The Super Brain"
In the second issue of *Sfären* (April 1972), Stieg contributed a science fiction story, "The Super Brain" ("Superhjärnan," around three thousand five hundred words). Set in 2174, it is told in the first person by a Michael November Collins, who two years earlier had been an Olympic gold medal sprinter. Collins receives a letter "through the mail tube, falling onto the breakfast table," with a government request to report for a medical examination at Boston University. When he goes, Collins meets Dr. Mark Wester, who refuses to tell him the purpose of the examination. Collins tries to refuse, but Wester says he has an order from the president demanding Collins's cooperation. Refusing will make him an enemy of the state, which may cost him twenty-five years.

Collins takes the examination and afterward Wester tells him its purpose. The greatest scientist of the day, Professor Hans Zägel, "born in Germany but fled to England when the Russians occupied Germany in 2136" and now an American, is eighty-six years old. He is on the verge of perfecting a brain transplant technique, which will require years of testing to be failsafe. But Zägel is dying, and so Collins, a supreme athlete, has been selected to provide a new body for Zägel's brain to make it possible for Zägel to finish his work.

Collins tries to escape but is caught. He is told that the operation is set for the same night, and he is allowed to see his wife but not his children. When the guards return, Collins follows them to the operating theater. Collins feels the sting of an injection and loses consciousness, hating Wester.

"The Super Brain" is a much more ambitious story than "The Wax Cabinet." Here, Stieg Larsson tries several nice touches, including unobtrusively giving details of the future in which the story is set, instead of doing so through exposition. The story is largely told in conversations between Collins and his wife or Collins and Dr. Wester. This is obviously intended to help strengthen characterization, but many lines feel unnatural or stilted.

The theme of "The Super Brain" is worth noting. The protagonist lives a comfortable life in a democratic and affluent society, but he discovers that in order to further its interests, the state is willing to suspend his legal rights, indeed to kill him. All is done with a veneer of politeness and the pretense of consent, but when the rights of the individual clash with the wishes of government, individual rights are dispensed with. In "The Super Brain," the message of the story is that the state is the enemy.

"Jensen's Crime"

Stieg's next story was again science fiction, this time set in Amsterdam in 2036. "Jensen's Crime" ("Jensens brott," about three thousand words) was published in *Sfären* 3 (August 1972). The story opens with a man called Jensen trying to escape from a posse with dogs. The hunters draw close and one of them knocks Jensen unconscious with a club. Jensen wakes up imprisoned, and guards armed with swords take him to a courtroom. We learn that his full name is Michel Jason Jensen. We also learn that Jensen is accused of witchcraft for having practiced "scientific methods."

The story now gives the background. In 2030, a major war occurred, with the two superpowers virtually annihilating each other. Jensen is a surgeon, originally from England, vacationing in Holland with his wife and daughter when the war starts, and staying to its end. During the atomic winter following the war, their daughter died but Jensen and his wife survived. When spring finally came, the survivors turned on those they believed had caused the holocaust—not the politicians or military, but the scientists who had created weapons of mass destruction. Mobs made no distinction between physicists and physicians; all science was banned, and those practicing science were condemned. Jensen stops practicing, but when his wife gives birth to a child, the complications almost kill them both. Jensen brings out his hidden instruments and performs a caesarean. This is his crime.

Jensen's defense is that he acted in accordance with his convictions, and to save lives. But in his world science is viewed as evil, and the practice of it as witchcraft. And so he is burned at the stake.

"Jensen's Crime" is a variation on a classic theme in science fiction: the fear of ignorance and superstition. With the rejection of science, what remains of the world is hurled back to the Dark Ages; when superstition reigns, progress is literally murdered. The dialogue is significantly stronger than in the earlier stories, but the story grinds to a halt while the background information is inserted, and this makes the whole less than satisfactory.

"The Last"

In *Sfären* 3, Stieg also published another very short story, "The Last" ("Den Siste," around seven hundred words). This one is told in the third person, with only a "he" as subject. It details how "he" limps along, severely wounded, trying to hurry but with nowhere to go. While fleeing, "he" remembers the fear and horror of a morning when alien monsters laid waste to "his" village, killing hundreds. The survivors had hidden in the ruins until this day when all that remained had been ground to dust and everyone killed—except "he," who managed to crawl away despite his wounds. But when the sun sets, "he" can go no further than the rock he's climbed.

The story switches to an epilogue, only a few lines long, where two workmen are taking a break from constructing a blacktop road through a forest. In the last sentence, we are told that on a small stone lies a dead ant.

This is one of many "ant" stories Stieg wrote, and to my knowledge the only one of them still in existence. "The Last" is an effective try at a "twist ending," where the last few words suddenly turn the story around, forcing the reader to view it from a different perspective. As for Stieg's penchant for writing stories about ants, I suspect that part of the fun may have been in the challenge to think up situations where the reader would automatically assume that the protagonist of the story was a human, until the last lines disclose him or her to be an ant.

"The Ninth Life"

Stieg Larsson's last story in *Sfären* was published in No. 4 (April 1973). "The Ninth Life" ("Det nionde livet," around one thousand five hundred words) is told by Geoffery Holden, who calls himself a half-alcoholic amateur author and earns his keep translating the worst entertainment novels possible. He tells about Annie, a slight, dark, and pretty girl without friends or acquaintances, living alone in a small apartment on money inherited from her father. Annie is a "telepath," able not only to read other's minds, but also to control them. The narrator tells of her loneliness and isolation, her withdrawal from the pressure of invading feelings and thoughts. He gives her a Siamese cat, which she names Socrates. He also tells the reader of Annie's conviction that a person's psychic energy endures after death.

Not having seen Annie for weeks, the narrator receives a letter from her saying that she had been wrong and that psychic life after death can persist only in physical form, and asking him to take care of Socrates. The narrator rushes to Annie's apartment to find she has hung herself. He takes Socrates home and opens a bottle of whisky when the phone rings. It's Annie, who tells him not to worry about her dying, and confessing that she loves him. When he has the call traced, the telephone company states that there was no call. Holden is put in a mental institution and the story ends with his wondering what has happened to Socrates, and asking Annie to help him, wherever she is.

"The Ninth Life" is an intriguing story, suffering mainly from being too short. The strongest part is the characterization of Annie and her relationship to the narrator; here Stieg made an effort to portray two isolated personalities clinging for support to each other. The story would have been stronger if this part had been extended, and if the ending had been made less ambiguous. The "nonexistent" phone call is easily explained by Annie's capacity to control the thoughts of others, which should also have occurred to the narrator, and so the internal logic of the story would have led to a different and more plausible end and made the story a sustained character study rather than one cut short by a pointless shock ending.

"Rendezvous in Dusk"

Stieg contributed two stories to other fanzines. In late 1973, *Cosmos Bulletin* announced a short story competition, with science fiction paperbacks as prizes. Coming home a bit drunk after a party, Stieg wrote a story he claimed to be unable to understand. So he sent it in, and in *Cosmos Bulletin* 21 (January 1974), Stieg Larsson's "Rendezvous in Dusk" ("Rendezvous i dunkel," around 2,750 words) was presented as the winner of the short story competition. As it turns out, there had only been ten entries. Stieg's story, the jury said, "treats a difficult subject in a professional manner."

"Rendezvous in Dusk," also science fiction, is the story of Sanders, who leaves his wife Susan and five-year-old Billy to go on the first expedition to Proxima Centauri, a trip lasting ten years. When he awakens from cold sleep, a disaster has occurred, the ship is wrecked, and some crew members may be dead. At the same time, details don't fit: an immense time seems to have passed, Sanders and other survivors seem to be simultaneously in their drifting ship and on a massive, alien prairie where a giant being towers to the sky, greeting them and asking them to join him. However, when Sanders does try to join the being, he is suddenly back on Earth, and Susan welcomes him home.

The story is told in fragments, memories from before the expedition interspersed with the unexplained events after the disaster. There is no doubt that Stieg had developed his writing skills by this point. The dialogue flows easily, the descriptive passages are more carefully phrased, and although the characters remain skeletal, they are distinctive. The story succeeds in hinting at mysterious forces being at work, but as Stieg himself said, the problem was that he himself had no idea of what these forces were or of their aim.

"The Duel"

One story was written much later than the others, and it is very different. In the last fanzine Stieg published, *Långfredagsnatt 1983*, three years after he otherwise stopped participating in fandom, he printed a semifactual story later revised for my own fanzine *Gafiac* No. 47 (September 1987). With the exception of a very long letter in the following issue, this story was to my knowledge Stieg's last contribution to any fanzine.

In "The Duel" ("Duellen," around two thousand words) Larsson puts himself as a character in the story. He is rereading Robert A. Heinlein's *The Moon Is a Harsh Mistress* at a table in a Stockholm café when a stranger enters, orders coffee, and joins Stieg even though only a single other chair is taken. The stranger also opens a book—L. Ron Hubbard's *Dianetics: The Modern Science of Mental Health*.

The stranger bares his teeth in a superior grin, gestures at Stieg's book, and asks, "Science fiction?" Stieg nods. After a silence, he makes a disdainful gesture at the stranger's book and asks, "Science fiction?" The stranger shakes his head, holds up the cover of his book, and declares, "Science."

The war of wills continues. Stieg cracks his finger joints by pressing his fingertips together and lights his pipe. The stranger carefully cracks each finger in turn by pulling them. Stieg calls Hubbard's book "nonsense," but the stranger calls Heinlein's novel "reactionary." After a further exchange Stieg crumples up a box of matches and drops it in an ashtray. The stranger retaliates by breaking a pencil in two. Stieg drains a refilled cup of coffee, burning his throat. His enemy does the same, but is shaken. Stieg gives him the coup de grâce by carefully raising his Heinlein novel, opening it, tearing out the title page, and letting it fall to the floor. His enemy stares at the mutilated book, then down at his own Hubbard volume. Without a word, he picks up his book and leaves.

After this, the only other customer in the shop remarks to the café owner's wife, "Good defense; excellent mental reflexes. Tomorrow we'll bring on the Mormon."

This story is, in my opinion, by far the best written of those Stieg published. In it, you can easily and unmistakably hear his spoken voice, though it is carefully crafted for reading. The story is both funny and quite tense; the careful choice of words, the understatements as well as the exaggerated effects of the two opponents' subtle thrusts, are well handled. By the mid 1980s, Stieg had most definitely learned how to create and sustain interest, mood, and tension, and to develop a simple idea into an engaging and memorable story.

Discovering Other Writers

Stieg was constantly discovering new writers. In English, Stieg—as well as Eva Gabrielsson, whose love for and knowledge of sf matched his—discovered Joe Haldeman, whose *The Forever War* was a response to Heinlein's *Starship Troopers*. They both also read Ursula K. Le Guin and the other new feminist sf writers who infused science fiction with new ideas and a social consciousness few authors previously had displayed. Some of these were Vonda N. McIntyre, Elizabeth A. Lynn, Pamela Sargent, Marge Piercy, and Lisa Tuttle.

The authors Stieg liked best were the radicals—Joanna Russ, whose *The Female Man* was an angry, irresistibly funny and brilliantly experimental novel, and Suzy McKee Charnas, in whose *Walk to the End of the World* women are kept as slaves in the male-dominated cities, while bands of free women dominate the wilderness and hunt men like animals. Stieg also enjoyed Delany's later novels including *Dhalgren* and *Triton*, the former a complex meditation on youth culture, the latter depicting the radically diverse social structures coexisting in a human colony on Triton.

Joan D. Vinge fascinated him because of her depiction of the alien, a recurring theme in her early fiction where the "alien" can be seen as a metaphor for those not belonging, regardless of whether they are women, are mentally or physically different, or belong to a different race.

In the reviews he published (mainly in *Science Fiction Forum* during 1979 and 1980), he lavished praise on Kate Wilhelm's *Where Late the Sweet Birds Sang* and characterized Wilhelm as an author who "always returns to the dangers which absolute power poses to both individuals and collectives."

Stieg was a great fan of Philip K. Dick, one of the most original and bitingly satirical authors within science fiction whose basic theme was the shifting nature of reality and the impossibility of finding an absolute one. Dick, tragically, died in 1982, only fifty-four years old, shortly after having seen the first major movie adapted from one of his novels, *Blade Runner* (based on *Do Androids Dream of Electric Sheep?*), and so never lived to experience his broader literary acceptance and, now, with a further dozen movies released or in production, commercial success as well. Eva Gabrielsson was also fascinated by Philip K. Dick and in 1979 she translated Dick's most famous novel, *The Man in the High Castle*, into Swedish. It is a brilliant, deeply humanistic novel set in an alternate world where the Axis powers won World War II and the U.S. is now divided along the Mississippi, its eastern part occupied by Germany and its western by Japan.

Stieg also wrote with great respect of Olaf Stapledon, and called his *Star Maker*, 1937, "science fiction at its very best: a speculative and fascinating fiction of ideas, an exciting tool for discussion and a source of inspiration." And he expressed great sympathy for the humanism of Clifford D. Simak.

In *Science Fiction Forum* 81 (March 1980), Stieg wrote a general biographic and literary overview of Frederik Pohl, interviewed him, and reviewed three of his novels. He obviously held Pohl in high regard. Frederik Pohl was born in 1919, grew up in Brooklyn, and began reading science fiction at nine. At fourteen he dropped out of school to help support his family. In 1936, Pohl joined the Young Communist League but left it in 1939, after the German-Soviet pact, since one of his reasons for joining had been his hatred for fascism.

Pohl's first novel, *The Space Merchants*, co-written with Cyril Kornbluth, was translated into Swedish in 1960; a savage satire on commercialism, it is set in a future where advertising agencies run the world. Stieg called Pohl's later *Gateway* powerful in both its bleakness and the splendor of its imagination, "one of the best sf novels I have ever read."

The Importance of Science Fiction to Him—and to Lisbeth Salander

Stieg's interest in science fiction remained strong throughout his life. When I invited Harlan Ellison to the Swedish Book Fair in 1992, Stieg was enthusiastic. Ellison is intransigent as a defender of civil liberties and an enemy of superstition, and one of science fiction's most emotionally powerful writers; he had been a favorite of Stieg's for many years. Stieg interviewed him for a very appreciative TT feature. Still later, Stieg was interested in the "cyberpunk" movement in sf, not least in Neal Stephenson, whose *Snow Crash* provided a model for the online "Hacker Republic" of which Lisbeth Salander is a citizen. When in 2004 I began editing the quarterly *Nova Science Fiction* magazine, Stieg applauded its efforts to publish women authors as well as stories dealing with gender issues.

For many years, Stieg tried writing science fiction novels. But the books that in the end made him famous are crime fiction. Nevertheless, influences from the science fiction he liked can be found in them. In Neal Stephenson's *Snow Crash* and *The Diamond Age*, the concept of a "distributed republic" is introduced; it means a "nation" where citizens and physical assets are scattered around the globe, often changing, in many loosely connected anarchist communities. The concept is adapted, and acknowledged, in the online, anarchist "Hacker Republic" in the Millennium novels, where Lisbeth Salander is a "citizen."

Other sf influences on the Millennium novels are less obvious but, I would argue, nevertheless important. Major themes—such as speculation about the future—may be missing but some subtle ones can be identified. Quite a few, I suspect, can be attributed to Robert A. Heinlein, whom Stieg read and reread for forty years. A recurring theme in Heinlein's work is that a young and inexperienced protagonist learns from a sympathetic older and wiser character. I wouldn't be surprised if this inspired Stieg to provide Lisbeth Salander with her wise guardian Holger Palmgren, or for that matter Mikael Blomkvist with Henrik Vanger.

Another Heinlein theme, which may well have inspired Stieg to reflect on these matters, is the idea of nondemanding and free consensual sex, a recurring theme in novels like *Stranger in a Strange Land*, *The Moon Is a Harsh Mistress*, and *Friday*. The heroine of *Friday,* incidentally, is a female secret agent, an extremely adept both fighter and problem solver who is also a master of disguise. She might have taught Salander a trick or two about changing her looks. But so might the heroine of Heinlein's *The Puppet Masters,* also an accomplished undercover agent. Other echoes of Heinlein, in my opinion, are visible in the storytelling structure of the Millennium novels, in the auctorial voice and in the integration of background with story.

As for Salander herself, Stieg wrote extensively on Joan D. Vinge's use of "alien" protagonists, through whose eyes society can be viewed as inimical and closed. Vinge's aliens in many cases were human women, placed outside society because of physical or mental differences. Lisbeth Salander could have been one of them. Just as she might be a sister of Joanna Russ's heroine Jael in *The Female Man,* an assassin who knows that she may well die by the hand of some man, but vows in that case to die with her hands tearing at his intestines.

We will never know what kind of science fiction Stieg might have written as a mature author. But given the closeness between him and his partner

Eva Gabrielsson, perhaps someday we may get a small inkling. When asked in an interview whether she also had considered writing crime fiction, Eva Gabrielsson recently said that she never had. If she turned to fiction at all, she said, it would be science fiction.

THE MAN WHO INHALED CRIME FICTION
by John-Henri Holmberg

Stieg Larsson became a reader of both science fiction and crime fiction at an early age. The pairing of the two literary fields is fairly common; they share a common ancestry. Both are rooted in the Enlightenment view of humanity, which holds that observation and rational thought are our only tools for acquiring knowledge of ourselves and the world. Science fiction applies this to society and the world at large; the classic detective story applies the same idea to individuals, dramatizing it into a quest for truth and justice. The author usually singled out as the originator of the detective story is Edgar Allan Poe, whose "The Murders in the Rue Morgue," written in 1841, features the first literary detective who solves crime through pure reason. Poe's heir was Sir Arthur Conan Doyle, creator of Sherlock Holmes. Both Poe and Doyle also wrote science fiction, and many later authors have also published in both fields.

When Larsson entered his teens there were relatively few science fiction titles available in Swedish, making it fairly easy to identify books he must have read and the themes that influenced him. But more than two hundred crime novels per year have been published in Sweden since around 1950, and by his midteens Larsson was already reading fiction in English. Here assumptions just won't do.

We know that Larsson's early enthusiasm for juvenile crime stories had him reading the "Twin Detectives" series by the Swedish pseudonymous author Sivar Ahlrud (Ivar Ahlstedt and Sid Roland Rommerud), with forty novels in print when Stieg was thirteen. Another author he talked about, and who was perhaps more important to him, was the prolific English children's writer Enid Blyton. Although never very successful in the United States, Blyton is ranked as the fifth most translated author in the world. She was immensely popular in Sweden in the 1950s and 1960s, although public libraries throughout the period refused to carry her books, considering them "stereotyped and badly written."

The series Stieg Larsson most often mentioned were the Famous Five and the Adventure books, mysteries in which four teens and one animal stumble on inexplicable or suspicious events and unravel them until they can deliver a solution to the authorities. In the Famous Five, the heroes are Dick, Julian, Ann, George (short for Georgina), and George's dog Tim. In the Adventure series the protagonists are Jack, Ann, Philip, Diana, and Jack's parrot Kiki. In their respective stories George and Diana compete actively with the boys in bravery as well as in solving the mysteries. The other two girls conform to traditional gender roles: they get frightened; need to be protected; and take care of the cooking, mending, and cleaning. George in particular is a strong-willed character, described as a tomboy. She wears "boys' clothes," hates household work and dolls, is unafraid, and likes action. Considering that the first Famous Five novels were written in the 1940s, their gender stereotyping, though strongly criticized, is hardly extreme and, given George as a major character, they in fact bend less in that direction than many other children's books of the period. Although formulaic, the stories are not badly told and the plots play fair.

Swedish children's author Astrid Lindgren was also among the writers Stieg read—in fact, had he not done so, he would have been unique among contemporary Swedes. Her work includes three novels about Pippi Långstrump (Pippi Longstocking); three about the boy detective Kalle Blomkvist (who in the English translations is renamed Bill Bergson); a high-fantasy novel *Mio, My Son*; and the tongue-in-cheek fantasies about Karlsson-on-the-Roof, a fat little man equipped with a propeller who makes friends with a lonely boy in a Stockholm apartment. Astrid Lindgren was long Sweden's most read author by far and Pippi is her most enduring character. Larsson once said that Lisbeth Salander was imagined as Pippi grown up.

The three Bill Bergson/Kalle Blomkvist novels are fairly sophisticated crime novels about murder, kidnapping, and other real and brutal crimes, informed by Lindgren's work as a secretary for a Stockholm University professor of criminology. The main character is an avid reader of crime stories and often compares himself to Agatha Christie's Hercule Poirot and Dorothy Sayers's Lord Peter Wimsey.

It is also most probable that Stieg read both Åke Holmberg's juvenile crime novels about private detective Ture Sventon (in translation Tam Sventon), humorous stories largely inspired by the Sherlock Holmes tradition, and Nils-Olof Franzén's internationally more successful series about Agaton Sax, a round man with a small moustache featured in eleven humorous and inventive private detective pastiches. Both series were phenomenally popular in Sweden during Stieg's childhood and early teens.

By the late 1960s, Stieg Larsson had graduated to adult crime fiction. An early love was the comic strip character Modesty Blaise, created by Peter O'Donnell in 1962 and introduced in Sweden in 1967, when the first of fourteen issues of a comic book called *Agent Modesty Blaise* was published. From 1971 onward, the strip appeared in a monthly anthology comic called *Agent X-9*. Stieg Larsson faithfully collected this comic for many years, and he also read O'Donnell's novels about Modesty Blaise, which appeared in Swedish as of 1965. Although not often noted in most discussions of the Millennium trilogy, she may well be at least as important an influence on Stieg's heroine as Pippi Longstocking.

Modesty Blaise is initially a girl without memories or name who in 1945 escapes from a displaced persons camp in Greece. Wandering around the Mediterranean, she learns to survive through her wits and strength. She befriends Lob, a Hungarian refugee scholar, who names her "Modesty"—the antithesis of everything she stands for. She herself later adopts "Blaise," after Merlin's tutor in the Arthurian saga. After giving her a comprehensive education, Lob dies and Modesty ends up in Tangier, where she takes control of a criminal gang and expands it to international scale as The Network.

At twenty-eight, having made a considerable fortune, Modesty retires to London with her right-hand man and friend (but never lover), Willie Garvin. Bored by living in lavish idleness, she starts accepting missions from Sir Gerald Tarrant, a friend who is also a head official of the British Secret Service. But in the total of ninety-nine comic strip stories, eleven novels, and eleven short stories written by O'Donnell, Modesty and Willie also help strangers in trouble, are haunted by criminals from their past in The Network, and regularly stumble into intrigue of all sorts. The Modesty Blaise stories are characterized by intelligent scripts, original ideas, and a genuinely outstanding heroine—fiercely independent, sexually ambiguous, and unconventional in her methods of fighting criminals.

By the age of twenty Stieg Larsson had graduated not only from juveniles but also from the standard, more traditional mysteries. In an essay entitled "Hardboiled," published in his and Rune Forsgren's fanzine *Fijagh!* 6 in

February 1976, he discusses three favorite authors, but begins by dismissing the Swedish publishing industry, talking about how Sweden is clueless in most literary areas. Instead of embracing the hard-boiled tradition, Swedish crime fiction had been detrimentally influenced by the British puzzle school, he says, and Swedish readers had to make do with what he calls the "incomprehensible" novels of Maria Lang and the "almost admirable disasters" of authors such as Stieg Trenter and Bo Balderson.

Since the authors named were generally considered among the foremost practitioners of crime fiction in Sweden, Stieg's dismissal is the more telling. He also stated unequivocally that just about the only Swedish crime authors he could stand were Maj Sjöwall and Per Wahlöö, creators of the ten Martin Beck novels. Sjöwall and Wahlöö wrote police procedurals of a kind new to Sweden. In their novels, murders are brutal, the day-to-day work of the policemen is grinding and ultimately defeating, the writing is terse and journalistic, and the books are explicitly political with a radical socialist slant. Stieg claimed to read Sjöwall and Wahlöö in American paperback editions because he felt that the kind of crime stories he liked had to be read in American English to sound realistic. (Whether this was literally true I have no idea. But he certainly said so.)

He then turned to the three crime authors he did admire: Dashiell Hammett, Raymond Chandler, and Ross Macdonald (pen name for Kenneth Millar). Picking these three is hardly original; within the hard-boiled school, Hammett was the primary creator, Chandler his direct descendant, and Macdonald their heir apparent. Stieg lauds their political acumen, their realism, their cynicism, their humor, and their central theme of loneliness and alienation. He names *Red Harvest* as his favorite Hammett novel, and praises Hammett's prose, but he also points out his weak plot structures. He calls *The Thin Man* slight and banal.

As for Chandler, Stieg views him as the author who developed and perfected Hammett's themes and ideas. He writes appreciatively of Chandler's dark images from the twilight side of life and of his social perspective, where readers can't always be certain whether the crime syndicate or the police is the worse enemy. He picks *The Long Goodbye* as Chandler's strongest novel and calls it one of the best American novels written, a masterpiece comparable to anything by Hemingway or Steinbeck. Nowhere else, he says, has the collapse of the American dream been as nakedly exposed.

However, if Hammett was the first and Chandler the greatest, Stieg considered Ross Macdonald the most interesting of the hard-boiled writers. The main difference between Macdonald and Chandler, in Stieg's view, is that while Chandler even in his later works kept writing about the 1940s, Macdonald placed his antihero Lew Archer firmly in the continuum of the present. He names *The Chill*, published in 1964, as Macdonald's supreme achievement, calling it a triumph as well as a crowning masterpiece of crime fiction.

Even before he had read Chandler and Macdonald, Larsson had already been trying his hand at not only science fiction but also crime fiction—or a combination of the two. In the second issue of his and Rune Forsgren's first fanzine, *Sfären*, published in early 1972 when Larsson was seventeen, Forsgren wrote teasingly:

Recently I asked Stieg how his latest novel was doing. I probably shouldn't, because he sure told me.

In Chapter 1, the hero pulls a girl out of the dirty waters of Nybroviken. Later he ends up at a police station in the company of another girl. Chapter 5 is very exciting! In it, he walks around looking for one of the girls, although I don't know which one of them. Main theme? There seems to be this mad scientist who plans to exterminate all of humanity except for a few chosen ones. A group of Stockholm teenagers find out about this, and then the whole whirligig is in motion.

I understand nothing, and the question seems to be how much of it Stieg understands. I tried to get him to explain, but all I got for my trouble was a spoiled night's sleep.

Still, I am convinced that within my honored friend Stieg hides a considerable auctorial talent. It's just a damned shame that it hides so well!

Between seventeen and twenty-one, Stieg Larsson learned to think ideologically, went from Maoism to becoming a political writer for the Trotskyist *Internationalen*, and from trying to write juvenile fiction to trying to write adult fiction. How his politics infused his reading is shown in a short essay printed in Rune Forsgren's fanzine *Fancy* 4, August 1973. In it Stieg vents his disgust at how political themes are handled in a handful of thrillers he had recently read, including the forty-ninth title in the Killmaster series purportedly written by the novels' hero, Nick Carter (in this case pen name for Jon Messman). In the novel *Operation Che Guevara*, the CIA learns that Guevara survived the confrontation in Bolivia in 1967 and is in fact living under an assumed name elsewhere in South America. Guevara is portrayed as a sadistic and homicidal maniac, and Nick Carter manages to track down and kill him. In another Killmaster novel, not named, Stieg notes that the plot incredibly involves Mao Zedong now having partnered with Martin Bormann and Swedish Stalinist Olof Palme to annihilate the U.S. population using a virus.

Another title, *Operation Annihilation*, in a book series spinoff from TV's "I Spy" series and written by John Tiger (a pen name for Walter Wager), is about China trying to start World War Three by blowing up an American city. Stieg calls it a reactionary, dishonest, absurd, and ridiculous story and wonders how any publisher would have the gall to print such junk.

Later, in his and Rune Forsgren's *Fijagh!* 5, 1975, Stieg recommends Ed McBain's (Evan Hunter) 1973 novel *Hail to the Chief,* which chronicles a youth gang war where Randall Nesbitt, the leader of the Yankee Reb gang, wants to achieve "peace with honor" by annihilating all opponents. The novel is a clever satire of President Richard Nixon, with parts of the Nesbitt character's defense almost directly quoted from Nixon; Stieg tells us that he has taken the novel to heart.

In the 1980s and 1990s, when he reviewed crime fiction for TT, the Swedish news agency where he worked as a graphic artist and feature writer, it was still obvious that Stieg primarily enjoyed hard-boiled and noir-inspired crime stories. Early on he mentioned being impressed by Frederick Forsyth's *The Odessa File* (1972), where a crime reporter attempts to find an ex-Nazi commander in modern-day Germany and discovers a secret organization called ODESSA (Organization of Previous SS-Members) that helps Nazi war criminals to change identity and escape to South America. It is hardly surprising that the anti-Nazi theme of the novel fascinated Stieg.

Among the authors I published as an editor and editorial director in the late 1980s and early 1990s, Larsson was particularly fond of James Ellroy, Sue Grafton, and Andrew Vachss. In Vachss's case, he was also impressed by the novelist's work as an activist and lawyer who represented abused children exclusively, and later invited Vachss to contribute an essay to *Expo*.

Among the authors published by other houses, his personal favorites included Liza Cody, Patricia Cornwell, Val McDermid, and Sara Paretsky. He also liked Laurie R. King's Kate Martinelli novels and Carol O'Connell's Kathy Mallory novels. In crime fiction, just as in science fiction, Stieg on the whole preferred female authors and female protagonists to male, and during the 1980s, women began making a strong showing in the previously male-dominated hard-boiled crime fiction field, just as they had done in science fiction during the 1970s.

That he liked Elizabeth George may seem surprising given that virtually all the other authors mentioned here belong to the grittier, streetwise school of crime fiction, whereas George, though American, must properly be placed in the traditional British school of mystery writing that includes Dorothy Sayers and Agatha Christie. But George's novels are not just loving pastiches, but also terse updates of the classics. Her tales of upper-class Thomas Lynley, a policeman by choice though born to riches (very much a descendant of Sayers's Lord Peter Wimsey), and his working-class sergeant Barbara Havers (a gender-conscious appropriation of Wimsey's faithful manservant Bunter), add complex social, emotional, psychological, and gender conflicts to the traditional detective story. That Stieg, well read in traditional crime fiction, would appreciate this is hardly surprising; in a sense, he does a similar thing in his Millennium novels, where each book intertwines two traditional plot structures. *The Girl with the Dragon Tattoo* combines a classic British manor murder mystery with a financial thriller, while the events within the plot are based not on traditional motives, but rather in the much darker issues of twisted sexuality, racial and gender hatred, and the lust for power.

Stieg Larsson was a lifelong constant reader. Apart from nonfiction, his great loves were science fiction and crime fiction. In both fields, he read both the classics and current authors. From reading came his own desire to write, and his favorite authors inspired his way of dealing with the technical elements of writing just as they inspired his characters and his integration of themes and plot. His subjects, however, stemmed from his political views and his uncompromising sense of justice and tolerance.

PART TWO

THE CLIMATE IS COLD, THE NIGHTS ARE LONG, THE LIQUOR IS HARD, AND THE CURTAINS ARE DRAWN

More than 150 years ago, *Uncle Tom's Cabin* helped lay the groundwork for the end of slavery. Let's hope that Larsson's novels help build pressure on trafficking as a modern echo of slavery. —Nicholas Kristof, *The New York Times*

Lisbeth Salander is one of the great female characters in fiction, dangerous as hell in spite of her waiflike appearance. The best thing about the late Larsson's Millennium trilogy is that the three books form one long, interconnected tale. And like Jo Rowling's Harry Potter series, it's a relentless, unputdownable narrative. —Stephen King

Lisbeth Salander has gone through so many terrible things and people had done so many things to her. But still she doesn't see herself as a victim. She doesn't feel pity for herself. She always finds a way to stand up and to decide what she wants to do and what kind of life she wants to live, and she does it and she never gives up.
—Noomi Rapace, the actress who plays Lisbeth Salander in the Scandinavian film trilogy, interviewed by Charlie Rose

The Girl Who Kicked the Hornet's Nest finally goes on sale (in the United States) this month. Except for *Harry Potter,* Americans haven't been so eager for a book since the early 1840s, when they thronged the docks in New York, hailing incoming ships for news of Little Nell in Charles Dickens's *Old Curiosity Shop.* —Charles McGrath, *The New York Times*

5. THE FATAL ATTRACTION OF NORDIC NOIR

INSPECTOR NORSE: WHY ARE NORDIC DETECTIVE NOVELS SO SUCCESSFUL?
from The Economist

The neat streets of Oslo are not a natural setting for crime fiction. Nor, with its cows and country smells, is the flat farming land of Sweden's southern tip. And Reykjavik, Iceland's capital, is now associated more with financial misjudgment than gruesome murder. Yet in the past decade Nordic crime writers have unleashed a wave of detective fiction that is right up there with the work of Dashiell Hammett, Patricia Highsmith, Elmore Leonard and the other crime greats. Nordic crime today is a publishing phenomenon. Stieg Larsson's Millennium trilogy alone has sold 27m copies, its publishers' latest figures show, in over 40 countries. The release this month in Britain and America of "The Girl with the Dragon Tattoo", the film of the first Larsson book, will only boost sales.

The transfer to the screen of his sprawling epic (the author died suddenly in 2004 just as the trilogy was being edited and translated) will cement the Nordics' renown. The more unruly subplots have been eliminated, leaving the hero, a middle-aged financial journalist named Mikael Blomkvist (Michael Nyqvist), and an emotionally damaged computer hacker, Lisbeth Salander (Noomi Rapace), at the centre of every scene. The small screen too has had a recent visit from the Swedish police. Starting in 2008, British television viewers have been treated to expensive adaptations of the books of Henning Mankell, featuring Kenneth Branagh as Kurt Wallander. The BBC series has reawakened interest in Mr Mankell's nine Wallander books, which make up a large slice of his worldwide sales of 30m in 40 languages.

Larsson and Mr. Mankell are the best-known Nordic crime writers outside the region. But several others are also beginning to gain recognition abroad, including K.O. Dahl and Karin Fossum from Norway and Åke Edwardson and Håkan Nesser of Sweden. Iceland, a Nordic country that is not strictly part of Scandinavia, boasts an award winner too. Arnaldur Indridason's *Silence of the Grave* won the British Crime Writers' Association Gold Dagger award in 2005. *The Devil's Star* by a Norwegian, Jo Nesbø, is published in America this month at the same time as a more recent novel, *The Snowman*, is coming out in Britain. A previous work, *Nemesis*, was nominated for the prestigious Edgar Allan Poe crime-writing award, a prize generally dominated by American authors.

Three factors underpin the success of Nordic crime fiction: language, heroes and setting. Niclas Salomonsson, a literary agent who represents almost all the up and coming Scandinavian crime writers, reckons it is the style of the books, "realistic, simple and precise . . . and stripped of unnecessary words", that has a lot to do with it. The plain, direct writing, devoid of metaphor, suits the genre well.

The Nordic detective is often careworn and rumpled. Mr Mankell's Wallander is gloomy, troubled and ambivalent about his father. Mr Indridason's Inspector Erlendur lives alone after a failed marriage, haunted by the death of his younger brother many years before in a blizzard that he survived. Mr Nesbø's leading man, Inspector Harry Hole—often horribly drunk—is defiant of his superiors yet loyal to his favored colleagues.

Most important is the setting. The countries that the Nordic writers call home are prosperous and organized, a "soft society" according to Mr Nesbø. But the protection offered by a cradle-to-grave welfare system hides a dark underside. As Mary Evans points out in her recent study, "The Imagination of Evil", the best Scandinavian fiction mines the seam that connects the insiders—the rich and powerful—and the outsiders, represented by the poor, the exploited and the vulnerable. Larsson is a master at depicting the relationship between business, social hypocrisy and criminal behavior, and his heroes do not want to be rescued through any form of conventional state intervention.

Analyzing Scandinavia and its psyche is nothing new; Henrik Ibsen did it over a century ago. But the greatest influence on these rising writers has been Per Wahlöö and Maj Sjöwall, a Swedish couple. Journalists and committed Marxists, they co-authored the ten-volume Martin Beck series between 1965 and 1975 with the aim of criticizing the country's welfare state. The central character is a likeable and dedicated policeman with a dry sense of humor. But the books, which closely study police procedure, feature an ensemble of his colleagues, all believable characters drawn with the lightest of touches. By turn entertaining and funny examinations of the day-to-day work of policemen, they are also gripping and complex thrillers.

The quality and popularity of crime fiction has given Nordic novelists a prestige that authors from other countries do not enjoy. This, in turn, has drawn in new writers. The next potential blockbuster could well be Leif G.W. Persson's *Fall of the Welfare State*—though a more enticing title is planned for its English-language debut. First published in Sweden in 2002, it is written by a professor of criminology who has been involved in many of Sweden's high-profile crime cases and is an epic and ambitious tale spanning several decades of Swedish history.

The cold, dark climate, where doors are bolted and curtains drawn, provides a perfect setting for crime writing. The nights are long, the liquor hard, the people, according to Mr Nesbø, "brought up to hide their feelings" and hold on to their secrets. If you are driving through Norway at dusk and see a farmhouse with its lights on and its doors open, do not stop, he warns, only half jokingly. You are as likely to be greeted by a crime scene as a warm welcome.

IKEA NOIR
by Brooks Riley

It seems hard to find a fan of Scandinavian crime fiction who isn't at the same time trying to explain the appeal of this genre. Is it that blood can also splatter on snow and a pristine landscape? The flawed, rumpled and vulnerable detectives who are more in tune with our times than a hard-boiled Sam Spade or Mickey Spillane? Or that the blend of Scandinavian street and place names and unique cultural habits provide just the right touch of exoticism on top of a society whose affluence, legal system, and values still make it recognizable and familiar to English-speaking readers? Brooks Riley, a fan of the genre well before Stieg Larsson came along, takes us on a tour d'horizon of Nordic noir. She also explains why she likes nothing better than to enter into the heart and mind of a Scandinavian writer well into the night—and why Larsson stands out so refreshingly from the rest of the pack.

Riley is a director, producer, film critic, editor, and screenwriter who lives and works in Germany.

Every night I travel to Scandinavia—to Sweden, Norway, Denmark, or Iceland. I climb into bed with a crime novel by Henning Mankell, Stieg Larsson, Arne Dahl, Jussi Adler-Olsen, Jo Nesbø, Arnaldur Indridason, or Åke Edwardson, and spend my last few waking moments in Ystad, Uppsala, Stockholm, or Gothenburg, in Bergen, Oslo, or Copenhagen, on the island of Gotland, or in Reykjavik.

There's something to be said for ending one's day somewhere else. After a few pages, sleep comes quickly, not because the books are soporific, but because the change of location paves the way for other landscapes to occupy my REM sleep.

Long before Stieg Larsson exploded onto the U.S. market, I became an avid reader of Scandinavian crime novels. It began with Henning Mankell,

---

An earlier version of this essay appeared on wowOwow.com and has been adapted by the author. Used with permission.

one of the first of the recent wave of Swedish crime writers to be translated into English. It continued with Jo Nesbø, the Norwegian rocker-turned-writer. After I had read them and the few other Scandinavian crime writers available in English at the time, I began my assault on the many more available in German translation, where Scandinavian mysteries have long been a healthy subgenre.

So, what do those Baltic-North Sea scribes have going for them that makes their books fly off the shelves? It's hard to say. Crime is not the first thing that comes to mind at the thought of Sweden or Norway. More likely it's fantastic fjords, social democracies, IKEA, Saab, H&M, saunas, pine forests, white interiors, Ingmar Bergman, dark winters, midnight suns. . . .

Dark winters? Midnight suns?

Dark winters: what to do with a truncated day when the sun wakes up around at eleven a.m., drags itself along the horizon, and then drops out of sight at three p.m.? Start a novel, to occupy all that time you're forced to be inside.

Midnight sun: what to do with those bright summer nights when you can't get to sleep because the sun that stayed for dinner just won't go home? Finish your novel.

That may be the key to why Scandinavian mysteries have become a red-cottage industry. Everybody's writing one, or so it seems. It may also have to do with the unsolved murder of Sweden's beloved head of state, Olof Palme, who in 1986 felt safe enough to go to the movies without his bodyguards and was gunned down on the street. From one minute to the next, Sweden was transformed from a sleepy, shirtsleeve democracy into the scene of a brutal crime. The loss of innocence suffered by the nation in that one shocking moment is a wound that still festers.

Are all these mystery novels a collective, cathartic response to the lingering frustration over the unsolved Palme case? Or is it that Scandinavians have come to the realization that something may be rotten in the states of Denmark, social utopian Sweden, or nouveau-très-riche Norway? Whatever the reason, none of these theories explains the immense popularity of these writers outside their own countries.

Stieg Larsson is the maestro of the page turner. I knew this at once, when sleep was a no-show after a few pages of bedtime reading. As I hurtled over the umlauts (a double whammy in the German translation) in *The Girl Who Kicked the Hornet's Nest*, my heart raced, and I willingly traded off a good night's sleep just to find out how it ended. At four in the morning, exhausted and wide awake, I closed the book on Stieg Larsson, just as the book was closed on him, alas, in his prime.

Larsson is not typical, however. His books are thrillers, and thrilling, to be sure. But there's hardly a cop in sight, and the genre-bending narratives he offers have more to do with high-octane investigative reporting, dangerous research, and a fast-paced, hair-raising form of vigilantism that targets a white-collar society's contemptible carbuncles. Larsson is story driven, almost never stopping to smell the smorgasbord. You join him on his joy ride, but you could be almost anywhere in the Western world.

The ghost of Larsson himself inhabits the character of Mikael Blomkvist: one can't help but wonder if his own early experience as witness to a rape condemned him to a life of compensatory, almost missionary service to the exposure of corruption and social injustices.

Ever since Larsson broke the Kindle e-book record, a number of other Scandinavian writers have been proclaimed "the next Stieg Larsson," especially on the covers of English translations. None of them is, although a few have attempted to up their body counts and raise the threshold of malevolence in their books. Jussi Adler Olsen's disappointing second Carl Mørck mystery *Fasandræberne* suffers from this unfortunate attempt to out-Larsson Larsson, offering a trio of interchangeable, vicious villains to rival Larsson's malignant menagerie, as well as a female vigilante as skillfully ruthless as Larsson's Lisbeth Salander, but without the hacker gene. The result is a story as predictable as it is unbelievable. Olsen manages to redeem himself only in the second half, by turning his attention back to Mørck and cohorts and away from the cardboard antagonists trumped up for his narrative.

While it is sad that Larsson's oeuvre is prematurely complete, it would be even sadder if Scandinavia suddenly started churning out Larsson imitations. There are too many good, original writers at work there, and their worth should not be measured by their similarity to Larsson. In the end, Larsson's greatest legacy may be in drawing attention to all those other fine tale spinners from the frozen north.

Americans have long enjoyed mysteries set in other countries, but most are written by American or British writers, who rely on their firsthand knowledge of the regions to present believable scenarios of native police work: Donna Leon (Venice), the late Michael Dibdin (various Italian cities), Robert Wilson (Lisbon, Sevilla). As good as these books are, they are fictional portrayals of the societies in which they take place, each offering an engaging verisimilitude that is picturesque but never quite authentic.

Enter the Vikings: when you read a Scandinavian crime story, you enter the heart and mind of a Scandinavian. They are a lot like us, but also not. Their homicide detectives are prone to depression (Edwardson), alcoholism

(Nesbø, Mankell), and failed marriages (Olsen, Nesbø, Indridason). They spend hours—and pages—longing to escape to places where life offers a reasonable number of daylight hours and tolerable temperatures (Edwardson). They eat existential angst for breakfast, and loneliness or guilt for dinner (Mankell). They tend to be good liberals, who let social injustices eat away at them (all). They are a surprisingly humorous bunch (Dahl, Olsen), given to sardonic observations, silent sarcasm, and gallows humor. Some of them are quite violent (Nesbø, Olsen), but righteous indignation fuels their fists.

Their cases have to do with racism, neo-Nazis, foreign mafias encroaching on the local economy, drug trafficking, political intrigues, old families, and new immigrants. Sound familiar? The patchwork ills of modern Scandinavian society are not so different from those of other Western democracies. The prism through which these ills are viewed, however, provides its own version of *verismo*. The private lives of the detectives are always two-stepping with the cases at hand. What's more, Scandinavians tend to brood a lot, and this is precisely where the books take on an extra dimension which has little to do with whatever crime may be driving the narrative engine:

I'm fond of Mankell's Wallander, who eats and drinks too much, listens to classical music, and tries to avoid bitter encounters with a father who has painted the same picture every day of his adult life.

I worry about Nesbø's Harry Hole, the tortured alcoholic who carries the guilt for his partner's death, but soldiers on, seeing the world through a bitter, highly customized, brilliantly written series of observations.

I delight in Olsen's cynical Carl Mørck, whose knee-jerk preconceptions about his new Arab assistant soon turn into grudging admiration and even a miser's mite of gratitude.

I even tolerate Edwardson's stolid Erik Winter, whose dogged dedication to a case sometimes takes the form of navel-gazing.

And then there are the places themselves: instead of exotic tourist attractions like Venice or Lisbon, you get gloomy Gothenburg, lofty Stockholm, provincial Ystad, wild-weathered Gotland, raunchy Reykjavik—a patchwork quilt of locations delivered with finesse by native writers exposing their chiaroscuro lands to closer scrutiny and a wider audience.

Publishers in America are now starting to flood the market with these writers. Soon, you too may be hanging out in Scandinavia every night. It's a trip worth taking.

THE SCANDINAVIAN INVASION
by Jordan Foster

The trickle has turned into a wave. Until the Stieg Larsson trilogy leaped to American best-seller lists in 2008—and stayed there—North American publishers treated Nordic noir mainly as a stepchild, bringing English-speaking readers only a small fraction of the books that were popular in their home countries. The most notable exceptions were the highly literate Martin Beck series written by the husband and wife team of Maj Sjöwall and Per Wahlöö in the 1960s and 1970s, the darkly compelling Inspector Kurt Wallander series by Henning Mankell begun in the 1990s and ending in 2011 (as well as Mankell's other books), and the one-hit wonder of Peter Høeg's masterpiece, Smilla's Sense of Snow, *published in 1992. Even these deservedly lionized authors rarely sold their individual titles in large numbers. But they paved the way for what followed; indeed, Mankell has said that he feels "like a locomotive."*

Since the unexpected wild breakout success of the Larsson novels, American publishers now can't get enough Nordic noir, spending hundreds of thousands of dollars to find the next Larsson, as is abundantly evident from this "inside baseball" article that appeared in Publishers Weekly, *the industry bible. Jordan Foster, a freelance writer who often writes for the magazine, introduces the wide range of Scandinavian writers and their work now hitting our shores.*

"Alas," this very magazine [*Publisher's Weekly*] lamented back in 2002, "Scandinavian dreariness just doesn't seem to have broad appeal to American readers." The review referred not to Stieg Larsson's tattooed hacker, Lisbeth Salander—who wouldn't explode onto the scene for another six years—but to the work of another Swede, Henning Mankell, and his series featuring Det. Insp. Kurt Wallander.

This article first appeared in a longer form in *Publishers Weekly*, November 22, 2010. Used with permission.

Mankell is an international best seller whose books have sold more than 35 million copies worldwide, yet his haunting, bleak Wallander series published in the U.S. by Knopf failed to capture America's attention in the same way the same imprint's 2007 acquisition of Larsson's Millennium trilogy would [45 million copies and counting].

American readers in 2008 gravitated to *The Girl with the Dragon Tattoo's* Salander, with all her razor-sharp edges, tattoos, antisocial tendencies, and lethal abilities to take out opponents with her fists or a few keystrokes. Wallander, on the other hand, is a middle-aged copper, on the road to diabetes when we first meet him. He's rumpled, irritable, and introspective to the point of brooding. Reviews continually praise Mankell's intricate plotting and his tackling of complex social and global issues, but point to the "pervasive Scandinavian gloom," describing his work as the "darkest of Swedish noir." Larsson's trilogy, on the other hand, is rife with violence, both physical and psychological.

But where did this wave of Scandinavian crime fiction originate? And where should readers who may have discovered Stockholm for the first time through the eyes of Salander go to get their next fix of Nordic noir? Unquestionably, the first grandmasters of Swedish detective fiction were Maj Sjöwall and Per Wahlöö, without whom there might be no Mankell or Larsson, certainly no Wallander or Salander. Beginning in 1965 with Roseanna (translated into English in 1967), the writing duo introduced the world to Stockholm police inspector Martin Beck. Over the next ten years, the couple wrote one book a year—winning an Edgar for Best Mystery in 1971 for *The Laughing Policeman*—concluding the series with *The Terrorists* in 1975, published a few months after Wahlöö died of cancer.

Committed Marxists, Sjöwall and Wahlöö used the Beck books as a way to address problems they saw in Swedish society. "Swedish society itself is the true spark of its crime writers' success," says bestseller Liza Marklund, who made her official American debut in 2010 with *The Postcard Killers*, coauthored with James Patterson. "Nowhere else can you live your life in complete safety, knowing that the state will care for you from cradle to grave. Where else can you find a better backdrop for a crime novel than here, in the most secure society on earth? Nowhere else are the contrasts sharper, the betrayals of authority bigger, the violence more unexpected than in Sweden." Beck also became a model for the flawed hero, a detective who's credible precisely because he's not superhuman in his ability to shrug off the horrors he sees on the job.

Stockholm is by no means the only locale, but it's a popular setting for murder and mayhem. The Swedish capital is home to series from Marklund, Leif G.W. Persson, and duo Anders Roslund and Börge Hellström. Marklund is one of Sweden's bestselling authors, and her series featuring journalist Annika Bengtzon has sold millions of copies worldwide. Pantheon debuted the first book in Persson's planned trilogy, *Between Summer's Longing and Winter's End,* a complex thriller based on the still unsolved 1986 assassination of Sweden's Prime Minister Olof Palme in 2010. Roslund and Hellström—a television journalist and an ex-con, respectively—set their series featuring veteran detective Ewert Grens in the seedy underbelly of Stockholm. Silver Oak published the second installment, *Three Seconds,* in 2011. [The authors are interviewed in chapter 6.—ed.]

Despite cosmopolitan Stockholm, readers still may associate Sweden with remote landscapes, and there are plenty of series set far off the beaten—and frozen—path. Mankell's Wallander series is set in Ystad, in southern Sweden, and Knopf will publish the final installment, *The Troubled Man,* in 2011. Åsa Larsson's series features tax lawyer Rebecca Martinsson, who returns to her hometown of Kiruna, the northernmost city in Sweden, and ends up staying. Delta published the third installment, *The Black Path,* in 2008. Camilla Läckberg, a best-selling Swedish crime writer who published her first and very successful novel before she was thirty, also sets her series in her hometown, Fjällbacka, a small fishing village. Pegasus published her English debut, *Ice Princess,* featuring writer Ericka Falck and cop Patrik Hedstrom, in 2010 and will bring out the second installment, *The Preacher,* in 2011.

Åke Edwardson's Insp. Erik Winter of Göteborg has much in common with Martin Beck—a fairly young man heading the police department—or Kurt Wallander—a fondness for music and a tendency toward shouldering enormous burdens. Also set in Göteborg is Helene Tursten's series featuring Det. Insp. Irene Huss of the Violent Crimes Division, a woman trying to juggle her work and family life. Soho Crime published *The Glass Devil* in 2007.

Norway

Norway has its share of bloody murders and brooding cops, thanks to a crop of top-notch contributors to the genre, including Karin Fossum, K.O. Dahl, and Jo Nesbø. Fossum, whose brand of haunting psychological suspense is often compared to Ruth Rendell's, writes a series featuring Insp. Konrad Sejer and his eager young assistant, Jacob Skarre, living in a small Norwegian mountain town. Harcourt will publish *Bad Intentions,* the seventh Inspector Sejer novel to be translated, in 2011.

Set in Norway's capital, K.O. Dahl's series features Chief Inspector Gunnarstranda and Det. Insp. Frank Frølich. Published in the US are *The Fourth Man, The Man in the Window* and, most recently, *The Last Fix* (book two). In 1994, Dahl's debut was one of only two first novels in Norway that were crime fiction. "Now the situation is quite the opposite," says Dahl. "Publishers, in Norway and abroad, [are] constantly searching for the next Millennium book. This may be why my books have reached more countries after the Larsson success."

Jo Nesbø—whose series featuring Det. Harry Hole is also set in Oslo—also credits Larsson with perhaps whetting the appetite for Scandinavian crime fiction. In terms of his sales abroad, explains Nesbø, "There is no doubt that he opened the doors for me and other Scandinavian writers to markets where Scandinavian crime wasn't already that established, meaning those readers are willing to give you a chance. But only one chance, so you'd better be good." Laconic Harry Hole fits the original Beck mold of the flawed detective, with a touch of Wallander's tendency to drink (hardly particular to Mankell's creation) and absorb all manner of work-related issues into an already rickety personal life. Knopf will publish the latest installment, *The Snowman,* in 2011.

Finland & Iceland

Finland and Iceland may not have the crime fiction output of their Nordic cousins, but they're both joining the growing tide of authors breaking into the English-speaking market. U.S. readers may be most familiar with criminal life in Finland through the work of American-born James Thompson, who has lived there for more than twelve years and sets his Insp. Kari Vaara series in the Lapland town of Kittilä. Putnam will publish the second installment of the Inspector Vaara series, *Lucifer's Tears,* in 2011.

Noted Icelandic crime writer Arnaldur Indridason series features Reykjavik's Det. Erlendur Sveinsson and his homicide team, though the brooding Erlendur prefers to work alone. While Indridason began the series in 1997, the first English translation didn't reach America until 2004, with *Jar City.* Minotaur published the sixth English installment, *Hypothermia,* in 2010. Another prominent name in Icelandic crime fiction is Yrsa Sigurdardóttir, whose heroine is Reykjavik lawyer Thóra Gudmundsdóttir. She defends a drug addict arrested for a murder with undertones of demonic worship in *Last Rituals* (2007) and investigates a shady land deal complete with a corpse in *My Soul to Take* (2009).

From Stockholm to Oslo, Ystad to Reykjavik, fictional crimes are being committed that will test the wits of this newly discovered army of Nordic crime-fighters. They've always been there, across the Atlantic, fighting their battles, shouldering burdens as heavy as any American copper has hefted. Some—Wallander, Erlendur, even the long dormant Beck—have crossed over for years and amassed loyal fans who eagerly await the next English install-ment, even if the delay stretches to years and the chronology is shot. But now, in the wake of a tattooed girl who played with fire and kicked a hornet's nest worth of political secrets, the trickle of Scandinavian crime fiction flowing westward has turned into a wave. And as much as the Larsson phenomenon can be credited for reinvigorating interest in crime fiction from the Nordic countries, there's no denying that, as fellow Swede Camilla Läckberg puts it, while "Larsson's books have helped my sales, I also believe that I wouldn't have had the success I've had if people didn't genuinely love my books."

6. MAKING WAVES: A ROUNDTABLE OF SWEDEN'S LEADING CRIME FICTION WRITERS

"WHAT YOU'RE AFRAID OF HAS ALREADY HAPPENED"
an interview with Anders Roslund and Börge Hellström

The Swedish crime-writing duo of Anders Roslund and Börge Hellström, writing under the name "Roslund Hellström," have been tipped as "the next Stieg Larsson" with their Ewert Grens series, which actually predates the Millennium books by seven years and has been successful in Sweden and Europe in its own right. The team made a breakthrough in the American book market in 2010 with their latest book, Three Seconds, *and a movie deal based on their novels is in the works.*

Anders Roslund is a prize-winning investigative journalist for Sweden's largest TV network who covered the rise of the right wing for its popular program Rapport *at the same time Larsson did as a reporter for the Swedish news agency TT and later at* Expo. *Their conversations were chiefly about how to survive the death threats and they each quickly became a source for the other.*

Börge Hellström, a reformed ex-con with several stints in jail behind him, is founder of a noted rehabilitation and crime prevention organization called KRIS (Criminals Return Into Society). A reformed criminal, he devotes much of his nonwriting time to counseling young lawbreakers and drug addicts.

Anders, you are well known for your long experience in reporting on Sweden's extreme right wing. You also knew Stieg Larsson.

Roslund: For years I worked for Swedish television. In the early '90s the extreme right was growing rapidly and so, as an investigative reporter for the biggest and most trusted TV station, I focused on it.

In about 1993 a mutual friend of Stieg's and mine recommended I contact him. He was working then at TT, a Swedish wire service, like your Associated Press. I'd heard of him and we may have met incidentally in a pub, but we didn't know each other. We were both looking into the same organizations and the same people, and we began to talk on the phone, almost always about how to survive the death threats we both had received. We met later, but it was always for professional reasons; we never socialized. What I most remember is that I could trust him to give me straight advice when I ran into trouble because of my reporting. He was one of the few guys with real knowledge.

Börge, you didn't know Stieg, but you bring your own colorful history to bear on the books.

Hellström: They say "write what you know," and that's what I've done. The first book, *The Beast,* is about a pedophile, and as a child I was sexually abused a couple of times by men. So I know how a child can react after that. A long time ago I also wasn't that good a person. I've been in jail twice in my life. But now it's been a long time since I was a criminal and a drug addict. Today I'm a totally accepted member of Swedish society. I have a driver's license, I am a member of the police board, a parole officer, and am licensed to carry a weapon. I have worked for years as a counselor to youthful offenders, helping them with their drug abuse problem and their way of thinking. That is the context in which I met Anders, who was doing a story on them.

Having both been in personal danger must also have had an impact on your writing.

Roslund: I was watched by the guys I was watching. These organizations were built on Nazi ideas. And they were aggressive, both with verbal and physical threats. For a while I was on the top of the list of those who should die.

Then it was phone calls. The threats came every day: I'm about to die, my family is about to die. I changed the number but three weeks later it was the same thing. It was never physical, until one day it was. It was not at all funny. From that point on my family and I started to move around a lot. Hotels, friends, other places. For a long time we had an armed bodyguard in our bedroom. It was a crazy time.

There was one night in '93 or '94 when we were moving from one hotel to another that my then three-year-old son was sitting on the floor, awake long past his bedtime, and, looking me in the eyes, said, "Daddy, what are we doing here?"

I decided that night: they were winning, and I didn't mind anymore. I'd been exposing them for three or four years; I had done my share. I couldn't live that life any longer, it just wasn't me anymore. From that point I went back to my ordinary reporting assignments, meaning just murderers.

Oh, just murderers.

Roslund: Murderers are more easygoing. I do still go back and report on the fascists now and then. Phone calls still come, but without the physical threats. If I publish a story I get three hundred emails or so, but just for a short while. I am no longer as worried because now they know I'm not the leading journalist on this subject anymore and there are too many other "enemies" to concentrate on. Also, they've learned. They don't shave their heads or walk around in army clothes. And when they're violent, it's in a much more sophisticated way.

Between your demanding day jobs, the promotional efforts in Europe and the U.S. for *Three Seconds,* an impending movie deal, and your starting the next book, life must be very hectic. How do you manage?

Roslund: I tend to be a driven person, but now I try hard to step back and focus on the "now," a goal of mine for years. On my right arm I have an old tattoo I'm trying to live up to that says just that—in Swedish of course: *Nu.* I can read it in the mirror every time I brush my teeth or wash my face. It's hard for any of us to do this in the face of reality but recently, and for the first time in my life, I've succeeded in actually living "now." I'm not thinking "Okay, this is good; what's next?" For me it's also actually a description of our authorship: to realize that we've come a long way. It's for real: let's stay here.

Hellström: I play guitar in a Swedish dance band and have played and sung since I was nine. I sing a lot of Siw Malquist songs. I call her the Swedish Connie Francis, and she was the first Swedish singer to first have a hit on the U.S. *Billboard* chart—well before ABBA!

Börge, I understand that among the first things you said to him when you first met was: "Well, Anders, what you're afraid of has already happened." Can you explain what you meant by that?

Hellström: I was in treatment seventeen years ago when a counselor first said that to me. She meant that my fear had conquered me. It's like I have a backpack with my history in it that will always be there. But I can make a choice whether to let it weigh me down, drag me backwards. I did some real bad things when I was younger, so I had to learn some way of not dwelling on them, to free my thinking for what I do today. Anders was threatened with grave danger in his career. I thought, he, too, can lessen his fears. That was twelve years ago and here we are, five books later.

The same advice turns up early in your new book, *Three Seconds*.

Hellström: The book starts with Ewert Grens, the police inspector who is our lead character in the series, going to the old age home where his wife lived for many years after she got badly injured—for which Grens blames himself and for which he carries an enormous amount of guilt. She has died now, but he still goes every Tuesday to the nursing home and looks up to the window where she once sat and looked out. The staff comes out to say, "Superintendent Grens, we love you, but please go away. Because what you are afraid of has already happened."

Grens thinks about this line for six hundred pages in Swedish and at the end he dares to go to her grave.

What else can we know about Grens?

Roslund: Grens is our kid. He's older than us but he's our kid because he's half Börge, half Anders. He's all our bad habits and good habits . . . or maybe just bad habits!

More seriously, Grens is a name, but it's also the word in Swedish for limit, for a border. So his name means what he copes with every day. He's always asking himself: Who has crossed the line? Who's right? Who's wrong? Who's the victim? Who's the perpetrator? Or both? He is a limping detective inspector, aging and obstinate, the sort who never gives up, who pursues the truth as far as he can and then some more when he realizes that a handful of colleagues have known it from that start.

Hellström: I've met policemen who were superintendents just like Ewert. He's a very grouchy person. Not bitter, but almost. But as Anders suggests, he is persistent in his quest for the truth, no matter what stands in his way. He won't stop until he has found the ones who have been protecting their secrets. It won't surprise you that he continually listens to Siw Malmquist, which of course helps make him very real to me.

Given your different histories, does one or the other of you do more than the other on these books?

Hellström: We get asked that a lot and our answer is always the same: I do 100 percent and Anders does 100 percent. That's the best way to describe our process. There's one language. What makes the job easier is that we both have had the right experience and have extremely good, high-level sources that we have developed over the years, and because of our success, each succeeding book opens more doors.

Americans used to have a mostly utopian image of Sweden, but crime fiction books like Stieg's, yours, and others deal with the underbelly of Swedish society. Why are those themes so popular?

Roslund: I think that if in this country we had stayed with the same kind of crime writing from the '70s, the '80s, and '90s, the genre would slowly have died. In the '90s when violence against immigrants was on the rise, traditional novelists did not address those realities. So we crime writers stepped in to fill the vacuum. Here was a chance to write a good mystery, and to reflect on society, and obviously the audience needed and welcomed it. We Swedes have helped evolve crime writing well beyond the classic Agatha Christie closed-door police procedurals.

Hellström: Our books reflect today's culture, and they have a duty to help us think about society's problems as well as individual violence: Why do people do it? Why does it happen here?

That "now" culture includes a resurgent neo-Nazi or at least extreme-right-wing movement.

Roslund: The overtly violent form it took in the '90s abated. Either we got control of it or the leaders were getting older or in prison or dying. But now the Sweden Democrats have arrived as the same party in another dress. They have been in Parliament for three months now and they're growing every day. In Malmö recently immigrants were shot and killed. This suits the extreme right and the Sweden Democrats perfectly.

It is also Stieg Larsson's worst nightmare—everything he worked against. Knock on anyone's door who lives outside Stockholm: there's so much hate. And this is just the start, I think you'll see more riots in the suburbs. It's a new thing, and I hope I'm wrong, but my kids and their kids will grow up in a new Sweden, a different Sweden.

Is it fair to say that neither of you are optimistic about the future of Sweden and its ability to solve these problems, or at least alleviate them?

Hellström: If all you do is read our five books, you should become very concerned about Swedish society. But I am not concerned. We're pointing out problems we see in our society, and saying: look at this. Do you like it? I hope we can solve the problems we write about, but I won't swear on it. I love Sweden. Not everyone, but almost. No, I am not concerned. Not yet.

Roslund: Well, I would like to move to the small island where I have my summer house, where there are twelve inhabitants [laughs]. Of course from my point of view, Sweden's still the very best place to grow up. But now it's not the kind of Sweden I want to grow old in.

LARS KEPLER: THE CHARACTER WHO CAME TO VISIT AND NEVER LEFT

an interview with Alexander and Alexandra Ahndoril

Alexander and Alexandra Ahndoril are the creators of "Lars Kepler," a nom de plume for their collaborative crime novels, The Hypnotist *(2009) and* The Paganini Contract *(2010), both best sellers in Sweden and in the top ten list of European fiction authors 2010.*

In their individual work Alexander is a novelist and playwright with nine novels and some twenty plays to his credit, including the best seller The Director, *a novel that follows the creation of Ingmar Bergman's film* Winter Light *and an experimental novel whose first sentence is 4,096 words, the next 2,048, and so on down to 1. Alexandra has published three novels based on historical figures as seen from the perspective of their families around them: astronomer Tycho Brahe, Saint Bridget of Sweden, and the socialist agitator August Palm. She is also a critic, writing primarily for one of Sweden's largest daily newspapers,* Göteborgs Posten. *They both belong to the small, select group of acclaimed literary authors in Sweden.*

Lars Kepler's The Hypnotist *will be published in English in the summer of 2011.*

You have each been immersed in your own literary worlds up to now, between you writing criticism, plays, and significant historical and literary fiction. What inspired you to write not only jointly, but in a totally different genre?

Alexander: We had always wanted to do something together. We tried once writing a play together, and a children's book, but we argued every time we tried.

Alexandra: It didn't work because we have very different literary styles and couldn't find a way to merge them. We just got angry with each other. We had to find a totally new genre and invent a character that was not us. It turned out to be Lars Kepler.

Let's pretend not to be Alexander and Alexandra. Let's call ourselves
Lars Kepler instead?

Alexandra: Yes, a person with a name that pays homage to both Stieg
Larsson and Johannes Kepler, the seventeenth-century German mathematician, astronomer, and astrologer. After we envisioned him we invited him
into our apartment and he is now very much alive in our house.

Alexander: We found out that he drinks tea. We prefer coffee. He eats
lemon biscuits, we never tried them before. And he has a very strong voice
and wants to write all the time.

Tea? Lemon biscuits? That sure is a long way from Blomkvist and
Salander's diet of pizza, fast-food hamburgers, and coffee. Nevertheless Larsson has clearly been a role model for you.

Alexandra: That's why Lars Kepler named himself after Stieg in tribute.
Larsson revitalized the genre and brought home the point that the better
way to reach people with your ideas is by creating crime fiction with strong
characters. We really like Stieg, but are trying to add something new. We
think Lars Kepler is interested in a much faster-paced story and also in taking the clichés of the genre and twisting them in a different way.

Alexander: What we have in common with Larsson is a narrative clarity
with extreme plots and a tone that is very sympathetic to the characters. We
think that he manages to keep that balance generally; he just touches the
extreme a little bit too much. A story must be possible, but it will be boring if it's totally probable. The challenge is to maximize the suspense without crossing the line to the impossible.

We also differ in that our entrance into crime fiction was not through
reading dozens of crime fiction books but through film. We've been watching
nearly one film a day for the past eighteen years as a way to relax from writing all day in isolation. Our thought was to try to transfer the way movies
tell a story into a text, to transfer the filmic kind of suggestion into a novel.

Alexandra: That is why we used the present tense for the narrator, which
we think is very filmlike and very rare in crime fiction. It is a way for the
reader to be truly inside the story.

Still, you seem to be in the mold of Larsson and almost every other
Scandinavian crime fiction writer these days in exposing the fact that
underneath its placid, lovely exterior is a society with a rising tide of
xenophobia, sex and drug trafficking, and so on.

Alexander: Dealing with such issues is precisely why we need crime novels. They expose the contradiction between the self-image and the reality of daily life.

Alexandra: It's inevitable for we Swedes to deal with strong social issues because our society has been considered almost perfect all over the world, with free health care, free schools, free universities, and so forth, but there are always something beneath the surface. And one strong voice to expose the dark waters is through crime novels. We are not really referring to older, formalistic crime novels, but in today's revitalized crime fiction. Our first book deals with family bonds that becomes dangerous when the society looks away; the second is on the huge gap of mankind between creating music and creating weapons.

Until recently, crime fiction was considered far down the cultural ladder from the so-called heights of "real literature."

Alexandra: It's true that there is a very long way between these two genres.

Alexander: But we no longer accept the differences—you can have bad high literature just as you can have good crime writing.

Shakespeare was very popular in his day. And no one would say that his work is not great literature, even though the masses understood it and responded to it.

Alexander: You shouldn't need an alibi to read a crime novel. Excitement is enough. There is a pleasure in reading this kind of novel because there is closure. The riddle gets a gratifying answer. The policeman takes the bad man away. Order has been restored.

Alexandra: In reality there are never such neat answers, of course. Good and bad are always mixed up. When you write literary novels you think of the feeling, the language, the aesthetic stuff. But in a crime novel, you think of plot. If a window is open it means you better close it.

Alexander: And if you have a gun, you better use it. But in a literary novel, you can have a gun and let the reader just speculate whether there is any meaning to it or not. It's so different.

Since readers in English haven't yet had a chance to read your books can you talk a little bit more about Lars Kepler's choice of a main character, Joona Linna?

Alexander: "Joona" is the Finnish version of Jonah, the biblical prophet who is cast into the sea and swallowed by a whale. Metaphorically, the whale is the plot and Jonah remains in him until he has solved the case, when he is thrown up on the shore again.

Alexandra: Finns represent the largest minority in Sweden and the accent is very beautiful to us Swedes. It's very melancholic, both sad and serious. For Swedes, it's a very attractive way of speaking.

How would you describe Joona's character?

Alexandra: He's not judgmental. He's not a man who thinks everything can be solved and wiped away with a gun. He is careful and follows the rules as long as possible, although his track record as an operative homicide investigator is unparalleled in Scandinavia. He is also sensitive, but he never gives up, he's incapable of leaving a case unsolved, a case is never cold to him. The obligation toward others is for him very personal as well as professional. When he sees a child that doesn't want to go home because her mother is drunk, he empathizes and carefully tries to help the girl. He says, "you can call me personally." All the while he is crying inside because he suffers from things in his past that make him feel very guilty. We will show what haunts him in our third and fourth books.

Alexander: It is very difficult for him to accept society but at the same time he would never judge a man or woman for their status, by the color of their skin, or anything else. His sole focus is to see that justice is done, whatever the obstacles.

It sounds as if it is now very natural for the two of you to work together in this new genre. And peaceful besides.

Alexander: Being each stuck behind our own desk was lonely. Some books took me seven years to write—seven years without showing the text to anybody, without input or discussion. That's pretty lonely. Now we can talk together and change the text twenty times a day, actually without arguing—it's fun and exciting.

Thank you, we appreciate your both taking the time to talk with us, especially since we know you are moving to a new apartment tomorrow. We hope Lars Kepler likes it.

Alexander: We do, too. Our first book was set in our old apartment and horrible crimes took place there.

WOMEN, CRIME NOVELS, AND SWEDEN . . . AND ZAMBIA . . . AND VIETNAM . . . AND POLAND . . . AND INDIA . . . AND . . .

an interview with Karin Alfredsson

Karin Alfredsson has played a major role in Sweden's public debate about women, men, and society. Her first nonfiction book, Who You Love You Beat *(1979), reported on violence against women. Her second,* Sex Sets Your Salary *(1980), was about gender-based inequality. Alfredsson's 2006 novel,* Beauty, Blessing and Hope, *won the Swedish Crime Writers Association Debut Award. Drawing on her knowledge gained in reporting on women's issues as a journalist, she has set her books in countries that include Zambia, Vietnam, Poland, and India. She is currently doing research in Dubai and Pakistan. Alfredsson also contributed another piece to this book, in which she details some of the real-life crimes against women in Sweden that may have influenced Stieg Larsson (see chapter 7).*

What got you started writing crime fiction, and what kind of stories are you telling?

I worked for many decades as a reporter, news editor, and journalism teacher all over the world. And wherever I've gone I always seemed to end up with an interest in the place of women in that society.

About seven years ago I was reporting on the situation of women in Africa and found myself very upset with the role of the Catholic Church there. The Church was working against abortion, against women's sexual rights, and against condoms in a part of the world that has so many problems with HIV and AIDS.

When I returned to Sweden I stopped being a recorder of events and got engaged in public debate instead. One morning I found myself sitting on a TV studio couch on Sweden's version of the *Today* program, arguing with a Catholic priest about the role of the Church in Africa. The influence of the Catholic Church in Africa is both broad and deep, and for African women that influence is often not positive. The Church is very involved in hospitals and the practice of medicine in many countries. In much of Africa, women are chattel and can't refuse sex. They are taught that the idea of birth control is morally wrong. These views have been supported by the Church, in my opinion. That started me thinking that perhaps these stories could be told in another way, not just the ordinary journalistic way where I was only reaching the people who already knew about these issues. That's how I became a crime novelist.

Tell us about Ellen Elg, the fictional Swedish gynecologist who is the lead character in all your books.
I chose her profession for two reasons. First, because I was planning to write a series of books, and it was plausible that a physician would move around in the world and find herself in different situations. Second, almost all oppression against women in the world is connected to the body, and to sexuality, so a gynecologist made sense.

My first novel, *Beauty, Blessing and Hope*, has her involved in a case about illegal abortions in Zambia. The second one, *Women on the Tenth Floor*, has Ellen working in a hospital in Vietnam. It's a story about prostitution, trafficking in babies, and men who are taking very young prostitutes to the tenth floor of a hotel and forcing them to do unspeakable things.

For my third book, I wanted to use a setting closer to home, so I put Ellen on a ship off the coast of Poland that offered abortions. Today we have an ironic and sad situation. In the '60s abortions were illegal in Sweden and Swedish women often went to then-communist Poland to have an abortion, since the procedure was legal and inexpensive there. Now Poland has opened up in many ways but when it comes to women, Poland has become more repressive. As a result of the policies of the Catholic Church, abortions are essentially no longer allowed in Poland. So now Polish women have to go abroad to have abortions outside of the reach of Polish law. Some of them come to Sweden. The title of my third crime novel is *9:37 PM*, the exact time of death for Pope John Paul II. In my opinion, John Paul II turned the clock back for women all over the world, especially in his native Poland.

Book four is called *The Sixth Goddess*, and deals with women's issues in India. I'm now working on number five.

The theme of "men who hate women" is central to Stieg Larsson's Millennium trilogy. What do you think of the way he handled that issue?
I love Lisbeth Salander. Stieg Larsson was a genius to have created such an extremely good character. I like that she is an outsider who doesn't obey the rules and that her psychology does not include any part of wanting to please.

She's not at all like me, because I want to please people quite a lot. Women almost always want to please someone. Perhaps some of us are strong enough to oppose bosses or perhaps fathers, but then we want to please a husband or our children.

Of course, we have to remind ourselves that Lisbeth is fictional—fictional to the extent that what she does is unbelievable. Her superhuman strength when she is fighting is also unrealistic. I'm not fond of violence in general and I don't have any serial killers in my books, nor any men who torture and kill people in their basement. My novels don't rely on violence. What makes them high impact is that they either *are* reality or it is entirely plausible that they *could be* reality.

On the other hand, it made me feel good when Salander takes revenge and puts a tattoo on Bjurman's chest. I have to say I like it when bad guys have to pay somehow.

If you were to encounter Lisbeth, would she be a friend of yours?
No, probably not. She's not really a friend of anyone, is she?

What do you think of Mikael Blomkvist?
I think he is the middle-aged Swedish man's wet dream. I'm a little disappointed in Stieg Larsson on that point.

But the purely come-as-you-are, go-as-you-are morality about sex applies to the female characters in Larsson's books, too, doesn't it?
Perhaps you can say this is a fantasy, too—one where women can just walk around and be free and have no obligations and no children and no dishes to wash.

"IT IS EASIER TO DISCUSS THE NUMBER OF WOMEN ON CORPORATE BOARDS THAN IT IS TO DISCUSS VIOLENCE AGAINST WOMEN"

an interview with Veronica von Schenck

Veronica von Schenck is a Swedish author of a series of crime novels featuring a fictional woman of mixed Swedish-Korean parentage who was raised in the U.S., worked as a profiler with the New York Police Department, and is now living in Stockholm. Born in 1971, von Schenck established her professional career as an editor of Swedish computer and event magazines. She had long dreamt of writing crime novels and finally decided to stop talking about it and just sit down and do it. She read Stieg Larsson's trilogy as she was writing her first crime novel and is quick to point out that in the few short years since Larsson's death, his style, plotting, and mix of entertainment and important social content has already had noticeable effects on many writers. In 2008, von Schenck published her first novel, Änglalik ("Angelic"). Her second novel, Kretsen ("Circuit"), followed in 2009, and she is currently finishing her third in the series.

Find out more about Veronica von Schenck and her novels at: www .altheasprofil.se.

You have chosen to feature a Korean-Swedish woman from New York as the central character in your crime novels. Why the multicultural background?

My crime novels thus far have featured Althea Sang-Min Molin. She has a Korean mother and a Swedish father, and divided her childhood between New York and Stockholm. Althea's mother is a photographer deeply involved in the New York arts scene. For a while, Althea was a police profiler in New York but, as a result of a frightening experience with a serial killer that continues to give her nightmares, she returned to Stockholm to start a new life.

I like the strength of people who come from mixed ethnic backgrounds and from troubled situations. I did not want my books peopled with blond, blue-eyed characters. I wanted the diversity of life experience to figure prominently in my writing.

I grew up with a Korean friend who was virtually my sister. Now, as an adult, I have a friend whose parents were born in Korea but she was born in Sweden. I think it is a huge strength that Sweden is becoming more diverse. In the past, I was always very pleased at how accepting Sweden was of this growing diversity. Of course, we always had a few problems, but nothing like the current situation. The election of the Sweden Democrats [the extreme-right-wing party that won twenty Parliament seats in 2010] makes it easier for others to express racist views and support racist policies. I thought no one would vote for the SD party. I was wrong—and I am very ashamed for Sweden.

Tell us about the plots in your first and second crime novels: *Angelic* **(***Änglalik***) and** *Circuit* **(***Kretsen***).**
In *Circuit*, Althea becomes embroiled in a tangled web of computer crime and a series of seemingly unrelated murders. She is contacted by the police and asked to look into these murders. Althea not only needs to understand the dark world of computer hacking inside banks, and the wave of cyber-crime that now threatens our financial system, but she also has to delve in to the human psyche to understand how far people will go to protect their reputation and cover up a crime.

Even before *Circuit* I was fascinated with the idea of the image that we have of ourselves. How far are we willing to go to keep up outward appearances and maintain our position in life? What would each of us be willing to do to keep the image of ourselves as "respected citizens"?

I had experience with computer hacking and IT security as the editor of a Swedish computing magazine before I started writing my novels. I think the issues involved with technology and privacy are very profound. Stieg Larsson was very concerned about this as well. In his novels, he brilliantly describes how vulnerable we are as individuals and as a society. Yet he was able to write about technology without being technical, and it is more powerful that way.

My debut novel was *Angelic*. In this story, the psychopathic serial killer is a photographer fascinated with a certain image of women who collects these women as murder victims. The corpses end up looking angelic. The story is really about surface and how we are fooled by superficial appearances.

Larsson died around the time you were working on your first novel. What impact did his books have on your thinking when you read them?

I first read Stieg Larsson while I was writing *Angelic*. I immediately felt his joy at writing—his will to entertain. I don't think he wrote his books to lecture. He clearly wrote them to entertain, which is what I try to do in my books. And yet, the "lecture" works better that way. He is able to make the points about the treatment of women in a very deep way, while letting the reader have the page-turning entertainment experience of reading a fast-paced novel. I particularly appreciate his consistent challenge of stereotypes, especially with the Lisbeth character. It has become a bit easier to have strong women characters in novels today, but very few truly tough women. Stieg Larsson was able to give us a tough and still fascinating character. Of course sometimes he goes overboard, like when Lisbeth is buried alive at the end of the second novel and she escapes anyway.

The use of explicit sexual violence in Stieg Larsson's books is troubling for any reader. I think he wanted the reader to be troubled. It is very close to the edge of exploitation in its explicitness, but it is on this side of the edge. In the end, the woman wins and gets revenge. I can understand what he is doing here. He is forcing the reader to encounter and react to the sexual violence of the real world, but in a very safe way in the context of a novel.

I actually have more of a problem with the picture he paints of uninhibited sexual relationships between the positive characters, the ones where violence is not present in the relationships. Is Stieg Larsson reestablishing the myth of Sweden as a place where everyone has sex freely without undertaking responsibilities to their partners? I am not sure about this portrayal. But at least very deep trust exists between the partners. This is true, for example, between Mikael Blomkvist and Erika Berger. They come together and go apart over the years, but there is always respect and trust between them.

Is the situation for women in Sweden as bleak as Larsson's novels suggest?

On the surface, Sweden is a very equal society. We don't want to believe that terrible problems exist for women—violence, abuse, trafficking. It is easier to discuss whether there are enough women on boards of directors of major corporations than it is to discuss violence against women. Yet there are very real problems for many women in abusive relationships or for those who become the victims of abuse. We need to face up to this as a political problem, as well as the more general issues about equality.

"CRIME FICTION SHOULD TASTE GOOD WHILE READING, BUT LEAVE A BITTER AFTERTASTE"
an interview with Katarina Wennstam

Katarina Wennstam is a well-known Swedish feminist, crime reporter, and author who is also in demand as a lecturer and consultant. Before turning her talents to crime fiction she had written two nonfiction books: the award-winning The Girl and the Guilt, *a book on society's tolerance of rape, and* The Real Rapist, *for which she interviewed young sex offenders to help psychologists and law enforcement officials better deal with them.*

In 2007, Wennstam published the first of her three thematically related novels about men's violence against women, all featuring prosecutor Madeleine Edwards. The first, Dirt *(2007), was about human trafficking and reached the Swedish best-seller lists. The second,* Dödergök *(2008), addresses domestic violence, and the third book,* The Alpha Male *(2010), deals with sexual harassment and violence in the film industry. The books have not yet been published in English. Wennstam is now planning a second crime fiction trilogy, this time featuring Shirin Sundin, a lawyer specializing in representing abused women.*

We spoke with her over coffee at Café Rival, one of Södermälm's trendiest spots. Photos of well-known Swedish cultural figures decorated the walls and ABBA provided the soundtrack.

Crime fiction in Sweden today seems preoccupied with social concerns such as violence against women, racism, and neo-Nazism. Why the particular focus on these issues?

These are some of the most important issues in society today. They all have to do with the contradiction between Sweden's benign self-image and its darker reality. Why is it that Swedish society believes that we are one of the most equal countries on earth yet we still have a big problem of men's violence against women?

We want to continue to believe in the social democratic dream that is Sweden: secure in your own home, secure out on the streets, no one is so poor that they don't have food for the day, and men and women are equal. That dream has been splintered. We imagine a utopia, but we still have Swedish men beating their wives to death. We have people like the former police chief Göran Lindberg, hailed as a model for his crusade to improve the criminal justice system's approach to crimes of violence against women, but who for years deceived girls into prostitution. [For more on this case see Wensstam's interview in chapter 9.—ed.] We've also had shootings and riots, especially in areas with a lot of immigrants. This too is a break with our benign self-image and is an increasingly troubling trend in society.

Do you think there's a difference in the way women and men write about these issues?
It is less about the *way* men and women write about these issues than it is the difference in the way the work is received. I really don't like to compare myself to Stieg Larsson because it's very hard to do that. But generally speaking, I think we both have a feminist agenda and write about similar issues. The difference is the way in which critics and the public want to personalize a woman's writing on these themes as a way of making it a little less dangerous.

For example, I always get the question, "Have you been raped? Have you been beaten? Have you been a victim?" If I'd have said, "Yeah, I've been raped. I've been beaten," then they would go, "Oh, then we can understand why you're writing about this," which personalizes it and somehow makes it of lesser importance in the eyes of many. But since I can answer, "No, I'm writing about this because I've been seeing it in trials when I'm reporting for television," I'm seen as a "professional woman" and not as a "female victim." It means people listen more diligently to what I have to say. Of course, nobody asks those questions of a white man in his forties. . . .

Another example: Larsson quotes the statistics on crimes against women put forward by the controversial Norwegian feminist scholar Eva Lundgren. But these figures have been debunked. Were I to have used them, journalists would have crucified me. But with Larsson it's "yeah, whatever."

I am not trying to make myself a victim. It's just a comment on the difference between writing on feminist issues when you are a man or a woman.

As a TV reporter, you were well known for reporting on men's violence against women. You also wrote two well-received nonfiction books about these problems. Why write about these issues again in a crime fiction context?

My nonfiction books became bigger than I ever would have hoped because they helped spark public and political debate that resulted in real change. They also helped my career as a lecturer, writer, and consultant on these issues. But after a couple of years I realized that I was at the end of a road in terms of reaching people. Outspoken feminism is still sometimes a kind of f-word in Sweden, just as it may have become in America. Nonfiction has its limitations; some doors are always closed. On the other hand, a lot of people buy a crime novel when they want to relax or go on vacation, including me.

So a page-turner with an agenda?

Yes. I'm writing about exactly the same things, using the same research methods and knowledge as before, but sort of hiding it away. Add some love, trial scenes, a good cop and bad cop, and people tend to swallow it differently. I want my books to taste good while readers are consuming them but leave them with a bitter aftertaste, a sense of discomfort. I am the same person as when I wrote nonfiction books, and as a television reporter before that. But now I take the same agenda and hide it inside the Trojan horse of the story. And I think the same thing applies to Stieg Larsson's books.

Tell us more about those Trojan horses.

So far I've written a trilogy: *Dirt, Dödergök,* and *The Alpha Male.* The first book is about lawyers, the second about police officers, and the third about the film industry. There's trafficking and sexual slavery. There's a family drama about a man with a teenage daughter buying sex; his wife knows there's something wrong but looks the other way. There's a policeman who beats up his wife, but is allowed to keep his job because the force doesn't care what he does in his free time. The last one is a sort of love story between a very young rising movie star and an industry alpha male type.

What's next, another trilogy?

I'm sort of sick of men's violence, so I said to myself after finishing *The Alpha Male* that I should write about something else for a while. I tried to write a feel-good book, but it didn't work out. I'm back to writing about what I know best. Shirin Sundin, a lawyer who was a character in my last book, is now getting a trilogy of her own. She is a Swedish woman with roots in the Middle East and an example of my desire to show people social possibilities that don't often get imagined or discussed. For example, I have created a black judge as a character in one of my books, even though there are no black judges yet in Sweden.

What's your evaluation of Lisbeth Salander? Do you consider her a true feminist?
Fundamentally, I love her as a character and role model and her creation is a historic event in the evolution of fiction. I have some reservations, however.

First of all, Salander basically steals over 2.5 billion kronor ($347 million). This is plain theft, though perhaps excusable as a kind of Robin Hood act since the victim, a very wealthy and very corrupt captain of industry, has himself victimized so many. Also, by portraying both Salander and Erika Berger as completely sexually free, Larsson may be musing on some ideal, but realistically he is making it a little too uncomplicated.

Were Larsson still alive he would have been seriously questioned on the matter: why does Salander use the money she stole to surgically enhance her breasts? Everything else about her says she wouldn't care how she looks to other men—or women. Sex is to satisfy her own lust, not to please someone else. But I would argue that if one goes into plastic surgery to do such a thing, it's not only for your own feelings of self-worth, but also to attract the attention of others, usually men.

Finally, and as vicariously satisfying as her actions are, feminism is not about beating people up, taking revenge, or turning yourself into an object of desire. It's not about keeping people out, or not nurturing them.

Sounds as if you would not want to spend time with Lisbeth in real life.
Would I want to go on a sailing trip with her? I don't think so. Maybe a dinner, when you can politely part afterward.

What might Stieg Larsson's next book or books have been about had he lived?
In the three books that we have been able to read there is not a whole lot about Nazi movements in Sweden, and Larsson was one of the most knowledgeable people in Europe about those matters. I think he would have broadened the agenda of his books on racist and multicultural issues, since he had more to say about those matters than most.

Will you continue to force people to confront the darker side of Swedish society?
In Sweden we have a long history of looking away. We're so very proud of not being in a war for two hundred years, but there's our very black history

of letting Germans and their trains go through Sweden to both Finland and Norway. I believe a lot of Afghans are being killed nowadays by a Swedish-made recoilless rifle carrying the name of our king Carl Gustaf. Facing up to who we are as a people and a society, particularly in the arena of women's rights, is a cause for which I will keep raising my voice.

7. HAS SWEDEN LOST ITS SWEDISHNESS?

WE'RE ALL SWEDES NOW: HOW THE WORLD CAUGHT UP WITH STIEG LARSSON
by Andrew Brown

"The great change in the last thirty years is that Swedishness doesn't look like Swedishness anymore," wrote Andrew Brown in his book, Fishing in Utopia, *winner of the 2009 Orwell Prize for political writing. Brown was referring to the increasing number of people in Sweden who look "exotic" (close to 20 percent of the population) and to the unfortunate parallel increase in intolerance that the sudden in-migration has bred. But it is also a metaphor for all the other realities intruding upon the now self-delusional dream of Swedish exceptionalism, among them increasing business and government corruption, a bloated and bureaucratic welfare state, racism, violence, and abuse against women. These themes are also at the heart of Larsson's Millennium trilogy, of course.*

Brown, who lived in Sweden for many years, is currently editor of the Belief section of The Guardian (U.K.). *His concern as well as affection for Sweden are obvious. He will also be among the first to tell you that although Sweden may call itself liberal, its "great distinguishing character is its narrowness." Yet, he says, yet . . .*

With the U.S. release this week of the final installment of Stieg Larsson's Millennium trilogy, the English-speaking world is again given a chance to indulge in a view of Scandinavia that is entirely dystopian. In Larsson's Sweden, the police are useless where they are not corrupt; the countryside is full of violent drug dealers; the rich are utterly unprincipled. It sounds like Mexico in the snow. This is no longer a clean, well-lighted place for Volvo owners. What went wrong?

This essay originally appealed in *Foreign Policy.* Used with permission of the author.

Crime fiction always exaggerates, and Swedish left-wing crime fiction, the tradition to which Larsson belongs, is a genre quite as stylized as Agatha Christie's. There will always be villainous millionaires and noble women. It is not enough to be a sadistic serial killer: you have to vote conservative as well. But what has changed since the genre was invented in the 1960s by the husband and wife team of Maj Sjöwall and Per Wahlöö is the overwhelming loss of confidence in the future, and in the state.

This does reflect reality.

The story of Sweden over the last fifty years has been one of a steady loss of exceptionalism. In some ways the outside world has grown more "Swedish"—we all wear seatbelts, drink less, and believe in gender equality. At the same time, Sweden has grown much more worldly—it drinks more, works and earns less, and struggles with the assimilation of immigrants. The Swedes themselves no longer believe in a Swedish model, or, when they do, it's very different from the heavily regulated "people's home" of myth. Last summer, I was on a panel with Pär Nuder, a Social Democrat intellectual and former finance minister whose description of the Swedish model was one of high taxes but minimal regulation; generous parental leave, but very high female employment; and a much greater reluctance to nationalize failing industries than is found in the rest of Europe, or in the United States for that matter. When Swedish car makers go bust, the state does not bail them out. Volvo is now owned by a Chinese company, and Saab by a Dutch maker of sports cars. Even the school system has been partly privatized, along with almost everything else that the state once owned.

The other point Nuder made was that Sweden is now a country with a sizeable immigrant population. Nearly a fifth of the Swedish population today are people either born abroad or the children of two immigrants, and this figure has risen by about a third in the last decade. Almost everyone from outside the EU has come as a refugee: over the last decade, the country took in nearly eighty thousand refugees from Iraq, which is nearly 1 percent of the population. But though they are not recruited as workers, they are expected to work, and the problem is that there is hardly any heavy industrial work for them to do.

In the far south of the country, where the refugees are concentrated, there is also a fair amount of anti-immigrant sentiment. The elections later this year may well see the Sweden Democrats, a xenophobic and populist party, enter Parliament for the first time, and they are already quite important in local politics. Larsson spent almost his entire working life combating such groups, and it is a remarkable fact that Sweden has not had any in Parliament before now, while both Denmark and Norway, with much lower levels of immigration, have. But there are some real tensions under the surface.

In Landskrona, a postindustrial town across the strait from Copenhagen that has never recovered from the collapse of its shipyard in the late 1970s, an elderly woman died this spring after she was assaulted over a parking place. To suffer from road rage is a great break with Swedish traditions anyway; in this case, however, the woman and her husband were native Swedes, the young man who hit them an immigrant. There was almost a riot when the case came to court, and the trial had to be moved to a neighboring city where passions aren't running so high.

If you look at the statistics, Sweden is not a particularly violent country, nor a particularly lenient one to criminals. It is in about the middle of the European averages for both figures. And while the homicide rate has been steadily declining in the United States over the past two decades, in Sweden there were 230 murders in 2009, up from 120 in 1990, when the country seemed a utopia. America still has more killings per capita, but there is a convergence here that doesn't flatter Sweden.

The whole of Europe has grown more violent, of course, as it has grown further away from the memories of war and the social disciplines it imposed. But for a long time, Sweden seemed detached from all the turmoil of the world below it on the map. This was enshrined in the idea of neutrality during the Cold War. But there's nothing very distinctive about that ideal now.

The great loss of Swedish independence and distinctiveness was the country's 1995 accession to the EU, which was forced on the country by the traumatic financial crisis of the early 1990s. At the same time, commercial television diminished the country's cultural autonomy; it is difficult now to remember just how rigorously the old state monopoly eschewed excitement. (Was I dreaming one Christmas when I lived there in the early 1980s that I saw a special Christmas broadcast of the year's most interesting weather forecasts?) It had always been a surprisingly Americanized country—if you want to see 1950s Cadillacs, go to the Swedish backwoods—but now it became once more a Germanized one, full of rather joyless consumerism. You could drive for a long way through the south of Sweden now without seeing anything that would be wildly out of place in Denmark, Holland, or northern Germany.

But there remains something distinctively Scandinavian about the country that cuts it off from the Anglo-Saxon mainstream. Swedes of any class have a sense of belonging, and of obligation to their country that is entirely different from the British or American attitudes toward the poor. Perhaps I know the wrong millionaires, but I have never met any rich Swedes who did not feel some sense of obligation to the poor, even when they were living in tax exile. It is not just a matter of charity, but of fellow feeling. That is not my experience in Britain or in the U.S., where riches are felt to turn you into a different, and possibly better, sort of person altogether, not least by their possessors.

Perhaps this moralism helps explain why Swedes were always much less secular than they appeared to be, even to themselves. Anything but the most notional Christianity had more or less died out among the middle classes by the 1980s, and the Swedish national church was disestablished at the millennium. Instead of imbibing myths about first-century Palestine, the people took in sermons about social progress and its culmination in twentieth-century Sweden. To some extent, those new myths were shared with the whole Western world. But it is in Sweden that their loss is most keenly felt, and the great efflorescence of dystopian crime fiction in the country is perhaps an expression of this loss.

It's also, of course, a new export industry. It is quite likely that there is a crime novel published for every single murder in Sweden: the country's Amazon.com equivalent says there have been 140 mysteries published there in the last six months. That's a statistic suggesting a country that is still, despite itself, pretty tolerable to live in.

"MEN WHO HATE WOMEN": THE NONFICTION CASE STUDIES THAT MAY HAVE INFLUENCED LARSSON

by Karin Alfredsson

Karin Alfredsson is a journalist and author who believes that women and men all over the world need to pull together to document and combat the kind of violence against women that Stieg Larsson dramatized so effectively in his novels. Here, she offers several Swedish case histories that may have inspired Larsson's depiction of "men who hate women," which was the original Swedish title Larsson gave the book we now know in English as The Girl with the Dragon Tattoo. *Alfredsson's literary debut came in 2006 with the thriller* Beauty, Blessing and Hope, *portraying the vulnerability of women in Sweden and Zambia, for which she was awarded the Swedish Crime Academy's Debutant Award. Since then she has published three crime thrillers featuring the fictional Swedish gynecologist Ellen Elg.*

Men who hate women can be found everywhere around the world. If you add up the number of men who murder or injure the women they claim to love, the total reaches several million. Every day, all across the world, terrible incidents of rape, abuse, violence, and murder occur. Sweden is no exception.

Sweden is a small country with 9 million inhabitants, internationally renowned for a good welfare system (well . . .), high taxes (true), many suicides (false), a high educational level (true in many ways), and—of course—gender equality. Year after year, Sweden tops the charts that rank "the world's most gender equal countries."

Still, some seventeen women are murdered every year in Sweden by men they have loved and trusted. I'm talking about husbands and ex-husbands, boyfriends and ex-boyfriends. The numbers are roughly the same from year to year, even though women's crisis centers have been expanded, laws are stricter, and the police better educated. And those are the cases where the authorities definitively know what happened. Obviously, there are more that are not counted.

As for domestic violence, the number of reported cases in Sweden has risen by 34 percent in the last ten years. Partly this is because more women have the courage to file a report and to leave their abusive partners. But experts believe that actual violence is also increasing. What famous cases of Swedish "men who hate women" may have inspired Stieg Larsson? Since I didn't know Stieg, I can only speculate, but here are three cases that attracted significant attention, echoes of which can be found in his books:

- **"The Geijer affair," 1977.**

From late 1969 until 1976, Sweden's Attorney General was a man named Lennart Geijer. He was renowned for his liberal views on correctional treatment. On November 18, 1977, Sweden's largest morning paper, *Dagens Nyheter,* published a statement claiming that the Swedish Security Service suspected Lennart Geijer of visiting prostitutes, making him a potential security threat. Social Democratic leader Olof Palme, who as prime minister should have received information about such suspicions, hit the roof, and forced the newspaper to retreat. Other politicians stood up to defend Geijer. The "machines of denial" triumphed. The newspaper had lied, Geijer was innocent.

We now know that the suspicions were correct and that in fact Palme had lied. In recent years, several former prostitutes and drug addicts have come forward to assert that when they were very young, Geijer was one of their customers, though no formal evidence to prove his guilt has ever been made public.

- **The Catrine da Costa murder, 1984.**

Catrine da Costa was an addict who supported herself as a prostitute in central Stockholm. On July 18, 1984, parts of her dismembered body were found in the suburbs outside of Stockholm. A few weeks later more bags filled with yet more body parts were found near the Karolinska Institute, a medical college. Her head, genitals, inner organs and one of her breasts were never found. The dismemberment was a professional job.

Two doctors, one a forensic pathologist (reportedly a regular customer of the city's prostitutes), were arrested but murder could not be proven. The doctors lost their licenses and have not regained them, despite many appeals. Police inspectors are still working on the case more than twenty-five years later.

- **The Fadime Sahindal murder, 2002.**

Fadime Sahindal was a twenty-seven-year-old woman of Kurdish ancestry who had arrived in Sweden as a refugee at the age of seven. Her attempt to live like an ordinary young Swedish woman, making her own choices about her life and loves, provoked her brother and father to abuse and threaten her for "bringing shame" upon the family. On several occasions she shared her story in newspapers, radio, and TV. As a result, she became a symbol of immigrant women subjected to so-called honor violence. In the autumn of 2001 she took part in an official seminar about honor violence held at the Swedish Parliament. On January 21, 2002, she decided to visit her mother and sisters in Uppsala. Her father was waiting in the staircase of her sister's apartment building, and shot her twice as she was leaving. She died instantly. The father was arrested, confessed, and was sentenced to life in prison.

However familiar Stieg Larsson may have been with the idea of powerful men abusing women, he would have been astounded by the double life of former county police commissioner Göran Lindberg. This case came to light after Larsson's death. A retired policeman, Göran Lindberg had once been a director at the Swedish police academy. His work to improve the conditions for female police officers and to fight against sexual harassment and gender inequality had made him something of a national celebrity. Among his fellow police officers he was known as Kapten Klänning (Captain Frock), a reference to his concern for female officers. But Lindberg was leading a double life, as a 2010 court proceeding proved. Underneath the veneer of his concern for women, he was actually a serial rapist and abuser of women. Although retired, he kept a locked room at the police academy where he stored, among other things, a bag full of provocative women's clothing and equipment used to tie up, whip, and blindfold his victims. In November 2010, he was sentenced to six years in prison following conviction on a number of serious sex offenses, including the rape of a vulnerable young girl.

By offering these examples I don't mean to say that Sweden is any worse than other countries when it comes to abuse and violence against women. We're probably better in many respects. Laws are more favorable to women's rights these days and nobody can say that the police don't care. But the facts remain that most of the women who have been murdered have a history of seeking help many times, both from the police and from social workers. Yet too often the authorities don't take women's fears seriously.

Is Sweden any different from the United States or other countries whose public society seems to support gender equality? In the USA, it's estimated that American women suffer some 5 million assaults of a physical or sexual nature every year. More than six hundred American women are raped or otherwise sexually assaulted on a daily basis, with at least half of these rapes committed by male acquaintances; in 20 percent of the cases, the rapist is a former or current partner. Shockingly, every year more than a thousand women in the United States are murdered by their partners. However frightening these statistics are about violence against women, the problems in both Sweden and the USA pale by comparison to other parts of the world. The facts set forth in a major 1994 health investigation by the World Bank, and confirmed in several subsequent reports, indicate that the fight against violence toward women is a global matter of life and death.

For women in all parts of the world between the ages of fifteen and forty-four—the demographic group that is often found at home with young children—rape and domestic violence is:

- more dangerous than cancer
- more than twice as dangerous as car accidents
- responsible for more death, disease, and suffering than malaria, breast cancer, and car accidents combined

In Pakistan, a country I visited recently in order to observe the situation regarding domestic violence, at least one and sometimes up to three women are murdered every day "in the name of honor." There, a murderer can escape punishment if the woman's family "forgives" the perpetrator. Since most honor murders are ordered by the head of the family and carried out within it, most are, of course, "forgiven."

There are no official statistics in Pakistan, but a report put together by a women's organization for the first half of 2010 shows 1099 kidnappings, 285 honor murders, and 719 "regular" murders. The unreported numbers are unquestionably much larger—and researchers haven't even tried to count everyday violence. A married woman must expect the occasional slap as part of the marital arrangement.

In South Africa, rape is also a common part of a woman's everyday life. In a survey taken of men, one in four admitted they had raped a woman at some point, and almost one in five admitted having done so in the previous year. Four in ten confessed to subjecting their partners to physical violence. The idea that lesbian women can be "cured" of their "unnatural behavior" through gang rapes has made it dangerous to confess one's sexual orientation in South Africa. Sometimes it is even lethal: many lesbian women have been murdered after such gang rapes.

Perhaps the true core of the problem lies here: that men hate—or at least hit/shoot/stab/rape/torture—women to maintain control over them and to maintain control over women's sexuality.

What is going on in a world where, in Sweden, Fadime Sahindal's father shoots his "immoral" daughter and, in Pakistan, a jilted fiancé throws acid into "his" woman's face? Where the former Swedish police academy director ties up his rape victim before giving her a beating? Where a gang of South African boys assaults a famous female football player, rapes her, and kills her by stabbing her twenty-five times? Where a little Iraqi boy shoots his big sister, believing he will save the family honor? Or where a Swedish truck driver attacks his former wife at her front door, pours gasoline over her, and sets her on fire?

It is time we recognized—as Stieg Larsson's fiction does—that abuse and violence against women is a major issue of our times that demands that we document and speak out about these cases and demand actions that can begin to turn this murderous tide.

NAZIS, SPIES, AND THE THRILLER WRITER'S "SCALPEL"
by Carl Loof

Carl Loof is a writer with one foot in Swedish and one in American cul-
ture. Having recently done extensive research on current issues concerning
the Jewish community in Sweden, anti-Semitism, and the under-discussed
influence of Swedish Nazi supporters in the World War II era, we asked
him to review some of the historical incidents and trends referenced in Stieg
Larsson's novels. His report follows.

In a society known for its high standard of living, economic stability, and low
criminality, the cultural phenomenon of Swedish crime fiction is best understood within the historical and political context of its most popular authors
and their work. Some of the best-known writers of the genre are staunch political activists from the Left, including Jan Guillou, Henning Mankell, and
the writing couple from the 1960s and 70s, Maj Sjöwall and Per Wahlöö, who
are often credited with giving birth to the Swedish crime novel. Many of
these authors view their books as a way to express their political viewpoints,
wrapped up in good storytelling. To paraphrase Sjöwall and Wahlöö, who
were dedicated communists, the crime novel can be viewed as an ideological
"scalpel" used to cut open the belly of the bourgeois-fashioned welfare state.
Larsson, although an active Trotskyist in the 1970s and '80s, seems much less
specifically ideological than other crime writers on the Left and much more
engaged with his storytelling. Nevertheless, to better understand his books, it
is useful to understand some of the allusions to historical events, well-known
individuals, and cultural phenomena familiar to his Swedish audience.

Swedish Upper-Class Nazism and the Vanger Family
In *The Girl with the Dragon Tattoo,* Larsson juxtaposes a series of brutal anti-
Semitic-tinged murders with one family's dark past. In certain ways, the
Vanger family becomes representative of the wider Swedish society, which has
only recently begun to investigate the history of Nazi influence on Sweden. At
the outbreak of World War II, Sweden and Germany shared strong economic
and cultural ties. German was the lingua franca of Swedish academia, the

arts, science, and business communities. Despite these close ties, Nazism gained only marginal public support in Sweden. Even at the height of their political success, far-right movements never gained more than 0.7 percent in the national election, or around twenty thousand votes. Awkward and fragmented, the movement was certainly hampered by a political message that seemed foreign and extreme to the Swedish public. But beneath the visible surface of society, proponents of the Third Reich sought to exploit shared Germanic cultural heritage and pointed to Sweden's homogeneity as an example of racial purity and Aryan superiority.

The "upper-class Nazism" exemplified by members of Larsson's Vanger family is a reflection of recent discoveries about prominent Swedish figures' flirtations with Nazism. National Socialism in Sweden was less a question of a mass movement and more one of networks of professors, lawyers, priests, doctors, civil servants, officers, and businessmen who worked to further Nazi ideas discreetly and secretly hoped for a German victory during the war. Although Sweden was officially "neutral" in World War II, the flow of iron ore from Sweden to Germany was important to the Nazi military machine and German soldiers were allowed passage across Sweden into Norway. Right after the war, researchers sought to expose Swedish Nazi sympathizers through "informative publication" of lists of individuals with ties to far-right groups. Since the 1990s greater efforts have been made by the Swedish government and research community to study the role played by Swedes in the context of Hitler's rise and fall. These efforts are largely thanks to Sweden's journalistic and academic community raising public awareness of the lack of information on the matter.

The ongoing current of anti-Semitism and the reality that Nazi sympathies have not disappeared came to light again in 2010 with the conviction of a Swedish neo-Nazi, Anders Högström, for coordinating the theft of the infamous "Arbeit Mach Frei" ("work makes you free") sign from the Auschwitz concentration camp in Poland. This bizarre incident of Nazi nostalgia, linked to powerful, wealthy figures with Nazi sympathies, certainly resonates with Larsson's warnings about the rise of neo-Nazism, which is uncharacteristic of Swedish society as a whole. During World War II, Sweden successfully protected its own Jewish population and those of neighboring countries, not to mention the thousands of Jews saved by Swedish diplomat Raoul Wallenberg. In 1944, Wallenberg traveled to Nazi-occupied Budapest, where by issuing "protective passports" and by renting buildings in the name of Sweden, he was able to prevent the deportation of over ten thousand victims, including the late Tom Lantos, who was an influential U.S. congressman until his death in 2008. In 1981, the U.S. Congress made Wallenberg an honorary citizen. Today, the United States Holocaust Memorial Museum in Washington, D.C., is located at One Hundred Raoul Wallenberg Place.

The Swedish Jewish Community

German-style Fascism never gained a real foothold in Sweden. There was no broad government-supported cultural anti-Semitism, and, while some anti-Semitic atrocities and incidents have taken place in Swedish history, they have never been tacitly encouraged by the state nor widely tolerated by the public.

Sizable Jewish communities in Sweden did not exist until 1775. Under a royal decree in 1782, Jews were permitted to settle, work, and worship only in Stockholm, Gothenburg, and Norrköping (similar restrictions were enforced against all non-Lutherans). Not until the mid-nineteenth century were Jews granted wider civil rights, and even then they were usually viewed as foreign nationals, as "Israelites" and "Hebrews," and part of the "Jewish nation."

Today's Jewish community is a vibrant and integrated part of Swedish society and is the largest in northern Europe. The country witnessed a remarkable growth in Jewish immigration over the past hundred years, including refugees from Russia, Poland, and Hungary, as well as survivors of the Holocaust, and, more recently, families from the Middle East and Latin America.

A central theme of Larsson's writing is the right to be different and to be free of religiosity. By developing individualistic Jewish characters throughout the Millennium trilogy, Larsson accentuates the Jewish community's significant role in Swedish intellectual, cultural, and business life, as well as their active role in promoting progressive social movements.

Larsson captures the essence of Sweden's Jewish community in his depiction of Inspector Jan Bublanski, whose nickname is both a Swedish pun that plays off of the word "bubble" as well as a play on the Yiddish term of endearment, "bubala." Like most Swedish Jews, Bublanski has an immigrant's background (Polish in his case), and is described, like most Swedes and Jews, as selective in his religious observance, although certainly aware of the high holidays and their traditions. Old laws once required all Jews to belong to one of the country's synagogues. In Stockholm, Larsson's Inspector Bublanski belongs to a congregation in Södermalm, which is most likely a reference to the Orthodox congregation Adat Israel on Paulsgatan. Larsson also makes reference to the diversity of the Jewish community through the Dragan

Armansky character, who is the CEO of Milton Security, and has a complex ethnic background that includes some Jewish heritage. He makes a similar point in referring to Bublanski's wife, Agnes, who is said to be Hungarian, and who most likely belongs to the group of Jewish refugees that arrived in Sweden during the 1950s. In *The Girl Who Kicked the Hornet's Nest*, we find Armansky and Bublanski holding a discreet private meeting in the synagogue on St. Paulsgatan.

The Wennerström Affair

Hans-Erik Wennerström, the corrupt fictional businessman in *The Girl with the Dragon Tattoo*, shares a surname with an infamous real-life Swede who spied for the Soviet Union and whose capture in the 1960s was a significant episode in Sweden's Cold War history. Larsson almost certainly picked this name for the evil businessman character because of the resonance between the financial corruption that is the focus of Larsson's story and the political corruption at the heart of the real-life Wennerström affair. Born into a prominent Swedish military family, Stig Wennerström was a colonel in the Swedish Air Force and served as a military attaché to Washington during the 1950s. In 1963, Wennerström was arrested on a bridge that was located, as if symbolically, between the Houses of Parliament and the Department of Foreign Affairs. Swedish intelligence recruited one of his house staff, who tipped off authorities about secret documents in the attic.

Wennerström was sentenced to life imprisonment for leaking Swedish air defense fighter jet plans to the Soviet military intelligence. Wennerström was paroled after twenty years in jail and was still alive when Larsson was writing his novels, although he has since died. Interestingly, this disgraced scion of the Swedish upper class had once been suspected of being a Nazi sympathizer and collaborator with the Germans, though this involvement was never proved.

WE'RE NOT LIKE ABBA AND IKEA: SOME SHOCKING TRUTHS ABOUT SWEDEN
by Stephen Armstrong

Stephen Armstrong, a freelance journalist and occasional radio documentary producer, has his own take on Sweden's so-called dark side. In this dispatch he writes about the new surge of Swedish culture, opines on the trilogy that ends with scenes of horror "beyond anything Hannibal Lecter could imagine," and interviews Henning Mankell, creator of the Wallander series and Larsson's most prominent forerunner.

"Part of Sweden's problem overseas is that everyone thinks we're like Abba and Ikea," says Stockholm-based stand-up comedian Magnus Betner. "We're a nation of beautiful people singing happy songs in stylish modernist apartments. But that's not how we Swedes see ourselves. We have a very, very dark side, and I think you're only just finding out about it now."

Betner, the vocal leader of Sweden's surprisingly large stand-up comedy scene, has just been booked into this summer's Edinburgh Festival where, consciously or not, he's part of a subtle cultural invasion by one of Europe's oddest nations. Everywhere you turn—in film, music, literature, fashion and design—there's a powerful Swedish presence.

Recently, for instance, impatient shoppers were hospitalized following a mob surge at a new Ikea store opening in North London. High-end style junkies, meanwhile, crave furniture from Frant, an all-girl interior design company. Clubbers across the UK queue for hours to hear hip DJ team Swedish House Mafia, who will dominate Ibiza this summer with their night at the island's fashionable nightclub, Pacha. In pop, on the other hand, Swede Max Martin has ruled the charts for the past 10 years—writing hits such as "Baby One More Time" for Britney Spears, "I Kissed a Girl" for Katy Perry, and "So What" for Pink.

Now there's a surge of interest in Swedish crime fiction, perhaps prompted by the BBC's wildly successful adaptation of the *Wallander* series of crime novels by Swedish author Henning Mankell, which stars Kenneth Branagh as the grumpy policeman. Mankell's compatriot, Stieg Larsson, meanwhile, died from a heart attack before seeing his international bestselling Millennium trilogy catapult him to the rank of second-bestselling writer on the planet.

This week sees the film adaptation of the first book in Larsson's trilogy, *The Girl with the Dragon Tattoo*, released in Britain. So far, more than 2.5 million Europeans have seen the movie, and *No Country for Old Men* producer Scott Rudin has just inked a deal to make the Hollywood version. By the time Rudin has finished, many millions more will have followed the story of investigative journalist Mikael Blomkvist and chaotic, freewheeling computer hacker Lisbeth Salander. What they find at the end of that story, however, may shock them.

Tattoo begins as a slow-moving, gently unfolding detective story but ends with scenes of horror beyond anything Hannibal Lecter could imagine. Throughout the book version, Larsson keeps dropping genuine figures relating to violent crimes against women in Sweden. The Swedish title for the book is *Men Who Hate Women*, and footnotes quote real-life incidents to explain how the fictional Salander—whose civil rights are removed at the whim of a judge—is based on real incidents.

Larsson, as with Betner and Mankell, spends much of the time pulling apart the stereotype of happy-ever-after, perfectly educated, socially democratic and joyfully tolerant Swedes enjoying wild sex lives and perfectly cooked meatballs. The Millennium trilogy tracks Blomkvist and Salander's attempts to uncover mysterious murders in neo-fascist billionaire families as well as state-sanctioned violent sexual abuse, pedophilia and rape. Larsson himself was a campaigning anti-Nazi journalist who set up his own version of the British anti-fascist magazine *Searchlight*, so you can see why he'd take this path. Mankell, however, was a well-established mainstream author before he created *Wallander*. He did so in order to investigate pedophile rings at the heart of Sweden's security services and expose public and institutionalized racism.

"*Wallander* was born in May 1989 out of a need to talk about xenophobia. So the story came first, then him," says Mankell. "I was writing the first novel out of anger at what was happening in Sweden at the time—the rise of xenophobia. That was my ambition. And, since acts of xenophobia are a crime, I needed a police officer.

"Even after the second and third books, I really wasn't thinking of a series. Then I realized I was creating a tool that could be used to tell stories about the situation in Sweden in the Nineties."

Wallander and Blomkvist also wade through some of the extremely unpleasant undercurrents beneath Sweden's tranquil social order. In Larsson and Mankell's stories, both men encounter Neo-Nazis who collude with Sap, the Swedish version of MI5 and MI6 combined. In their version of Sweden, racism is rife, violence against women is commonplace, while the trafficking of children for sex is facilitated by highly placed lawyers and doctors.

One would be forgiven for dismissing these plotlines as pure fantasy. After all, in 2007 Sweden was rated best practicing democracy by *The Economist*, least corrupt nation by Transparency International, most equal in gender relations by the World Economic Forum, and most generous donor of overseas development aid by the OECD. Even the legend that the country has an unusually high suicide rate isn't true. Coming about 35th in the world, Sweden comes in lower than France, Germany, Australia and New Zealand. And yet, can it merely be coincidence that last year's runaway Swedish movie hit, *Let the Right One In*, portrayed a child vampire as a more innocent and sympathetic figure than the bullying, ignorant authority figures she encounters in 1980s Swedish society?

In 2007, the U.S. State Department recorded 6,192 cases of child abuse in Sweden by November of that year. It also reported homophobic crime was on the rise, and tens of thousands of rapes and domestic violence incidents in a population of just nine million. "Violence against women remains a problem," its report concluded. Likewise, a 2006 report from the group Global Monitoring on the commercial sexual exploitation of children found systemic faults in Sweden, including allowing child pornography to be viewed, although not downloaded, and failing to care properly for children caught up in sex trafficking.

Little of this would come as a surprise to Larsson, Blomkvist or Salander, who encounter all of this and more while investigating the brutal murder of a child, apparently at the hands of her rich, Nazi-sympathizing family. "Sweden has yet to come to terms with its Nazi past," says Anna Blondell, who runs a Swedish restaurant in London. "We were neutral during the war, and our Nazi party still lives on. In fact, I think it will do well at the next election, under a different name. Many people in the older generation were very sympathetic to Nazi ideas like eugenics but, unlike Germany, we have not been so open about this."

Certainly the country practiced forced sterilization of women deemed unfit to be mothers until as recently as 1975. Branded low class, or mentally slow, they were kept in Institutes for Misled and Morally Neglected Children, where they were eventually "treated." In 1997, the government admitted that 60,000 women had been sterilized.

Meanwhile, Ikea founder and Sweden's richest man Ingvar Kamprad revealed his youthful Nazi sympathies in 1994, confessing to a nine-year friendship with Per Engdahl, the openly pro-Nazi leader of the Neo-Swedish movement. Kamprad claimed he couldn't remember if he'd joined the Nordic Youth, Sweden's equivalent of the Hitler Youth. He apologized to staff in an open letter: "Perhaps you find something in your youth you now, so long afterward, think was ridiculous and stupid."

Kamprad also admitted to a widespread Swedish vice—alcoholism. In a bid to restrain binge drinking, the government has a monopoly on off-licenses and closes them at 7 p.m. Drinking in the streets is illegal. Copenhagen, just over the water from the Swedish town of Malmö, receives hordes of booze-cruise Swedes every weekend.

So have we got Sweden all wrong? Is it still essentially a nation of Vikings? Mankell bristles at the suggestion. "I would like to emphasize that Sweden is a very decent society to live in," he insists. "It would be ridiculous to say anything else. But we could have been better today if we had been different before—if we hadn't thrown a few babies out with some of our bathwater. I would like to change that and we can only change by discussing. We know that if our system of justice doesn't work, democracy is doomed. I think we are worried about that, so maybe that is why detective stories are so popular in Sweden.

"Until recently it was a very cold isolated culture. Our art can't bring about social change, but you cannot have social change without arts."

THE MAN WHO BLEW UP THE WELFARE STATE
by Ian MacDougall

That Stieg Larsson took on the issues of violence against women and neo-Nazism in Swedish society is by now a given, and central to most of the discussion about the Millennium trilogy. What has been overlooked, says Ian MacDougall, formerly a reporter in the Oslo bureau of The Associated Press, is that Larsson also took on what is arguably an even larger target: the State itself. By doing so, MacDougal argues, Larsson has truly separated himself from the more traditional Swedish crime fiction.

To read the 1,802 pages of the Swedish crime novelist Stieg Larsson's Millennium trilogy is to be told that, for all their perceived virtue, the institutions of social democracy are a farce. In Larsson's books, American readers will find the Sweden they expect: the welfare-state comforts, Volvo security, and Ikea practicality for which the country is known. But they will also find a country they didn't expect. In this Sweden, the country's well-polished façade belies a broken apparatus of government whose rusty flywheels are little more than the playthings of crooks. The doctors are crooked. The bureaucrats are crooked. The newspapermen are crooked. The industrialists and businessmen, laid bare by merciless transparency laws, are nevertheless crooked. The police and the prosecutors are crooked. And the criminals, of course, are crooked, though not always: it's often the case that criminal acts committed by do-gooders in the name of justice—from petty larceny to massive bank fraud—are the only means by which to overcome the comprehensive failure of the world's most comprehensive welfare system.

In Larsson's trilogy it's also the case that most, if not all, of these crooks hate women. The first volume's Swedish title is *Män Som Hatar Kvinnor*—in English, *Men Who Hate Women*—a title international publishers chose to tone down. (The French put the problem in the past tense, *Men Who Didn't Love Women*.) Sweden may have attained heights of gender equality only dreamed of in other parts of the world but, if we're to believe Larsson, that

---

apparent moral superiority is merely cosmetic, concealing pervasive misogyny at every level of society.

These are Larsson's twin themes: the failure of the welfare state to do right by its people and the failure of men to do right by women.

For even the most casual reader of Swedish crime fiction, Larsson's themes will come as no surprise. Swedish crime fiction—and in our historical moment, Sweden is the crime fiction capital of the world, with growing suburbs in Denmark and Norway—owes its greatest debt to its British forebear, whose plots it cheerfully rips off. But the Swedish model distinguishes itself by infusing these plots with a social and political consciousness. Agatha Christie, the paradigmatic British crime novelist, was more likely to deploy ethnic stereotypes than to interrogate or denounce them. If Swedish crime fiction also owes a certain debt to Dashiell Hammett and Raymond Chandler, the great chroniclers of New Deal America, who certainly did try for something of a social consciousness, the Swedes show how Sam Spade and Philip Marlowe might have faired under the sunny gaze of a full-size welfare state. The Americans, studying the decay of cloudless Depression California, grew hard-boiled; their Swedish counterparts, pale-skinned but with Bergman-sized consciences, practically fry.

The Swedish crime novelist par excellence is Henning Mankell. His Inspector Kurt Wallander novels of the 1990s are widely credited with setting off the current wave of Swedish crime fiction, a geo-literary subgenre so distinctive the Germans have given it a neologism: *Schwedenkrimi*. Mankell has dominated the genre ever since, and he and his heirs are no strangers to novels that tackle moral issues. Mankell addressed misogyny in *The Fifth Woman,* and his literary progeny—not to mention earlier Swedish crime novelists, notably the husband-wife team of Maj Sjöwall and Per Wahlöö—are also well known for critiques of Western socialism. As Slavoj Žižek notes in a recent essay in the *London Review of Books,* the leitmotif of Mankell's crime fiction oeuvre has always been "the long and painful decay of the Swedish welfare state." Like the stench of decomposing trash, murder mysteries seem to radiate from the welfare state as it rots in the Scandinavian snow.

Together with the quaint aesthetics of the Scandinavian countryside, this socialist backdrop is precisely what makes the genre work. It's shocking enough when a bloated corpse turns up floating in Stockholm's pristine, well-managed waterways or when a serial killer disrupts the huddles of little red cottages that dot the Swedish countryside. The lingonberry jam on the detective's afternoon waffles looks a darker shade of red; the friendly smile of the average Jens on the street twists into a sinister grin. But the complicity of the welfare state heightens the tension.

The system has a hand in all aspects of Swedish life. If you can't trust the system, what can you trust? In the best Swedish crime novels, including Larsson's, the cradle-to-grave welfare system takes care of its wards. But you start to wonder just which meaning of "to take care of" that phrase refers to and whether the all-too-visible hand of the state isn't rocking the cradle over an open grave.

While adhering strictly to the classic plot structures—the locked-room mystery, the police procedural, the courtroom drama—the Millennium trilogy masterfully produces the tension that sets the Swedish subgenre apart. Larsson's ascent is all the more remarkable because he tackled fairly sophisticated subject matter—from minute problems distinct to the Swedish welfare state to European sex trafficking to the global problem of misogyny—and resisted the urge to prescribe hasty or cliché cures for the social ills he described. Larsson's sentences, well preserved by Reg Keeland's English translation, possess all the elegance of a grocery-store thriller. More importantly, Larsson has distinguished himself by refusing to stand in Mankell's shadow, no small feat for a Swedish crime writer.

The Millennium trilogy never conforms to the sullen-eyed worldviews and depressive, introspective detectives that characterize the genre. His protagonists—the beleaguered lefty journalist Mikael Blomkvist and the tortured punk hacker Lisbeth Salander (of dragon tattoo fame)—aren't beaten down by the unjust world they encounter. They're outraged by it. And their outrage is justified by the fact that Larsson brings the ostensibly protective welfare state to the fore, making it not just a backdrop but a central force and, in a way, a villain. A different kind of villain calls for a different kind of protagonist, and it's no coincidence that Larsson gave his lead roles to a journalist and a hacker rather than a detective and a femme fatale. Blomkvist and Salander both observe like classic detectives, but unlike them, Blomkvist and Salander make their observations public. The whodunit becomes the exposé.

In Larsson's three novels, Blomkvist and Salander expose not only a vast host of Volvo-driving, H&M-clad villains—bad guys large and small, government officials and petty criminals—that apparently scheme at all levels of Swedish society, but also the institutions that allow those villains to operate. And in each of the sequels, the number of villains multiplies,

their ties to the welfare state growing increasingly proximate. Indeed, there
are so many corrupt men who hate women in every corner of Larsson's Sweden that to present them all in a concise manner would be impossible.
They range from editors of major dailies to the members of Scandinavia's
ubiquitous biker gangs to police to lawyers to medical doctors to criminal
masterminds right out of a Roger Moore–era James Bond film. The one
thing that unites this mélange of women-hating crooks is that the welfare
state sponsors or at least supports their crimes. The state itself is the greatest villain.

The final volume of the Millennium trilogy, *The Girl Who Kicked the
Hornet's Nest,* is titled, in Swedish, *Luftslottet Som Sprängdes,* literally *The Castle
in the Air That Got Blown Up.* The title suggests the point at which Larsson
departs from his contemporaries. The typical Swedish detective solves the
crime but leaves intact what facilitates it—the broken institutions of the
welfare state. The castle in the air, the delusion of a perfect progressive utopia, persists after the case is closed. For Larsson the story's not over until the
state's blown up, if only in the reader's mind.

Although there is an obvious analogy to recent American forays into the
crime genre, like the HBO series *The Wire,* this only points to what sets
Larsson apart—a particularly Scandinavian optimism that insists it's never
too late to effect real change. Larsson, unlike David Simon, doesn't see insti-
tutional dysfunction as a tragic wheel driven around by some essential human
flaw. Larsson the idealist believes that an opposing force, if applied strongly
enough, can slow that wheel, if not bring it to a grinding halt.

The welfare state, like any utopia, is never finished. For many years
now, crime has been on the rise in Sweden. Close to a fifth of the population is unemployed or on long-term sick leave or disability, paid for by the
state. Immigrants have been arriving since the 1950s and Sweden's Minis-
try of Integration and Gender Equality still hasn't figured out how to as-
similate them. The Swedish industrial base has all but crumbled. To believe
in the *gemütlichkeit* of the "people's home"—as the Swedes call their welfare
state—amid all these inadequacies is to give up on the future, to make the
perfectible present into a dystopia by accepting its failures along with its
successes.

We see the real nature of Larsson's refusal to acquiesce amid Sweden's
undeniable achievements in the conclusion to his final novel. The acquittal
of the wrongly accused Salander isn't enough. Nor is the arrest of the misogynistic government agents who used the welfare state to frame her. The

sign that the novel has begun to draw to a close is the introduction of an investigative series on Sweden's TV4 that promises to expose these agents and the institutions they manipulated. Only when the story's out in the open can the crime even begin to be solved.

LEFT: Eva Gabrielsson worked with the Nørrebro Teater in Copenhagen, Denmark, to dramatize *The Girl with the Dragon Tattoo,* 2010 to 2011. *(Miklos Szaboo/Nørrebro Teater)*

BOTTOM: Performance still from the play *Men Who Hate Women.* Lisbeth Salander (played by Signe Egholm Olsen) has just tattooed Nils Bjurman (played by Max Hansen), Nørrebro Teater, Copenhagen, Denmark. *(Miklos Szaboo/Nørrebro Teater)*

LEFT: Stieg Larsson at work at the TT feature and photo desk as a graphic illustrator, Stockholm, 1984. *(Leif Bloom/Scanpix/Sipa Press)*

BOTTOM LEFT: Stieg Larsson at work as a news graphic illustrator at TT, where he worked for twenty years, 1984. *(Leif Bloom/Scanpix/Sipa Press)*

BOTTOM RIGHT: Stieg Larsson in a newly opened science fiction bookstore in Stockholm in the late 1970s. *(John-Henri Holmberg)*

TOP: The view from Blomkvist's small attic apartment includes the Stockholm Court House, far left, in which the trials of first Blomkvist and later Salander occur. City hall, far right, is home of the annual Nobel Prize dinner. (*Julie O'Connor*)

BOTTOM: The view from Lisbeth's Fiskargatan apartment building of the Gröna Lund amusement park and its roller coaster, at right. (*Julie O'Connor*)

TOP: Stieg Larsson photographed by childhood playmate Bo Lindh after Stieg had moved to his parents' apartment in Umeå. *(Bo Lindh)*

ABOVE LEFT: Stieg Larsson photographed by childhood playmate Bo Lindh. Stieg is on the left, and Harry Bäckström is on the right. *(Bo Lindh)*

ABOVE RIGHT: Stieg Larsson, during his school years in 1975, accompanied his classmates on a ski weekend but stayed indoors typing his senior thesis on the 1968 Paris uprising. *(Annika Nordström)*

TOP: The apartment building at Bellmansgatan 1 was built in 1888 and has beautiful views of the water and city. It is said to be home to Mikael Blomkvist. (*Julie O'Connor*)

BOTTOM: The luxurious penthouse at Fiskargatan 9 is said to be the twenty-one-room home of Lisbeth Salander. Originally known as Scandal House for blocking the view of Catherine Church, seen at right. (*Julie O'Connor*)

ABOVE: The spectacular night view from Lisbeth's apartment building at Fiskargatan. (*Julie O'Connor*)

LEFT: Fiskargatan 9 turret. Salander's apartment nameplate reads V. Kulla, a reference to Pippi Longstocking's home, Villa Villekulla. (*Julie O'Connor*)

OPPOSITE MIDDLE: Mellqvist Kaffebar, Hornsgatan 78. Baristas still remember Larsson writing here. In the 1990s, *Expo* had an office above the cafe. (*Julie O'Connor*)

OPPOSITE BOTTOM: Kvarnen, Tjärhovsgatan 4. Kvarnen, or "Windmill," is a restaurant and nightclub founded in 1908. Lisbeth's friends in the girl band Evil Fingers play here. (*Julie O'Connor*)

TOP: Billy's Pan Pizza is a favorite of both Lisbeth and Mikael. It comes frozen and is microwavable. (*Julie O'Connor*)

BOTTOM: The 7-Eleven at Götgatan 25, where Lisbeth Salander and Mikael Blomkvist shop. (*Julie O'Connor*)

LEFT: Paolo Roberto—already famous in Sweden as a champion boxer, actor, and cookbook author—is now also newly famous as a heroic character in the Millennium trilogy. (*Julie O'Connor*)

BOTTOM: Södra Teatern, Mosebacke 1, Lisbeth Salander and Annika Giannini meet at the Södra bar upstairs. The summer terrace has breathtaking Stockholm views. (*Julie O'Connor*)

The *Expo* magazine fifteenth-year anniversary celebration was held on November 10, 2010, at the Södra Theater. (*Julie O'Connor*)

TOP: Lundabron, or Lunda Bridge, leads to the street where Lisbeth Salander grew up. (*Julie O'Connor*)

BOTTOM: *The Sisters* sculpture in Mosebacke Square by Nils Sjögren is a reminder of Lisbeth and her sister Camilla. (*Julie O'Connor*)

TOP: Two tabloid newspaper props. (*Julie O'Connor*)

BOTTOM: The Stockholm City Museum displays props from the original Swedish movies, such as these newspaper front pages. Start your Millennium tour here. Reserve early for a guided tour, or buy their official map to discover the key locations on your own. (*Julie O'Connor*)

TOP: Stockholm City Museum display of mock Millennium covers used as props in the original movie. (*Julie O'Connor*)

BOTTOM: Milton Security, the company Lisbeth Salander worked for as a freelancer, is thought to be housed in one of the concrete, glass, and steel buildings of Slussen. (*Julie O'Connor*)

Adat Jisrael Synagogue, St. Paulsgatan 13, where Dragan Armansky meets Detective Inspector Jan Bublanski, a member of its congregation. (*Julie O'Connor*)

The Stockholm City Museum, Ryssgården, Slussen, was once a seventeenth-century palace. Millennium tours are given in multiple languages.
(*Julie O'Connor*)

Anders Roslund

Karin Alfredsson

Robert Aschberg

Alexandra and Alexander Ahndoril

Börge Hellström

Katarina Wennstam

"A DARK SWEDEN, WITH DISHONEST, GREEDY, CYNICAL, CHILD-ABUSING, AND WOMEN-HATING MEN"
by Mian Lodalen

Mian Lodalen is a Swedish feminist and gay rights activist. She is a columnist and essayist, as well as an author of fiction and nonfiction. Her first novel, written in 2003, tells the story of a journalist trying to find true love—or at least good sex—in Stockholm. Her latest, the widely praised Tiger *(2010), portrays the sexual awakening of a teenage girl in a strongly religious community. Lodalen regularly writes columns on the gay community and the struggle over achieving equality for women.*

I'm no crime fiction enthusiast. However, Stieg Larsson's novels captured me immediately. At the height of the hysteria surrounding his novels you simply had to read them, and they proved irresistible.

Considering his work at *Expo,* it is hardly surprising that Stieg wrote perceptively about the dark underside of Swedish society. It's more notable that he also captures the world of big business, high finance, and the upper class so convincingly. Having had the privilege (or dubious pleasure) of spending long periods in both these worlds, I've noted that not even the upper class itself manages to depict itself in so believable a fashion. But in my opinion, Stieg does capture it convincingly.

Stieg Larsson writes about a dark Sweden, with dishonest, greedy, cynical, child-abusing and women-hating men at the highest levels of society, who have no compunctions about exploiting the weakest. Some might believe this to be grossly exaggerated, but during the last few years Sweden has been rocked by numerous scandals indicating that Stieg Larsson's view of the country is spot on. Consider:

- Lundin Petroleum is a Swedish oil company heavily involved in Sudan. At the behest of oil prospectors, the Sudanese government had systematically terrorized the inhabitants of the oil-rich southern part of the country in order to force them to move. Tens of thousands have been killed and hundreds of thousands have been driven from their homes. Swedish foreign minister Carl Bildt was a member of the Lundin Petroleum Board of Directors from 2000 to late 2006, when he joined the government. In June 2010, District Attorney Magnus Elving ordered an investigation into the possibility that Swedes may have been party to the crimes against humanity committed in Sudan's south.

- From 2002 on, one of Sweden's oldest and largest insurance companies, Skandia, was rocked by scandal after scandal: many of its highest executives had illegally used company funds to acquire huge downtown apartments or renovate their existing apartments and houses, grant themselves huge bonuses, and so on. In November 2003, the board of directors and the CEO were forced to resign and several of them were prosecuted. Skandia stock dropped dramatically and in 2006 the company was bought by South African Old Mutual.

- In 2004, Knutby, a town of about five hundred people only sixty-five miles from Stockholm, suddenly hit the headlines when the local, charismatic Pentecostal vicar, Helge Fossmo, was indicted for conspiracy to commit murder, and his family's nanny was charged with murder and attempted murder. Reverend Fossmo, it turned out, had managed to convince the nanny, with whom he had a sexual relationship, that God wanted her to murder his wife as well as the husband of yet another lover of his. Further investigations disclosed that his church had been run as a totalitarian dictatorship, its two priests proscribing in minute detail what their followers were allowed to think and do.

- One of the major sex scandals of 2009 was the indictment of three highly placed corporate managers for procuring, rape, and aiding in rape. These men had engaged in simulated or actual gang rapes of teenage girls.

- Shortly before the 2010 general election, two Social Democrat candidates running for Stockholm's local government assembly were arrested for entertaining prostitutes in an apartment belonging to the Swedish Trade Union Confederation.

- In January 2010, former police commissioner and principal of the Swedish Police Academy Göran Lindberg was arrested for aggravated rape, rape, and attempted rape of a minor as well as procurement. The arrest occurred when Lindberg was on his way to meet a fourteen-year-old girl with whom he had arranged to have sex. Adding insult to injury, Göran Lindberg was for many years considered the foremost advocate of women's equality within the Swedish police. He is now serving a six-year jail sentence.

- In March 2010, an award-winning TV special told the story of fourteen-year-old "Linnea" in Bjästa, a town of less than two thousand. In 2009, she was raped by a fifteen-year-old boy, who later committed a second rape. Although he was found guilty and has been sentenced for both, virtually all of the community chose to blame Linnea and the other girl. The rapist was forgiven by the school and the local church, and many locals had joined a Facebook group supporting him.

So how true is the portrait of Sweden given by Stieg Larsson? Every Swede is much too aware of the answer—or should be. He viewed patriarchal society as a global problem, but chose to place his stories in Sweden since he considered our country to be ruled by the same structures as the rest of the world. The idealized image of Sweden as a country with full equality has been justly tarnished by his works.

As for the protagonists in Stieg Larsson's novels, you can of course perceive the characters of Lisbeth Salander, Miriam Wu, and Mikael Blomkvist as the wet dream of a straight white male. My view, however, is that within the literary universe created by Stieg they remain totally believable. And although Blomkvist acts like any horny male, and in that respect contributes nothing new to sexual politics, he happily lacks the vanity and prestige usually typical of straight male fictional heroes.

As for Salander, I know women who are autonomous, highly educated, hackers and martial arts experts with a black belt in karate or some other combat sport, and who like to sleep with both men and women. So apart from her fictional talents, such as winning fights against five opponents, impossible even for males, I consider Salander a believable character.

It is difficult to measure her importance in terms of sexual politics. Her importance may be greater in countries other than Sweden, as we are a people who, in spite of all, are reasonably willing to "accept" that individuals are attracted to others of the same gender. Still, many bisexuals are stigmatized by both the hetero and the gay community, which makes it a blessing that Stieg let Salander be attracted to both women and men. The best thing about her sexuality is that she partakes of partners on her own terms. Regardless of both "Swedish sin" and Swedish equality, I hardly believe that hetero feminists consider Sweden to have achieved sexual equality. Perhaps it never will. But in that respect, Salander is a true role model! I smile just thinking about her.

At the 2008 annual Swedish Gay Gala, Stieg Larsson was given a posthumous award for *The Girl Who Kicked the Hornet's Nest*. Lisbeth Salander played a major part in earning him that award, which was accepted by Stieg's life partner, Eva Gabrielsson. There was a standing ovation when she said, "I come here on behalf of Stieg, since Stieg would have come on behalf of Lisbeth."

Is Sweden realistically and believably portrayed in Stieg's novels? Yes, sadly so. The same norms exist here as in other countries. Girls and women both are subjected to patriarchal oppression perpetrated by males of all classes, from street thugs to police commissioners, company presidents, politicians, priests, fathers, scout masters, soldiers, and headmasters.

Consequently, I agree with Stieg Larsson. He was a Swedish counterpart to Michael Moore, a white intellectual middle-class male saying what feminists scream themselves hoarse about while they are seldom or never listened to. But Stieg is now read by millions of people. I feel a genuine sadness that he was not given the opportunity to continue the work of enlightenment he began.

8. ENGROSSED IN THE WORLD OF STIEG LARSSON

THE DEATH OF STIEG LARSSON: MYSTERIES WITHIN THE MYSTERIES
by Laura Gordon Kutnick

The most far-reaching questions about the Millennium trilogy extend beyond the book covers to the circumstances surrounding the death of the author and the bitter battle that has ensued over his financial and intellectual legacy. One reader among the many Stieg Larsson devotees who found the author's life story (and death story) even more interesting than the novels is Laura Gordon Kutnick, who has been on her own quest to think through the many unsolved mysteries about Larsson and to look for ideas, if not ultimately satisfying answers, in the texts of the novels themselves. What follows is her remarkable analysis of the pervasive questions about Stieg Larsson that loom over the Millennium trilogy—and the ironic, eerie, and prophetic words about them that come directly from Larsson's own fiction.

Is there any chance that something other than natural causes was responsible for Stieg Larsson's apparent death of a heart attack at the age of fifty after climbing seven flights of stairs to his office on a day when the elevator was suddenly out?
Larsson's cause of death is known to be myocardial infarction (heart attack), and everyone close to him, regardless of which corner they are in about the issues concerning his legacy, accepts this cause of death as definitive. Yet speculation about his untimely demise continues. Larsson faced numerous documented death threats in the last decade of his life. These arose from his crusading work to expose neo-Nazis and right-wing extremists. Quite conscious of these threats, he lived a life of constant countermeasures and precautions, even writing a handbook for investigative journalists on how to avoid being killed by right-wingers while in the course of researching and exposing them.

His death occurred on the anniversary of Kristallnacht, just before he was to speak at a commemoration of that horrible 1938 "night of the broken glass" in Hitler's Germany. A small minority of commentators have wondered out loud whether Larsson met with foul play. Some consider it uncanny that he had been threatened by extremists outside the magazine's office previously and had narrowly escaped with his life by running down the back stairwell. Larsson's friend, Kurdo Baksi, recalls that Larsson had wondered just days before his death whether he should seek police protection for the Kristallnacht event.

For most conspiracy theorists—and Larsson's own novels, of course, are filled with extensive webs of conspiracies—it is all too coincidental that he would die at the comparatively young age of fifty and on such a historic date of particular relevance to the very neo-Nazis who had often threatened him. It also seems strangely coincidental that his death would have occurred only a few months after he had signed an unprecedented three-book publishing contract and just after he received a major motion picture contract. Even among those close to him, there are different understandings about whether he was buried or cremated. The details and location of his final resting place are undisclosed, since his colleagues were concerned that a public monument might lead to neo-Nazi desecration attempts against it. Yet this lack of disclosure adds to the aura of mystery surrounding Larsson's death.

What of the treatment of Eva Gabrielsson, Larsson's lifetime partner and companion since they were teenagers together?

How deeply ironic that a set of best-selling contemporary crime novels, which owe much of their popularity to their streak of moral conscience against the mistreatment and abuse of women, would end up at the heart of a controversy over the apparent trampling of the rights of the author's female partner by his male relatives? In her inability to be allowed a voice in Stieg Larsson's literary and intellectual legacy, as well as in her disenfranchisement from the billion-dollar industry that has sprung up around Larsson's estate, Eva Gabrielsson seems to embody Stieg Larsson's message about society's pattern of patriarchy and injustice against women. All the power, control, and money are flowing to Larsson's father and brother—his two officially recognized heirs. Having read much of the published record about Larsson's relationships, I find no evidence of emotional closeness with these two individuals during Larsson's adulthood and quite a bit of evidence that his relationships with them were, at a minimum, troubled. Meanwhile, the woman he spent thirty-two years sharing everything with is left with virtually nothing and is marginalized even in the discussion of how Larsson's ideas and writings—to which she contributed—should be managed in the future. And this in a country that prides itself on its many progressive steps toward formal gender equality. Just as Lisbeth Salander is abused by many of the men in her life, especially her father and brother, Eva Gabrielsson is telling us she is the moral and financial victim of her father-in-law and brother-in-law.

What about the mysterious "fourth book," the one that Stieg had completed anywhere from 160–200 pages (or more) of at the time of his death?
It was said to be on his laptop. There are varying stories about how complete the book is, where the laptop is now, and what became of his notes and outlines for other books—perhaps as many as ten titles—featuring Lisbeth Salander, Mikael Blomkvist, and other Millennium trilogy characters. Among those who knew Eva and Stieg, some believe Gabrielsson was not just Larsson's life partner, but also his collaborator.

In her own memoir, *Millennium, Stieg and Me*, published in early 2011 in French and Swedish, Gabrielsson details some of the parts of the Millennium trilogy that were based on her research or ideas and says, "Just as we had a common language, we often wrote as a team." In recent interviews, Gabrielsson speaks of wanting to undertake the completion of the fourth novel. Who has the rights to this material? Who, if anyone, will finish the story and publish the book? Eva Gabrielsson says she wants to do it. She has even announced the provocative title, *God's Vengeance*. Joakim Larsson has said he won't permit Eva's publication of the book.

There is one more question that needs to be given some consideration, however improbable: **Is there any chance that Stieg Larsson is not dead?** Like Huck Finn and Tom Sawyer hidden in the church, attending their own funeral, and listening to speeches about themselves, could Stieg Larsson have merely disappeared for a long while? After all, many of Larsson's characters are known for their disappearing acts. In *The Girl with the Dragon Tattoo*, almost everyone thought Harriet Vanger was dead when she disappeared at age sixteen, yet Mikael Blomkvist locates her four decades later. To believe that Larsson is alive and in hiding somewhere would require acceptance of the idea that a vast conspiracy of people close to him (who are at extreme odds over other matters) had joined together to cover up his disappearance. The disappearance theory more plausibly belongs in the realm of Larsson's own fiction. And yet, as we shall see, it remains disturbingly eerie that he would have written time and time again, in each of the three novels, about people who disappear for long periods of time and are presumed dead . . . but then come back into view.

These questions have become so central to the mythology of Stieg Larsson that they continue to swirl through the minds of the 50 million buyers of the books and many others who haven't even read the books but have been drawn into the web of intrigue surrounding them. The UK's *Daily Mail* affixed one of the longest yet best headlines to the story: *"The True Mystery Story Behind the Girl with the Dragon Tattoo: Suddenly, EVERYONE Is Reading Stieg Larsson's Thrillers but His Own Life Was Just as Intriguing as His Fiction. Was He Murdered? Did His Partner ACTUALLY Write the Books? and Why Hasn't She Had a Penny after His Death?"*

If we assume the basic facts of the Larsson death are true—he died from a heart attack; he did not meet with foul play; he is really dead and not in self-imposed exile; the battle between the Larsson family and Eva Gabrielsson is not part of a *Hornet's Nest*–like cabal, but only the product of human frailty, corporate interests, and greed—then we only have to acknowledge that art often mimics life in excruciating detail. Dozens of eerily disturbing clues in Larsson's books point to incidents and situations that now appear almost like forecasts or predictions.

A close reading of *Tattoo, Fire,* and *Hornet's Nest* yields an amazing number of specific references to:

- Characters who disappear for long periods of time while the rest of the world thinks they are dead
- Characters who experience sudden medical problems, several of whom die of sudden heart attacks
- Sibling and family situations that mirror the experiences of the key people in Larsson's own life
- Estate law, wills, and inheritance issues

If you read the references assembled below carefully, it becomes hard to think Larsson didn't, at the very least, have some strong intuitive premonitions about what might happen after the publication of the books. And his track record at procrastination was good: He had, after all, presciently predicted the rise and parliamentary success of the Sweden Democrats years before they became an electoral force.

Sibling and Family Issues in the Millennium Mirror

Stieg Larsson (aka Karl Stig Larsson) is a thinly veiled version of his fictional doppelganger, Mikael Blomkvist (aka Carl Mikael Blomkvist). They are both left-wing journalists who grew up poor working-class boys from the Swedish countryside far outside Stockholm. Very early in the plot of *Tattoo,* Blomkvist is hired by Henrik Vanger to serve as the biographer of this fictional family of Swedish industrialists. But just as Stieg Larsson has a hidden agenda in writing his crime novels—to expose and take a stand against the abuse of women in the course of writing entertaining potboilers—the fictional Blomkvist is asked by Vanger to take on a hidden agenda as well: finding out what happened to his beloved niece Harriet who disappeared from the Vanger family summer compound on remote Hedeby Island at the age of sixteen in 1966.

Harriet is said to have vanished "without a trace." All these years later, Henrik still wonders if she "could have gone off of her own free will . . . (or) had an accident and died . . . (or) committed suicide . . . (or) been the victim of a crime."

Blomkvist discovers, much to his surprise, that he is personally connected to the Vanger story and to Harriet Vanger herself. He learns that his father worked for Henrik Vanger and that, as a small child, his baby-sitter was none other than Harriet herself. Perhaps Larsson is trying to tell us that he too has a personal connection to the stories he is telling. Larsson's own presence looms in the Vanger family photo Blomkvist looks at like "the photographer's shadow . . . in the left bottom corner." Blomkvist increasingly sees the Vanger family saga as a "locked-room mystery in island format," which refers to a genre made famous by Agatha Christie, and is one of several genres at play within the Millennium trilogy.

The parallels are clear: Hedeby, although fictional, is said to be a remote island; the area where Larsson actually grew up is in the remote extreme north of Sweden. Harriet has traumatic experiences with her own father and brother, but she feels at home, comfortable, and close to her uncle Henrik. Larsson, meanwhile, was at best distant from his father and brother growing up. His parents sent him to live with his grandparents and rarely saw him in his early years, while his brother stayed with his parents after his birth. On the other hand, Larsson's friends say he was very close to his grandfather, Severin Boström, and that Severin ended up a major force in his life. Thus, the relationship between Harriet and her elderly uncle Henrik can be viewed as a kind of parallel to the story of Stieg and his grandfather.

In one of the novel's many prophetic observations, Blomkvist worries that Henrik Vanger may die before the biography is published. (In *Hornet's*

Nest, investigative journalist Dag Svensson will be murdered before *his* book is finished.) In the end, of course, it is Larsson who turns out to be dead before his books are published.

Meanwhile, another Vanger family member raises the specter of disappearance early in *Dragon Tattoo*. Cecilia Vanger, another niece of Henrik's, is fearful that Blomkvist's biography will reveal her family to be as dysfunctional as it is. (Patriarch Henrik has already predicted that Blomkvist will conclude that the goings-on among the Vangers will make Shakespeare's tragedies look like "light entertainment.") Cecilia poses a telling question: "Will I have to go into exile or emigrate when the book comes out?"

Blomkvist's meticulous exploration of all the reasons why Harriet may have disappeared in 1966 may be providing Larsson with a way to explore his own personal childhood issues.

Upon receiving a typewriter for his twelfth birthday, the young Stieg Larsson was exiled from his family's apartment because his typing kept people up. Instead of sharing a room with his younger brother, Joakim, the family found a room for Stieg in the windowless basement of their apartment building. All this occurs right around 1966, the year picked for Harriet's fictional disappearance. Once he obtains that typewriter, Stieg Larsson begins the process of becoming a writer and separating himself from his family.

Over and over, Larsson sets up family dynamics in his novels where father/son duos jointly attack the unfavored offspring, driving them away—and worse. Harriet, Lisbeth, and other characters are victims of *both* father and brother. In Stieg's case, it seems more that he simply did not fit in with his family and, from an early age, had to find a way out into a new life.

Do the terrifying scenes in the Millennium trilogy of Blomkvist being tortured in the windowless basement of Martin Vanger's house or Lisbeth Salander being removed from her mother's custody—at age twelve, when she is sent into solitary confinement at a psychiatric hospital after trying to murder her father—have their origins, at least metaphorically, in the active imagination of Larsson's lonely childhood years?

Stieg Larsson had one real-life sibling—his younger brother, Joakim. He had no sister. Yet when Larsson sat down to write the Millennium trilogy, he invented for Blomkvist not a brother, but a wonderful younger *sister* with whom Blomkvist is very close, Annika Giannini. We meet Annika when Blomkvist is sharing Christmas dinner with her family, something Larsson apparently did not do often with his own family who stayed in remote Umeå after Stieg and Eva moved to Stockholm in the late 1970s. Indeed, many of

Larsson's friends in Stockholm say they didn't even know he had a brother until Joakim appeared at the memorial meeting in 2004. Stieg rarely visited Umeå after moving to Stockholm, and his father and brother rarely left the remote frozen north of Sweden to come to see him in the capital city.

Adding to this tapestry of sibling issues, consider these ways in which Larsson's art mirrors his life: Lisbeth has a sister—a twin in fact, Camilla—yet most people who know Lisbeth don't know she has a sister at all. Zalachenko, Lisbeth's father, clearly favored Camilla (much as Erland Larsson appears to have favored Joakim over Stieg). Lisbeth hasn't seen Camilla since they had a fight on their seventeenth birthday. Coincidentally, seventeen is about the age Stieg Larsson really started living life on his own apart from his family.

Annika is among Larsson's most morally rigorous characters. She is a crusader for women's rights and ends up being of tremendous help to Blomkvist, including taking, and winning, Lisbeth's court case. Is it coincidence or premonition that Larsson's real-life brother would end up not only of no help in protecting Eva's rights, but leading the effort to deny Eva a meaningful role in Stieg's intellectual and financial estate? Annika, the imagined sister, appears to be the antithesis of Joakim, the real-life brother.

Disappearing Acts

The Millennium trilogy is filled with references to illusion, deception, magic, and disappearing acts: Blomkvist sees himself as an illusionist; Salander's ability to gather information through hacking is said to be "sheer magic"; Zalachenko is "an expert in disguise and deception." Indeed, when Zalachenko wants the Section for Special Analysis gang to solve a problem, he says, "Fuck the forensic evidence. It's a matter of how the investigation is carried out and how the facts are presented . . . wave your magic wand and make all this disappear. . . ."

Blomkvist discovers the key visual clue that will lead to solving Harriet Vanger's disappearance when he notices the worried look on her face in a photo that suggests something disturbing just outside the frame. Many of the enigmas of the Millennium trilogy are solved when clues are revealed to be in unconventional places. A photograph is only important because of the date on the back; what everyone thinks are phone numbers in a diary turn out to be encoded Bible verses; tattooed statements appear on a rapist's belly; identifying insignias are cut out of a motorcycle jacket. Perhaps there is something disturbing in Stieg's past, just outside the frame of all that has been written about him, which gnawed at him and troubled him.

When the fictional Blomkvist writes a fictional book about evil doings in high places, it bears more than superficial resemblances to the Millennium trilogy that would begin to be published just after Larsson's death. Blomkvist enjoys using reverse psychology to get media attention. He promotes his book through his own absence: "It was a brick of a book, 608 pages. . . . The first edition of two thousand copies was virtually guaranteed to be a losing proposition, but the print run actually sold out in a couple of days. . . . *Blomkvist's extraordinary absence* was part of the media strategy that he and Berger put together. Every newspaper in the country was looking for him . . ." (emphasis added). The rumors about Blomkvist "assumed legendary proportions." He was described "as a hero in such ludicrously flattering terms that he was quite embarrassed."

The parallels to the wild success of Larsson's posthumously published novels are obvious. Soon after Larsson wrote these words extolling Blomkvist's clever ploy to garner media attention for his book by absenting himself from the promotional circuit, Larsson, the first-time novelist, would himself be "absent" from the promotional circuit, having died just before the first novel of the trilogy went to press. Yet he would get some of the best media coverage a first-time novelist has ever received, on the way to his books joining the ranks of the all-time leading best sellers.

Skeptical of this media fanfare surrounding Larsson's books, reviewer Chauncey Mabe accuses the deceased author of fabricating a PR trail that "metastasize(s)" his legend: "Apart from being dead and all, Stieg Larsson is living the life. Seldom has a writer gotten to eat so much of his cake and have it too. . . ." Did Larsson drop the crumbs from this cake for us to find, Hansel and Gretel style?

Although Larsson understood the media very well, he was personally anything but a media monger. He "refused point blank to be photographed," according to his friend Kurdo Baksi. Anonymity was vital to Larsson, says Baksi. So too "was the possibility of making a difference without being noticed. . . . It is . . . difficult to imagine how he would have handled his success as an author." The fictional visions of Blomkvist's superstardom as a journalist—TV interviews, invitations to all the best parties, everyone in Sweden knowing exactly who he was and what he had done to bring down Wennerström—are probably as much of a Larsson fantasy as the many women who seek out Blomkvist for sex without commitment.

So many of Larsson's fictional characters go "off the radar" that it is hard to ignore the nagging suspicion, no matter how incredible it may seem, that

Larsson himself might have disappeared rather than died. In *Tattoo,* Henrik Vanger really should have figured out from the pressed flower cards he gets every year on his birthday that Harriet is still alive and that it is she who is sending these cards to him. Instead, despite all the years of investigation and thought about the mystery of these cards, he chooses to believe that Harriet's murderer is taunting him by sending them. By opening *Tattoo* with this obvious ruse as a prelude, is Stieg Larsson trying to communicate something to his readers about his own vitality and disappearance? Is he counting on the reader to pursue his maze of well-placed clues?

After all, Harriet Vanger vanishes to Australia, which is about as far away from Sweden as you can get on planet earth. She starts a new life under a new name, even while most everyone in her family, including her much loved uncle Henrik, assumes she has met with foul play. She comes back to Sweden and to her uncle Henrik only after Blomkvist tracks her down almost *four decades* after her disappearance, and only because he is able to assure her that her evil brother Martin is dead and no longer a danger to her.

The theme of disappearance from view is repeated throughout Larsson's novels:

- Harald Vanger becomes "an invisible but ever present spirit who affected life in the village by his absence."
- Henrik Vanger, the family's "twenty-point stag," makes a public appearance after a self-imposed exile of twenty years.
- After Mikael Blomkvist's "professional reputation . . . imploded . . . his means of recovering was to hide himself away in a tiny town in the deep country, chasing ghosts."
- Hans-Erik Wennerström seeks exile when his "labyrinth of corporations owned by one another" tumbles like a house of cards.
- Miriam Wu can't be located by the police.
- Ronald Niedermann evades a massive manhunt for him all over Scandinavia and Germany by hiding out in a dilapidated factory owned by Zalachenko, back home in Sweden.
- Zalachenko, a 1976 defector from the highest ranks of Soviet intelligence, is given a new name and a new life in Sweden by the ultrasecret "Section" inside SAPO, the Swedish secret security police. We never find out why no one from the Soviet side ever inquires or figures out what happened to this missing high-ranking intelligence officer. Nor do we learn how this Soviet émigré, set up by the

Section as a Swedish businessman named Karl Axel Bodin, never aroused interest in who he really was, despite his involvement with numerous unsavory characters for the last twenty-five years.

- Employees of this ultrasecret "Section for Special Analysis," who handle "the most secret of the secret" information, regularly disappear. The Section itself operates completely hidden from public view for several decades, with its membership and activities not even known to prime ministers and senior Swedish political leaders. Section members Gullberg and Clinton reactivate themselves out of retirement where their past activities have been completely covered up and hidden.

- The Ranta brothers go on a "little vacation" to disappear from police scrutiny.

- Holger Palmgren, Lisbeth's one guardian who was a positive force in her life, is presumed by many to be dead after suffering a major stroke. However, he is actually recovering and will come back to play a pivotal role in Lisbeth's trial.

- Salander's twin, Camilla, has never been heard from again after the fight on the sisters' seventeenth birthday. Some sources believe Larsson imagined Camilla in Canada, and say that she may figure in the fourth Larsson novel, which itself has "disappeared."

- Lisbeth disappears on a globe-hopping, life-re-creating tour of beaches, sunshine, alcohol, and sex, after acquiring a large fortune Robin Hood style. Under a new name and identity, and using her Gibraltar money manager as a cutout for the real estate transaction, she sets up house in the luxury apartment at Fiskargatan 9, only to be forced on the run again. Meanwhile, Blomkvist adopts Lisbeth's apartment as his own. By walking there via circuitous routes, he is able to disappear into it regularly and use it as a safe house while he is conducting his investigative work.

- Toward the end of *Fire,* Lisbeth has been buried alive. Yet she claws her way out of the grave Niedermann has dug for her, and goes on to survive even a bullet to the brain. It is as if she had a near-death experience and is reborn with a new life.

For Blomkvist, like Larsson, death threats are a regular occurrence. The need to disappear, carry out evasive maneuvers, or work in safe houses are all routine parts of daily life. The office back stairwell becomes a reliable escape hatch. "Blomkvist left the Millennium offices at 10:30 pm . . . took the stairs down to the ground floor, but instead of going out onto the street he turned left and went through the basement. . . . Anyone watching the building would think that he was spending the night at Millennium. . . ."

Kurdo Baksi says of the real-life threat level faced by Larsson, "It is hard to imagine any other Swede being threatened more often than he was during the last twenty years of his life." Unlike Henrik Vanger who received pressed flowers once a year on Harriet's birthday, Larsson received threatening and anonymous letters frequently. Exactly fifty-six days before Larsson's death "a woman with clear neo-Nazi links (responsible for killing other left-wing journalists) collected passport pictures of him" as well as his home address. Baksi says he advised Larsson to go into hiding and, for the first time, Stieg agreed it would be a good idea.

Larsson's characters frequently need to figure out how to lead untraceable lives. The idea of seeking anonymity by hiding in plain sight lies at the core of Stieg Larsson's geographical landscapes, whether it be a remote global location like Australia, Grenada, or Gibraltar, or within the microcosm of Stockholm's streets. Larsson's characters escape detection by creating new identities, establishing hidden residences, flying to uninhabited islands, stealing hard drives and duplicating files, changing external appearance, or just using the back stairwell. So if all Larsson's characters go MIA so often and so well—and then come back from hiding places, self-imposed exile, and near-death experiences—why not the author himself?

More Than Aware of His Own Mortality

By the third volume of the trilogy, Blomkvist becomes aware of his poor health habits and is becoming conscious of his own mortality. Like Larsson, Blomkvist is a chain smoker, overly dependent on caffeine and junk food. His self-imposed workload deprives him of exercise and sleep. According to Erika Berger, who half jokingly offers to write his obituary in *Fire,* he takes unnecessary risks. "I'm not sure if you know this, but sometimes I really worry about you," Erika tells him.

In *Hornet's Nest,* after Blomkvist and Monica Figuerola sleep together, Monica tries to encourage her new out-of-shape lover to go running with her. Blomkvist replies: "If I tried to go at your pace, I'd have a heart attack on Norr Mälarstrand." (The *Expo* office, where Larsson experienced his 2004 heart attack, is barely a mile away from Norr Mälarstrand.) Later that day, Blomkvist *needs* to run in order to catch the diabolical Dr. Teleborian in the act of conspiracy against Lisbeth. Blomkvist has just learned about a meeting at a café in the Central Station. To get there in time, he has to run. The narrator tells us: "When he reached Slussplan he was badly out of breath. Maybe Figuerola had a point. He was not going to make it."

Larsson's characters regularly suffer heart and other medical problems:

- In *Fire,* a frightened Blomkvist must guess at and punch in an unknown security code to break into Salander's penthouse. After he succeeds with this mission impossible, he looks as though he has "just avoided a heart attack." Inside the apartment, he feels as though "someone were squeezing his heart."
- In *Dragon,* Henrik Vanger suffers a major heart attack.
- In *Hornet's Nest,* when Frederic Clinton is called into action for the Section long after his retirement, he tells his old friend Evert Gullberg that he is an unlikely prospect for another mission, since he is on dialysis nine hours every other day. He points out that he can't even "go up stairs without gasping for breath." Gullberg replies that if climbing the office stairs is a problem, the agency will insure a working elevator or else they will arrange for Clinton to be carried on a stretcher. In this discussion of elevator versus stairs versus stretcher for a man constantly out of breath, we have yet another eerie premonition of November 9, 2004, when Larsson would apparently find the elevator at his real-life magazine, *Expo,* out of order, climb the seven flights of stairs, experience a heart attack, and be carried out of *Expo's* headquarters on a stretcher.
- Inspector Paulsson, the incompetent policeman who arrives on the frenzied scene at Zalachenko's farmhouse in Gosseberga and handcuffs Blomkvist in *Hornet's Nest,* turns out to be taking heavy doses of antidepressants and ends up collapsing and being admitted to the hospital suffering from exhaustion. He never appears again in the novel.
- After three weeks of fifteen-hour workdays as the new editor in chief of *Svenska Morgen-Posten,* Erika Berger suffers heart palpitations. She was "halfway to her car when she felt such strong heart palpitations that she had to stop and lean against a wall. She felt sick." She tells Blomkvist minutes later that "three weeks at SMP have already done me in."
- On the May day when Erika has her heart palpations, we have already encountered the former chief editor of SMP, Håkan Morander, whom she was hired to replace. Morander's heart trouble was the reason why SMP needed a new editor. Morander knew that if

he didn't retire soon, he was going to have a heart attack. Erika was supposed to work with Morander through a transition period before his formal retirement. However, on day three of Erika's new job, Morander, who works in a glassed-in office, "leaned forward, grabbed the back of a chair, and held on to it for a few seconds before he collapsed to the floor. He was dead before the ambulance arrived."

The image of the editor in chief of a newspaper collapsing and dying of a heart attack in view of his colleagues is, at a minimum, another eerie premonition of what would happen to Stieg Larsson after he climbed the stairs to *Expo* that November day in 2004, less than a year after he had written this scene for *Hornet's Nest,* the last of the three books. For another eerie premonition, consider that St. Görans hospital where Erika and Mikael are rushed after they suffer injuries in the shootout at Samir's Cauldron is the very same hospital where Stieg Larsson was pronounced dead after being rushed there by ambulance after his heart attack on the stairs at *Expo.*

Wills, Estates, Inheritance Issues

The absence of a will is one of the more publicized pieces of the posthumous puzzle. On the one hand, we know that Larsson made very little money during his career at TT and *Expo,* and that he and Eva as a couple had few possessions. Moreover, they had no children to worry about providing for. So it is easy to lump Larsson in with the millions of people in affluent countries all over the world who should give thought to the possibility of their own death, and should write up a will, but don't ever do it for various reasons. Yet the obvious arguments that might apply to other people (laziness, inertia, procrastination, avoidance) don't apply so easily to Stieg Larsson.

Consider, for example, these facts:

- Even when he was in his twenties and had almost nothing in the way of material wealth, he drafted a will before his trip to Eritrea, leaving the nothing he had to the Trotskyist group he was then associated with. He never signed this will, nor was it witnessed, so it was never considered in the legal proceedings after his 2004 death, in addition to the fact that it was several decades out of date. Very few people bother to scrawl even a few lines of a will when they are in their twenties. But Larsson did. So the idea that he didn't think it was important or relevant to have a will is undermined by his own young adult behavior.

- Before leaving for Africa in the 1970s, Larsson wrote a note to Eva to be opened on his death. It was not a will, and she only opened it many years later. It was a love letter reflecting his romantic side. But it also revealed the type of final thoughts that would be associated with someone unafraid to confront their own mortality and very concerned about how his lover should carry on with his blessings after his death. Eva read this letter at the 2004 memorial meeting for Stieg and it is referenced in John-Henri Holmberg's biography of Larsson in this book.

- After Larsson sold the novels to Norstedts in 2004 for what is reportedly the biggest advance ever paid to a first-time Swedish crime novelist, there was apparently a lot of discussion both between Stieg and Eva and between Stieg and Norstedts about financial planning. Stieg and Eva often discussed the house they were going to build with the money (which Eva, the architect, was designing as a "writer's cottage"), the causes they intended to support, and the need for a will. Eva explained to the *Daily Mail* in a 2010 interview, "The publisher, it was decided, would also draw up a will to decide what would happen to Stieg's estate in the event of his death." In retrospect, one can see many reasons why the publisher might prefer to deal with the business-and-money-oriented Joakim, versus the moral-principle-oriented Eva, but apparently no will was ever drawn up. Dying intestate in Sweden, as opposed to most other Western countries, means the blood relatives inherit everything; the common-law spouse or cohabiting person gets nothing and can't even make a case for why they should get something.

Inheritance and wills are referred to multiple times in Larsson's books, so it seems odd that Stieg would fail to understand that Sweden's Special Act of Cohabitation did not provide for Eva to be his heir if he did not specify that desire in a formal will. Are the repeated references to the rights of inheritance in the novels just coincidental? Or are they another intriguing set of premonitions? Consider these specific, detailed discussions of inheritance law:

- In *Tattoo,* a mere forty-three pages into what will eventually be fifteen hundred pages of the Millennium trilogy, when Larsson is first beginning to sketch out the vast scope of his plot, he already wants us to know that Blomkvist, a man of almost no luxuries in life, *inherited* a summer cabin by the water. The cabin is said to be in Sandhamn, a resort haven in the finest area of "the archipelago," the watery spray of thousands of islands not far from Stockholm where affluent Swedes like to sail and spend summer holidays. (This is the cabin where Blomkvist frequently goes to write and think, but also where he has been known to take women he gets serious about, including Erika and Lisbeth.)

- Having hacked into every bit of personal information about Blomkvist available online, Lisbeth explains to Henrik Vanger's representative Frode that Blomkvist's uncle bought the Sandhamn cabin (otherwise unaffordable today) back in the 1940s when normal mortals could still afford such things. Larsson is at pains to tell us very early in the story that what little Blomkvist family property exists has been divided amicably between Mikael and his sister, Annika. Mikael got their uncle's cabin in Sandhamn; Annika got their parents' apartment in Lilla Essingen. It is an amazing detail of a fictional character's biography to focus on at the opening of the story. Hanging over this detail is the real-life specter of the bitter feud between the Larssons and Eva Gabrielsson that continues to play out in the Swedish tabloids almost seven years after Stieg's death and even as I write this.

- The politics of family inheritance is central to the plot of *Tattoo.* Both at the beginning of the book and at the end, we learn how the Vanger family dynasty is ruled by the laws of inheritance. Larsson gives us a short course on several centuries of family history, laying stress on one particular problem: how female heirs' ownership was really in name only. It was decided at a certain point that shares in the Vanger family company had to stay in the family. While female heirs were entitled to receive shares, male relatives lobbied and manipulated the women in order to aggregate voting power and control the direction of the company. We are even treated to this bit of dialogue:

> "Do you know anything about the old inheritance laws?" Vanger asks Blomkvist.
>
> "No," answers Blomkvist.
>
> "I'm confused about it too," says Vanger.
>
> Then, after listening to Henrik recount the story of the last century of the Vanger family history, share ownership, and control of the business, Blomkvist concludes, "It sounds medieval."

Knowing nothing about inheritance law? Being confused about inheritance law? Thinking inheritance law, and the absurd outcomes it dictates, sound "medieval"? This could be Stieg Larsson contemplating the results of his own unwillingness to write a will and specify Eva Gabrielsson as his heir. The real-life outcome—that Eva has no rights because she and Stieg were not formally married—is "medieval" indeed. In the end of *Tattoo,* the aggrieved, abused Harriet and other family members will experience something of a fairy tale ending. Henrik is happy that Harriet will become CEO, and that she has put together a substantial voting bloc of company stock, having inherited her mother's and her brother's shares. No such luck—yet—for Eva Gabrielsson.

- Each book in the Millennium trilogy manages to focus at some point in the narrative on inheritance. In *Fire,* we are told about the death of Lisbeth's mother whose meager estate includes the apartment on Lundagatan where Lisbeth grew up. Lisbeth will basically give the apartment to Miriam Wu after Lisbeth moves to Fiskargatan, precipitating a whole stream of plot points.

- We also get to enjoy a wonderfully humorous digression when Lisbeth recruits a money manager in Gibraltar for her millions, and the instructions she gives Jeremy MacMillan about how she wants her money managed. While not technically an inheritance (since she basically cyber-siphoned the money out of Wennerström's account), the story treats her relationship to this vast fortune as if she had inherited it.

- In *Hornet's Nest,* wills, estates, and inheritance are discussed in *eight* separate places. Annika has a very specific discussion with Lisbeth about her father, the criminal Zalachenko, who has died. His estate goes by law to his daughters. Lisbeth doesn't need the money from her dead father and doesn't want it. She tells Annika: "I don't want any inheritance from my father. Do whatever the hell you want with it." But Giannini is so dedicated both to her client and to moral principle, she won't let Lisbeth make a hasty choice. She tells her in effect: Go through the proper procedure, take control of the assets, and then decide what you want to do with it. Annika is very concerned to make sure Lisbeth divides the estate equally with her sister Camilla, even though no one knows where to find Camilla. In other words, Annika insists Lisbeth take responsibility and action to protect her absent sister's rights, even though Lisbeth doesn't want to be bothered with the inheritance and it doesn't mean anything to her. Arguably, Joakim and Erland's behavior toward Eva has been exactly the opposite.

Joakim Larsson has been overtly dismissive of Eva and has gone on the counterattack to defend his behavior and his father's. At one point in 2010, Joakim told an interviewer, "We don't think she [Eva] is qualified to manage the rights to the books. Eva won't talk to us because we won't do exactly as she wants. We have become the enemy. . . ." His words echo Annika Giannini's counsel to Salander concerning her "brother" Blomkvist: "I don't want to get involved in a big drama between you and my brother. If you have a problem with him, you'll have to work it out. But for the record, he's not your enemy." It is as though this feuding were right out of the fourth volume of the Millennium trilogy, which it very well could be.

Missing Laptops, Missing Books

In one of the most incredible ironies/premonitions of *Hornet's Nest*, a missing laptop and an unpublished book become important to the fictional plot, just as today we continue to live with the mystery of where Stieg Larsson's laptop is and who, if anyone, will finish and publish the fourth novel said to have had its first 160–200 pages left on the laptop. In *Hornet's Nest*, Larsson creates a plot that includes the murder of Dag Svensson, an investigative journalist, and his girlfriend, Mia Johansson. They are murdered by those seeking to quash publication of Dag's forthcoming exposé on the sex-trafficking business, which is going to lead inextricably to the fact that Zalachenko and Niedermann are now deeply involved with that business, and that Zalachenko has been protected by a secret cabal in the government.

Blomkvist, in his role as Dag's editor at *Millennium,* takes on the responsibility of insuring the book will be published, despite this heinous attempt to silence Dag and Mia. He also makes sure he gets a hold of Dag's all-important laptop that has the critical research documents and notes for the book on it. The whole story of the dead writer, the laptop, and the unfinished book provides more eerie and uncanny parallels to the events of Larssons's life and death. Of special note:

- While it is "Dag's book" on the laptop, Mia, his girlfriend with whom he lives, is well known to have contributed substantively to it. Mia was researching the sex traffic for an academic thesis she was writing. Her interviews with girls and women sold in to Baltic prostitution rings provide the starting point for the book Dag is writing, just as Eva's research on subjects as diverse as architecture and unfair trade practices in Swedish companies figure prominently in Larsson's books.

- Unlike the way the real-life story plays out, Blomkvist visits Svensson's next of kin to insure their permission to publish the book posthumously while informing them they will receive royalties. Blomkvist is exceedingly respectful of the family and making sure the best outcome is obtained for everyone—and that the book is published.

- Blomkvist has no problem finishing the work that Dag and Mia had started. Indeed, he sees it as his obligation to their memory, just as Eva Gabrielsson has proposed finishing the fourth book in Stieg's memory. "In light of what has happened, the book will have to be extensively reworked," Blomkvist declares at one point. Eva Gabrielsson might make the same comment today about Stieg's fourth novel.

Unfortunately the smooth executive functioning of Blomkvist, who saves the laptop, finishes the research, puzzles out what it all means, handles everything just right, and not only publishes the book in the end but solves the murders, is nowhere to be seen in the clumsy handling of Larsson's own affairs in real life. While the case is easy to make that Erland and Joakim have not treated Eva Gabrielsson properly, the fact is that Stieg Larsson, who experienced all these premonitions about his own death, about unfinished books, and about inheritance battles, took none of the steps he should have taken to prevent this "hornet's nest" of problems from arising.

Gabrielsson claims Stieg's father and brother have not only connived to cut her out of Larsson's financial and intellectual inheritance, but that they are also actively preventing her from exercising what she perceives as her moral right as Larsson's companion, collaborator, researcher, and keeper of his spirit, to complete the fourth book and publish it.

In her own book, Eva Gabrielsson asserts her desire and capability to finish the fourth book and publish it. She says she has been involved in this book from its beginning, telling Larsson fans that Salander will be back, and *revenge* will be a major theme. According to Gabrielsson, Salander "little by little frees herself from her ghosts and her enemies" over the course of the novel. Is this now a premonition about Eva's life, in the way that some of the passages we have reviewed above were premonitions about Stieg's life? And what of this provocative challenge from Eva's French co-writer of her memoir, about Eva's version of the fourth book:

> "All of us loving Millennium . . . can look forward to meeting its heroes again, and the enemies of Lisbeth Salander and Mikael Blomkvist can start trembling. The book's title will be *God's Vengeance*. The enemy is advised that Eva, the salsa dancer beheld by the Eternal, is prepared to finish the work and lead the dance on their graves."

The unsolved riddles of Stieg Larsson's life, death, and aftermath remind me of Fermat's famous notation about his mysterious mathematical theorem, the solution for which became the holy grail of mathematicians for three and a half centuries after Fermat's death. Lisbeth Salander works on solving the enigma of Fermat's Last Theorem in various passages of *Fire*. Ultimately, she does solve it (although genuine experts dismiss Larsson's depiction of her mathematical work and are critical of his explanation of the real-world proof that mathematician Andrew Wiles finally produced in the 1990s). The origins of the mystery of Fermat's theorem lie in his handwritten scribbles in his copy of the *Arithmetica* of Diophantus, where he famously wrote (in Latin) in a passage quoted by Larsson in *Fire*: "I have found the most marvelous solution, but there is not enough room in the margin of this book to write it here."

Think about Blomkvist looking carefully at the 1966 photograph of Harriet Vanger, realizing what no one else had seen no matter how many times they had viewed that picture: that Harriet was staring at something just outside the frame of the photo, and that something caused her to be scared, and possibly to run. No wonder Larsson is fascinated by a 350-year search for the proof to Fermat's theorem, the answer for which lay outside the margin of Fermat's copy of the book. Larsson was interested in people on the margins of society, whether they were neo-Nazis or their immigrant victims, or secret agents in the government, or alienated, troubled young people like Lisbeth.

Larsson also understood how dangerous knowledge could be. I will mention just one more eerie premonition from *Tattoo*. Early in the book, Blomkvist gets the call from Dirch Frode, the lawyer who represents Henrik Vanger.

Frode is tasked with enticing Blomkvist to come to Hedestad, meet Henrik Vanger, and take on Vanger's project to look into Harriet's disappearance. It is Frode, who as family consigliere has previously checked out Blomkvist with Milton Security, where Dragan Armansky has asked Lisbeth Salander to do the background check. Salander, of course, will hack into computer systems and learn everything there is to know about Blomkvist, compiling a dossier that will impress Frode. And this is all prior to Lisbeth actually meeting Mikael.

When Frode places his first call to Blomkvist, Mikael at first thinks Frode might be a crackpot of some type. This triggers a memory on Blomkvist's part of a time when he had listened to a lecture at the ABF hall on the anniversary of the assassination of Prime Minister Olof Palme. (Larsson's own memorial meeting would be held in the very same ABF hall in 2004.) The lecture Blomkvist attends at ABF is said to be a serious analysis of the assassination of Palme, Sweden's equivalent of the JFK assassination in American history. Both in terms of the national tragedy Sweden experienced, as well as the conspiracy theories that have been advanced in the years since the still unsolved 1986 murder, Palme's death eats at Sweden's soul much as JFK's death has troubled America's psyche for fifty years.

At this meeting attended by Blomkvist, many amateur sleuths have shown up with their own theories about who killed Palme. One woman announces, "I know who murdered Olof Palme." When it is suggested that, if she has this information, she should give it to the official investigation committee, she replies, "I can't. It's too dangerous."

In another essay in this volume originally written for *Vanity Fair,* Christopher Hitchens notes that there are numerous speculative theories about who might have wanted to murder Stieg Larsson and that there is at least one blogger "preoccupied with the theory that Prime Minister Palme's uncaught assassin was behind the death of Larsson too."

Like Fermat whose proof couldn't be written in the margins, like the woman who believed she knew who killed Olof Palme but could not say who it was, some of the answers to the riddles of Stieg Larsson's life may be in the books themselves, even if they are "outside the frame" and hard to find. Whether Larsson's death was a tragic irony or ironic tragedy remains shrouded behind an enormous smokescreen that makes it impossible to say what is reality and what is the mirror image. Unlike so many contemporary writers whose talents have been subordinated to the powers of technology and the wonders of the media, Stieg Larsson was extraordinary in creating his own special effects.

Blomkvist believes, as I am sure Larsson believed, that investigative reports, articles, and books can be "a declaration of war." Crusading journalists
wield their power like a "lance," dropping it with the power of a "bomb."
Larsson's photo stands alone on the jacket flap like a beacon, as a constant
reminder of his own absence. What readers can't help but wonder is if, in
these semifantastical versions of his own life, Stieg Larsson was trying to reveal something so potent he had to conceal it in a novel and then disappear
from view?

While Larsson's life remains an enigma, many believe the fourth volume might offer some closure.

"Everybody's talking about the fourth book," Larsson's friend Per Jarl
told Nathaniel Rich, who wrote a piece on Larsson for *Rolling Stone* in 2010.
"Does it exist, what is it about? For me, it's very clear what the fourth book
is. The fourth book started the day he died: It's everything that's happened
afterward, all this fucking mess, all the rumors. . . . The fourth book is happening right now."

LISBETH SALANDER IS THE CURE TO ELIZABETH GILBERT
by Lizzie Skurnick

Lisbeth and Elizabeth, twin sisters in name, both riding high on the best-seller lists. Both forced to deal with "issues," and both needing to deal with the men in their lives. Both cheered on in their struggles by legions of fans. But what are we to make of it when these two women, the fictional Swedish vigilante and the real-life American wanderer, are conjoined atop the best-seller lists and in the movie megaplexes by their immense popularity, despite their completely different temperaments and their diametrically opposed approaches to seeking truth? This is the question pondered by Lizzie Skurnick, teen lit columnist for Jezebel.com, culture critic, and the author of ten teen books.

When a genuine cultural phenomenon emerges for the most part through word of mouth, the boom can be bewildering to those of us who aren't immediately swept up. My first adult experience of this, aside from the rush toward Brazilians, was *Eat, Pray, Love,* the story of a journalist and newly minted divorcee who ditches New York to rediscover her appetite for, well, everything.

Its ubiquity rendered it compulsory. It was unavoidable on public transport. People led with it at parties. Sometimes, someone would put a hand on my arm, as if about to utter a caring bit of insight. No. "Have you read *Eat, Pray, Love?*"

Finally, a friend pressed it into my hands just before I boarded a train for three hours. I felt mildly assaulted by Elizabeth Gilbert's rhapsodic flights of self-examination, but not particularly worse for the wear. Who was I to talk? I was off for three months of prefunded gadding about myself. Arranging gadding about can be kind of a pain. Perhaps that's why millions of people with jobs and families preferred the vicarious rewards of someone else's semiedited, insight-rich journey.

A version of this essay originally appeared on Jezebel.com (Gawker Media) and has been adapted by the author. Used with permission.

But how to explain the equal—if not greater—global reach of Lisbeth Salander, Gilbert's polar opposite?

Like with *EPL*, I first turned to the *The Girl with the Dragon Tattoo* and Millennium series through assignment. I'd been sent it seventeen times, and it had struck me as the kind of frothy mystery I generally had completely no time to read. I was thinking it was a charming urban mystery, à la *Westing Game* meets *Basil E. Frankweiler*. I was thinking screwball. I was thinking mystical. I think—forgive me, associative '80s brain—I was kind of thinking *The Golden Child*.

Well. Stieg Larsson! Shut my mouth.

There are many things I am prepared for the American reading public to enjoy, but here are a few I am not. Graphic anal rape with butt plug. Unironic disquisitions on journalistic ethics, or the principles of mathematics. Police meetings in which cops respond to assertions with statements like, "Sounds reasonable to me." Lines like, "At that instant he began to loathe Lisbeth Salander with an intensity that blazed like red-hot steel." Swedish family trees. Sweden. Lots of purchasing of IKEA goods and lattes. (I know we like these things IRL, but as things that are supposed to provide narrative *momentum*.) Sweden. So much Sweden! People with Swedish names! In civilized Swedish threesomes.

But I was beginning to understand that Larsson's trilogy, for the faithful, is sort of the literary equivalent of the IKEA meatball: lumpy, congealed, yet addictively, improbably delicious. But our interest in Salander?

Alternately enthused and agonized, Elizabeth Gilbert's appeal is straightforward. She's the frazzled seeker who makes good, now softly emanating inner peace onscreen in the person of Julia Roberts, America's sweetheart. She importunes the citizens of the world to provide her with life's meaning—and, improbably, it is granted.

Sullen and socially allergic, Salander is on a quest as well—to escape from herself. She has no need for self-reflection—she's been told through social agencies exactly who she is through her entire adolescent life. She's pathologically avoidant of intimacy and scoffs at love. Secretly accessing secret lives of friends and enemies through the comfort of a remote server, she knows everything—except what lies in her—ach!—hard drive of a heart.

If you have so much as glanced through a copy of *Bitch* magazine, it is pretty easy to rattle off Salander's less-than-kosher characteristics. In a recent piece on Tiger Beatdown titled "The Girl with the Lots of Creepy Disturbing Torture That Pissed Me Off: On Stieg Larsson," one writer called the skinny, childlike Salander "masturbation fodder for dudes who want to pretend they aren't sleazy," then continues: "Boy, is that a new one in the universe. The super hot damaged skinny white chick with a bunch of tattoos who kicks ass."

Yes, it is, but Salander is not by any definition a "skinny white chick with a bunch of tattoos who kicks ass." As a character, she's far more in the tradition of Monk, or Asimov's Wendell Urth, a genius whose superdeductive powers, whose analytic strengths, are counterbalanced by a hefty dose of emotional idiocy. To be frank, she's creepy. Sure, it's nice that a ninety-pound girl can taser the balls of two bikers, but one hopes she'll be able to carve out some space between lunacy and genius. (And re: Steig. We must remember the poor author begins every chapter with a variation of, "Every day, men do something horrible to a number of women in Sweden, if not the world, and *a pox upon them*," and that he titled his own book *Men Who Hate Women*.)

But we titled ours *The Girl with the Dragon Tattoo*, and it's the girl's hypervigilant, emotionally unfulfilling life we're consumed with, just as we were consumed with Gilbert's hyper-self-consumed search for emotional fulfillment. Is Salander's hostile, embattled avenger the responsive yin to Gilbert's sunny, drifting yang? Are we avoiding some golden mean of literary womanhood, or is the appeal their clumsy extremes? Should everyone read *Olive Kitteridge* and rethink the whole thing? Because while, in their intensity, the two ladies are irresistible for pilgrims and partisans, for the trend avoidant among us, it seems only that Gilbert might want to ease up on the spiritual plundering, while Salander get some *Eat, Pray, Love*.

But it remains to be seen whether a character who actually could do both would be interesting to anyone at all.

A READER'S ODYSSEY
by MeraLee Goldman

Every reader's story about how they discovered the Stieg Larsson trilogy and how they experienced it as a reader is different. But getting wrapped up in the stories and reading one book right after the next has been a common phenomenon for millions of people. In the review that follows, MeraLee Goldman, former mayor of Beverly Hills, California, and that city's cultural ambassador, tells her personal experience of how she encountered The Girl with the Dragon Tattoo *and the reader's odyssey that followed.*

I was sitting in my doctor's office, awaiting my annual flu shot, and deeply engrossed in reading a very serious book on my Kindle. My doctor came out to greet me, noticed me reading, and said "I've just finished the best novel I've ever read—you must call it up right now on your Kindle—the title is *The Girl with the Dragon Tattoo.*" I replied that I had recently seen that book in the bookstore, and passed it up because I could tell that it really wasn't my kind of book—whereupon he told me that he wasn't going to invite me into his office for my flu shot until I had called it up on my Kindle, and read at least the first chapter.

Well, what's a girl to do? My doctor and I are old friends and I didn't want to offend him—so I called up a "sample," certain that I wasn't going to like it, and began to read. By the time he came back, ten minutes later, I had read enough to be totally involved in the location, the lead characters, and the story, and had already canceled the "sample" and bought the book.

I would find it difficult to say the Millennium trilogy novels were "the best books I've ever read." (For many years, I have reserved that designation for the Alexandria quartet of novels by Lawrence Durrell.) Nevertheless, I became deeply involved in *The Girl with the Dragon Tattoo.* I finished reading it a day later, on a plane from California to New York. I not only liked it a lot, but I wanted a lot more—more of frigid Sweden, more of the very peculiar characters, and perhaps even some partial resolution to the plot threads still hanging loose all around me.

Sitting on the tarmac, waiting to deplane (and quite grateful for the wireless Kindle bookstore, which can deliver a book in under a minute), I bought *The Girl Who Played with Fire* and continued reading book two in the taxi on my way into the city. I was among the fortunate few that didn't have to wait for the third book, as one of my daughters was working on a film in London and brought it to me as a birthday gift only a few days later—well before its U.S. publication. *The Girl Who Kicked the Hornet's Nest* immediately commanded all my free time over that weekend. At the end, I was once again reluctant to be finished with these characters and their world, but now there was no more—or was there? Any possibility would be comforting!

Now that some time has passed, allowing me to think more deeply about the very dense "world" Steig Larsson created, I wondered why these three books were so engrossing, so compelling, and so demanding of my complete attention. What universal element might lay within them, which led so rapidly to such an extraordinary number of devoted readers? After all, the setting is in a distant country where I have spent very little time, the heroine/antihero character is unlike anyone I've ever known or ever will know, and the ongoing plot incorporates a lot of violence and some very questionable legal antics—definitely not the sort of things I usually enjoy reading about. Ah—but those are precisely the reasons these books captivated my attention, and why they have been so popular and so enjoyed by all those readers all over the world. It is the exotic nature of an unfamiliar setting, and the even more bizarre and peculiar nature of the main character and her life. Readers are presented with a window into the soul, the personality, the extraordinarily violent life, and a world that totally envelopes someone totally foreign to the world the rest of us live in.

The rather traditional "locked room mystery" aspect of the first book compels the careful reader to figure out the solution. By then you are eager to learn more about these people and what happens next. I found the second book somewhat disappointing and inconclusive. In retrospect, the second book seems to be merely a short bridge between the intriguingly mysterious aspect of the first book and the real message of the plot underneath it all, which doesn't emerge in full until the third book. It is in the third book that Larsson lets his readers in on the real reason he wrote what I believe is one long book, rather than three connected books. Having worked in a political world for most of my life, his concern with political corruption and deception resonated deeply for me.

As I finished reading the third book, sensing I was at the end of an odyssey, but still reluctant to part with the characters, their lives, and the strange setting, I realized that the compelling element that drew me deeper and deeper into this literary experience was that it is, in essence, about injustice, with only a modicum of redemption. The powerful way this story of injustice is told resonates with what exists in much of the world we live in, if we are, in fact, paying close attention to the real world around us.

9. STIEG LARSSON RE-IMAGINED

THE GIRL WHO PLAYED WITH LARSSON
by Craig Faustus Buck

Why would a working nonfiction writer play craps by putting years into a series of dark mystery novels on spec? If he were trying to temper a midlife crisis, a sports car would be more practical and probably cheaper. Yet here I sit with the dice in my hand. Because of that folly, the editors of this book have asked me to try to extrapolate from my experience and venture some educated guesses about why Stieg Larsson went on his midlife literary bender and what lessons he might have learned along the way.

I toyed with writing a mystery novel in college. It remains unfinished, and deservedly so, but the fiction seed was planted. After graduation I put my literary aspirations aside to pursue freelance journalism but the seed never died, it just went into hibernation.

For thirty-five years I had what many would consider a successful writing career, first in magazines, then nonfiction books, then television drama. But the bug to write a novel is like having malaria. It may go into remission but it never quite leaves your body. I spent most of my life working for overseers—editors, publishers, producers, studio executives, and the like. Over time, this sort of work tends to aggravate the authorial virus. My defenses finally crumbled two years ago and I sat down to write my debut novel, a noir mystery called *Go Down Hard*.

Stieg Larsson followed a similar path, getting hooked on writing fiction in his youth, in his case sci-fi, but then moving on to the more serious work of advocacy journalism. After several decades of this he, too, lost his resistance to the bug. He said he did it for the money, but I suspect he also suffered from what I call gravitas fatigue, a nonfiction writing syndrome that comes from the strain of having to waterproof every fact you assert in your work. The problem was surely exacerbated by the death threats he received from some of his political targets. Larsson must have hungered to write something that could free him from the pressures of righteousness, editorial scrutiny, and fact-checking, a work of fiction unconstrained by anything but his imagination. Succumbing to the same sort of literary relapse that I did, Larsson embarked on his first novel.

The amount of effort and dedication required to complete a publishable novel is like the pain of childbirth: if you'd known what it was going to be like beforehand, you might have reconsidered. It's hard to imagine that Stieg Larsson would have willingly dived into *The Girl with the Dragon Tattoo* if he'd known it was going to consume him for close to three-quarters of a million words. I was ready to collapse after completing the rough draft of *Go Down Hard,* and it came in at only a hundred thousand words, every one of them labored over and carefully selected.

I started my novel with the idea of reworking an old script that had two major characters in a desperate conflict that built to a climactic twist. By the time I'd finished the rough draft of the book, my original antagonist and protagonist had become minor characters, their conflict had been relegated to unexplored backstory, and their shocking conclusion no longer existed. In fact, none of my novel's main characters, locations, or storylines survived from the original screenplay. This all evolved to my surprise. Unlike any other writing I've ever tackled, novel writing proved to be unpredictable, startling, and revelatory.

Writing *Go Down Hard* turned out to be a two-year road trip, but before the end of the first week my characters unbuckled their seatbelts and hijacked the bus. They took control of the wheel and drove me right off the map to destinations I had neither planned nor imagined. The road had more curves than a small intestine so I couldn't see where we were headed. By the time I'd finished the first quarter of the book, I had no idea whodunit anymore. I realized I was just along for the ride.

I'm pretty sure Stieg Larsson experienced much the same thing. Exposé journalism would have done little to prepare him for the capricious independence of fictional characters, especially tortured anti-heros like Lisbeth Salander who, when they grab the wheel, steer straight over cliffs.

Another thing Larsson's political writing didn't prime him for was humor. He cut his teeth on political exposés about right-wing extremists. This sort of writing is, by nature, earnest and cheerless. That was a hard habit to drop when he turned to fiction. Larsson peppered his books with didactic rants and irrelevant tangents with nary a punch line in sight (though I've been told his editors, translators, and publishers saw fit to remove some of his more humorous asides, digressions, and plays on words in Swedish).

Like the bleak themes of the Millennium trilogy, those of *Go Down Hard* were spawned from the power of childhood abuse to distort adult behavior (the topic of the first two nonfiction books I co-authored, *Betrayal of Innocence: Incest and Its Devastation* and *Toxic Parents*). Nothing funny there. But that doesn't mean a character can't try to cope by cracking wise or appreciating the irony. Good noir should be mysterious, dark, and droll. Tension may be the reader's entrée, but you need sides of comic relief to round out the meal.

I learned this lesson writing TV mysteries and dramas. Stieg Larsson never had that opportunity. As a result, although I couldn't put his books down, I often felt as if I were reading a cross between an appliance manual and *Das Kapital*. If the varied reviews and blogs are any indication, I'm not alone in this love-hate relationship with the Millennium trilogy. So why are Larsson's books so wildly popular? Why are his readers so obsessively loyal? Why have so many millions of copies been sold?

I could conjecture about the compelling uniqueness of the victim-turned-avenger Lisbeth Salander, about the allure of a steadfast crusader for justice like Mikael Blomkvist, about the appeal of gripping stories that pit good versus evil, or about the enticement of the cliché-smashing dark side of Scandinavia. But the fact is, no one knows why these books took off as they did and, unfortunately, my experience doesn't help me identify with the scale of Larsson's success. At least not yet (okay, it's unlikely, but can't a guy dream?).

What I can identify with, and respect, is the grueling effort required to write a complex yet consistent fifteen-hundred-page trilogy. Doing so on spec would have made the task doubly harrowing. Enduring this protracted odyssey with an impulsive, headstrong navigator like Lisbeth Salander must have been torturous. Larsson's family and friends think he died of natural causes. Having walked a few feet in his shoes, I'm not so sure.

NOW PLAYING: LISBETH SALANDER, HOLLYWOOD, AND FEMINISM
by Melissa Silverstein

The powerful Swedish film adaptations of the three Millennium novels have won critical and box office success in Europe and the U.S. They are likely to be best remembered for the way Noomi Rapace became Lisbeth Salander personified. The actress seems to have walked right into the novels, grabbed hold of the Lisbeth character, and never let go.

Nevertheless, Hollywood is already bragging that it can do better. Director David Fincher served notice that while he knew it would be sacrilege to some, the script will take a different turn than the book—as will the ending—and "his" Salander (Rooney Mara) will be much more aggressive.

Melissa Silverstein, writer, blogger, marketing consultant, and expert in the area of social media regarding women and Hollywood, previews the new film from a feminist perspective. Silverstein is the founder and editor of Women and Hollywood (blogs.indiewire.com/womenandhollywood) as well as the producer and co-founder of the Athena Film Festival, a celebration of women and leadership.

On December 21, 2011, Sony Pictures Entertainment will release *The Girl with the Dragon Tattoo,* the first of three films based on Stieg Larsson's Millennium trilogy. Two elements of the release signal an exciting moment for Hollywood feminism. First, by conferring a Christmas release on the film, Sony is saying this is an important picture, and one they see as having significant commercial appeal. The team assembled to make the film—director David Fincher, writer Steven Zaillian, and producer Scott Rudin—has an impressive awards pedigree, suggesting this film could also be an awards contender. Second, the fact that Sony Pictures announced the film as the first in a "three-picture adaptation" means they believe in the franchise, are in this for the long haul, and are going to invest significant amounts of money to make these pictures a success. Sony chief Amy Pascal—who incidentally is the only woman running a major studio—said in an interview with *The Wrap* last summer that the films are a "big tentpole franchise" and that she wants to get all three of them out as quickly as possible.

When a studio chief calls a movie like *The Girl with the Dragon Tattoo* a "big tentpole franchise," it's a moment of celebration for anyone who spends her time watching how Hollywood treats women. Franchises are pretty much reserved for guys. Most of the franchises of late are based on comic book characters or video games targeted at men and boys. The Millennium trilogy franchise is interesting to watch because it is a franchise led by a female and, yes, feminist character—a rare feat in Hollywood today. The only other films that come to mind that are led by women include the Angelina Jolie *Lara Croft: Tomb Raider* films, the *Sex and the City* films, and the *Twilight* saga. Whether or not any of them would qualify as a feminist franchise is a debate for another day.

For those movie fans who have been enthralled by the Stieg Larsson books, a Hollywood adaptation might seem like a no-brainer. But not so for this film, and not just because the lead is a woman. She is a woman unlike any Hollywood has seen before. She kicks ass (literally), barely speaks, barely smiles, is rude, has a ton of tattoos and piercings, and is a socially introverted bisexual hacker. To say that she is outside the typical Hollywood female role would be a grand understatement.

And the fact that she *is* so "un-Hollywood" is something that worries Lisbeth's large fan base. People are musing about what Hollywood will do to the story as well as to Lisbeth. Will it be toned down? Will she be less of a badass? Will she be less of a feminist? Will she be made more palatable to bring in men who might otherwise see her as too strong a female character for their tastes? Though none of these questions will be answered until the film opens in December, they're worth considering.

A couple of clues about Hollywood's take on Lisbeth have emerged. One clue we have is from Amy Pascal of Sony herself in the interview with *The Wrap* about preserving the authenticity of the story. She stated: "We're doing the books . . . we're going to really do this, in all their glory. Otherwise why do it? They're very R-rated movies. It's the shock of what's really going on underneath the surface of society. If you don't actually make good on that, you haven't told the story."

Another clue is the casting of Rooney Mara as Lisbeth. Mara, before this year, was a virtual unknown, and now she is the star of one of the most highly anticipated films of 2011. Her biggest part to date was as one of the only women of note in the film *The Social Network,* which also happens to be directed by her *Dragon Tattoo* director David Fincher. In the first scene of that film, she hits it out of the park in a brutal evisceration of and breakup with her boyfriend, Facebook founder Mark Zuckerberg (played by Jesse Eisenberg). If Mara can channel that anger and amp it up a few thousand notches then she could be a great Lisbeth. Other positive news is that early stills from the set, and a recent spread in *W* magazine, show Mara as Lisbeth with piercings, ripped leggings, and wearing heavy-duty, thigh-high, tie-up boots made for kicking ass.

One challenge facing Mara and the American version of the film is Swedish actress Noomi Rapace's iconic portrayal of Lisbeth in the European Millennium films. Rapace, who previously spent most of her career working in Europe, has become the new "it girl" here in Hollywood. Let's not lose the irony in this. A woman who is known in the U.S. for playing a role in Swedish films based on Swedish books (albeit incredibly successful Swedish books) has become the toast of the town. Hollywood was so enthralled by her performance, as well as the character, that she was able to secure meetings with high-profile directors and win a part in the *Sherlock Holmes* sequel alongside Robert Downey, Jr. In an interview given while promoting *The Girl Who Kicked the Hornet's Nest,* Rapace revealed that people are often surprised that she is so different from her character. She said, "it surprises me over and over when people say, 'Oh, you are not like her at all.' No, it was a role." It's kind of funny that not only does the character of Lisbeth defy expectations, but the woman who played her also shatters other stereotypes of how a woman who plays a strong character on screen should look and be off camera.

Another remarkable thing to note is that all three Swedish films were released in a single calendar year in the U.S. The Harry Potter films have been with us for over a decade, and the *Twilight* saga will probably end up lasting about five years. But since the Millennium trilogy films had already been released in Europe to huge success—according to boxofficemojo.com, the three films have grossed overseas a total of $188 million—the decision was made to release the full trilogy in the U.S. in 2010 as the obsession with the books and Lisbeth was cresting.

The fascination with Lisbeth crosses genders, which is one reason why the film can be a commercial success. Specifically, though, the character has become a kind of women's obsession, especially for feminists who either reject or embrace her. Many people, myself included, believe that Lisbeth is a feminist character (interestingly created by a man, clearly sprinkled with a little fairy dust by his partner of over thirty years, Eva Gabrielsson, as she revealed in her recent interviews). Lisbeth is like an avenging angel for all women who have been wronged by society. How can a feminist not fall in love with a guy who has the guts to create a character that has been so screwed by the system yet retains the strength to come back and get revenge on the people who have done her wrong? On the other side of the argument are others who are adamant that a man could never have created Lisbeth and her story because they are both too feminist. Still others also believe that Lisbeth is a victim, and they are very angry and disturbed by the violence depicted against women—particularly in the first novel and film (titled *Men Who Hate Women* in their native Sweden). True, the violence is disturbing and hard to watch. But it doesn't mean that it isn't feminist.

The debate about Lisbeth, the book, the films, and their relationship to feminism is one of the most exciting things about the upcoming film. 2010 might go down as the year when America—both men and women—became obsessed with books with a new feminist icon, but 2011 could go down as the year when Hollywood somehow releases a feminist film that becomes a big mainstream hit. Bring it on.

NOOMI VERSUS ROONEY: THE RUMBLE IN THE CELLULOID JUNGLE
by Paul Berger

The challenge: who will best portray Lisbeth Salander on-screen, one of the great female characters in fiction? She, the affectless, horny, cyberpunk hacker (Nathaniel Rich, Rolling Stone). Someone dangerous as hell in spite of her waiflike appearance (Stephen King, USA Today). A feminist version of Dirty Harry (Jenny McPhee, Bookslut.com). A brilliant twenty-four-year-old computer hacker with the social skills of a feral cat; a mix of Pippi Longstocking, Buffy the Vampire Slayer, and Bill Gates (Deirdre Donahue, USA Today). Someone with a photographic memory, a violent temper, and some serious intimacy issues (Alex Berenson, The New York Times). And, a merciless dark angel of twenty-first-century kick-ass feminism (Andrew O'Hehir, Salon.com).

The venue: somewhere between Stieg Larsson's imagination, a far-less-than utopian Sweden, and a punked-out Hollywood fantasy. The contestants: a proven champion, Noomi Rapace, versus a little-known upstart, Rooney Mara. The stakes: tens of millions of dollars, potential Oscar glory, a decade-long film franchise, or a forgettable remake. The judges? Millions of Stieg Larsson fans.

Paul Berger, freelance journalist and frequent contributor to Burstein and de Keijzer's Secrets series, weighs in with a ringside preview.

The Danish director Niels Arden Oplev usually agonizes over the casting for his movies, but he admits that it took longer than usual, literally months, to find his Lisbeth Salander. Oplev's main concern about Noomi Rapace, the actress who eventually landed the role, was that she was too good looking. Delicate, with soft skin and fine cheekbones, Rapace did indeed seem an odd choice for the brooding, almost boyish, Salander, who spends large parts of Stieg Larsson's epic tale meting out, or on the receiving end, of brutal acts of physical and sexual violence. But anyone who has seen Oplev's film, *The Girl with the Dragon Tattoo*, or its sequels, knows that Rapace is the reason why the movies are almost as successful as Larsson's books. Hollywood's remake of *The*

Girl with the Dragon Tattoo, directed by David Fincher and starring Rooney Mara and Daniel Craig, faces all the obstacles that confronted Oplev, plus one more: to many of Larsson's fans Rapace *is* Salander.

Book-to-movie adaptations are a tricky business. Though fans of Stieg Larsson's three novels may find fault with the Swedish movies (stripped of some telling details and subplots and with a relatively weak supporting cast), few would disagree that they are faithful to Larsson's dark and urgent storytelling. Ably shot and competently acted, the three Scandinavian films were a runaway success for their genre, grossing some $211 million worldwide. Each dominated European theaters when first released. Their U.S. box office showing was a relatively modest $23 million—still an impressive sum given that they are foreign films with English subtitles. Hollywood stands to earn vastly more for its David Fincher remake, but can Rooney Mara even begin to match the impact of Rapace's performance?

Rapace is not your typical Swede. Her father is a Spanish flamenco singer and her mother, who appeared in the Scandinavian "Tattoo" film as Lisbeth's mother, Agneta, is a Swedish actress. At the age of five, Rapace's mother took her to Iceland with her stepfather, where the would-be actress developed into a punk and a rebel as a teen. That rebellious streak, Rapace told *Charlie Rose,* is something that she felt she had in common with Salander. "She doesn't feel pity for herself," said Rapace. "She always finds a way to stand up and to decide what she wants to do and what kind of life she wants to live . . . she never gives up."

Some have accused the films of hatred toward women—what Mariella Frostrup, writing in *Harper's Bazaar,* described as "Larsson's misogynistic fantasies." But Rapace sees Salander as a strong female role model. "I think that most women in the world have been longing for somebody like her," she told Charlie Rose, "somebody who . . . doesn't take any shit." Audiences agree; they root for the comeuppance, feeling empowered by the pixie hacker who refuses to play victim. No one, not even Niedermann, the nasty blond giant who literally feels no pain, scares her. Violent revenge may not be moral, but the audience feels it's deserved.

Apart from Larsson, few people have spent as much time inhabiting Salander's mind as Rapace. The actress may have a soft face, but in interviews she quickly assumes an intensity that suggests the Salander that lurks within. For her role in the movie, she refused a conventional audition. Instead, she turned up for her meeting with Oplev dressed in men's clothing. She told the director that she wanted to own the part: to do her own stunts, train as a kickboxer, get a motorcycle license, and have Salander's piercings.

Over the following seven months, the already svelte, five-foot-two actress went on a strict diet, cutting out bread, potatoes, candy, and alcohol. She lost twelve pounds and trained five days a week with a Serbian kickboxer. "I wanted to get rid of my female softness," she told *The Telegraph*. "I wanted to be more like a boy in my body." Rapace cut her hair, had her eyebrow pierced and a bull ring inserted through her nose, and worked on channeling her inner aggression. "I think that everybody in a way has some kind of animal inside and it's sometimes good to let it out," she told National Public Radio. Rapace went on to shoot all three films in the space of one year. At a champagne party to celebrate the end of filming, she kept having to run to the bathroom to be sick. "It was like my body was throwing Lisbeth out of me," she revealed in an interview on *The Girl with the Dragon Tattoo* DVD.

The physical and emotional sacrifices clearly paid off. "Watching Rapace burrow deep inside Lisbeth's damaged mind, body and soul is its own sort of twisted pleasure," wrote *LA Times* critic Betsy Sharkey. *The New Yorker*'s Joan Acocella noted that Rapace's eyes alone communicate "something like a five-act tragedy."

Held against such a benchmark performance, can Rooney Mara measure up? She certainly wants to be judged on her own terms. "I don't categorize our version as a remake," she said upon landing the role. "I don't plan on 'borrowing' anything. I plan on giving my own interpretation of the character." Like Rapace, Mara embarked on a punishing regimen to prepare for her portrayal of Salander. She took motorcycle and kickboxing lessons and even outpierced her forerunner by having not just her eyebrow and nose, but also her lip and nipple pierced.

Here Comes Hollywood

Film critic Roger Ebert of the *Chicago Sun-Times* was on point when he said that while the plot is important, "These films are really about personality, dialogue and the possibility that the state has placed itself outside the law. That leads to an oppressive, doom-laden atmosphere that the characters move through with apprehension."

David Fincher, the director chosen for the American Sony production, is widely acknowledged as an expert when it comes to oppressive, doom-laden atmospheres. Three of his best movies, *Se7en*, *Fight Club,* and *Zodiac,* revolve around murky central characters who are at once repulsive and magnetic, part hero, part villain. If audiences think the Swedish movies are bleak, wait until they get the Fincher treatment. Fincher has let it be known, via an interview with the hip fashion magazine *W,* that his Salander is more aggressive than the one already in the public consciousness. "They wanted me to do *Zodiac* because *Se7en* was successful and both are about serial killers," Fincher told the magazine. "Now they offer me *Girl with the Dragon Tattoo*. They think, no one does perv quite like this guy."

But "perv" would be doing a disservice to Larsson's creation. The sexual violence in his novels is meant to repel, not titillate; the retribution is meant as a moral lesson, not just a revenge fantasy. And while the Swedish movies hew to the plot, *W* also reported that screenwriter Steve Zaillian will offer a script that deviates from the book with an ending that, in journalist Lynn Hirschberg's report on her conversation with Fincher, "has been completely changed. . . . It's been made more interesting." But it is Salander who drives these films forward. So, ultimately, the success of the movies will stand or fall on Fincher's choice for the lead role.

Oplev's choice was an actress experienced on stage and screen. Noomi Rapace had already garnered acclaim for her award-winning portrayal of a troubled teen mother in the 2007 Danish film *Daisy Diamond*. Rooney Mara, on the other hand, is an unknown quantity who earlier starred in a forgettable remake of *A Nightmare on Elm Street*. But Mara caught Fincher's eye, and had a short and memorable role in the early part of the Fincher-directed 2010 box office hit *The Social Network*. Good as she was as Mark Zuckerberg's girlfriend in that film, it is still difficult to extrapolate from there to the complexity of Lisbeth Salander. Fincher is brilliant and Mara talented, so all we can say for sure is the answer is yet to be revealed.

The two women's upbringings are markedly different as well. Rapace's teens and twenties, a good part of them living in Iceland, were marked by rebellion. "When I was fourteen, I had piercings, I dyed my hair blonde," Rapace told *The Telegraph*. "I looked terrible. I just wanted to get drunk every day." She left home at fifteen, married early, and had a son. She has hinted in interviews that she drew on dark times in her past for inspiration. Mara, on the other hand, is a single, twenty-five-year-old scion of two football families, the Rooneys (majority owners of the Pittsburgh Steelers) and the Maras (her father Timothy is the vice president of player evaluation at the New York Giants). She recently moved out of an apartment that she shared with her sister.

Rapace walked boldly into her audition, already inhabiting the role. Mara was more cautious, telling *W* magazine: "Before I read the book, I didn't think I could do it. I locked myself in a room for a week and read all three books, and decided I really wanted to be Lisbeth. But I thought I had no shot at it."

Rapace fought openly with Oplev on the set over what Lisbeth would do or say. When actor Peter Andersson, who played Lisbeth's despicable legal guardian, Bjurman, held back during a rape scene, Rapace screamed at Andersson: "Damn it, just hit me!" according to *The Los Angeles Times*. "Noomi," Oplev noted, "is the kind of actor who would rather get punched for real."

Early indications are that Fincher will be the director with a capital "D" and has already stamped his imprint on Larsson's creation. His Salander is, by turns, sexier and more androgynous than the Swedish version, "a mash-up of 70's cyberpunk and spooky Eighties goth with a dash of S&M temptress," said *W* magazine.

Posters for the Oplev movie in the U.S. and Europe depict a punk-dressed Rapace, with an intense face that also reveals complexity. Prerelease rumors for the U.S. version have Fincher pushing for a naked image of Mara on the promotional materials; *W* carried an image of Mara wearing nothing but a headband from her waist up, with her arms crossed over her breasts.

It is now Mara's turn to put her stamp on the character of Salander. Can she be as painfully, frustratingly closed-off from the outside world as her Swedish counterpart? And at the same time show the kind of tenderness and emotional growth that Larsson has also embedded in his masterful creation (think Salander's kindness toward her former guardian and her mother, and her willingness to begin to open up to Blomkvist)?

Mara will have to dig deep to come up with just the right mix of sexy, punk, dark, and unforgiving when she enters the ring—yet demonstrate that Salander also has a vulnerable side.

Larsson's fans won't take their Lisbeth any other way.

"NO ONE ASKED *HIM* HOW HE FELT ABOUT BEING RAPED ON CAMERA"
an interview with Katarina Wennstam

Katarina Wennstam is a journalist, author, and feminist who has focused much of her work on raising social awareness of violence against women. Through television, nonfiction, and now crime fiction, she is among the most interesting voices in Sweden calling attention to the issue, which she says should be looked at primarily as a broad social problem, rather than a chiefly criminal one.

Wennstam started her career in 1997 as a crime reporter at a local news station in Stockholm, and then moved to the national network SVT and joined Rapport *(Report), the most watched news show in Sweden. She reported on crime stories and trials, gradually focusing on stories of men's violence against women, including rape, gang rapes, and date rapes. She also covered the 2003 assassination of the greatly admired Swedish foreign minister, Anna Lindh, whom she talks about below.*

In 2001 Wennstam took some time off from television to write her first book, The Girl and the Guilt, *which deals with society's perception of rape victims. Her second nonfiction work,* A Real Rapist, *features interviews with convicted rapists. She has picked up these themes and developed them further in her crime fiction, which we discuss with her in chapter 6.*

Sweden is ranked among the top countries in the world when it comes to the quality of life for women. Yet crimes by men against women keep grabbing the headlines and pervading current crime fiction. Why the discrepancy?

It is true that for the last fifty years Sweden has been one of the best countries in the world for a woman to give birth, get married, get a divorce, get an education, and find work. But that doesn't change the fact that we still have more than four thousand reported rapes per year in a country with a relatively small population of 9 million. Denmark, which has about 60 percent of Sweden's population, only has around seven hundred reported rapes per year—about 18 percent of Sweden's reported rape cases. It is likely that Sweden's high numbers are due in part to the fact that 70 to 80 percent of rapes are reported here, but it's still a dark number. [With eighty-nine thousand cases of forcible rape reported in the U.S. in 2009, American statistics on rape are only about two-thirds of Sweden's on a per capita basis, but the FBI estimates that only 40 percent of the cases are reported as opposed to Sweden's much higher percentage—ed.]

There are also cases where women are killed simply for being a woman. The most famous example is Anna Lindh, the very popular Social Democratic politician who served as Minister for Foreign Affairs from 1998 until her assassination in 2003. I really miss her as a role model. She would likely have become the first female prime minister of Sweden. It is my opinion that she was killed not for political or personal reasons but by a man whose only known motive was that he hated women and singled her out as an example because she was so visible while campaigning for the Swedish referendum on the question of joining the European Monetary Union, which followed a few days later.

Further, I think the security police were naïve in ignoring the fact that in addition to her being as powerful a political figure as she was, her being a woman was in and of itself a threat against her life and security.

You have said that acts like these are not just criminal ones, but social ones.
One of the hardest things for people to realize is that men who are violent against women are not lonely islands in the big ocean of society. My opinion is that every man who is violent against a woman implicitly asks, "Can I do this?" The problem is that society often says "yes." After all, "she's drunk," or "she's dressing too provocatively," or "she's acting like a whore," or "she got pregnant," or "she couldn't get pregnant," or dozens of other irrational rationalizations for attacking a woman.

From my ten years of crime reporting, I developed a saying: society has the crimes that it deserves, but the people who are victims of those crimes never deserve it. If a man beats his wife nearly to death, he carries the sole responsibility. He is the one who is choosing to not seek help. He's the one who's responsible for not being able to end the discussion in words and using fists instead. But if people know what is going on in that relationship and don't act on it, he's implicitly getting permission from society. He's living in a society that says a woman's life is not worth as much as a man's.

Lisbeth Salander certainly redressed that imbalance in *The Girl with the Dragon Tattoo* when she took revenge on Nils Bjurman after he had raped her. The scene was so graphic that some feminists believed Larsson crossed the line into voyeurism. What do you think?

When you write realistically about rape, as Larsson did, most people reading the text will recognize it as a terrible thing. But I think you must always know that some people who read those passages don't react like the rest of us—they might get a kick out of it. Should you not tell the story explicitly because of those people? No. You have to find the right balance. Larsson found that balance in my opinion.

What about the way the rape was portrayed in the Swedish film version of *The Girl with the Dragon Tattoo*?

When I went to see the film the audience almost cheered when Salander rapes and mutilates her guardian, Bjurman, because they hated Bjurman so much for raping her. I can understand why they would. Still, it left me with quite a peculiar feeling because I don't really believe in that sort of revenge. Would you say hooray if someone went out and really did what Lisbeth Salander is doing, even in revenge? No. Everyone would just put her in jail.

There is a deeper issue here. One of the first questions the press asked Noomi Rapace, who played Lisbeth Salander, was, "How are you going to do the rape scene?" No one asked that question of Peter Anderson, the man who played Nils Bjurman. No one asked this male actor, "How do you feel? Do you think it was terrible to do that? Did it destroy your sex life?" Those are all questions that have been asked of Rapace, even though I think that the scene where Bjurman is raped by Salander is actually much more explicit than the rape of Salander by Bjurman.

You have written about how rape is portrayed in well-known films. What's your conclusion?

Once you start looking at rape scenes in movies it's like, "Oh my god," because so many movies have them in it, especially American ones. If you take, for example, Charlize Theron in *Monster* or Hilary Swank in *Boys Don't Cry,* who are screaming because they are being raped, then you can show their breasts or their near-naked bodies in a way that you would never see in a movie that is not X-rated. If she is screaming out of lust, you can't show it. But if she's being raped, you can show it.

That provides filmmakers an incentive to show rape. And there are quite

a few women stars who were never acknowledged as truly talented until they
had done a rape scene. It's the film world's rite of passage: you have to be
raped on camera to become known as a great actor.

**Speaking of a double standard, tell us about the big scandal sur-
rounding the case of Göran Lindberg, the police commander, that
came to light in 2010 and sounds like a story right out of the pages of
a Stieg Larsson novel.**
Lindberg was in the top ten of Swedish policemen. He was head of the Police
Academy in Stockholm and then police chief in Uppsala, our fourth biggest
city. He was known all over Sweden for promoting female police officers and
for the awareness campaigns and training programs he ran on gender equality and sexual harassment within police departments and among violent
offenders. After he retired, but while he still had an office at the Police Academy, they found out that he was a serial rapist and committed girls to prostitution. Apparently he kept the tools of his perversions right there in his
office in the academy. When my feminist friends and I read about it, our
reaction was, "This is what Larsson's talking about in his novels."

You had some personal experience relating to Lindberg. . . .
I am often asked to give talks to police departments and groups in prison
about violence against women. In late 2010 one of the teachers, who had
been working on the investigation of Lindberg, turned to me after a lesson
and said, "Do you want to see his old room?"

So we walked into the office where he had been planning all these crimes,
the very room where he had been writing to the girls, sending them text mes-
sages, and maybe even meeting them; he had locks all over the doors. The
creepy part came when the teacher asked me, "Do you know what books we
found over here on the shelf? Your books, *The Girl and the Guilt* and *The Real
Rapist,* with a lot of underlining and dog-eared pages." I was stunned, and I
wondered which way he might have read them. Did he read them as a teaching tool? Or did he read them thinking, "I would like to try that with some
of my girls"? It was a very strange feeling.

It sounds like the plot of a novel.
You can never make up a criminal like Göran Lindberg. Lindberg had a big
pile of Post-It notes with names of young girls—fourteen, fifteen, sixteen,
seventeen-year-old girls—that he e-mailed, met, and bought sex from. Some
of them he almost killed trying to strangle them or sitting on their faces. If

I created a character like him in a novel—an outwardly profeminist police official who secretly rapes and tortures young girls in his office—people would go, "Oh, come on, really? That's a little bit over the top." But there you have him in real life.

Is a feminist consciousness making any progress toward the mainstream in Sweden? It sounds as if there's still a long way to go.
Feminism is moving forward. Even women who were on the forefront of the fight for women's rights in the 1960s remark on the difference between then and now. Back then the focus was directed to our sexuality and economic independence. Now we can move on the other issues, among the primary ones being men's violence against women. Plus, although feminism has traditionally been a women's issue here as well as in America, today we have men who are engaged in the debates and raising their voices. It's often two steps forward and one back, but the overall trend is still positive.

What do you see as the steps backward? And forward?
There's a whole group of young women in Sweden today who are heavily influenced, almost victimized, by the music video industry and the pornography industry, which teach them that their looks, behavior, and self-worth should be measured against what a man or boy thinks of them.

On the other hand there is what I call "generation Grynet." Grynet is the central character on the most popular kid's show on Swedish National Television for the past ten years. Her mantra is, "Don't take any shit from others." You own your sexuality. You own your brain. My daughter is a big fan of the show. So was Noomi Rapace, I think. When Rapace told an interviewer, "Lisbeth Salander wouldn't take any shit," those words could have come directly out of Grynet's mouth.

Of course these two trends are often mixed up with each other, but the point is that there is now a whole group of young girls who are feminists, who know their rights. If someone puts a hand up between their legs in school, they go directly to the principal and say, "Do you know what this guy did?" And she has about five or ten girlfriends behind her saying, "Well, we don't accept this." So you have all these girls who are much more feministic than I was when I was a teenager in the '80s. They are strong, well educated, and know their rights.

But there's a long way to go.

LISBETH SALANDER BROUGHT TO LIFE ON STAGE
by John-Henri Holmberg

The first stage production of a Stieg Larsson novel had its premier at the Nørrebro Theater in Copenhagen, Denmark, in December 2010. Using the Danish version of Stieg's original title for his novel, *Mænd der hader kvinder* (*Men Who Hate Women*), the play is based on *The Girl with the Dragon Tattoo* and written by Vivian Nielsen. Throughout the writing, production, and rehearsal process, Eva Gabrielsson, Stieg Larsson's lifetime companion, worked closely with director Kim Bjarke.

The play was produced as a series of tableaux, connected by the monologues of a character known as "The Woman." This character was created to comment on and give perspective to what happens on stage, but the audience gradually learns that she is also one of the characters in the story.

The play was a complex production, involving forty-seven set changes accomplished by means of a turning stage. Much of the novel's intricate plot was simplified or excluded in order to focus sharply on the essential contrast between consensual and nondemanding sex on the one hand and forced sex as a manifestation of power on the other. "We are focusing on oppression and rape," director Kim Bjarke said.

On stage, the story is not about solving the disappearance of Harriet Vanger. It is about women robbed of their childhood, who are, in the end, strong enough to come into their own as liberated individuals. It is also about seeking and obtaining revenge. More abstractly, it is a play about a society falling apart, where rules of behavior have been dissolved and replaced by an abuse of power symbolized by men's violence against women.

Danish reviewers lavished praise on the production, which may travel to London and elsewhere in the future.

THE MYSTERY OF THE FOURTH BOOK
by John-Henri Holmberg

Among the questions constantly asked since the success of the three Millennium novels is: Where is the fourth novel? And will there ever be more to read about Lisbeth Salander and Mikael Blomkvist? Speculations about a fourth novel, perhaps even a fifth, have been fueled both by a number of statements made by Stieg Larsson himself and by later comments from the principals involved in the tragic aftermath to his death. But what unpublished material actually exists? And what would the next book(s) have been about?

The Manuscript

Stieg Larsson was interviewed about his novels only a single time, on October 27, 2004, exactly two weeks before his death. The only journalist to interview him about the Millennium novels was Lasse Winkler, editor in chief of *Svensk Bokhandel,* the journal of the Swedish publishing industry. In it, Stieg was asked why he kept writing his novels without submitting more than the first one to a single publisher. He replied, "I wrote them for fun. I didn't write them with the conviction that they would be published. And things don't really all come together until you get to the third book. Now the foundation is in place. And I can go on to write as many books as I like about these characters." Then he added: "My original synopsis was for five books."

Lasse Winkler asked if it's true that a fourth novel in the series is almost finished.

"Yes," Stieg replied, "I'm a fast writer and crime novels are easy to do. It's much harder to write a 1,000 word article, where everything has to be 100 percent correct." According to Winkler, Stieg said that, "at least 150 pages of the fourth book exist."

In e-mails, however, Stieg Larsson told others that much more than 150 pages had been written. His last e-mail to his brother Joakim Larsson, written on October 20, 2004, and published in January 2011, states: "Three novels are finished and handed in [to the publisher], and the fourth one almost finished."

In July 2004, Stieg e-mailed me: "Strangely enough, I'm currently simultaneously writing the third, fourth, and fifth [novels], and right now the
fifth feels most entertaining; I've completed around 100 pages of the ending
of that book and have 300 to go."

And in the last e-mail I received from Stieg, written on October 15, 2004,
he was considerably more explicit: "I am 320 pages into Salander 4 and hope
to be finished in December." He goes on to note that "according to my synopsis, it should end up as 440 pages," a statement which is significant in that it
at least explicitly claims that Stieg had developed fairly detailed synopses for
the novel(s) he intended to follow the first three in the Millennium series. But
if he did, no one so far has admitted to having seen this material. In the same
e-mail, he further told me that he had rearranged the order of the books: "this
one was actually meant to be Salander 5, but [was] much more fun to write,
so I've changed the beginning a bit to make it fit to the ending of the third."

While all of these different statements suggest that a good deal of additional material for future novels had been written by Stieg Larsson prior to his
death, they don't reconcile with each other as to the exact amount actually
completed. On October 15, Stieg wrote me that he had written some 320
pages, including the ending, of his fourth novel. On October 20, he told Joakim that the fourth book will be "finished soon." But on October 27, he says
to Lasse Winkler that "at least 150 pages" of the fourth book exist.

What to believe? Stieg may, of course, have been overstating the amount
of finished text in his October e-mail to me. But back in July he had already told me he had written around 100 pages of the ending of the book,
and in October he is quite explicit about which parts of the book have been
done, and about both how long it was supposed to be and what remained to
be written. What he tells Joakim five days later does not contradict what he
wrote me. The contradiction occurs in the Lasse Winkler interview, a week
after his e-mail to me. But here Stieg knew that he was speaking for publication, and it is quite possible that he wanted to give himself more leeway.
Things were happening fast enough as it was. As evident from Norstedts's
e-mail correspondence with Stieg referenced in *On Stieg Larsson,* the companion volume issued in the U.S. as part of the 2010 boxed set of the Millennium trilogy published by Knopf, Stieg's Swedish publisher wanted him to
spend more time on the editing of the three finished books. Perhaps Stieg
simply didn't want his publisher to learn that instead of concentrating on the
edits to the earlier novels, he was writing the next one.

The mystery of the fourth and future books has been enhanced by con-
flicting statements made after Stieg's death. Stieg's father, Erland Larsson,

says that immediately after Stieg's death, in Eva Gabrielsson and Stieg's apartment, he held the manuscript for the fourth novel in his hands. "It was the two-thirds of it then existing," Erland Larsson says. "It was a printout, but it disappeared."

The other principal who talked of the fourth novel is Stieg's partner, Eva Gabrielsson, who in her book *Millennium, Stieg and Me* writes that the day after Stieg's death, Eva's sister took his satchel to the *Expo* office. The bag contained his calendar with his meetings and other commitments, notes made for the next issue of *Expo,* and a laptop computer. Eva Gabrielsson writes that the computer belonged to *Expo,* and contained Stieg's writings, correspondence, research, sources, and so on. For more than six months it stayed in the *Expo* office, unused since no one had its access code. Eva Gabrielsson writes: "The fourth part of Millennium is probably in that computer. When we went off on vacation that summer, Stieg had written around 160 pages. . . . He probably didn't have time to write more than around 50 more pages before his death. Thus, the manuscript is maybe somewhat over 200 pages."

As to further volumes in the Millennium series, the situation is even more unclear. In the e-mail to me quoted above, Stieg said that he was writing the fourth and fifth novels simultaneously while also finalizing the third. He further indicated he had become more interested in the fifth book, and therefore switched things around and made it the fourth. This could reasonably mean that what existed of the initial fourth book was now set aside for the fifth. He also made reference to a synopsis, calling for the fourth novel to be 440 pages. In an earlier e-mail to me, he had mentioned that he now had "an outline for ten novels" in the Millennium series, reasonably meaning seven more books in addition to the three published. And in Lasse Winkler's interview, Stieg says that his "original synopsis was for five books," but that he now feels he can go on to write as many as he likes.

In diametrical contrast, however, Eva Gabrielsson states in her book that apart from what she estimates as "maybe somewhat over 200 pages" of the fourth novel, "there are no further texts." In interviews, she has also said that, "there is the beginning of a book. People don't seem to understand that it's a fragment. It's something between a sketchbook and a manuscript," and that there are no synopses or outlines for further books in the series. But she has also stated that she has not read what does exist of the fourth novel, nor looked at or had access to the laptop computer Stieg used.

What is certain, then, is that Stieg had started the fourth novel and that he had written a minimum of "somewhat over 200 pages" of it. According to what Stieg wrote and said during the last weeks of his life, he may have written almost twice that much, including the ending, and there may also be a plan for the complete novel. If all of what he said in his e-mails is assumed to be true, there may also be outlines for further novels and possibly even some first-draft text meant to be used for what would have become the fifth Millennium novel.

The Story

Do we know anything about Stieg's ideas for his intended further novels? Yes, a little, from two sources.

We do know where he intended to place the action. In an e-mail to me on October 16, 2004, he wrote in detail about a remote Canadian location: "The plot is set 120 kilometers north of Sachs Harbour, on Banks Island in the month of September." He did not go into any details about the actual story, but he did add a few amusing facts, typical of his passion for this kind of minutiae, almost regardless of what it happened to be about: "Did you know by the way that 134 people live in Sachs Harbour, whose only contact with the outside world is a postal plane twice a week when weather permits?"

He went on to catalogue the number of musk-ox (48,000), wild flowers (80), and polar bears (1,500) and the most common means of transport ("a mini-tractor with giant wheels (in the summer) and a snow scooter in the winter") and inform me that they closed the school "when the temperature drops below minus 40 Centigrade." He ended with a typical Stieg-ism: "This just in case you happen to feel a sudden need of an all-round education."

That tells us the setting, which is exotic enough. Banks Island, at twenty-seven thousand square miles, is Canada's fifth and the world's twenty-fourth largest island. It is part of Canada's Northwest Territories and situated in the Canadian Arctic Archipelago. (Since Stieg wrote his e-mail in 2004, however, the island's population has grown—by two people.)

Some clues to the actual story come from Eva Gabrielsson. She says that "Lisbeth [Salander] gradually frees herself from both her demons and her enemies." Each time she has managed to extract her revenge on someone who has hurt her, physically or mentally, she will remove one of her tattoos that represents that particular hurt. "Tattoos are a kind of war paint to Lisbeth Salander."

Eva Gabrielsson adds that for Lisbeth, "the large city is her jungle. She acts instinctively, like an animal, and is quick to interpret situations and avoid dangers. One of her T-shirts bears the warning, 'I am also an alien.'" She adds one final provocative teaser: the title of the fourth novel, if ever published, will be *God's Vengeance*.

Much more than this, Eva Gabrielsson is not willing to say at this time. She has said that she is willing to finish and publish the fourth Millennium novel, provided Stieg Larsson's heirs (his father Erland Larsson and brother Joakim Larsson) sign over to her the right to hold in trust and manage Stieg's literary legacy.

Can anything more be surmised about what Stieg intended to happen in the plots and character development of future stories? Given the deletion of Lisbeth's tattoos, as revealed by Eva Gabrielsson, there are both questions and surmises possible. In the first three novels, we are told that Lisbeth has nine tattoos. Among these, we learn the details of several of them, including: the huge dragon on her back (if we account for the correct translation into English of the Swedish original text—see my commentary on this subject in chapter 2), a wasp on her neck, one loop around an ankle and another around her left biceps, a Chinese sign on her hip, and a rose on her calf. We also learn that at the age of twelve, when she was put into the psychiatric "care" of Dr. Teleborian, she did not yet have any of these tattoos. Consequently between the age of fourteen (approximately), when she got out of the hospital, and age twenty-four, when we first meet her in *The Girl with the Dragon Tattoo*, she has acquired her nine tattoos.

By the end of the Millennium trilogy, she has already erased one of them, the wasp on her neck. If we assume that the act of removing a tattoo is a symbol of having laid one of her ghosts to rest, the wasp tattoo should reasonably have symbolized the deceitfulness of Bjurman, the lawyer who refused her access to her money unless she paid for it in sex, on whom she revenges herself and who is then killed. Careful readers of the Millennium books will perhaps feel suspicious of this, as they'll remember that Lisbeth removes the wasp tattoo during her stay in Genoa in *The Girl Who Played with Fire*, and that the reason given in the book for this was that she felt it made her too conspicuous. My guess, however, would be that the notion of having Salander view her tattoos as symbols of her tormentors occurred to Stieg after the three first novels were finished. An afterthought of this kind would in no way be particularly unusual for a writer working on a multinovel series, and when he got down to explaining the symbolism of the tattoos, he would have convinced us in retrospect that the wasp was not only conspicuous, but also a symbol of Bjurman and so had served a dual purpose.

At least one of her other tattoos probably symbolizes the vast pain of her childhood, when her father, Alexander Zalachenko, abused and almost murdered her mother. In *The Girl Who Kicked the Hornet's Nest,* Zalachenko is killed, his death at least indirectly a consequence of Lisbeth's actions. She has taken vengeance on him, and another tattoo will most probably be removed.

Seven remain—perfect for a ten-novel series needing a further seven books. Working further along the same line of reasoning, one of the tattoos would almost certainly represent Lisbeth's deprivation and abuse at the hands of psychiatrist Peter Teleborian. While it is true that Teleborian is disgraced at the end of Lisbeth's trial in the third novel, to the point of almost certainly being deprived of his license to practice, and that he will be charged with possession of child pornography, it is not clear that he will truly be brought to justice, since Swedish laws would probably deliver him to prison for one or two years at the most. Is this vengeance enough for Lisbeth Salander's suffering at his hands? Or will she meet him again, this time for a final duel?

A possible clue to some of the other villains Lisbeth will meet is given by her father, Zalachenko, who, in his encounter with Lisbeth toward the end of *The Girl Who Played with Fire,* informs her that she has in fact "at least" seven more siblings (presumably most or all of them half-siblings) in addition to her full sister, Camilla, and her half-brother, Niedermann, the blond giant who attempts to kill and bury her at the end of the book. Like Niedermann, her siblings are said by Zalachenko to be engaged in various aspects of the international crime syndicate he has built. It is difficult to believe that in mentioning these siblings or half-siblings briefly in the second novel, Stieg did not intend for her to meet with them at some point in her future adventures.

Characters, Relationships, Settings

As to the personal and romantic relationships in the novels, the published three books at least settle some possible questions and hint at other developments. Will Lisbeth Salander and Mikael Blomkvist ever become a couple? No, they will not. Salander's development in the three published novels, on the psychological level, form a series of arcs from dependence to independence; mentally (from the beginning when we are told that she has been diagnosed as suffering from Asperger's syndrome to the final book where the diagnosis is removed and she is declared fully competent); economically (she has to ask permission even to use her own money in the first book, but by the end of the trilogy she is wealthy beyond most people's dreams); socially (she develops from virtually without social contacts to being able to cope much better with them); and emotionally (she goes from refusing any emotional attachments, to fixating on Blomkvist, to finally coming to terms with her fixation and freeing herself from it, which means that she will again be able to treat him as a friend, and perhaps even occasional lover).

Central to this process of character development is the idea that Salander achieves independence and self-sufficiency. And in accordance with Stieg Larsson's elsewhere discussed theme of nondemanding and noncontrolling sexual relations, this is what she is now able fully to achieve. When coming fully into her own, Salander has no further need to feel dependent on Blomkvist, and so she is able to treat him as a trusted friend without needing either to be jealous of his other friends and lovers, or to avoid him in order to confirm her self-sufficiency.

Salander, interpreted in this way, is actually a fascinating character, to my knowledge unique in Swedish literature: a woman who not only refuses to be a victim but who also refuses to accept any of the other traditional roles ascribed to female characters. She is not nurturing, not weak, not sentimental, not preoccupied with her emotions, not longing for a male, a steady relationship, children, or domesticity. What she is instead is a fully functioning, active, and self-sufficient individual, ready to choose her own goals and live on her own terms, neither subservient to nor dominating others, but ready to take her revenge on those who wrong her. She is, I suspect, Stieg's idealized human being—regardless of gender.

Another question is, will Mikael Blomkvist and Monica Figuerola become a couple? Yes, probably, to the extent that their shared view of intimate relationships as, again, noncontrolling and nondemanding allows it. Monica Figuerola is introduced in the last of the three published novels, and she is clearly built up to be an important character. She matches Blomkvist and almost Salander in intelligence, self-sufficiency, bravery, and fierceness. Nobody should be surprised if she was slated to appear repeatedly in later novels—or even if at some point she happened to end up in bed with Lisbeth Salander instead of Mikael Blomkvist.

As for settings, most of the action in the first three novels takes place in Stockholm and almost entirely in Sweden, with the exceptions of Lisbeth's excursions to Genoa, Grenada, Gibraltar, and some pleasure travel around the world. Stieg Larsson loved travel, geography, exotic locations, and historical and cultural minutiae, so we can surmise he would have incorporated many other locations—and indeed, we have already seen the specific references that point to Canada as critical to the fourth novel. Stieg had traveled the Siberian railway, was fascinated by Africa, and was very familiar with many cities and places in Europe. Add to this that the economic success of his first three novels would have made it possible for him to go anywhere and experience almost anything, and it becomes a virtual certainty that later novels would have been rich in international settings. But they would have been chosen with care and imagination, as was the case with Banks Island, which few people are likely to have ever heard of. My guess is that Stieg would have much preferred to place his characters in exotic, little known, and therefore intriguing locations rather than just having them visit well-known places. Everyone has been to London; if he wanted to place a story in Britain, he would have thought it much more fun to have Lisbeth face down an adversary in Llandrindod Wells.

However, granted that Stieg would have loved to surprise and delight his readers with intriguing and unusual international settings, he would also have adhered to the logic of his novels and their main characters. While Lisbeth has been set free to be a wandering spirit, going off wherever she likes on the spur of the moment, Mikael Blomkvist does have a magazine to run and will continue to do so. *Millennium,* to Blomkvist, is not a day job or a necessary obligation, but a passion. Whatever the number of novels Stieg might have written, Mikael Blomkvist would have remained based in *Millennium*'s editorial offices, which (unless an anonymous donation from a bank in Gibraltar makes it possible for the magazine to go international, pull up stakes, and move to London or New York) will almost certainly remain in Stockholm. And so, at least as far as one of their continuing protagonists would be concerned, any further Millennium novels would also have had at least one foot firmly planted in Sweden.

PART THREE

HOW STIG BECAME STIEG: AN INTIMATE PORTRAIT

I cannot think of another modern writer who so successfully turns his politics away from a preachy manifesto and into a dynamic narrative device.
—Nick Cohen, *The Guardian* (U.K.)

It's easy to feel these days that the bad are never punished, so high is the quota of stupidity or malignity in the world. In a simple, old-fashioned way, Larson's reporter hero, Mikael Blomkvist, pursues the wicked with the energy of a Tintin. But a combination of Larsson's storytelling genius and his own strongly held leftish views has enabled him to outdo Herge. Where the chilly Belgian cartoonist, protestations notwithstanding, wrote boys' comic books, Larsson has created a wholly believable fantasy book for adults which also expresses a coherent view of how the world, if we so wanted, might be.
—Nick Fraser, *The Independent* (U.K.)

Salander doesn't particularly like to be around people. But she is no sociopath. The primary diagnostic feature of sociopathy is callousness—lack of feeling—toward others. Lisbeth falls in love with Mikael. She bring gifts—cake and perfume—to her mother, who is in a home for the mentally impaired. She operates outside society but not outside morality.
—Joan Acocella, *The New Yorker*

Lisbeth Salander [is] a pierced and tattooed street urchin with the body of Patti Smith and the brain of Stephen Hawking.
—Billy Frolick, *The Huffington Post*

10. "I ARRIVED IN STOCKHOLM WITH A COLD AUTUMN WIND, A BOTTLE OF WINE IN MY BAG, AND MY GLASSES MISTED BY RAIN."

THE STIEG LARSSON STORY
by John-Henri Holmberg

Hundreds of newspaper and magazine articles have been written about Stieg Larsson since his death in 2004. Several TV reports and documentaries have aired, and multiple biographies and guidebooks to his novels have been published. We can assure you, however, that nothing you have read before about the life, times, ideas, influences, writings, relationships, commitments, beliefs, and passions of Stieg Larsson have the combined power of authenticity and objectivity that John-Henri Holmberg brings to the following three-part biography of Larsson.

Holmberg knew Larsson as a friend for more than three decades since they first met when Larsson was only seventeen years old. They shared a passion for science fiction, as well as for big ideas and political debates. They usually disagreed about the specifics of their politics—Larsson gravitated toward Maoism and then Trotskyism in his early years; Holmberg, having read Ayn Rand in his early teens, became one of the first Swedish libertarians. But they shared a passion for individual freedom, personal morality, and personal responsibility that would prove more lasting than some of their early political engagements. Holmberg also knew Eva Gabrielsson since shortly after Stieg and she came together in the beginning years of what would prove to be a life partnership. Holmberg's path would take him into editing, translating, publishing, and reviewing crime novels for leading Swedish newspapers. These would prove to be useful skills both for advising and supporting his friend when Stieg turned to writing the Millennium trilogy in the 2002–4 period, as well as for understanding and appreciating the immensity of Larsson's creative accomplishments and his intellectual legacy after Larsson's death.

To assemble this biography for our readers, Holmberg interviewed many of Larsson's friends from all periods of his life and went deep into his own voluminous archives of vintage fanzines from the 1970s, as well as correspondence and e-mail over many years with Larsson. He also mined the vast piles of media articles that have appeared in the Swedish press to better understand fact and fiction concerning everything that has happened since Larsson's death.

From their first meeting in 1972 to their last dinner together in the summer of 2004 at John-Henri Holmberg's home, these two friends shared a great deal intellectually, many good times, and some of life's twists and turns. Here, Holmberg brings his friend to life for those of us who did not know him, while informing us of key details in Stieg Larsson's life experiences that allow readers to better understand the Millennium novels.

—Dan Burstein & Arne de Keijzer

Part I: Living at Home

Let me tell you about the Stieg Larsson I knew, who was many things—funny, bright, principled, unafraid, hungry for knowledge, a steadfast friend and unforgiving enemy, more than anything else consistent. He held strong opinions and convictions, all based on the fundamentals of his character. So perhaps before we talk about the things he believed in we should talk about what he *was*. Many who knew us both were surprised by our friendship, since the things we believed in might seem diametrically opposed—he a revolutionary communist, I an individualist libertarian. Yet I suspect that our friendship grew out of fundamental similarities, and that our political views reflected a similar vision of human liberty.

It's Stieg's story I'll try to tell. But my views will influence how I interpret him. So I will tell you a little of my own background, then some about Stieg's, and how I imagine his experiences may have given him an outlook similar to mine.

Individualism

Boys become socialized early, settling into hierarchical patterns when they start running with other boys. They learn to compete for position and to accept the results of this competition. Perhaps this is an inherited trait in males; perhaps you learn it when playing with other boys. If inherited, perhaps it's a gene Stieg and I both lacked. If learned, perhaps neither of us learned it: Stieg grew up in a very small community, with only a single other child his own age, and I spent too much time from age three to eleven sick in bed. Instead, both of us learned to entertain ourselves, to feel content when alone, even to need being along to feel whole. It also made us into voracious readers.

People like Stieg and I became what others call individualists or sometimes loners—persons who do not rely primarily on others for their sustenance or self-respect, and feel no need to embrace the opinions of their peers or of any authorities.

Individualism at an early age is both a blessing and a curse. It can provide strength, but inevitably it makes you an outsider when you find yourself among people who neither share your interests nor respect your integrity. While living in the home of his maternal grandparents, Stieg learned to make his own choices and live on his own terms even as a very young boy. It seems a reasonable guess that in many ways, he was treated as an adult. He started drinking coffee. He began staying up late reading or, later, writing.

When later he moved in with his parents, he spoke a dialect difficult to understand in their home town of Umeå. In Jan-Erik Pettersson's book about Stieg, his father Erland says of his son in that earlier period, "He lived pretty freely up in Bjursele, up there I guess he did pretty much whatever he felt like. So I guess the rules we had here were a bit more strict." How to interpret that word, *strict*? Two facts should be noted. One is that to my knowledge Stieg never said a bad word about either of his parents, Erland and Vivianne Larsson, and was deeply affected when his mother died. The other is that he quickly freed himself from many of the rules imposed on him when he came to live with them shortly before turning nine. Stieg's individualism was evident early on.

Feminism

Fairly early in life, boys and girls begin seeking primarily the companionship of others of their own sex. Later on, most men and women continue to lead partly separate lives, having close friends of their own sex, behaving differently to others depending on their gender. From this, I suspect, springs the view that it's impossible for men and women ever fully to understand each other.

I grew up ill, without playmates. My father worked days and in his spare time pursued a lifelong interest in sports. In my childhood memories he is a late-night shadow, smelling of fresh air and tobacco, and whispering good night. But my mother was always present, talking, reading, and later discussing things with me. My older half-sister Birthe and her partner Inger were also frequent guests; creative, artistic women of wide interests and as far as I could judge the happiest of all couples in my parents' circle of friends. In practice, my mother was my single real parent; my half-sister and her partner were role models.

Stieg Larsson spent the years from infancy to almost nine with his maternal grandparents, Tekla and Severin Boström. The first couple of years they lived in a village called Ursviken, while Severin Boström worked at the Rönnskär copper mill. In 1957, when Stieg turned three, Severin quit the mill for health reasons and they moved to Bjursele, the village where Tekla Boström had grown up, a cluster of some twenty houses at the edge of a lake. Here Severin Boström supported his family by repairing bicycles, motorbikes, utilities, and farm equipment, doing odd jobs, hunting and fishing. The Boströms bought an old farmhouse on a hill outside the village, surrounded by forest. The farm was called Måggliden—*måg* is an old Swedish word for son-in-law, *lid* means hillock or slope—the Son-in-law's Hillock.

From around three until nearly nine Stieg lived here in a village of less than sixty inhabitants. I mentioned that he had only one playmate his own age. That single friend was a girl. And there was always Tekla, his grandmother, strong, competent, and compassionate.

Is it strange that neither Stieg nor I learned to think ill of women, or consider them a different species?

Science Fiction

A third early influence was his love of science fiction. Today, science fiction is everywhere. This was not always the case, especially in Sweden, where science fiction was long considered both inherently substandard literature and an unhealthy influence on the young. Nor was sf commercially successful: both its speculative nature and its individualistic, romantic, and heroic themes fell outside a Swedish preference for social realism.

In the 1950s, however, a few publishers hoped to create a market for science fiction in Sweden. During that decade a few score novels were published, and two sf magazines were launched, one surviving for a dozen years. Those of us who stumbled upon science fiction then and fell under its thrall soon realized we were in trouble. Classmates shunned us for talking about weird stuff. Adults told us to put childish nonsense aside and grow up. Teachers said that we ought to read real literature about current problems.

Genuine sf enthusiasts were not deterred. Our solution was to seek out other sf readers. Science fiction fandom was born. Soon it became a sanctuary for sf-reading teenagers shunned by their peers with more mundane inclinations. Being a science fiction fan set you apart from others, regardless of age. At least in your own view, you had an open mind; theirs were closed. Knowing they held unfounded prejudices made you less inclined to let their views influence you.

Science fiction also immersed you in the values of the authors you read. Of course, sf authors hold no single political or moral views. But most twentieth-century authors of science fiction share a number of specific ideas. The most important:

- Nothing is permanent; the only certainty is change. Today this may not sound very dramatic. But fifty years ago the majority of people everywhere believed that values, morality, and social structures were inherently true, and would remain basically unchanged.

- We can understand the world, but only by means of our intelligence; reason and science are our only means of comprehending and influencing reality. This is more or less the Enlightenment view, which broke the stranglehold of religion, led to the American and French revolutions, and led to the scientific and technological advances of the last centuries. Even today it challenges many; in science fiction, it was an absolute.

- Tolerance and understanding are primary virtues. Whether other space-faring beings look like giant tarantulas, have eighteen sexes, or are crystalline rather than organic is irrelevant as long as they are sentient, self-aware, and intelligent. With this as a fundamental conviction, the notion that the color of someone's skin, sex, sexual orientation, or beliefs should make even the slightest difference to their humanity is simply ridiculous.

These were views that young sf fans like Stieg and I learned in the 1960s. Can you visualize this young boy living with his mother's parents outside a small village in the far north, a neighbor girl his best friend? He's thin and wears glasses, is a voracious reader and has an active imagination, fueled by the stories he reads. He has learned to think for himself and been influenced by his reading, but also by his family, particularly by his grandfather Severin Boström.

Raised by His Grandparents

Why did Stieg spend the first almost nine years of his life with his maternal grandparents, who were already in their midforties when he was born? Stieg's parents, Erland Larsson and Vivianne Boström, grew up in Skellefteå, one of the larger cities in Västerbotten, Sweden's second most northerly province. They met at an outdoor dance in 1953. Both were seventeen years old and they soon started dating. By the end of the year, Vivianne was pregnant. On August 15, 1954, in the harbor suburb Skelleftehamn, she gave birth to a son who was named Karl Stig-Erland Larsson (Stieg's birth name). The parents lived in a small, noninsulated apartment. Erland began each day by lighting a fire in the old-fashioned masonry heater before leaving for work at Rönnskärsverken, one of Sweden's dirtiest factories—a melting plant producing gold, copper, lead, silver, zinc, selenium, and other metals, and in the process generating by-products like sulfuric acid and sulfur dioxide. A local saying was that a real Rönnskär worker sneezes blood.

Erland Larsson soon decided to quit and move to Stockholm to train as a retail decorator. He and Vivianne sublet a room in a Stockholm suburb where they shared the kitchen and bathroom with their landlord. Stieg stayed with Vivianne's parents.

Stieg's father now says that the idea was that Stieg would stay with the Boströms only until he and Vivianne had found more suitable housing. Whatever the intention, Stieg remained with his maternal grandparents not only while Erland and Vivianne lived in Stockholm and later Uppsala, where Erland was employed as a decorator, but also after they moved to Umeå in 1956. There, in the largest city in Västerbotten, Erland was employed as a decorator by Åhléns Department Store. Vivianne went to work as a clerk in fashion shop.

Erland and Vivianne found an apartment and in 1957 had a second son, Joakim. They now also married. In interviews, Stieg's father has said that he and Vivianne wanted Stieg to live with them, but that Stieg was rooted at his grandparents'. So for five years Stieg stayed in Bjursele while his parents and new brother lived some 75 miles away in Umeå.

During those years, Stieg's grandfather Severin became a role model. In that remote and sparsely populated part of Sweden the weather is severe, with long cold winters and pervasive darkness. The soil is poor. But here you also find rich mines, vast primeval forests, and huge rivers. It is a harsh land, demanding much of its occupants; those who came here worked hard, with little reward for their labor. The miners, loggers, railroaders, fishermen, and hunters were quick to embrace the ideas of the early socialist union agitators; later many became communists. Severin was one of the radicals, a communist of the Stalinist school.

During World War II, particularly after the German attack on the Soviet Union, communists were considered undesirable in the Swedish army. Sweden was officially neutral, but unofficially it bent over backward to accommodate German requests. Throughout the war, millions of Germans traveled on Swedish railroads to Norway, Denmark, and Finland. Sweden supplied the German garrison at Narvik, Norway, sold iron, steel, ball bearings, and other goods to Germany, and censored anti-Nazi and anti-German views—not only in print, but even in public speech. Karl Gerhard, one of Sweden's foremost stage artists, was famously not allowed to perform his anti-Nazi song "The Infamous Trojan Horse" in his 1940 Stockholm cabaret.

Authorities believed that communists in the armed forces might stir up anti-German feelings by committing acts of sabotage and thus threaten Sweden's relations to Germany. Since Sweden had a military draft system, draftees labeled "untrustworthy elements" by the secret police were inducted as "work troops" and placed in guarded internment camps. The first such camp was opened at Storsien in 1939; in all, fourteen such camps operated in Sweden, the last two closing in 1948. Historians believe that some three thousand Swedes were kept in the camps, most of them communists, others active in radical trade unions or so-called pro-English groups, all critical of Swedish policies.

Severin Boström was one of the "untrustworthy elements" incarcerated in the camps. Some unnecessary controversy surrounds Severin's experience with the camps. In interviews Erland Larsson has said, "Certainly he was a communist, you can safely call him a Stalinist. . . . But he was never . . . in any camp." Eva Gabrielsson, on the other hand, states that Severin, after being "interned in the Norbotten concentration camp Storsien . . . found it difficult to be accepted in society." She continued: "It was this that Stieg carried with him: the desire to guard the equal rights of all individuals, to fight for democracy and freedom of speech, to make sure that what happened to his grandfather was never repeated in Sweden."

No one doubts Boström's communist convictions, or that during the war they might well have led to his internment. But Swedish military archives contain no reliable records of those interned in the camps. It is possible, if unlikely, that Severin Boström was never interned but heard accounts of the camps and retold them as his own. Even if that were so, the effect on the young Stieg Larsson would have been the same. Hearing about Sweden's wartime censorship, Nazi-appeasing policies, and internment of dissidents, he learned a lesson he would never forget: that below the veneer of openness, re-spect for individual rights, and uncompromising neutrality, the Swedish es-tablishment was just as likely as any other to sacrifice its citizens to hold on to power. Stieg never forgot that lesson, as he never forgot Severin Boström. A decade after his grandfather's death, Stieg was publishing writings and draw-ings using the pen name Severin both in political magazines and in fanzines.

School Days

In August 1961, Stieg celebrated his seventh birthday and a few days later started school in a village called Pjärsön, a mile or two from Mäggliden. This was the norm; Swedish children start school at seven (indeed, until recently they were generally not allowed to start earlier). The following year, when Stieg was in second grade, Severin Boström died of a sudden heart attack at the age of fifty-six. Stieg continued living with his grandmother Tekla for another year and a half until completing second grade, but by the summer of 1963, shortly before his ninth birthday, he moved in with his parents in the city of Umeå. Grandmother Tekla moved in too for a while, to smooth the transition.

Stieg now attended Hagaskolan, a modern school in central Umeå for preschool through ninth grade. After finishing the obligatory nine years in 1970, Stieg went to a two-year vocational school, graduating in late spring 1972. The idea was for him to start his work life then, as a vocational di-ploma did not qualify him for higher studies.

Before and during the years he spent with his parents and younger brother, Stieg developed many of the interests and habits he would retain for life. He was a science fiction reader, and like most young sf fans he was also fascinated by astronomy, space travel, science, and technology. He made star charts using his own small telescope as well as a more powerful one at school. He had an amazing capacity to absorb facts about a subject that interested him, as for example when he engaged in an extended debate on the pros and cons of nu-clear power with fellow science fiction fan and friend Kjell Rynefors, a profes-sor of physical chemistry in Gothenburg who considered Stieg a worthy opponent.

Stieg was also an avid mystery reader, having been captivated by the juve-nile novel series Tvillingdetektiverna (The Twin Detectives) by Sivar Ahlrud. This immensely popular series featured the twins Klas and Göran from the north of Sweden, and their Stockholm cousin Hubert. While Hubert is the classical nerd hero with an appeal for smart but nonathletic young readers—bespectacled, well-behaved and a straight A student in all subjects except physical education and music—the twins are notorious troublemakers, sure to appeal to every child's wish to rebel. For a science fiction fan, the books also provided an excellent bridge to crime fiction, since several combined science fiction motifs with mystery plots. Early on, Stieg also loved the juvenile mysteries of Enid Blyton. From these early favorites, Stieg's reading habit quickly moved on to adult crime fiction, mixed happily with science fiction.

He loved writing and drawing, and at a very early age began producing his own magazines. Before his tenth birthday, Stieg "published" a magazine written and illustrated by hand and sold or given away to relatives and neighbors. Around this time he also began writing stories, mainly science fiction, and before he was seventeen he had begun and in some cases completed several juvenile novels, all later discarded. Most were typed; Stieg received his first typewriter at twelve and soon got into the habit of writing late into the evenings. This became a problem since he shared a room with his younger brother, so the family rented a small room for Stieg in the basement of the tenement house where they lived.

Thus already at twelve Stieg lived largely by himself, spending evenings in his basement room with his shortwave radio equipment, his books, and his typewriter. As far as is known, none of Stieg's writings from this period survive; many times he described destroying his early writings after happening upon a few stories, rereading them, and shuddering at the thought of anyone else ever laying hands on such painfully bad teenage attempts.

Another of Stieg's interests was DXing—the hobby of tuning in distant radio signals and collecting written verifications from the stations heard, or making two-way contact with other amateurs. Stieg was so fascinated that he joined the Umeå Shortwave Club, which also gave him a chance to write for its mimeographed magazine *Distance*.

Stieg had strong convictions and stood by them. Classmates tell of a boy who went his own ways, but was always around to help when needed. One, unnamed, says, "If someone was bullied, he would try to solve the problem. Never by fighting, but by talking." But at school, he sometimes did get into fights; at least he claimed that his gold tooth was a token of one of them.

Stieg also demanded that his parents countersign his resignation from the official Church of Sweden well before he reached the age of consent, eighteen, when he would be allowed to leave the church without parental permission. They did not share his atheism, and according to his father, Stieg quarreled for hours with his mother about his wish to leave the church. The important thing seems to have been the argument; having won it, Stieg apparently never bothered to hand in his resignation.

Closely related to both his atheism and his respect for reason was his equally strong contempt for all forms of superstition and pseudoscience. He loved Martin Gardner's *Fads and Fallacies in the Name of Science,* a brilliant collection of essays debunking numerous pseudoscientific frauds, including flying saucers, Dianetics, ESP research, astrology, creationism, and flat-earth theories. In one of the book's chapters Gardner declares the pseudoscientific racial theories of such purported scientists as Hans F. K. Günther, Charles Carroll, and Lothrop Stoddard "on a level with" flat-earth theory "but . . . capable of causing infinitely more suffering." Already in his teens, Stieg Larsson knew that racism was an affront not just to morality and human dignity, but to reason, science, and reality.

Activism

Stieg also gradually became politically active. Doubtless he had heard politics being discussed throughout his life. His grandfather had been a pro-Soviet communist; his parents were members of the Social Democratic party and his mother represented the party on the Umeå city council. The Social Democratic party is a nonrevolutionary socialist party based in the trade union movement and was the dominant force in Swedish politics from the early 1930s into the 2000s; they created the modern Swedish welfare state. Either alone or with some minority party support, they continuously held government power from 1932 to 1976 (and have held it for twenty-one of the thirty-four years since).

One effect of this dominance, not obvious to the party's older supporters, was that by the 1960s, young Swedes could hardly view the Social Democrats as a movement for radical reform. For decades already, they had been the establishment.

Stieg Larsson had listened to his grandfather's stories of wartime internment. During the war, legendary Social Democratic leader Per Albin Hansson had been prime minister. Given Severin's opinions and experiences, he would hardly have praised Hansson or his party. And in the mid-1960s, the political issue engaging most young Swedes became the war in Vietnam.

With a huge influx of American forces in 1965, the Vietnam War attracted growing international attention. Vietnam became the first televised war. TV viewers could watch people being bombed, shot, and burned to death. The impact was enormous. During 1965, a number of Swedish political organizations arranged protests against the U.S. war effort, among them the Swedish branch of the World Peace Council, the Swedish Communist Party, and the Social Democratic student organization. These groups demanded a negotiated peace between the two parts of Vietnam, a view reflecting the wishes of the Soviet Union, but contrary to what the Chinese hoped for.

In 1965 a new movement was started in Sweden: the DFFG, or "United FNL Groups." Officially, these were small groups of concerned individuals without political affiliation but united in their support of the National Liberation Front. In reality, they were organized by an anti-Soviet, pro-Maoist splinter group within the Communist Party that was formalized in 1967 as the Marxist-Leninist Communist League. Ideologically, DFFG rejected pacifism as a strategy for third-world conflicts—the position advocated, for example, by the Social Democratic Party in power in Sweden. Pacifism would lead to a continued imperialist presence in former colonies, they argued; only armed victory by revolutionaries could guarantee true sovereignty. Instead of calling for "Peace in Vietnam," as did other protesters, the DFFG demands were "U.S. Out of Vietnam" and "The People of Vietnam on Their Own Terms."

The support of intellectuals with easy media access hastened the growth of the DFFG; by the end of 1967, the organization had more than two hundred local chapters and could muster demonstrations of over ten thousand participants in many cities. At its height, the DFFG reached hundreds of thousands of Swedes, most in their late teens or twenties. But the DFFG was also a classic example of a united front strategy, where revolutionaries join with others in a common cause and try to convert the others to their ideas. The DFFG, true to the strategy, actively used study circles to promote the ideology of its core organizers.

Stieg Larsson began meeting DFFG activists in the streets of Umeå. They were selling their magazine, collecting money for the NLF, organizing rallies and demonstrations, and gathering signatures in support of their demands. On TV, he could watch the war they protested. By early 1969, fifteen-year-old Stieg was a DFFG sympathizer who had begun groping for a political stand. Soon he joined the Umeå DFFG, started wearing the NLF yellow star button, and gradually became more involved in the DFFG.

In Umeå the DFFG was not dominated solely by Maoists, as in most of Sweden, but also heavily influenced by Trotskyites. After World War II, the Swedish Trotskyite movement had officially dissolved, its members joining either the Social Democrats or the communists to work underground, influencing the larger parties from the inside. By the late 1960s, the Trotskyites felt that the time had come to break cover and begin working openly again. In 1969 they formed Revolutionary Marxists and, for a period, Maoists and Trotskyites worked side by side in the DFFG.

1968 and 1969 were dramatic years in Sweden, as elsewhere in the West. Increasing affluence made it possible for many Swedes to travel abroad for the first time, leading to greater awareness of conditions outside the country. Small incidents, like the police breakup of an anti-American demonstration on Hötorget in central Stockholm in June 1965, had gained symbolic importance as proof of the repressive nature of the state. 1968 saw further clashes between demonstrators and establishment. In early May street fighting in the small town of Båstad ended only after demonstrators protesting apartheid managed to force the cancelation of a Davis Cup tennis match between Sweden and Rhodesia. In May radical students occupied Stockholm University's student union building.

The Social Democratic government was accused of collaborating with reactionaries to preserve a nonegalitarian status quo. Within years, radical theater companies, progressive music groups, anti-establishment magazines, radical publishers and bookshops sprang up around the country. Young Swedes of both sexes wore their hair long and sported Palestinian *keffiyeh* as a symbol of their solidarity with third-world peoples. The Soviet invasion of Czechoslovakia in August 1968 further alienated young radicals from Moscow's version of communism, strengthening the Maoist and Trotskyite influence within the protest movements, as demonstrators protested both American and Soviet imperialism.

In many countries May Day is celebrated as a workers' day, partly in memory of the Chicago Haymarket Riot of 1886. In Sweden, the day was declared a public holiday in 1939, and demonstrations are held in virtually every town, the largest organized by the Social Democratic party, often in cooperation with the major trade unions. In 1969, as every year, Stieg Larsson's parents took part in the Umeå Social Democratic demonstration. The Social Democrats ruled the country, and the two most powerful party men were Tage Erlander, prime minister for more than twenty years, and Arne Geijer, secretary general of the Swedish Trade Union Confederation for more than a dozen. The Social Democrats hailed their heroes, but among the revolutionary groups with whom Stieg Larsson was marching that year, one of the most chanted slogans was: "Tage and Geijer, Lackeys of Nixon!"

Meeting Eva

In the fall of 1972, while Stieg Larsson was greeting those arriving at the door to a public DFFG meeting held in a school building in Umeå, he started up a conversation with two sisters who had come to attend their first DFFG meeting. Stieg immediately recruited them as members of his own local group.

He and the older of the two sisters, Eva Gabrielsson, hit it off immediately. They enjoyed each other's company while selling the DFFG magazine *Vietnambulletinen,* putting up posters, collecting contributions, and discussing endlessly. Gradually wanting to deepen their political understanding, the two began going to meetings and seminars arranged by the Maoist cadre within the DFFG. Stieg became committed to the Maoist view, but Eva felt it too simplistic and dictatorial; she chose the Trotskyites. Their political arguments were heated, but gradually Stieg came to share the view that the Maoists lacked a sense of the complexity of political and economic problems. By the fall of 1974, he had broken with the Maoists and gradually came to adopt the Trotskyite viewpoint. Soon he became active in the party and began writing in *Internationalen,* the Trotskyite outreach magazine. Eva Gabrielsson had already left the party by the time she moved from Umeå in 1977; in her opinion, critical thinking was more important than strict adherence to doctrine. But Stieg remained a party member and *Internationalen* contributor for many years.

It is perhaps not difficult to understand the attraction of Trotsky's imaginative, emotional, and visionary utopianism on a young science fiction fan looking for the intellectual tools to make sense of the world. Among those of Trotsky's books published in Sweden in the late '60s was his 1924 classic, *Literature and Revolution,* which ends:

> It is difficult to predict the extent of self-government which the man of the future may reach or the heights to which he may carry his technique. Social construction and psycho-physical self-education will become two aspects of one and the same process. All the arts—literature, drama, painting, music and architecture will lend this process beautiful form. . . . Man will become immeasurably stronger, wiser and subtler; his body will become more harmonized, his movements more rhythmic, his voice more musical. The forms of life will become dynamically dramatic. The average human type will rise to the heights of an Aristotle, a Goethe, or a Marx.

Heady words. Not least for a young science fiction reader, who in Trotsky's words could hear echoes of the visions of mankind's future found in the sf novels of H. G. Wells or British philosopher and author Olaf Stapledon.

Sometime in the late 1960s, another experience further cemented many of Stieg's views. On a camping ground near Umeå, he saw boys of around his own age, some of them his friends, rape a young girl. In Kurdo Baksi's book about his relationship with Stieg, where the story was first revealed, Baksi called it "one of the worst memories Stieg ever told me." Eva Gabrielsson, however, says that she told Baksi about the rape only after Stieg's death. As far as I know, Eva was the only person Stieg ever spoke to about it. In interviews given outside of Sweden in late 2010, Kurdo Baksi has also claimed that the rape victim's name was Lisbeth. No one else, however, seems to have heard of her name, and Baksi has so far never said this publicly in Sweden, nor does he name her in the Swedish edition of his book.

Stieg did nothing, and afterward did not report it. But he broke all contact with the rapists. When he next saw the girl, he asked her forgiveness. She told him that he was no better than the others, and to get lost.

Kurdo Baksi theorizes that this experience was the driving force behind Stieg's feminist convictions as well as his three novels. I doubt it. I believe that respect for women as persons of equal value was a conviction Stieg had long since formed, and that this conviction led to the shame he felt and to his need to ask forgiveness. I also believe that the theme of his novels—men's hatred for women—grew not out of a single experience, but from a lifetime of thinking about and observing the reality and pervasiveness of sexism. Still, he would never have forgotten what he saw, and I have no doubt that Stieg was deeply ashamed of not interfering. The experience may well have made him pledge that in an even remotely similar situation he *would* act, regardless of cost, a commitment that may have helped him to act fearlessly later in life.

In late August 1969, Stieg Larsson began ninth grade. It was his last year of obligatory school. In August 1970, he would be sixteen years old and start vocational school, which would prepare him for life as an adult. But in many ways he was already an adult. He had been uprooted when his grandfather died, leaving the house, village, school, and almost everyone he knew for Umeå to live with parents and a brother he had seldom seen. His views, habits, and interests had been questioned, but he had stood up for them. His refusal to give up his writing, DXing, and late hours had earned him a room of his own, even if it was in the cellar.

In the fall of 1970, at sixteen, he drew the consequences of all this and moved out of his parents' apartment to live on his own. Stieg Larsson was on the threshold of making his own way in the world.

Part II: On His Own: Life in Umeå

In August 1970, Stieg Larsson celebrated his sixteenth birthday. He was still Stig, and he would remain so for another four years. After nine years of primary school he was now in vocational school with a further two years left before getting a job. He moved out of his parents' home and into a one-room apartment in a building diagonally across from theirs on Ersmarksgatan in downtown Umeå.

It was also the year when Stieg joined the Umeå Shortwave Club, abbreviated UKVK. The club, and the hobby of DXing (trying to receive distant radio stations via shortwave), enjoyed its heyday in the 1950s, with around a hundred shortwave clubs in Sweden. Many of them published member magazines, mostly mimeographed or otherwise duplicated in at most a few hundred copies. The Umeå club magazine *Substantial* was published throughout the 1950s but had folded in the early 1960s. In 1968, UKVK started a new club magazine, *Distance*.

Stieg Larsson took to UKVK as a fish takes to water. The radio club not only gave him other shortwave enthusiasts to talk with, but it provided two even more important things: a magazine to write for, and new friends who shared his enthusiasm for science fiction. In particular, Stieg was drawn to Tommy Lindgren, a contributor to *Distance* since its first issues, and Rune Forsgren, a relative newcomer who wrote his first pieces for *Distance* in the February 1970 issue. That issue also had its first contribution by Jacques de Laval, who gives this insider's picture of the club:

> The atmosphere around the club magazine *Distance* was characterized by enthusiasm in those years from 1970 and on. UKVK had a clubroom in the Old Customs Building in Umeå, and a lot of what was written for the magazine was typed there. Many contributed to getting the magazine out and there was a festive feeling to it all.
>
> The magazine was published monthly. When *Distance* appeared on the DXing amateur magazine scene, the most advanced DXing in Sweden was largely performed within a closed and elitist group belonging to the Arctic DX Club, who carefully kept secret the knowledge they had managed to gain. *Distance* broke their monopoly by getting hold of and then publishing what they had learned, doing so in an uppity tone of voice.
>
> What was important was that *Distance* attracted contributors who were primarily interested in writing and in having fun producing a magazine, rather than in DXing in itself. Many pennames were used and many fictitious characters were invented, partly in jest, partly in order to keep secret exactly who had managed to figure out the techniques used by the members of Arctic.

By the mid '70s, *Distance* had more than two hundred readers spread over all of Sweden, with some in Finland, Norway, and Denmark. Issues were up to forty pages. Two- and three-color printing was sometimes attempted. Some of the content was similar to what you generally find in science fiction fanzines. Some of it was not. There were many humorous pieces, for example. Made-up people were presented and written about as if they were real, sometimes over several issues, after which they were used in totally absurd stories. For a while, *Distance* promoted a Woodstock-like music festival to be held in a small village called Botsmark. People interested in attending began to ask for further information and tickets, but of course the whole thing was just made up.

When the heat and smoke made us gasp for air in the Old Customs Building, the editorial staff escaped to some nearby coffee shop. We tried to get there as close as possible to when that day's layer cakes passed their "best-by" sales time, which was in the last hour before closing. By then the counter lady would sometimes sell a cake cheaply, or even give it away, to poor but hungry steady customers like us.

Neither Stieg, Rune Forsgren, nor I were hard-core DXers. We primarily worked on the magazine because we liked doing it and because we enjoyed the fun atmosphere within the editorial group. We all tried to improve our writing and Rune became adept at using the mimeograph machine.

Stieg and Rune belonged to a clique within the UKVK that liked to play minigolf during the summer months. I believe Rune was also one of those who came up with the idea that UKVK should form a volleyball team, which for a few seasons played in the local club circuit. We did volleyball with the same kind of happy enthusiasm we did the magazine. I can't remember us ever winning a game.

Stieg's first contribution to *Distance* was published in the March 1970 issue; after that, he was a steady contributor. He seldom wrote about DXing, instead delivering items such as a short humorous piece about problems at home when a fuse had blown, news about radio astronomy and space exploration, and a spoof horoscope. In issues 8 and 9 he published a substantial report of a ten-day bus trip to the Soviet Union he took with his father that ended in Moscow. While there, Stieg interviewed the head of Radio Moscow's Swedish-language broadcast. He ended his report with a tribute to Lenin, writing that probably no man will ever again mean as much to any country.

Stig Becomes Stieg

Stieg joined other organizations in 1970 as well. One of them was the Umeå NLF group, the local chapter of the countrywide Swedish DFFG, which supported the National Liberation Front in South Vietnam. The first NLF meeting he attended was a large one, to which all members and newcomers had been invited. Stieg later wrote that he felt awkward and nervous. People sat in a large circle, and before the meeting officially began all were asked to stand up and give their names.

As Stieg later told the story, when his turn finally came he rose and said, "Stig Larsson, Inner City Base Group." Then the young man sitting next to him, whom he had never met, rose and in a much softer voice said, "Stig Larsson . . ." as well, and everyone laughed.

This, according to Stieg, was how Stieg Larsson met Stig Larsson, and the potential confusion between the two would make him change the spelling of his name.

According to Stieg, he gradually came to know the other Stig Larsson. The similarities between them didn't end with their both joining the DFFG at the same time, going to the same first group meeting, or sitting next to each other. Both Stig Larssons hoped to write for publication, aiming to begin by selling to the locally published newspapers. Both also worked as visual artists, which they discovered in 1973 when the local city council culture board placed the contributions by the two Stig Larssons almost next to each other in an exhibition, with the result that they were assumed either to be the same person, or to have done each other's work.

By 1974, the other Stig Larsson had begun reviewing movies professionally, and people began either complimenting or disagreeing with Stieg Larsson on his opinions. After our Stieg Larsson published an essay on paperback crime novels in the daily *Västerbottens Folkblad,* the other Stig Larsson received both the compliments and insults. They sometimes received each other's mail, and when Stieg Larsson began receiving threatening claims for overdue library books borrowed by Stig Larsson, he felt the time had come to act.

As Stieg tells the story, he met with Stig and they amicably decided to differentiate their names. In writing, Stieg would add the "e" to his first name. As compensation, he said, they agreed that since the different spelling wouldn't be noticeable in conversation, Stieg would be referred to as "Stig-One," while the other Stig would agree to be called "Stig-Twopointfour." In fanzines published during the first months of 1975, Stieg sometimes spelled his name the old way, sometimes the new. But from the end of spring that year, he was always Stieg. In later years, he told the story often, and with variations, but the basics remained the same.

As for the other Stig Larsson, he in time became a highly regarded Swedish novelist, poet, playwright, and film director. In a recent inininterview, Stig Larsson says that he and Stieg did indeed sometimes receive each other's mail. But Stig Larsson denies they ever met to discuss any kind of name change.

"It seems implausible that I should have forgotten it. It's theoretically possible that it happened, but I don't believe it since I never used to get very drunk," Stig Larsson said, adding that, "another possible reason was that we never belonged to the same groups, including the leftist ones." More than thirty years later, as a major Swedish author, Stig Larsson has read Stieg Larsson's novels and calls them "brilliant." He adds, "He could describe mundane things—as ordinary as making coffee in your kitchen—and still maintain the tension of the story. If you can do that, you're damned good."

Stieg was an entertaining storyteller who liked to improve on the anecdotes he told about himself. At the same time—and this deserves to be stressed—he was a very private man, in a sense even secretive. He talked about his ideas, his reading, funny things happening to him, but very seldom about his feelings, childhood, or relations to others. When reminiscing or recounting anecdotes, his aim was usually to make a point, to entertain or to get a laugh, and he would embroider accordingly. The stories he told in public were mostly amusing but totally innocuous, in the sense that he always kept confidences and never disclosed anything very private about himself or anyone he felt close to. My guess here is that the Stig Larsson version of the name change is likely the factually correct one. But regardless of whether Stieg more or less made up his story, one fact remains: Stieg Larsson was an individualist, and certain enough of himself that he refused to be mistaken for anyone else.

Steig Larsson, At Home in His New World

Sixteen-year-old Stieg Larsson had found a new world in Umeå. He now lived in his own apartment, made new friends who shared his interests, and immersed himself in schoolwork, politics, reading, movies (which had become one of his passions), and writing for the DXing club magazine. Soon he would start writing for another group to which he already belonged without knowing it: science fiction fandom.

He was an intellectual in need of ideas that could help him understand, analyze, and act. He had also grown up with the communist ideas of his

Stieg Discovers Science Fiction Fandom

Via the DX club, Stieg met Rune Forsgren, Tommy Lindgren, and Jacques de Laval. They were all science fiction readers and quickly became inseparable. They talked of books, authors, and movies. Before long Rune Forsgren discovered they were not alone. He had stumbled on the existence not only of other Swedes interested in science fiction, but of the whole world of science fiction fandom, where people formed clubs, arranged conventions, corresponded, and published their own magazines. When a truly enthusiastic science fiction reader discovers fandom, the first step is to send for copies of fanzines. In the fall of 1971, the budding Umeå fans received their first. [For a more detailed look at the impact of science fiction on Larsson as a reader and writer, see Holmberg's analysis in chapter 4.]

In general, 1971 was not a notable year for Swedish fanzine publishing. Only around twenty-five issues of seven ongoing fanzines were published. One of these was *Jules Verne-magasinet,* a 1940s commercial magazine restarted as a fanzine in 1969. It became the link connecting the four lonely Umeå souls with Swedish fandom.

They all soon avidly read *Jules Verne-magasinet,* and Stieg tried contributing to it. This attempt of his eventually led to the "discovery" of two "previously unknown" manuscripts. Many years after he published the last issue of his *Jules Verne-magasinet* in 1971, Bertil Falk, its owner, donated two boxes containing the magazine's editorial archives to the Swedish national library, *Kungliga biblioteket* in Stockholm. When the material was finally processed in June 2010, Stieg Larsson's submissions turned up. Most likely the two very short science fiction stories written by the then-seventeen-year-old had been rejected but never returned. (Another librarian would later discover *published* Stieg Larsson stories in a donation of more than ten thousand fanzines, but the two discoveries were mixed up in the press.)

After Rune Forsgren's discovery of the rest of Swedish fandom, the Umeå fans—particularly Rune and Stieg—quickly became involved in it. They began planning future activities, not least a fanzine of their own, and before school started in the fall of 1971, Rune, Stieg, and Tommy celebrated by taking a ferry trip to Finland. On the boat, sixteen-year-old Stieg for the first time in his life had a drink in a bar.

Strieg's New Spheres

In January 1972, Rune published the first issue of *Sfären* ("The Sphere"), wi' Stieg Larsson and Tommy Lindgren listed as co-editors. The issue had sixt pages of typewritten text plus illustrations. Short stories dominated the maternal grandfather; when trying to find his own political identi[ty], looked to the left, first gravitating to Maoism. But as someone who had [wide-]ranging interests, the closed mind-sets and blind obedience characteris[tic of] many political groups in the end repulsed him. I can't help but suspect [that] one reason for his final choice of Trotskyism was that Trotsky's aesth[etic] was much more inclusive than that of other socialist ideologues. Ot[her] revolutionary movements often imposed what their members could read [and] watch. Only social realism was permitted for those belonging to most Ma[ox]ist or Stalinist groups, for example.

Stieg would not have accepted that. He read science fiction and crim[e] fiction, preferably of the American, hard-boiled variety. He also read com-ics, his favorite being a monthly called *Agent X-9*, an anthology comic fea-turing Stieg's particular favorite, Peter O'Donnell's *Modesty Blaise*, a British crime and adventure strip (and series of novels) about a smart, rich, self-sufficient, and deadly female protagonist of ambiguous sexuality.

And he loved movies—Stanley Kubrick's science fiction films, *Dr. Strange-love* and *2001: A Space Odyssey* among them, though the young Stieg felt that Kubrick included too much gratuitous violence in *A Clockwork Orange*. He also liked American crime movies and considered Roman Polanski's *China-town* one of the greatest films made. Ever eclectic, he also thought highly of Italian director Sergio Leone's westerns.

This was not what most serious communists read or watched. But, again, Stieg would not compromise with his conviction that each individual must decide for him- or herself what to read, listen to, watch, enjoy. He was a life-long enemy of every form of censorship, a stand that put him at odds with most Swedes, who applauded the various "limits" to free speech introduced in the mid-1980s that banned "the depiction of sexual violence or force," "the depiction of children in a sexual context," and "the public display of Nazi symbols." Stieg deplored these efforts to legislate thought and expression. Regarding the law against Nazi symbols, for example, he said that it would be so much simpler and more convenient to have Nazis walking around sporting swastikas than to be forced to identify them from their ravings. It was a joke, of course. But only in part.

Already before the age of eighteen, Stieg had declared himself an antiracist and a feminist. To do so at the beginning of the 1970s was far from common. Swedes believed themselves to be free of racism; therefore to be actively against it was needless. Stieg knew better. And at that time, only women were femi-nists, while men might quietly sympathize with their position. Stieg knew that it would take more than just sympathy to overcome men's hatred for women.

tent. Stieg published one, "The Wax Cabinet," five pages long, and Tommy Lindgren another. The issue also contained a humorous column and a short editorial by Rune Forsgren, a couple of poems, and a half-page protest against weapons of mass destruction by Stieg. *Sfären* was the first new Swedish fanzine in more than two years. It caused quite a stir, and most comments were emphatically positive.

On April 28, Rune and Stieg boarded a bus for the overnight trip to Stockholm to attend their first science fiction convention and meet some of the other fans with whom they were now in contact. The convention, called SF•72, with its three days of programming and some 180 attendees, was the largest in Sweden up to that time.

Rune Forsgren's convention report, published in *Sfären* number 3, mentions that most programs were enjoyed but he also talks about the all-night hotel room parties where fans discussed "the Vietnam War, fanzine publishing, and the convention program."

I was one of the members of the convention organizing committee, and one of those all-night talkers. I retain an impression of Stieg as a thin, soft-spoken, dark-haired boy with a narrow face, metal-framed round glasses, and a ready smile. At a time when many of us had long hair and beards and wore jeans and beads, Stieg dressed more traditionally in pants, shirt, tie, and leather vest, and wore his hair in an inch-long crew cut. But this, too, was a uniform. At the time, young Swedes active in the various leftist organizations tended to adopt what they believed to be a "proletarian" dress code, breaking less with traditional middle-class dress than those who tried to emulate American hippie informality.

During the convention lectures, debates, and other program items, I have no memory of Stieg taking part in discussions or asking questions. He sat silently, listening. But with a dozen other fans in a hotel room at night, drinking wine or whisky while the tobacco smoke gradually thickened into an opaque smog, he proved an engaging, dedicated, and above all a calm and reasonable debater, an excellent raconteur and a very funny guy. Small groups were his forte. Stieg was never self-asserting; he loved discussions, but his weapons of choice were facts, logic, humor, and reason, not grand gestures or stirring exhortations.

Stieg's personality changed surprisingly little over the years, at least as far as I could discern. He was seventeen in the spring of 1972; when he moved to Stockholm he was twenty-three. Over the five intervening years we met at several sf conventions, and he remained the same. For most of us, our late teens and early twenties are characterized by dramatic changes.

This is when we irrevocably stop being children and perhaps even become adults. Stieg was no child at seventeen, and perhaps never became wholly adult. I say that not to diminish him but in admiration. His enthusiasm, curiosity, and joy for life remained intact.

Ayn Rand once wrote, "To hold an unchanging youth is to reach, at the end, the vision with which one started." She could have been thinking of Stieg. At seventeen, he lived to write, learn, discuss, analyze, publish, tell stories, and do the things that felt right and necessary to him, regardless of whether or not others agreed with him, and regardless of whether or not they brought him fame or riches. He had no sense of prestige and no interest in money. As long as there was enough to buy books, pay rent, and keep himself in coffee and tobacco, he enjoyed life. This also meant that he had no great interest in long-range plans or career goals, didn't want to be tied down by responsibilities, and intensely disliked accounting and other kinds of organizational paperwork.

As for my quoting Rand to characterize Stieg—an author and philosopher he generally abhorred because of her crusading procapitalism but at least one of whose novels, *The Fountainhead,* he actually said he rather liked for its style and portrait of a hero uncompromisingly true to his artistic vision— view it as an example of the kind of banter we exchanged. He would have appreciated it, just as I did when in a fanzine he called me "a damned red. A commie. Yes, that's what you are. Just rearrange your views a bit [. . .] and you're ready to join any liberation movement around."

Stieg was well read at his extreme side of the political spectrum, and he liked quoting the writers he appreciated. So was I, and so did I. My impression was that he both enjoyed our banter and was exasperated by it because while our views were often based in similar analyses, and expressed similar sentiments, they nevertheless often reflected diametrically opposing points of view. Fascinatingly, the libertarians I quoted and the communist writers he preferred often sounded surprisingly similar.

Stieg and Eva

In the fall of 1972, Stieg met the most important person in his life—Eva Gabrielsson, who was to become his lifetime partner, both personally and intellectually.

Stieg and Eva met through the Vietnam protest movement, but they soon found they had far more in common than their political views. Eva loved books, writing, and the visual arts. She was also a science fiction fan in her own right. She and Stieg shared outlooks, convictions, interests, and even favorite authors and movies, while still retaining their distinct individuality.

Stieg and Eva were not just partners in the sense that word is normally used. They were intensely and joyfully involved in each other's lives, feelings, thoughts, and creative work. Stieg and Eva did far more than just sleep, eat, and do dishes together (and they *did* do the dishes together, since both hated dishes, though Stieg liked to clean house and Eva to cook). They actually *lived* together, which is both much harder and much more scarce.

In her own right, on her own terms, Eva was as actively involved as Stieg in politics, science fiction fandom, working, writing, thinking, and debating. They continually discussed everything, both privately and with others. With others, they never behaved in the way so many heterosexual couples do, the man mostly talking to other men, the woman to other women. Stieg and Eva stayed together, greeted friends together, talked and discussed with women and men alike, often filling in for each other, completing each other's thoughts or statements, adding arguments to what the other had just said. They worked and functioned as a team, and were inseparable.

I have never met another couple functioning in quite the same way. Stieg and Eva grew together, yet were separate, responsible adults, each with his or her own agenda, responsibilities, and work, each recognizing and respecting this within their ongoing relationship. This means that they traveled both together and separately, that they lived both together and separately, that they worked both together and separately, as circumstances, commitments, and professional considerations allowed or necessitated. Neither of them demanded that the other give up his or her interests, friendships, or assignments. Sometimes that meant being separated for some time. Nor did either of them ever demand that the other subordinate his or her interests or wishes. What Stieg and Eva had was a working, intensely involved, yet totally non-submissive relationship of equals.

I have no doubts that after Stieg and Eva began living together in the fall of 1974, in a very real sense Stieg was a contributor to everything Eva wrote or did, and Eva to whatever Stieg did or wrote. Theirs was anything but a silent partnership. It was a partnership of constant analyzing, discussing, giving and taking, embellishing, adding and questioning, suggesting and creating. This pertains as much to Stieg's three Millennium novels as to everything else he wrote. Of course Stieg himself *typed* his three novels—but he *wrote* them in the same way he wrote everything else: in an ongoing, fruitful, and irreplaceable interplay with Eva, who was present throughout their creation.

He Continues His Education

In a sense, Stieg was lucky not to get his wish in 1972.

In the spring he had graduated from vocational school, but instead of going to work, as would normally be expected, he wanted a drastic change. So he applied to the Stockholm School of Journalism, which selected students from sample writings and in-depth interviews. His application was turned down. He could have reapplied but as far as is known, he never did. Perhaps the first rejection discouraged him.

Luckily, he almost immediately found a job as the replacement for a dishwasher in the Metropol diner who had a penchant for pyromania and was duly incarcerated for his actions. Later on, Stieg delivered newspapers and took other short-term jobs.

With Eva, Rune, Tommy, and sometimes others, he hung out in the downtown Umeå coffee shops—Mekka, the NK store cafeteria, and one at the EPA department store. They talked endlessly, planned their fanzines, discussed the books they read, and joked. Simultaneously, both Eva and Stieg started studying politics in earnest.

Meanwhile, Stieg had made friends in both his fandom and political circles who, unlike him, had not stopped their education, and for whom going on to gymnasium [in Sweden, gymnasium is a secondary school] and academic studies was natural and desirable. Stieg's parents and grandparents had a working-class background, where theoretical studies were not part of life. But Stieg decided to break with this tradition. He would go back to school, complete gymnasium, and so at least become eligible for university admission.

Consequently, in 1973 Stieg started gymnasium at Dragonskolan, a large and centrally located school. He chose the social sciences curriculum, where in addition to foreign languages, history, mathematics, and science, he would study political science, psychology, philosophy, and sociology. He graduated in two years instead of the normal three. One of his last-year classmates, Ingela Mattsson-Löfbom, described him this way in a recent interview: "Round eyeglasses, a skin vest and a shoulder bag. That's what he almost always wore, but then again, so did many in those days." She also noticed that there was one thing he always kept within reach—his typewriter, which he carried around the way many nowadays tote their laptops.

During the final gymnasium term, in early 1975, part of the class joined a study circle centered on a novel by Vilhelm Moberg, a major Swedish novelist with a strong liberal streak who is best known for his Emigrants series, which follows a group of Swedes who are making a new life in America. The study circle ended with a trip to Kittelfjäll, a famous ski resort, where every-one spent the days skiing—except Stieg Larsson. Avoiding the slopes, he stayed indoors writing an essay on the 1968 Paris student uprising. "Stieg was strongly engaged in politics," Ingela Mattsson-Löfbom said. "He was very knowledgeable in political issues, and liked to show it. He loved discussions, but never became angry or aggressive; he was positive and kind. He had an immense integrity. Still, although he was open, you never knew very much about him."

Humor, Stieg-style

However serious he was about his writing and his political and cultural discussions, Stieg also knew how to have fun. Consider his instigation of the Good Friday Night tradition, one that became legendary among the hand-ful of people who happened to hear about it.

Until 1969, Good Friday in Sweden was by law a strict religious holiday. Shops and restaurants were closed. The radio channels played only classical and religious music. Even cinemas were closed, with the occasional exception of one showing David Lean's and George Stevens's *The Greatest Story Ever Told*.

Even after the entertainment ban was rescinded little changed in smaller towns. According to Stieg, Umeå was one of them. "Scholars of religion as well as Bible thumpers claim that Good Friday was the day when Jesus a lot of years ago was nailed to a wooden cross and became part of the holy spirit or something," he wrote. "For some inconceivable reason the Swedish state even in this secular century agrees with the church that this hardly memo-rable event should be celebrated." And so, on Good Friday, virtually all life-sustaining social functions ceased for twenty-four hours, something that "those of us who are atheists can hardly view as anything but an unfair kick in the groin."

On Good Friday evening 1973, Stieg, Tommy, and Rune drove around Umeå hoping to find something, anything, to do. There was nothing. They ended up at Tommy's, where they spent the evening talking and joking, meanwhile typing up some of what they said. The next morning Stieg re-typed the manuscript on stencils, printed it, and brought a few copies of the fanzine to his evening job as usher at the Saga Cinema. According to Stieg, not a drop of alcohol had been consumed, but when transcribing the haphaz-ard conversation he happened—by pure chance, or so he claimed—to have misspelled a word, which altered the last sentence to read, "We solemnly and truthfully declare that during the creation of this fanzine, all three of us . . . were absolutely suber!"

He phoned Rune and Tommy from the cinema to come by and get their copies of the fanzine with their rambling conversation, which he claimed to have mailed to most of the Swedish fans they knew. The joke backfired totally. Rune and Tommy were furious, convinced that Stieg had made them look like idiots to many of their friends. In the end, readers liked it and Rune and Tommy relented.

So the Good Friday Night celebration, and a fanzine containing whatever those present felt like typing down from their conversation, became a tradition. In 1974 Rune Forsgren had moved to attend school in Vindeln some thirty miles away. Stieg went there for a few days, working on the science fiction novel he kept writing for years before finally discarding it, and on Good Friday night Tommy Lindgren, Eva Gabrielsson, and Eva's sister showed up for the party. More or less successful repeats were held in 1975 and 1976. By then in its fourth year, the Good Friday Night party tradition had led to weak imitations in other parts of Sweden, where fans were hopelessly envious of what they imagined to be Umeå fandom's black masses and unimaginable debauchery.

On Good Friday 1977 Stieg was on his way to Eritrea and in 1978 Stieg and Eva had moved to Stockholm. The tradition was dead—or so everyone believed, until Stieg and Eva managed to get a late flight to Umeå and unexpectedly rang Rune's doorbell. But no fanzine was produced, just as none had been produced in 1977. And by Good Friday 1979, Tommy was in Copenhagen, Rune in Umeå, Stieg in Stockholm, and Eva down with German measles at her sister's in Uppsala. At midnight, Tommy phoned Stieg and Stieg phoned Rune, but how could that be called a party? The last gasp came in 1983, when Stieg phoned Tommy, Rune, and a few others to collect quotes for a tenth-anniversary issue of his *Långfredagsnatt* fanzine. But after that the Good Friday feasting and fanzine tradition was definitely over.

Neither extreme political groups nor sf fandom are spared fanatics. Stieg, with his intensity, fascination with facts, and great enthusiasm, had characteristics that might have driven him toward the edge, but he also had traits that very effectively saved him from that fate. One of these was that he had many different interests—so different that some viewed them as contradictory. Another, that he was independent and self-confident enough not to be swayed by group pressure or by the opinions of others. And, third, that he had humor and self-irony to spare.

In *Distance,* he made up nonexisting club members and wrote about their antics to poke fun at his own hobby. Later he, Eva, Tommy, and Eva's sister were viewed with great suspicion in DFFG when it was discovered that they had amused themselves by making up two ideologically warring communist factions, and written and printed issues of the secret magazines of these factions, *The Foot Front* and *The Paw,* in which they vehemently denounced each other. Stieg thought that their parody of the ideological squabbles within the revolutionary left was both funny and worth thinking about. But the party bosses seemed to suspect the writers as class enemies in disguise.

In the science fiction fanzines, humor and self-parody were not only accepted but applauded. An informal, amusing column would often gain more praise than a worked-out essay or piece of fiction. The Good Friday parody fanzines are examples of the kind of absurdities Stieg not only thought up, but put a lot of work into sharing with his friends.

What united his commitment to politics, his hobby of DXing, and his reveling in fandom was that they all allowed Stieg to write and draw, and to have his work published. Nobody could doubt that he was readying himself to work in print, but as to how, opinions differed. Rune Forsgren believed that Stieg would be an artist. "Even back then you could see that he had talent, but the novels he finally published are on an entirely different level. What happened is truly incredible. If someone had asked me to guess back then, I would have pegged him to become an illustrator instead. He could do a finished drawing in three minutes."

Stieg always sketched, but gradually his drawing turned more into doodling while his writing became dominant. The wish to express himself in words was stronger than the lure of art.

Living with Eva and Others

In August 1974, Stieg Larsson took a decisive step by moving from his one-room apartment to a flat on Mariehemsvägen, which he and Eva would share with Tommy Lindgren and Eva's sister. By this time Stieg had rejected Maoism and instead joined the Trotskyite Revolutionary Marxists. He soon became a regular contributor to the outreach weekly *Mullvaden* ("The Mole"), in 1975 renamed *Internationalen,* and for a time was one of its editors. During the roughly fifteen years he wrote for the magazine, often under his "Severin" penname, its print run increased from six hundred copies in 1971–1973 to two thousand nine hundred copies in 1976, then declined again. Contributors were never paid.

Also in 1974 Stieg and his friend Rune Forsgren started a new fanzine, *Fijagh!* [an acronym for "Fandom Is Just a Goddamned Hobby!"], of which they published eight issues from September 1974 to December 1976, a ninth belatedly appearing in 1978. In the second issue, Rune wrote about the collective on Mariehemsvägen:

> Take their library. Actually it's a closet, around eleven feet square. It's where they keep books, newspapers, comics, magazines, and a lot of other stuff. Quite a lot is sf and a fair amount is politics. But the selection is pretty strange. Or maybe I should put that in another way. Let me try to explain.
>
> They have four copies of *The Pentagon Papers,* three copies of Edgar Snow's *Red Star Over China,* as many of Carr's *Socialism in One Country* and also three of Harry Magdoff's *The Age of Imperialism.* But there is nothing by Sven Lindqvist. And if we're to take a look at areas related to sf, there is nothing by Kafka or Carl Johan Holzhausen. True, there is a copy of [Holzhausen's] *Språnget* in there, but I've long suspected that it is my copy.
>
> Their record collection is equally skewed. Just a lot of King Crimson and similar noise. Nothing by Blå Tåget, only a single Melanie album and no Latin American folk music. In all truth, not even Røde Mor is represented.
>
> Though in all honesty they do have a couple of albums you can bear listening to. A few by Dylan, Nynningen, maybe one or two more. But not many. I could donate my Røde Mor collection. But it feels too much like throwing pearls before swine.

A Stint in the Military

In late spring 1975 Stieg passed his gymnasium exam and went into military service, mandatory in Sweden at the time. In order to live close enough to be able sometimes to get home from his army regiment, the Umeå-based I-20 (20th Infantry), he moved from the collective to a small apartment on Rådhusesplanaden. In his writings, he expressed exasperation at military life and a nostalgic longing for earlier days.

Not unexpectedly, Stieg viewed military service through his Trotskyite filter, which favored learning the use of weapons since at the right historical moment a final, armed conflict between oppressed and oppressors was inevitable. Learning military skills was part of preparing yourself for the revolution. Plus, conscripted soldiers were ideal targets for recruitment.

Stieg went off to I-20 with that double agenda. He learned to use weapons, and tried to convert other conscripts, in part by selling *Röd soldat* ["Red Soldier"] in the barracks—a Trotskyite magazine aimed specifically at draftees and intended to imbue them with a feeling of class solidarity.

After basic training Stieg had been slated for transfer two hundred miles north to the Royal Life Company regiment in Boden for squad leader training. But he had been expressing his revulsion at military life in no uncertain terms—a whole valuable year would be wasted on "parades, imbecile commanders, stupid NCO's, shining shoes, making beds, getting sinusitis and abrasions and back pains, caring for weapons, being degraded, staring at blue and yellow flags, getting punished, being powerless, wasting time and getting drunk." He summed up his feelings as, "Fucking idiots. I just can't stand in straight lines, I just can't march, I just can't stand at attention . . . I just can't waste my time on imbecile nonsense."

Stieg was never transferred to Life Company. He claimed that after a month he had managed to make himself so irritating that his company commander, Captain Grafström, called him a danger to discipline and morale. Stieg fulfilled his military training at the Umeå regiment in constant clash with the system and with constant minor but irritating and tiring physical problems.

Stieg Larsson left military life in late spring 1976 and went to work at Hörnefors paper mill, some twenty miles south of Umeå, where he lived at a single men's hostel. He continued writing. He published in *Internationalen* and in a few sf fanzines, but his attempts at fiction seldom satisfied him and remained unpublished. He wanted to do something meaningful. He decided to go to Eritrea.

African Adventures

Stieg had always been fascinated by Africa. His first try at getting there failed miserably; his idea was to hitchhike, but he got only as far as Stockholm before losing his money, and he was forced to return home after two days. He made his second try in the summer of 1973. It was another ill-fated trip but nonetheless had a lasting and powerful impact on him. Stieg hitched rides south via France and Spain to Algeria, where he met and joined a group of youths intending to cross the Sahara and continue to Niger. But their truck broke down and the person sent to buy spare parts disappeared with their money. In the end they had to walk back to Oran. Stieg returned by hitching rides through Europe again, selling his jacket to get money for food, and arriving home half-starved and penniless.

But Africa had lost none of its attraction. In the summer of 1974 he went again, this time with Eva. Decades later he still would often hint at the stories he could tell of his trips—of backpacking cross-country, of renting a room in an Addis Ababa brothel (and while there, on Easter in 1977, writing a Hemingwayesque short story about an organization so secret that not even its members know whom they are killing, or to what end), of making friends with a giraffe in the Khartoum State Zoo, and of getting lost in the jungle around Lake Victoria. Sometimes he claimed to have written much of this down, just never having gotten around to polishing it enough for publication.

All this set the stage for his decision to travel to Eritrea in 1977.

After fifty years of being colonized by Italy, Eritrea became a British protectorate during World War II and remained so until 1952, when the UN passed a resolution to federate it with Ethiopia. The stronger Ethiopia controlled all the major ministries and quickly established its dominance. In 1958, the main Ethiopian language became the only official one, in 1960 the Eritrean flag was banned, and in late 1962 Eritrea was directly annexed. The EPLF (Eritrean People's Liberation Front) now took to arms, and a thirty-year struggle began, ending in EPLF victory in 1991. Tragedy followed. The EPLF leader Isaias Afewerki tightened his hold on the country, banned all other political parties, introduced harsh censorship, and persecuted his opponents. In short, one dictatorship was replaced by another.

No one could foresee this outcome in 1977 when Stieg decided to go. But drought had added starvation to the brutalities of war, and the situation in Eritrea was desperate. Stieg had met representatives of the EPLF movement and wanted to help. So he went to Eritrea as a courier, carrying documents and, according to some, cash.

Stieg knew that the trip would be dangerous, perhaps lethal. Before setting out, he wrote two documents and sealed them, writing "NB! Personal. Not to be opened until after my death" on the envelope. They remained sealed for almost thirty years.

One of the documents was his last will, stating in part: "I wrote that I was not a wealthy person and I hardly leave any large amount of money. However I wish that whatever monetary assets I have (and on this I am absolutely decided) shall be given to the Umeå branch of the Communist Workers' League."

The will was signed but not witnessed. According to legal experts, it might have been considered valid if Stieg had died during the 1977 trip. But as he returned and lived for another twenty-seven years, the document had lost all possible validity. When the will became public in 2008, after much public speculation, the Communist Workers' League—now named The Socialist Party ("Socialistiska Partiet"), and with only some twenty active members left in Umeå—declined to lay claim to any of Stieg's inheritance. It also attacked a Swedish legal system that would not permit Eva to be his heir:

> Stieg's books and other writings criticized not only racism and right-wing extremism. They were equally critical of patriarchal society and of the oppression of women. There are many women—as well as men—who live together but for various reasons do not marry, and who are thus victimized by these discriminatory laws. [. . .] The reactionary Swedish law, putting marriage above all other forms of relations, same-sex as well as heterosexual, must be totally reformed. Individuals must have the right to live together as they choose without risking insecurity or injustice.

The other document written and sealed by Stieg was a moving letter to Eva in which he deeply committed himself to her. It was read aloud by her at the memorial held for Stieg in Stockholm on the day of his funeral service.

Leaving these two documents, in which he gave his nonexistent money to the Trotskyite cause and his deepest feelings to Eva, Stieg in February left for Eritrea and war. He traveled via Moscow to Sudan and on to Addis Ababa, where he said that he was interrogated at the British Consulate about troop movements he might have witnessed while crossing the country. He refused to cooperate and made his way on to Asmara in Eritrea where he found his EPLF guerrilla contact and was taken to a training camp in a mountain region. There, by chance, he ended up training a company of women soldiers to fire grenades, a skill he himself had learned while in the Swedish army.

One of the features of the EPLF most appreciated by Stieg Larsson was that the organization actively encouraged women to take part in the armed struggle, and to do so on equal footing with men. In the strongly traditional, patriarchal Eritrean society, EPLF was a force for women's liberation, and up to one-third of its fighting forces consisted of women, which Stieg applauded. That after the rebels' final victory these outspoken and self-confident women would be forced back into silent submission was to Stieg proof of almost incomprehensible hypocrisy.

Did he take part in actual fighting? Yes, according to his friend Graeme Atkinson, European editor of *Searchlight* magazine, for which Stieg became the Scandinavian correspondent in the early 1980s. Atkinson has said,

Stieg was a revolutionary socialist and he believed in a better life, and equality for all. The fact of the crushing poverty in Africa appalled him. He went [to Eritrea] to aid the struggle. That meant in the end being involved in fighting and he faced live bullets. He was an amazingly courageous man. He told me a lot about it, but never boasting. A lot of what he saw left me deeply shocked.

Rather surprisingly, the mention of Stieg's months in Eritrea caused headlines in late 2010 when it was "uncovered." The trip had never been kept secret, even if he seldom talked of the things he had seen publicly. But the memories stayed with him. An acquaintance has mentioned that sometime in the 1990s Stieg spoke of having been part of a detail looking for survivors after an attack. He saw a foot sticking out of a pile of debris, tried pulling at it—and found himself holding a blasted-off leg in his hands.

Illness put an end to Stieg's time in Eritrea. He contracted malaria and later developed a kidney inflammation, which had to be treated at a hospital in Addis Ababa. When he was well enough to travel he went by bus to Kenya, continued to Uganda, and finally managed to return home in July.

Time to Move On

In Umeå, nothing was as before. By the late summer of '77 many of Stieg Larsson's friends had moved away. He spent long afternoons playing chess with Eva Gabrielsson's brother in Nya Konditoriet, a coffee shop, regularly losing. He had a strong nostalgic streak, and the changes in his hometown and life made him feel ill at ease. He had expressed similar feelings in writing as early as 1975, longing for childhood, blue skies, warm summers, the first pop concert, teen romances, his secret, unreachable loves for Judy Garland, Veronica Lake, Pier Angeli, Monica Vitti in her film role as Modesty Blaise. . . .

In August, Eva Gabrielsson moved to Stockholm to study architecture. Stieg wrote, self-ironically, that as she could no longer support him economically, he in desperation went to the employment office to ask for work. They found a job for him at the Post Office sorting facility in Stockholm. The employment agency paid for his relocation and Stieg and Eva moved in together in a student room.

Stieg Larsson was twenty-three years old. He had finally arrived in the city where he would make his name.

Part III: Stieg in Stockholm

"I arrived in Stockholm with a cold autumn wind, a bottle of wine in my bag and my glasses misted by rain," Stieg Larsson wrote. Eva Gabrielsson had come to Stockholm to study architecture at the Royal Institute of Technology; Stieg arrived a couple of months later, after his return from Eritrea. Eva had managed to get a small student apartment in Rinkeby, a suburb north of the city, considered by many older Stockholmers to be an immigrant ghetto but appreciated by others for its diversity, street stands, small restaurants, and mixture of nationalities, cultures, and traditions. Stieg and Eva stayed in that apartment for six years, then moved to a larger apartment in the same area for another six. In 1991, they moved for the last time, to a small condominium apartment in the southwestern part of Stockholm, where Eva still lives.

The employment counselor in Umeå told Stieg that to actually get the job arranged for him at the Post Office, he had first to pass a medical examination. And if Stieg didn't get the job, or lost it within six months, he would have to repay the relocation cost.

So Stieg reported to the Post Office medical office, failed the examination, retook it, and passed. The doctors wondered about his low blood count. Stieg told them it might be due to his malaria. The doctors were enthusiastic. They seldom got the chance to work on interesting ailments. Stieg envisioned an endless process of blood samples, proddings, and pinchings. But he got the job and a promise not to be laid off until the doctors had finished their tests. And he said that malaria was the best chronic disease to have, since attacks were sudden, irregular, and unpredictable. This meant that whenever he didn't feel like reporting to work, he could phone in claiming a sudden attack. Who could say that he didn't have one?

Stieg's job sorting mail was an economic necessity but boring. He became involved in the trade union at his workplace and continued writing for *Internationalen,* where one of his pet subjects was to attack the growing wave of new age superstitions. He and Eva became more active in sf fandom than ever before. And during his two years of postal employment he spent much of his time in Stockholm coffee shops, where he wrote or saw friends. This was when he began talking about writing the definitive guide to the hundreds of cafés in Stockholm. For a while, asking him about this project was a standing joke, as was his usual reply that sadly another dozen had opened in the last week and so his notes had again become obsolete.

As for the mail sorting, whenever someone complained about not having received some piece of mail, Stieg liked to tell about the occasional sudden halts of the conveyor belt in the sorting room. Mail, he said, was transported on a conveyor belt on several levels past numerous workstations, and every so often the belt would just stop. When it did, Stieg claimed, everyone knew what had happened. Mail kept dropping off the belt down into the machinery below the floor, where it was ground to a pulp. When enough pulp had collected—it only took a few thousand letters, Stieg said—the machinery would stop and the workers would open trapdoors in the floor and remove the pulped paper with shovels, after which the belt was restarted and sorting continued. Stieg would put on an innocent face and add that there was no need to worry. After all, it didn't happen all that often. Only a couple of times a week.

Stieg wanted to write for a living, but thus far had failed. To be published commercially at all, he believed, you had to adapt your writing to bourgeois readers, which meant that even at best you could only express pseudoradical ideas, never truly radical. He knew at least three fellow sf fans writing pornography for the growing men's magazine market, but rejected that option. Pornography, just as formula-written as Wild West or crime novels, demands a total absence of any challenge to bourgeois morality, including its denigration of women, and Stieg refused to sell out his ideals.

In late 1979 Stieg quit the Post Office to work for the TT news agency, housed on the top floors of one of the five 240-foot so-called skyscrapers in downtown Stockholm. TT (*Tidningarnas Telegrambyrå,* "The Newspapers' Telegram Bureau") is the dominant Swedish news agency, formed in 1921. Stieg's first TT job was as a typist and proofreader. Later he got the chance to stand in for an absent graphics artist and so got the chance to prove his proficiency in drawing maps and diagrams. He was offered a steady job and ended up staying at TT for twenty years until 1999. Apart from maps and diagrams he did freehand drawings and caricatures. For the first ten years Stieg worked manually, with India ink pens and dry transfer letter sheets. From 1987, desktop publishing made inking diagrams by hand obsolete.

Not long after he started at TT, Stieg became fascinated by developments on the small island of Grenada at the southern end of the Grenadines island chain in the southeastern Caribbean. In 1974, near the end of the British decolonization process, Grenada was granted independence. The government headed by Eric Gairy soon proved corrupt. Gairy wasted national resources on such wild tangents as hunting for UFOs and he wasted his time asking the UN to acknowledge a universal god and create a flying saucer research agency. The New Jewel Movement, led by Maurice Bishop, opposed Gairy, and in 1979 staged an armed coup. Gairy was deposed and Bishop declared himself prime minister. Bishop undertook a variety of ambitious social and economic policy measures. He rewrote laws to promote gender equality. He reformed the school system and lowered the inflated civil servant salaries.

In 1981 Stieg and Eva went to Grenada to study the reforms and express their solidarity with Bishop's policies. They met many Grenadians, including Bishop himself. Back in Sweden, they joined the Grenadakommittén (Grenada Committee) and founded its magazine, *Free Grenada,* which was published until 1985. Stieg and Eva also wrote enthusiastically in *Internationalen* about the virtually unknown Grenadine revolution. In *The Girl Who Played with Fire,* Stieg lets Lisbeth Salander meet a Grenadian who tells her about Gairy and Bishop from Stieg's perspective.

Maurice Bishop embraced a nonorthodox Marxism and hoped to modernize and industrialize the island, but his government needed foreign aid, and received it from Cuba. As Cuban influence grew, so did the military forces urged on Bishop by the Cubans, while opposition was banned and dissidents jailed.

The end was quick. The government split into two factions, one loyal to Bishop, the other to his associate Bernard Coard. The Coard faction demanded a strictly Leninist policy and closed the only independent newspaper in Grenada. Bishop opposed this, was accused of bourgeois tendencies, and in October 1983 was placed under house arrest. A crowd of citizens freed him, and the Coard faction sent soldiers to capture Bishop. On October 19, Bishop and seven others, including cabinet members, were captured and shot. The army commander, Hudson Austin, earlier a Coard supporter, now formed a military government with himself at its head. The replacement of Bishop's moderate socialist government by a Cuban-backed militant one worried the American administration, and on October 25 the U.S. invaded Grenada, jailing Austin, Coard, and others implicated in Bishop's murder. During this time Eva Gabrielsson worked with Stieg at TT to make extra money. On the day of the American invasion, they got hold of a Grenada phone book, called Grenadians, and asked them to describe what was going on. Until telephone access was cut, TT alone provided eyewitness accounts of the invasion in Sweden.

Outlets for His Writing

Around this time, Stieg found new outlets for his writing. One was at his place of employment. TT wanted to expand its output and set up a new department to handle feature material, both text and images. In 1984 TT moved to offices close to the Stockholm Courthouse, and TT-Reportage began operations. The head of the new department was Kenneth Ahlborn, who realized that Stieg Larsson had broad interests and was very capable of writing about them. Stieg began writing essays, mainly intended as Sunday supplement material. He wrote about new age fads and pseudoscientific superstitions, debunking nonsense like the Bermuda Triangle. He also wrote about literature, interviewing authors and for many years doing overviews of new crime novels.

Kenneth Ahlborn says in retrospect that,

> Stieg wrote entertaining articles about authors, illustrators, or amusing, well-researched trivia. I can only remember two or three articles about what you could even call politics. He wrote a presentation of a British organization keeping tab on neo-Nazis, and on another occasion wrote about a young man who had infiltrated neo-Nazi circles in Sweden under cover. A third article was a review of a British book detailing how right-wingers infiltrate soccer supporter clubs.

There has been some confusion about the extent of Stieg's feature writing while at TT. According to Ahlborn, features until 1992 were photocopied and sent out by mail, to be typeset by the newspapers that used this material. The archive of noncomputerized feature material was lost in 2006, when TT moved to its current offices on Stockholm's south side, but Ahlborn estimates the number of feature articles mailed by 1992 at around a thousand, and states that over fifty were written by Stieg Larsson. The computer archives from 1993 on include over thirty further features by Stieg. A total of eighty or ninety features in fifteen years may not seem very impressive. But Stieg's main work at TT was as a graphic artist, illustrating news.

Two controversies concerning Stieg's work at TT surfaced in early 2010. One concerned his reliability as a journalist. In his book about Stieg, Kurdo Baksi made several unflattering claims. One was that Stieg "committed misconduct at TT" when writing about Nazi threats in a news article sent on October 17, 1999. "His text lacked the neutrality, impartiality and relevance you must demand from a professional journalist," Baksi writes. "It was an incredible overstep."

Was it? Kenneth Ahlborn replied in print that the article sketched the background to the so-called Sätra murder, where two Nazis killed unionist Björn Söderberg in 1999. Stieg had by then been writing for *Expo* for years and had expert knowledge of how Nazi groups worked. Ahlborn points out that Stieg's text is "irreproachably written," that the two persons quoted,

David Lagerlöf and city councilor Björn Fries, are both relevant to the theme and clearly identified. It was a known fact that Swedish Nazis kept track of their enemies, and it was relevant to write about this. Ahlborn highlights the key passage from Stieg's article: "Among those registered by Anti-AFA [a secret, neo-Nazi information network] are the two journalists in Nacka whose car was blown up in a bombing last summer, members of the *Expo* magazine editorial staff, known antiracist debaters, as well as persons working for the authorities." That Stieg was a member of the *Expo* staff was public knowledge, and Stieg's superiors at TT were well aware of it. It was also the cause of Baksi's charge: that instead of identifying himself as one of those threatened, Stieg wrote about the situation as if he were not personally involved. But the ethics questions here are far from clear cut. Stieg's article was purely descriptive, and he was not involved in the events leading to the murder of Björn Söderberg. So did he really compromise his journalistic objectivity by not naming himself as one of those of whom Nazis kept track? Baksi claims so; the TT editors at the time did not think so.

The other, absurd controversy began with an article in *Dagens Nyheter,* Sweden's largest daily, timed to coincide with the publication of Baksi's book. Anders Hellberg, a night editor at TT during the last years of the 1970s and the first of the 1980s, wrote that, "Stieg Larsson was an impressive researcher, very knowledgeable and imaginative, but writing wasn't his strong point. This raises the question who really wrote the Millennium trilogy." Hellberg says that he worked as editor and responsible TT publisher on the night shift from eleven p.m. until six a.m. He and Stieg had offices on different floors. Stieg, he said,

> showed me captions and descriptions he had written for his graphics and asked me to check them. "I'm not all that good at it, you know," he sometimes said about the writing part. And I could see for a fact . . . that he simply couldn't write. His language was stiff, the words were often put in the wrong order, his sentences were badly constructed and his syntax was sometimes entirely wrong—in other words, his prose had to be rewritten to work professionally. . . . Stieg's friend Kurdo Baksi now suggests the same thing in his book. . . . When he says that Stieg was "a mediocre journalist," he obviously means his weakness as a writer.

Is there any substance to Hellberg's claims? No. Stieg wrote for publication from the age of seventeen, and by the time Hellberg met him eight years later had published hundreds of texts in fanzines, political journals, and newspapers. Anyone can read Stieg's early writings and judge whether their author might not, after thirty years of further practice, be capable of writing the Millennium books. In a TV confrontation about Hellberg's claims, I asked him to substantiate them. He replied that he hadn't saved any of Stieg's bad captions, but that he "was there, at the time, and read what he wrote, which none of you who deny what I say were." I replied that I was indeed "there at the time" and showed him a pile of Stieg's 1970s fanzines. Hellberg paled, and the debate on whether Stieg Larsson was really the author of his novels ended.

Had Anders Hellberg bothered looking, a single easily available work should have convinced him. In 1987, Stieg Larsson on one of his few freelance assignments traveled the Trans-Siberian railroad for the newly launched travel magazine *Vagabond,* a trip resulting in the fourteen-page essay "9001 Kilometers to Beijing" in *Vagabond* no. 2 1987—a funny and thoughtful text mixing fluent and inventive personal reflections, historical fact, descriptive reporting, and colorful observations in a kaleidoscopic, memorable whole.

Even so, Hellberg's accusations did reflect the views of a number of TT managers. Stieg had a champion in Kenneth Ahlborn, but he faced opposition from others throughout his twenty years at TT. Stieg wanted to switch from graphic art to reporting, but despite the popularity of his feature writing and the support given him by the working journalists at TT, management refused. In the end, when the economic crisis in print media during the late 1990s forced TT to cut costs, management decided inexplicably to disband Ahlborn's feature department, which was one of the few TT units actually still turning a profit. TT offered a number of employees severance pay to quit. Stieg took the offer.

Stieg had not been the most punctual of TT employees. Perhaps this may have been a reason for some managers to dislike him, as they may have felt that he let *Expo* and his outside interests take precedence. Ahlborn has commented,

> Stieg was often late for work, sometimes several hours, but otherwise very disciplined and would work past his quitting time for at least as many hours as he had been late, usually longer. I knew, of course, that his late arrivals were not due to secret alcoholism, a lack of respect for TT or anything of that kind; during evenings and nights, he was performing a kind of guardian duty aimed at neo-Nazis and other forces of darkness.

An Intolerance for Intolerance

Stieg was impressed by the British *Searchlight* magazine, and he became its Swedish correspondent in 1983. Searchlight consists of three branches: the monthly *Searchlight* magazine, where Stieg wrote pseudonymously until his death; Searchlight information services, a research and investigation organization to which he contributed greatly; and Searchlight Educational Trust, dedicated to teaching the dangers of fascism and racism. In his work for Searchlight, the idea for what would later become *Expo* no doubt began to develop.

Stieg Larsson formed his views on morality and politics early in life. Although he gained knowledge and experience over the years, and refined his analysis and understanding, his basic outlook never changed in any dramatic sense. From the beginning, he hated intolerance and injustice. At a time when few males called themselves feminists, the teenage Stieg Larsson proudly did. At a time when most Swedes had little knowledge of third-world countries, Stieg was a true internationalist, willing to take risks for causes receiving little or no attention, such as the Eritrean revolt or Maurice Bishop's efforts in Grenada. In this he worked alongside Eva Gabrielsson, whose dedication was no less than Stieg's. Just as Eva had done in the 1970s, Stieg later came to leave the revolutionary groups to which he belonged. Like Eva, he came to feel that they placed ideology before moral principles. In his work for Searchlight and *Expo* as well as in his Millennium novels, Stieg chose the fight against intolerance as his main battle, while placing less emphasis on any specific ideological viewpoint as time went on.

Stieg also become fascinated by those who not only did not share his values, but worked actively against them. In fanzines, Stieg had encountered Lars-Göran Hedengård, a fellow science fiction fan who opposed everything Stieg and most others believed in. There are people who seriously believe that "whites are superior to all others," that "women should be subservient to males," and that "opinions different from mine should be banned by law." Lars-Göran Hedengård in his midteens was well on his way to becoming one of those people. How had he formed those views? How many shared them? And would they try to implement them? I can't claim that meeting Hedengård was what made Stieg aware of racist and fascist organizations and individuals. Even in Umeå, considered a hotbed of radicalism, there was a small branch of the explicitly Nazi Nordiska Rikspartiet ("Nordic Reich Party"), and, as early as high school, Stieg wanted to write a paper on Swedish neo-Nazism. During part of the 1970s, armed guards had to protect the Stockholm Hillel School and Jewish Center, while synagogues and Jewish graveyards were defaced. To Stieg, that people could embrace racism was outrageous. That some tried to excuse it by claiming solidarity with the Palestinians was worse, as in doing so they also smeared those principles of equality and justice Stieg held as absolute.

After World War II, overt fascism all but disappeared in Sweden, but it returned during the late 1970s and 1980s. Stieg viewed this as extremely dangerous, particularly as immigration was also increasing and immigrants were frequently the victims of neo-Nazi attacks.

As he began to do research on neo-Nazi groups, I suspect that Stieg found it interesting to discuss with me his work mapping the extreme right wing at least in part because of my different experiences and sources. He knew the left-wing organizations from firsthand experience. I had worked with and knew many conservatives and liberals. In 1977, I was hired by the Moderate Party (a traditionally conservative party, but since 1970, it had been led by the very liberal Gösta Bohman, and from 1976, had been part of the coalition government) to be editor of its member magazine. I worked at the party offices in Stockholm's Old Town. When in late 1981 Gösta Bohman had to resign as party leader due to the severe Alzheimer's developed by his wife, his successor, Ulf Adelsohn, wanted no ideological conflicts and so fired the handful of neoliberals, myself included. (It should perhaps be noted that "liberal" is today a term used in the U.S. for views that in Europe are normally called "social democratic," while in Europe, "liberal" indicates views related to those of the original liberals, like Adam Smith, John Stuart Mill, and Tom Paine, albeit usually diluted. In the 1970s, "neoliberalism" appeared in Europe, and this was closely related to what in the U.S. is often called "libertarianism.")

I went to work for Timbro, a publishing house set up to spread works and ideas favoring a liberal political climate. Stieg often dropped in to see me, both at the Moderate Party headquarters and at Timbro, although he would usually put a red star on his lapel just for the occasion. But by this time our friendship was deeply rooted. In fact, I know the moment when Stieg became a friend for life. Sometime in 1978, we were sitting at my kitchen table and I asked him to tell me what made his particular group different from all other communist fractions. He said, "I think the big difference is that when all the others are out in the streets, fighting and hanging you right-wingers from the lamp posts, we will remain in our cellar, trying to figure out if it really is the right historical moment."

He reached the same conclusion about me at a party I gave around Christmas in 1978 or perhaps it was early 1979. A lot of people were milling around, drinking and talking. The doorbell rang. Outside stood several people I was fleetingly acquainted with and who must have heard of the party from someone else. They had brought along Christopher Jolin, who had become notorious for his 1972 book *Vänstervridningen* ("The Left Turn"), in which he argued that communists dominated many Swedish newspapers as well as public radio and TV. That view could be and was discussed and debated. But later Jolin became involved with the racist Keep Sweden Swedish group ("Bevara Sverige Svenskt"), characterized by Stieg Larsson and Anna-Lena Lodenius in their pioneering book about the extreme right as "the first modern Swedish antiimmigrant party."

At the door to my apartment, I told the visitors that, since I didn't know them or their views, they were welcome to join the party, but since I did know what views Jolin was now spreading, I would not have him in my home. As far as I remember, they all left. Apparently Stieg witnessed this nondramatic scene and found it significant. Stieg was impressed with the fact that I took a stand of principle over who I would allow to enter my home and that I would not allow in someone like Jolin, who later wrote that "racial mixing leads to a decrease in the general intelligence and creativity of the population." In all honesty, I can't see that there was anything to be impressed by; on the contrary, I think he would have been right to drop me instantly as a friend if I *had* let Jolin in.

In 1982, a demonstration against racism in Stockholm led to the founding of a coalition against racism, which by 1985 had grown into Riksförbundet Stoppa Rasismen (the National Organization to Stop Racism). The organization also published a magazine, *Stoppa Rasismen,* and Stieg Larsson became one of its contributors. He now wrote continuously about the extreme right and racism also in *Searchlight* and *Internationalen.* Over the following years he worked hard at mapping the sympathizers and fast-changing organizations of the extreme right. But all this was unpaid, voluntary work; his only income was from TT. Meanwhile, Eva, after receiving her degree in 1986, went to work as an architect and CAD operator for builder Ohlsson & Skarne.

In 1988, journalist Anna-Lena Lodenius and philosopher Sven Ove Hansson had written a book about Swedish right-wing ideas, *Operation högervridning (Operation Right Turn).* The publisher was interested in a second book giving an overview of right-wing organizations. Stieg Larsson wanted to write it, but the publisher wanted him to do it in cooperation with Lodenius, who had strong connections to the Social Democratic party, which also owned the publishing company. The product of their collaboration turned out to be the book *Extremhögern (The Extreme Right),* which was published in 1991.

Co-writing the book was harder than either author had assumed. In the end, they split the book to work individually on different parts, Stieg writing the international outlook chapters. On publication, the book received major media attention, but Stieg felt unfairly passed by since Lodenius reaped much of the secondary benefits of the book, establishing herself as a media and lecture expert on right-wing extremism. The book also made both authors targets for hate mail from right-wing sympathizers; on that point they were seemingly treated equally. This was the time period when Stieg began to feel actively threatened. The situation worsened as neo-Nazi organizations like White Aryan Resistance began issuing death warrants.

Earlier, Stieg had often joked about charting individuals and organizations. I well remember the time he came to visit at the Timbro offices, carrying an evening tabloid. "Look," he said, "they've charted all of you closet libertarian extremists." And so they had. The paper contained a graph purporting to show the various organizations and individuals involved in the "ideological conspiracy" to turn Sweden into a more liberal country. Only most of it was wrong.

"They don't know half of it," I said, "and what they've got is wrong."

"Thought so," Stieg said. "Why don't you straighten it out for me?"

So I did. We left the office for one of his beloved coffee shops, and I drew him a diagram showing the constituent parts of the network of liberal organizations, think-tanks and so on, their links to political parties and their public outlets.

A few years later Stieg still joked about finding his name on the death lists of fascist organizations (and could pretend to be upset when one of them had left him out of their ten worst enemies list), but he steadily became more careful and took the threats more seriously. By this point, he had left the Trotskyite group he had been affiliated with after almost twenty years. The reason he gave was that, in his opinion, this party put theory before practice: it supported a number of third-world governments because of their avowed ideals, but despite their obvious disregard for human rights.

Violence against immigrants was increasing. Refugees were not allowed to work and had to live in government camps while waiting to learn if they would be given the right to stay. In the early 1990s almost a hundred attacks on refugee camps or individual immigrants were committed. Neither the traditional media nor the authorities wanted to acknowledge that these bombings, incidents of arson, and cross burnings formed a pattern of organized violence aimed at immigrants.

The Founding of *Expo*

The surge of racist sentiments and growing public appearance of fascist and racist organizations created an ominous atmosphere. A group of journalists upset by these developments, including Stieg Larsson, occasionally discussed the situation at the Press Club, the bar and restaurant in the Association of Swedish Journalists building. They talked of starting a magazine to call attention to it, but nothing happened. Then, *Stoppa Rasismen* wanted to include a more analytical supplement, specializing in detailed exposures of fascist and racist organizations. From the word "exposure," the name *Expo*—though initially written as *"eXpo"*—was derived. The project was headed by Andreas Rosenlund and Stieg Larsson, and after three issues, the decision was made that *Expo* ought to be independent. First one small office on Stockholm's south side was rented, then another and a third. The magazine was owned by a nonprofit foundation, formed by the mostly very young journalists working on it. It was first named the Hill Foundation as a tribute to Roy Hill who, on behalf of *Searchlight,* had infiltrated British fascist organizations. In 1995, it was changed to the Expo Foundation.

Initially, bylines in *Expo* gave only initials ("By S. Larsson"). A fictitious person, "M. Karlsson," was listed as editor in chief, and a post office box was the only address. The *Expo* group was well aware that it was challenging dangerous enemies. *Expo* was quickly recognized both as extremely well informed and as an impressive exponent of investigative journalism. But it also became a prime adversary to those it set out to expose. As early as 1996, retailers and organizations that had sold or supported *Expo* were attacked, while the printing shop producing the magazine had its windows broken and swastikas spray-painted on its walls. In response to this obvious attack on freedom of the press, a unique cooperative venture between the two major afternoon tabloids, the Social-Democrat *Aftonbladet* and the liberal *Expressen,* was launched. Together, they published *Expo*'s third 1996 issue as a supplement on June 10, in a print run of over 800,000 copies.

Unfortunately, neither the media uproar surrounding the attacks on the magazine nor the free issue distributed by the two daily papers did much for sales. By the end of 1996 *Expo*'s sales were declining. The magazine applied to the Swedish Arts Council for a grant of around US$100,000 to cover rent and one full-time salary, but only around US$3,000 was approved. The *Expo* group refused the money in frustration. By the end of 1997, only three out of those who had worked on *Expo* remained. With no money and almost no staff, *Expo* seemed on the verge of extinction.

Stieg Larsson didn't want this. He believed the informational archive on right-wing extremism he had built over the years, by far the most comprehensive in the country, must be preserved, but just as important was the continued existence of a magazine devoted to exposing the activities of racists and ultranationalists. He managed to continue the magazine, first as a small supplement to the Norwegian antiracist magazine *Monitor,* later as an insert in a quarterly published by Kurdo Baksi.

Baksi had come to Sweden with his family at age fifteen in 1980. In 1987, he had started the antiracist magazine *SvartVitt* (*BlackWhite*). In 1992 he was the main organizer of a strike set for February 21 of that year, in reaction to the "Laser Man" racist shootings. The idea was for all immigrants to go on strike under the slogan, "Without Immigrants, Sweden Will Stand Still." But Stieg called to tell Baksi that he had the wrong idea. "Racism is not an immigrant problem," he said, "it's a Swedish problem." He wanted Baksi to welcome everyone in the country to strike in order to show their solidarity with Swedes of immigrant background. Baksi did as Stieg suggested. The strike slogan has since become a standard phrase to point out the importance of immigrants and their children, who by now make up close to 20 percent of the Swedish population.

According to Baksi's account, he and Stieg next met in late fall 1992, and saw each other occasionally after that. Their collaboration was a curious one—Stieg Larsson wrote an unknown number of essays, articles, and appeals, which Baksi signed and published in magazines or newspapers. Stieg felt that the important thing was to get his views spread, and that Baksi, as an immigrant debater, had a better chance of getting them in print. In May 1998, Stieg convinced Baksi to include *Expo* in his *SvartVitt* magazine. The *Expo* group would produce a number of print-ready page originals for each *SvartVitt* deadline, to be printed on colored stock and stapled into Baksi's magazine. Neither editorial staff would interfere with the other.

The collaboration began in 1999. The merged magazines, now called *SvartVitt med Expo,* was published quarterly until Baksi folded *SvartVitt* at the end of 2002. Since then *Expo* has continued as a quarterly. The original logotype with the large X was designed by Stieg, but disappeared when the layout was redesigned in 2004.

Coping with the Growing Neo-Nazi Threat

The growing threat posed by neo-Nazis was made explicit in 1999. On May 28 of that year, Tony Olsson, a founder of the Nazi NRA (interpreted to mean "National Revolutionary Army"), who had been sentenced for conspiracy to murder, escaped from jail. He and two fellow Nazis, Jackie

Arklöv and Andreas Axelsson, robbed a bank that day and killed two police officers with shots to the backs of their heads. Stieg Larsson wrote about this in *Expo,* quoting the extreme right-wing international "Blood and Honor network,", which had declared, "The gunfight between national socialists liberating bank funds and ZOG-troopers is a just vengeance for the police murder of patriot Martin Krusell in Malmö in 1991." ("ZOG" is an acronym used by the right wing for "Zionist occupied government.") On June 28, a car bomb exploded in the Stockholm suburb of Nacka, seriously harming a journalist and his eight-year-old son. Both the journalist and his partner had written for *Expo;* they were living undercover and had police protection at the time of the incident. On October 12, trade union activist Björn Söderberg was shot to death outside his apartment in another suburb. Söderberg had refused to let his coworkers play white power music at work. He had also disclosed to the press that one of the local union board members was a known Nazi. The murder of Söderberg took place soon after the Nazi was removed from the board and fired.

Stieg responded to these attacks not only by covering them in articles, but by writing a short book for journalists about how to protect yourself when working on stories concerning potentially violent persons or groups. This was published as *Överleva deadline—handbok för hotade journalister (Surviving Deadline—Manual for Threatened Journalists)* by the Association of Swedish Journalists in 2000. It's a hands-on manual, discussing various forms of threats, the reasons for them, and the different psychology of those who threaten. When a threat is perceived as serious and when the threatening party can be assumed to have the determination and means to act, a number of defensive moves are recommended. One particular step recommended in the handbook was to check if your passport picture has been requested by someone. Until 2004, passport photos were public documents and could be requested by anyone. Stieg knew that shortly before the murder of Björn Söderberg, someone using the name "Peter Karlsson" had requested the photos of some twenty people, among them not only Söderberg, but Stieg Larsson as well. Other advice included: never answer the phone in person; install a safety door; do not post your name on your door; always check who is outside before opening, and much more.

Stieg and Eva followed most of this advice in their personal lives. Eva installed a safety door. Stieg made it a habit to arrive unpredictably for meetings. He avoided walking the same route twice in a row. He avoided being photographed. In public places, he usually sat facing the door with his back to a wall. When *Expo* moved to a new location, its offices were on the top floor of a tenement house close to police headquarters, and only the very common name "Larsson" was listed in the building directory. The apartment where Stieg and Eva lived was marked only with the name Gabrielsson.

Stieg was not new to subterfuge and to security measures. The revolutionary communist groups in Sweden at the beginning of the 1970s were monitored by the secret police. Knowing this, Stieg had to be careful when he did things like smuggle copies of the Trotskyite *Röd Soldat* (*Red Soldier*) magazine to other drafted soldiers.

Stieg had received threats since 1982 and was well aware of having enemies who had proven themselves willing and able to kill. To some, taking present-day Nazis that seriously might seem melodramatic. But even the virulent hatred expressed by Swedish "white power" rock bands like Blood and Honor, Somalia Kickers, SS Totenkopf, and White Warriors tells only a fraction of the story. Theirs are the equivalent of PG-rated hate videos, compared to the XXX one Stieg once played for me at *Expo*, and which he thought ought to be included in the school curriculum. It showed a group of young males, naked to the waist, with shaven heads and Nazi tattoos, performing on stage to screaming admirers a song endlessly repeating the phrase, "kill a nigger." Spliced in were film sequences showing black people being shot, stabbed, burned, and hung. Stieg's view was that as long as this kind of abomination is watched only in secret, by half-drunk, angry, and alienated young men, it might be cheered. But if shown in the open, where those sympathetic to it have to defend it against those who are not, it would be defused.

Stieg believed each individual to be responsible for his or her actions, and that each of us has the sole right to decide which risks to take and how to act to be true to our convictions. In his book about Stieg, Kurdo Baksi writes about being upset when he discovered that Stieg had accepted the idea of young *Expo* contributors infiltrating fascist organizations to gather information. Baksi says this is unacceptable, since the young journalists might have come to harm, and that Stieg should have prevented them from taking such risks. To me, the chapter ("The Infiltrator") indicates a surprising lack of understanding of Stieg's way of thinking. Stieg would have discussed such projects with the journalists. He would have made sure that they understood the dangers involved, knew which rules to follow, and had access to a backup. After that, he would have considered them responsible for their own decisions and supported their choice.

Another area where Stieg differed from many was in his rejection of ageism and paternalism. To him, thoughts like, "He's only sixteen, but I ought to talk to him as if he were an adult" would have been alien and absurd; of course you treat all individuals equally. An adult is a person who by his or her choices and acts takes adult responsibility. The idea that someone else should make decisions for you, or prevent you from making your own, was immoral in Stieg's judgment.

The Meaning and Mess of Life

Although unafraid for himself, Stieg worried that his work might endanger Eva. She had not made the decision to risk her life by exposing fascists. She had "only" made the decision to live with Stieg Larsson. The views they shared meant that she accepted his right to make his own choices within their relationship, just as she had the same right to choose for herself. But this did not mean that he was free to ignore her safety in making his choices.

Much has been made of the fact that Stieg and Eva never married. Among other reasons for their decision not to marry, Stieg and Eva's security concerns were important, although perhaps incomprehensible to those who don't know the Swedish system. Since 1947, all Swedes have been issued a ten-digit "personal number." This number is your primary identification code. It is the basis for all records and it is cross-referenced with your credit cards, library card, bank accounts, rental contracts, school grades, and income tax returns. Anyone who knows your number can find your phone numbers, address, place of employment, parents, car make, siblings, children, criminal record, and rate of growth while in day care. They can easily find your marriage record, your spouse's personal number—and so on. Unauthorized persons are not supposed to be able to retrieve all this information. But under Swedish freedom-of-information laws, a considerable amount of information in public databases must be disclosed on demand. There are also glitches in the system. A frightening number of women living with protected identities have been found and murdered by their tormentors through the simple expedient of asking some public agency for copies of correspondence. This is not supposed to happen. But it does, again and again.

If you want to be secretly married, Sweden is not the place to try. As I knew Stieg and Eva, at least during the first many years of their relationship, they both felt that marriage as an institution was an outmoded patriarchal women's trap. And later, when they perhaps felt differently, the risks to which formal marriage would expose them had become real concerns. Even so, Stieg always called Eva "my wife."

Stieg and Eva lived full, busy lives. But in summers, they tried to take time off together, sometimes renting a cottage in the Stockholm archipelago where they walked, wrote, talked, and rested. They sailed the *Josefine,* their mahogany motorboat, or rented a sailing boat. Eva Gabrielsson has written:

> Life with Stieg was a mess but hung together. Our circle of friends and collaborators was a speckled international crew that grew and changed through life. Always there were new unholy groups of nerds from all possible fields of knowledge and with different ethnic, religious, political and social backgrounds, ages and occupations. It didn't make life simple. In the academic world it is called inter-disciplinary. In real life it's a cross draft. It was very refreshing. Stieg viewed this confluence of individuals as a kind of dynamic harmony. Not everyone else did. Quarrels could be explosive. Stieg viewed that kind of thing calmly. "It's their problem," he said. Respect and tolerance were his way of life, though it should be said that he was better at that than most people, myself included.

And of course Stieg and Eva had their arguments. Stieg was uninterested in money, bookkeeping, keeping regular hours, or interrupting his writing or his discussions for any reason. Eva did their tax returns and saw to practical day-to-day necessities. When money was scarce, Eva prepared lunch boxes for them. Stieg would "forget" his; he liked eating in coffee shops or fast-food joints. It was up to Eva to somehow make ends meet. Twice during the chaotic 1990s, she has said, she walked out on him in exasperation, living for a few weeks with friends. But they had grown together. She held on.

Both of them loved working. And enviably, they were able to work at things they loved doing, and would have done as hobbies otherwise. If they never married, they ought to have written wills. But Stieg never made much money nor owned much of any economic value. When Stieg said in 1977 that, "I'm still broke, but the move to Stockholm has brought at least one good thing with it. I can again let Eva support me," he was making a joke out of a fact. During his years of employment he hardly enjoyed lavish wages.

After quitting TT Stieg received over a year's wages in severance payment, but he had to use this money not only for his personal expenses but also to help finance *Expo.* He once told me that if the magazine happened to have any money, he would draw a salary of around SEK10,000 a month— about US$1,500. The laptop Stieg used both at work and at home belonged to *Expo.* His thousands of mostly paperback books had little secondhand value. I suspect that with so little in the way of material possessions or money, Stieg felt the need for a will less than pressing, even as he grew older.

By the end of 1999, Stieg Larsson could finally work full-time at *Expo*. The magazine was still an insert in *SvartVitt,* but there was no lack of work. Since the late 1990s, he had also become a sought-after lecturer. He began appearing on TV and radio. He spoke at schools and symposia, gave advice and information to politicians, journalists, debaters, researchers, and police officials. The Expo Foundation became the Swedish partner in the European Racism and Xenophobia Information Network, RAXEN, coordinated by an agency of the European Union, which entailed providing both reports and continuous information. Stieg was very much involved in this work, as well as in numerous new projects.

Taking on the "Sweden Democrats"—Who Are Anything But Democratic

In 1988, a new political party was formed, called Sverigedemokraterna ("The Sweden Democrats" or "SD"). Among its founders were Leif Ericsson, earlier a founder of the "Keep Sweden Swedish" anti-immigrant organization, and Anders Klarström, previously active in the Nordic Reich Party. Nothing much distinguished the Sweden Democrats from other minuscule right-wing groups, but they kept growing. In the 1988 elections, the party received only 1,118 votes; by 1994 their vote count reached 13,594 and they won five seats on local councils. By 1998, the numbers were up to 19,624 votes and eight local council seats. A new leader was at work trying to make the party somewhat more respectable, by banning "uniform-like" dress and curbing openly racist statements.

By the late '90s, the SD had become by far the strongest of Swedish anti-immigrant organizations. Stieg felt that something had to be done about it. He was worried the party might make racism palatable in Sweden, disguised as a critique of "overly liberal immigration regulations." Stieg decided that *Expo* must start a campaign to expose the fascist roots of the new party, and to write a book about it in cooperation with *Expo*'s youngest staffer, twenty-one-year old Mikael Ekman. In June 2001, they signed a contract for the book. From early July, they basically lived at *Expo,* writing and checking facts around the clock. In November 2001, the 364-page book was put on sale and caused considerable attention, as did *Expo*'s campaign against the Sweden Democrats. But Stieg was never naïve enough to believe that exposure could put an end to the party. What he hoped for was damage control. In many European countries, anti-immigrant parties had been elected to Parliament and gained considerable influence. Stieg's hope was to spread enough information about the racist nature of the Sweden Democrat ideas to keep them small.

Even while many political experts dismissed the idea that the SD could gain a following in Sweden, Stieg predicted that the SD party would gain enough votes to win some seats in the Parliament after the 2006 election. He turned out to be wrong, but only by one election cycle. In 2006, they won 2.9 percent of the vote. Since the cutoff for representation in the Swedish Parliament is 4 percent of the vote, seats eluded them. But in the 2010 election, the Sweden Democrats won 5.7 percent, giving them twenty seats in the Swedish Parliament. *Expo* has continued the work Stieg started by exposing the party's roots in overtly racist and fascist groups, and by countering its simplistic agenda of solving all problems by limiting immigration.

Honor Crimes

When *SvartVitt* folded at the end of 2002, *Expo* continued on its own. Since 1998, Stieg had been officially editor in chief. The magazine clearly had problems. Money was scarce, as always, and Stieg was not an administrator. The situation was precarious and sometimes chaotic. Soon he was also troubled by a sudden debate that began filling the Swedish media over "honor crimes," "honor killings," and "cultures of honor."

On January 21, 2002, twenty-six-year-old Fadime Sahindal was shot to death by her father in central Uppsala. She had left her Kurdish family after refusing to submit to their views on morality. She had become a public figure after giving a speech to the Swedish Parliament about the plight of young women in many immigrant families. Her father said that she had dishonored her family by openly criticizing its morality and flaunting her independence, leaving him no choice but to kill her. Her murder was also a reminder of the 1999 killing of nineteen-year old Pela Atroshi by two of her uncles.

The media debate over honor crimes was deeply worrying to Stieg. His view was that all intolerance stems from the same source, regardless of whether the group selected for persecution happens to be distinguished by its color, gender, sexual preferences, or any other arbitrary attribute. But the "honor murders" debate seemed on the verge of muddling this truth. Feminists were accusing men from certain cultures of persecuting women, while antiracists defending cultural acceptance ran the risk of being perceived as indifferent to men's abuse of women.

Stieg wanted to help turn the debate away from this potentially damaging polarization of feminist and antiracist views. In collaboration with journalist Cecilia Englund, employed by the Expo Foundation as its RAXEN liaison, he edited *Debatten om hedersmord: Feminism eller rasism* (*The Honor*

Murder Debate: Feminism or Racism), a book to which nine writers contributed.

In his own essay for the book, Stieg began by describing the brutal murder of Melissa Nordell, a twenty-two-year-old fashion model, by her thirty-seven-year-old boyfriend. Both were ordinary Swedes, and the murder was an ordinary Swedish "family tragedy," the term commonly used by media to describe men's violence against women with whom they are in extended relationships. Stieg's point, which he emphasized by calling Melissa Nordell and Fadime Sahindal "sisters in death," was that both had fallen victim to the same male wish to control women and their sexuality. In an ironic paragraph, he compares media treatment of the two murders:

> The murder of Melissa according to the media . . . was a cruel and planned torture killing, but also an obvious "act of insanity" based in jealousy. Her boyfriend simply couldn't tolerate that Melissa wanted to choose her own path and shape her future regardless of his wishes. While the murder of Fadime was a "culturally conditioned honor killing." Her father simply couldn't tolerate that Fadime wanted to choose her own path and shape her future regardless of his wishes.

Stieg's point was that male violence against women stems from a male desire to control women's bodies and choices, a desire given its cultural and political expression in the patriarchal social structure dominating the world. Claiming that murders of women within some cultures are "culturally conditioned," while murders of women within others are not, is simply a form a xenophobia, he argued; it's the equivalent of saying, "Native Swedes commit murder because they're crazy, but immigrants commit murder because they're immigrants." Or, in other words, with Swedish criminals, blame is individual; with non-Swedish criminals, blame is collective. And that, in Stieg's view, was racism.

Reactions to the anthology were mixed. Many noted that the book was not an impartial appraisal of the debate; almost all contributors basically shared the views expressed by Stieg. Others objected to the implied denial of "cultures of honor" as an existing reality.

I suspect that Stieg for once was blinded by his conviction that claiming some cultural characteristics inferior to others implies a form of racism. But cultural patterns do influence individual behavior. And rigidly sexist cultural patterns, enacted in law and exalted in religion, make social change much more difficult to effect. For this reason, to those of us who place a supreme value on individual human rights, cultural relativism is not possible. In my opinion, this part of the equation was missing from Stieg's analysis. But I should add that he did not agree when we discussed this.

The Storyteller

All of us need to relax and refresh our thinking from time to time. Stieg was no exception. To the outsider, the difference between what he did at work and in his free time may have seemed negligible. Whether working or relaxing, what Stieg actually did was read voraciously and write endlessly. But shifting focus, working on different texts and thinking about different problems, gave him the relaxation necessary to feed his energy and enthusiasm. He loved what he spent his time doing, and for most of his adult life he did almost only what he loved.

One thing he loved doing was telling stories.

He told them in different ways. In his teens, he wrote fiction. When he was with his friends, he told anecdotes or stories he had heard, made up, or experienced. And in the 1990s, when during his last years at TT he began using e-mail, he amused himself by writing word sketches or brief stories, sometimes inspired by news items, sometimes invented. He sent these "prose doodles" to people he thought might appreciate them.

In July 2002, Stieg Larsson and Eva Gabrielsson rented a cottage in the Stockholm archipelago. Eva was writing a book on Per Olof Hallman, the pioneering architect and city planner who was a main creator both of modern Stockholm and other Swedish cities. They set up their laptops on opposite sides of the kitchen table, and, while Eva began working, Stieg wondered what to do. One of them remembered a story fragment he had written in 1997 about an old man who on each birthday for over forty years receives a framed flower from an unknown sender. "Why don't you go on with that story," Eva said. "I've wondered who sends him those flowers."

"So have I," Stieg said. And he got down to writing.

That fragment from 1997, in edited form, is the prologue to the first of Stieg's crime novels, *The Girl with the Dragon Tattoo*. He wrote parts of the book during their summer vacation that year, discussing scenes and themes with Eva while she discussed with him the architectural and social visions of Stockholmers a century earlier. Her knowledge of Hallman found its way into Stieg's novel. Most sympathetic characters live in parts of Stockholm designed by Hallman. This was how they worked when together—writing, juggling ideas, joking, and writing some more while the light held, then walking, reading, having coffee, and talking about where their writing was going.

So it began. So it continued. Eva worked full-time and continued with her book in her spare time; Stieg wrote his as a relaxation from work, from problems at *Expo,* and from his many other commitments. During the spring of 2003 the first novel was finished and the second begun. The first was sent off to Piratförlaget, but it was rejected unread. In the summer of 2003, in another rented cottage, Eva continued writing about the creation of modern Sweden, while Stieg was by now well into *The Girl Who Played with Fire.*

Stieg's working habits have by now become common knowledge. But much said about his lifestyle seems judgmental rather than descriptive. Certainly he kept unusual hours. Certainly he smoked a lot—when I first knew him in the seventies, mostly a pipe, later mainly cigarettes, for a while rolling them himself. And he drank a lot of coffee, although in the seventies he more often had tea. But among the freelance writers I've known, none of this would be uncommon. If anything distinguished Stieg, it was that he drank very little liquor. After the first few years on his own in Umeå, he came to dislike feeling drunk. Wine with food or a good single-malt whisky, certainly. But not to excess and usually chased by some more coffee. As for food, he viewed it mainly as a necessity. Not that he couldn't appreciate great cooking; he just didn't consider it worth the time, trouble, or cost when a hamburger or pizza would do just as well. In general, he thought the "point" to eating was to get energy to do more interesting things.

Stieg was thin, wiry, and boyish. At forty, he still looked like a man in his twenties. After that, he filled out a bit, gaining rounder cheeks and a belly. He disliked exercise, but he did walk and never got a driver's license. He said that he seldom slept longer than six hours. That's hardly unique. In the last few years, being his own employer at *Expo,* Stieg's working day might well start by waking at noon or later, having coffee, smoking the day's first cigarettes, packing his computer and whatever else he might need, then taking the bus, having breakfast in a café somewhere, and arriving at *Expo* at two or later in the afternoon. Unless there were lectures or other commitments, he might stay at *Expo* until midnight or later, always with a cup of coffee and an overflowing ashtray on his desk, before again packing his computer and returning home. Once back home, he would set up his computer, check his mail, and work on his novels until he grew too tired to go on.

Early in 2004, the second novel was done, ending on a cliffhanger—the heroine almost dead, the murderers on the loose. Stieg let Robert Aschberg read the two books. Aschberg is a journalist and TV host and was a strong supporter of *Expo.* He had published several books. After reading Stieg's manuscripts, Aschberg showed them to his publisher, Norstedts, one of the largest Swedish publishing houses.

The manuscripts were read by legendary Norstedts publisher Lasse Bergström, who was retired but was retained as a consultant. In his report, Bergström wrote: "He has a kind of encyclopedic gift for literary tension and entertainment. . . . I find it hard to think of an equivalent of Lisbeth Salander anywhere in the worlds of crime novels or films."

Stieg was offered a three-book contract, promising that the third novel would be finished in the summer. On April 28, 2004, Stieg received the contract from Norstedts. He phoned me to ask if I would take a look at it, since I had a fair amount of experience as a publisher.

He mailed me the contract. Two things were notable. It was a combined hardcover and paperback contract for all three novels. The advance was close to US$85,000, unusually high for Swedish publishing. Norstedts was anxious not to miss out on Stieg's books. Apart from the unusually high advance, the royalty percentages were standard. I suggested to him that, since the publisher obviously thought his books would do well, he might be able to negotiate a higher royalty. He said that he thought the publisher would make a greater effort to sell his books if they stood to profit more, and that might well make a bigger difference than a couple of percent. This was typical; from the beginning, Stieg was certain that his novels would find a large audience. But then everyone who read them in manuscript, myself included, told him that they would, so he hardly had any reason to doubt it.

The second notable thing about the contract was the agenting rider attached to it. Norstedts wanted to handle all subsidiary rights to Stieg's novels. They also wanted a hefty piece of the action; the fee stated in the contract was 35 percent on income from secondary sales.

I told Stieg that he really had three options. He could retain subsidiary rights and get a freelance agent to handle them for him. This would give him a larger degree of control as well as a larger piece of the profits, since literary agents normally charge from 15 to 25 percent. The percentage proposed by Norstedts was unusually high for Swedish Publishing. He could suggest changes to the contract, either to retain more personal control of his work, or to lower their percentage, or both.

I made another suggestion: he might simply ask for a clause that the contract should run for a limited period and then be renegotiated. Stieg said he would think about it and talk it over with Eva. In the end, I understand that he just signed the contract and didn't try to change the terms. Using the most conservative estimates, his novels have earned around $70 million in royalties by now—with much more on the way. That means his novels have enriched Norstedts by $25 million, while the rest has gone to Stieg's father and brother.

As for the novels, Stieg e-mailed them to me in manuscript form. I printed them out as they arrived and read each one at the kitchen table, beginning after dinner and finishing late at night. When reviewing the first of them, I said that Stieg's novel was the best first Swedish crime novel published, and superior to most crime fiction written in the country. This is not to say that Stieg's novels are perfect. They aren't. He was sometimes a sloppy writer, and the novels improve as he gets into his stride and becomes more certain of his themes, ideas, and characters. I would have loved to see the books he might have written further on in the series. He talked of doing at least ten. If the first three were impressive, I suspect the last three would have been amazing.

Stieg finished the first draft of the third novel in July but didn't send it to Norstedts until August 11. During the summer of 2004, he, Eva, and Eva's sister traveled in Sweden. Stieg and Eva had discussed how to use the money from the novels and decided to spend the income from the first book on a house of their own—a small cottage in the Stockholm archipelago. Eva was working on a large planning project in Dalarna, commuting weekly from Stockholm. She spent weekdays at work, getting home by a three-hour train trip for the weekends. Stieg was already working on the fourth and fifth of his novels. In July, as usual, they both took a couple of weeks off from work, this time driving south, and on July 31, 2004, they came to visit at my home.

I live with my family in a village on the sound separating Sweden from Denmark. Stieg, Eva, and Eva's sister spent the afternoon and much of the night, having dinner and talking into the small hours. The night was warm, we sat outdoors on the patio, life was good, we drank whisky and smoked, joked and talked about politics and literature, about Stieg's novels, about xenophobia and the seeming impossibility of tolerance even in this new millennium. The moon rose and began sinking. The smoke from our cigarettes kept the mosquitoes at bay and Stieg was exuberant. "Finally I'll be able to take it easy sometimes," he said. "I'll finance *Expo* with some of the money from my novels. We'll be able to hire more people. And I'll be able to just write what I feel like."

It was the last time I saw Stieg.

On August 15, Stieg turned fifty. A party was planned, but postponed. There was too much else to do. He worked at *Expo* as usual, gave lectures, attended conferences in Switzerland and Israel. He continued writing the fourth and fifth Millennium novels. With Daniel Poohl, he began a brief handbook on racism for the Malmö Museum. On weekends he and Eva talked about the cottage they by now had decided to design and build themselves. Stieg kept in touch via e-mails, often talking about his books, and I recommended his first three novels in very strong terms to another old friend, Otto Penzler, founder of *The Armchair Detective* and Mysterious Press.

On November 9, 2004, Stieg went to *Expo* to meet a Grenadian associate at around two in the afternoon. When he entered the office he was pale and sweating. A co-worker asked if he was ill, if they should call an ambulance. Stieg said that perhaps they should, he felt a pain in his chest. Then he collapsed. The ambulance arrived quickly and during the short trip to St. Göran's hospital, only a few blocks away, the paramedics kept asking Stieg for his name, his age, the year. Once he responded, saying, "I'm fifty, damn it!" At the hospital, doctors worked on him for almost an hour but finally gave up. At 4:22, Stieg Larsson was declared dead.

Early November 2004 was exceptionally warm for that time of year in Sweden. In the afternoon of Wednesday, November 10, I was standing in line by an ice cream truck with my two youngest children. My mobile rang. Eva told me that Stieg was dead. I was stunned. He was one of the most vital, optimistic, exuberant persons I had ever known. My children told me that I grew very pale. I felt numb.

The next time I saw Eva was on December 10, the day of Stieg's funeral service, a nonreligious ceremony at the Forest cemetery just south of Stockholm. Later the same day over a hundred friends and acquaintances gathered at a memorial in downtown Stockholm. People from around the world were present, representatives of liberation movements and antiracist organizations, people from underground groups and government offices, people in publishing, journalism, academia. Stieg had made a difference. His burial was a few days later, in private, and the place has not been made public. Stieg needs no swastikas defiling his grave.

At the memorial meeting, Eva read from the letter he had left her when going off to Eritrea more than twenty-seven years earlier, and which had remained sealed until she found and read it after his death. He had written:

I want you to remember me, but I don't want you to grieve for me. If I truly meant something to you, and I know I did, I am sure that you feel pain now that you've learned of my death. But if I truly meant something to you, you also know that I don't want you to be in pain. Don't forget me, but live on. Live your life. In time, the pain will pass, even if right now it doesn't feel as if it would. So live in peace, my beloved friend, live, love, hate, and go on

fighting. I had many faults and lacks, but I hope also a few good points.
You, Eva, woke a love within me I could never truly express in words. Take
care of yourself, Eva. Go have a cup of coffee. It's all over now. Thank you
for a wonderful time. You made me very happy.

I knew Stieg for more than thirty years, and I've known Eva for almost
as long. They were inseparable. They had grown together as few couples ever
do. Neither was complete without the other, but not in the sense of owning
or controlling each other; theirs was a continuing relationship of choice.
They were truly enviable.

When I last saw Stieg at my home on that almost tropical summer evening, he told me what he had decided. He wanted all rights to his novels to
be owned by a company controlled equally by him and Eva. The idea was
for it to pay them salaries and otherwise contribute to causes they deemed
worthy. Income from the first novel would enable them to build a small
house by the sea, to relax and write. Income from later books would be their
pension money, but only a reasonable amount; the rest would be used to
fund *Expo* for the foreseeable future, to help finance women's safe houses in
Sweden, and to further other of their causes.

Stieg said that he would ask Norstedts to have its legal department fix the
documents necessary to set this up. I can only assume that he did as he said.
But at the time of his death, no such documents had been signed. What happened instead is a tragedy.

PART FOUR

THE MILLENNIUM FILES

The crux of the books is a kind of gender war. Salander tortures men, beats them up, leaves them for dead. But, according to the moral world Larsson establishes, they deserve it. Larsson's nasty achievement is that you root for comeuppance. Did that wife-beater that Salander attacked just get sucked away by a freak tornado? Good riddance!
—Wesley Morris, *The Boston Globe*

In the Millennium trilogy, the boundary between private and public blur while the intertwining of different media and genres intensifies. Communications in Larsson's fictional universe are constantly and strikingly mediated and indirect: e-mailing, texting, programming, scanning, bugging, word processing, and talking on cell phones. When people speak face-to-face, we can be sure that the dialogue is soon interrupted by one of the ubiquitous media technologies.   —Magnus Peterson, *SVD* (Sweden)

Lisbeth Salander, Stieg Larsson's fierce pixie of a heroine, is one of the most original characters in a thriller to come along in a while—a gamin, Audrey Hepburn look-alike but with tattoos and piercings, the take-no-prisoners attitude of Lara Croft, and the cool, unsentimental intellect of Mr. Spock. She is the vulnerable victim turned vigilante; a willfully antisocial girl, once labeled mentally incompetent by the state's social services system, who has proved herself to be as incandescently proficient as any video game warrior.   —Michiko Kakutani, *The New York Times*

11. A MILLENNIUM SMORGASBORD

THOUGHT PROVOCATIONS AND REFLECTIONS AFTER READING STIEG LARSSON'S TRILOGY
by Dan Burstein

Lisbeth's moral compass . . . Zalachenko . . . Photographic memory . . .
Stieg Larsson's niece . . . The girl with the golf club . . . Kafka's ghost . . .
The Millennium spirit(s) . . . Lisbeth and Asperger's syndrome . . . and
more . . .

Lisbeth's moral compass doesn't point to murder: Readers who race
through the Millennium books frequently draw the conclusion that Lisbeth
will stop at nothing to achieve her version of vengeance, retribution, and
justice vis-à-vis any bad guy she meets. She is skilled at martial arts, has a
superheroine's familiarity with the tools of the violence trade, and a particularly well-tuned ability to inflict extreme pain on men who outweigh her by
a factor of two or three without giving it a second thought. However, whenever possible, she intentionally and consciously stops short of murder. Stieg
Larsson goes to a lot of trouble to show us that whenever Lisbeth believes a
death sentence is warranted, she sets it in motion but tries to steer clear of
the technical act of murder itself.

Take the death of Wennerström in *Tattoo,* for example. The authorities
are looking for him after Blomkvist's exposé is published. Lisbeth knows
exactly where he is day by day, having hacked into all his computers and
e-mail. She plunders his bank account and transfers his money to her control. Then she monitors him on the run for months.

After six months, she tires of tracking Wennerström. She thinks about
calling the police but reconfirms her principle of not talking to them. She
reminds herself that Wennerström did bad things to women, in addition to
being a major financial criminal. Once she triggers the memory of Wennerström's violence toward women, she makes her decision to eliminate him.
But she is not going to do it herself. In a pattern we will see several more

times, she picks up the phone and calls an unnamed attorney in Miami. (We can infer that the attorney works for Colombian drug dealers whose debts have not been paid by Wennerström because Lisbeth has stolen the funds he needs to make good.) She tells the attorney's secretary where to find Wennerström, who is in the Spanish resort city of Marbella. Four days later, Wennerström's dead body is found in an apartment in Marbella. Lisbeth watches a TV news report on Wennerström's demise for a few minutes. Then she switches off the TV and makes herself coffee and a sandwich.

Martin Vanger's death at the end of *Tattoo* gets similar Salander treatment. When Lisbeth rescues Blomkvist from Vanger's basement torture chamber, she viciously attacks Vanger with a golf club, cracking his bones and causing him to howl in pain. But she doesn't actually kill him. Bloodied, crazed, and maniacal, Martin Vanger escapes in his vehicle. Salander gives chase on her motorcycle. She watches Vanger essentially commit suicide by increasing his speed and slamming into an oncoming truck. She didn't kill this horrible man who is evil incarnate, and has tortured and murdered so many women. He killed himself.

When it comes to Dr. Richard Forbes, the corrupt evangelist who Lisbeth deduces is trying to kill his wife, Geraldine, for her money in the early pages of *Fire,* something similar happens. With Hurricane Matilda blowing in and everyone in Grenada seeking shelter, Lisbeth prevents Forbes from seizing the moment to murder Geraldine. In a beachfront confrontation illuminated by occasional flashes of lightning, Lisbeth saves Geraldine before Forbes can deliver another blow to her skull with the pipe he is wielding. Lisbeth then cracks a chair leg over the back of Forbes's head, gathers up Geraldine, and, together with George, her sixteen-year-old Grenadian boyfriend, drags Geraldine to safety. Meanwhile, in one more flash of lightning, Lisbeth sees a tornado funnel forming and witnesses Dr. Forbes swept up by "the finger of God" and out to sea—never to be seen or heard from again. Lisbeth delivered a blow to the back of Forbes's head, but she didn't kill him. That was a job for God's vengeance.

Even when it comes to three of the people in Lisbeth's life who have most horribly abused her, she doesn't kill. In *Tattoo,* she extracts vengeance from her evil guardian Bjurman by giving him a serious taste of his own sexual violation medicine and by tattooing him across the belly with the message: "I AM A SADISTIC PIG, A PERVERT, AND A RAPIST." But while she punishes Bjurman with a hellish trauma that he relives every day for the rest of his life, she does not kill him. For the time being, she makes use of him. Later, in *Fire,* after Bjurman tries to arrange for Lisbeth's murder, he is killed by Niedermann, who is afraid Bjurman knew too much.

Lisbeth tries to kill her father, Zalachenko, in the farmhouse in Gosseberga at the end of *Fire* but ends up wielding the axe only to wound him severely, while she is almost killed herself by Zala's bullet to her brain. In the hospital at the opening of *Hornet's Nest,* where Lisbeth and Zala are in nearby rooms, it isn't clear who will first succeed in finishing off the other. But Gullberg breaks into Zala's room and kills him before he can give away the secrets of the "Section." Much as Lisbeth would have liked to kill Zala—she had tried as early as age twelve—in the end, it is Gullberg who accomplishes the task.

The pattern continues in the epilogue to *Hornet's Nest.* Lisbeth finds Niedermann holed up in the dilapidated warehouse owned by Zala (and recently on Lisbeth's inventory of inherited property after Zala's death). It was here that the women in Zala's trafficking network were housed in a state of sexual slavery and then murdered. Lisbeth takes on her half-brother Niedermann, the giant who feels no pain, ultimately nailing his feet to the floor with an industrial nail gun. She thinks about killing him, but decides not to. Instead, as with Wennerström in *Tattoo,* she makes some phone calls. First she calls the criminal motorcycle gang that is also looking for Niedermann. Then she calls the police who have been on an unsuccessful manhunt for Niedermann. Having set up the killing of Niedermann by the motorcycle gang, followed by the arrest of the gang members by the police, Lisbeth goes to a nearby shop, has a coffee and a sandwich, and goes home to take a hot bath. She concludes that she is "free" and that the painful story that began on the day of her birth is now over.

Lisbeth's culpability in these deaths is an interesting matter for philosophers, legal experts, and ordinary readers to consider and debate. But Stieg Larsson is very careful to set up the plot in each case so that Lisbeth's actions are always justified; she is always ready and willing to do what it takes to eliminate these scourges from the human race, but, in the end, she somehow manages to avoid actually doing the killing herself.

Blondie and Blomkvist: In the middle of *The Girl Who Played with Fire,* Blomkvist makes some coffee and mulls over what he really knows about Lisbeth Salander. He puts on his CD player and we learn that he is listening to Debbie Harry singing her 1999 hit "Maria." Aside from the fact that "Maria" was a fairly recent hit song at the time Larsson was writing this passage (most probably in 2003), why did he make this particular allusion? Could it be that he was starting his writing career over again as a crime novelist after more than twenty-five years as a politically engaged journalist? When Debbie Harry, the lead singer of Blondie, reached no. 1 on the U.K. charts with "Maria," she was fifty-three and the oldest female singer to have a no. 1 hit. She was restarting Blondie more than twenty-five years after the group split up. The song itself, with its lyrics about a young girl who basically "doesn't care," has many resonances with Salander, the person Blomkvist is thinking about at that moment and trying desperately to contact: "She moves like she don't care/You've gotta see her/She's like a millionaire . . ."

Hedeby Island: Most of the locations mentioned or described in Stieg Larsson's trilogy are real. In *The Girl with the Dragon Tattoo,* however, much of the action takes place in a purely imaginary location: Hedeby Island. It is here that the Vanger family has its compound. In the frozen Hedeby winter, Blomkvist and Salander team up to try to solve the mystery of Harriet Vanger's disappearance in 1966. As a Swedish island, Hedeby is fictional, but Larsson probably drew the name from the fictional village of Hedeby in a trilogy of novels by one of Sweden's major modern authors, Sven Delblanc. These were also made into one of the most popular TV series shown in Sweden, *Hedebyborna (The Hedeby Folks),* running from 1978 through 1982. Set before and during WWII, the story portrays the prewar "traditional" Sweden, depicting the vast chasm between peasants and barons, then goes on to indicate the transformation of Swedish society from a class-based to an egalitarian one. In a popular vote run by a radio show in 2010, *Hedebyborna* was voted the best Swedish TV series ever made.

There's also another connection: the old Viking town of Hedeby located in modern-day Germany, just south of the Danish border. Meaning "hearthland" in old Norse (Larsson's Hedeby serves as hearth and home to the dysfunctional Vangers in Larsson's story), this Hedeby was known as far back as the era of Alfred the Great. Even a millennium ago, it was famous for its bridges over the Schlei inlet. In Larsson's fictional Hedeby, the accident on the bridge connecting the island to the mainland looms large as providing the cover for Harriet's disappearance.

Zalachenko's not real, but Karl Axel Bodin is: When "the Section" sets Soviet defector Alexander Zalachenko (Lisbeth's father) up with a new name and a new identity in Sweden, he becomes known as Karl Axel Bodin. A real historical character by that name was undoubtedly borrowed by Larsson from his reading of Nazi history in Sweden. The real Karl Axel Bodin is said to have been a Nazi sympathizer who left Sweden during the war to join the Waffen-SS in Norway. At the end of the war, he and a friend stole a car in an attempt to escape from Norway, where there would be retribution against the Nazi supporters, and to get back to "neutral" Sweden. A gunfight erupted over the stolen car in which the car owner and Bodin's friend were shot. Bodin escaped to Sweden.

Harvard University Press probably wishes they had published this book: In the beginning of *The Girl Who Played with Fire,* Lisbeth Salander has become fascinated with spherical astronomy and is reading a book on that subject said to be called *Dimensions in Mathematics,* apparently written by L. C. Parnault and published by Harvard University Press in 1999. Although the citation sounds plausible, it turns out there is no such book. Harvard received so many inquiries that they felt compelled to issue the following statement in February of 2009, via Harvard University Press's blog:

> *Dimensions in Mathematics*—a phantom, a chimera: Readers who will have snagged a copy of Stieg Larsson's newest thriller *The Girl Who Played with Fire* . . . will have noticed that female protagonist Lisbeth Salander satisfies her nascent interest in spherical astronomy with the help of a book titled "Dimensions in Mathematics," written by one L. C. Parnault and apparently published by Harvard University Press in 1999.
>
> Unfortunately for those of you who would like to follow in Lisbeth's footsteps and penetrate the "dimensions of mathematics" for yourselves, you'll have to turn somewhere other than the work of the esteemed Dr. Parnault, for as far as we can tell, and if our memories and our computers have not completely failed us, HUP has in fact published no such work, in 1999 or at any other time. Thus it seems that Mr. Larsson, whose Scandinavian crime fiction has won him a good deal of posthumous fame, leaves us with more than just fictional mysteries. . . .

Photographic memory: In *Tattoo,* Blomkvist discovers Salander has a "photographic memory" when he realizes she knows every word of a passage

from Leviticus relevant to decoding the vicious unsolved murders they are
investigating, even though she had virtually no previous knowledge of the
Bible. When he asks her about it, she becomes obviously uncomfortable and
angry. Her extraordinary memory comes in helpful on multiple occasions
throughout the trilogy. In *Hornet's Nest,* we learn that Lisbeth's father, Zalachenko, is also said to have a photographic memory. Worth noting: there
is significant debate among brain researchers over whether anything like
"photographic memory" (or "eidetic memory," to use the scientific term) actually exists. Those who think it does exist don't usually believe it is heritable, although a recent study has suggested that extraordinary memory for
recognizing faces is a heritable trait.

Photographic memory (or near-photographic memory) is sometimes associated with autism (as in the case of Dustin Hoffman's famous role as
Raymond Babbitt in *Rain Man*), particularly with people who experience
Asperger's syndrome. We know that Larsson was interested in exploring Asperger's syndrome in his novels, and at various times described the Lisbeth
character as "suffering from Asperger's."

Photographic memory is also a trait used in many crime, science fiction,
and superhero stories, as well as in thrillers and literature and film across
many genres. Robert Langdon, of *Da Vinci Code* fame, is thought to have
a photographic memory. The same is true for Will (Matt Damon) in *Good
Will Hunting,* Dr. Lexie Grey in *Grey's Anatomy,* Captain Davidson, an Ursula K. Le Guin character, and, at various times in various presentations,
Superman, Batman, Wonder Woman, and Sherlock Holmes.

Was Stieg Larsson's niece Therese a model for Lisbeth? Stieg Larsson
didn't have children of his own. He appears to have been an intellectual
pied piper to a group of young people in the 1990s—but they were almost
all young men who wanted to work with him at *Expo* on researching, exposing, infiltrating, and fighting the neo-Nazis. So where did he get his deep
insights into the character of this unusual young woman, Lisbeth Salander? From many life experiences, from much reading, from thinking
about Pippi Longstocking as a young adult, as he told several friends and
interviewers . . . but one more important influence may have been Larsson's
niece, Therese, the daughter of his brother Joakim.

Now in her midtwenties, Therese would have been in her teens when
Larsson was writing *The Girl with the Dragon Tattoo.* According to Nathaniel
Rich, the first U.S.-based journalist to interview Therese Larsson, her uncle

Stieg was aware that she had often talked of getting a dragon tattoo, and that in the end, she had chosen to have a "large rose . . . tattooed on her shoulder." Rich's report, which appeared in *Rolling Stone,* suggests that the teenage niece in the remote north of Sweden and the middle-aged uncle in the capital city with adventurous life stories to tell had a special relationship, which included exchanging a lot of e-mails. "Larsson didn't visit Umeå often. . . . But he corresponded regularly with his niece by e-mail, Therese sending short notes and receiving what seemed to her like novel-length responses. He was an adult she could confide in, a role model and teacher who wasn't a parent, with whom she could discuss life as a teenager in Umeå."

According to Rich's account, Larsson e-mailed Therese with questions that seemed designed to fit into his research for the character of Lisbeth. The responses he received included information about Therese's struggles with anorexia and her interest in kickboxing. Rich quotes Stieg Larsson as telling his niece, "Lisbeth Salander is like you"—soft on the outside but hard on the inside. The same quote appears in a 2008 article from the Swedish newspaper *Expressen,* which went on to say that "Stieg Larsson used his niece as a model when writing his books . . ."

The *Expressen* article also says, "In hundreds of e-mails they discussed all that courses through the mind of a teenager." In 2009, with the Millennium books huge global best sellers and Lisbeth Salander arguably the most famous Swede who never lived, the Swedish newspaper *Dagens Nyheter* weighed in with a report indicating that Therese said that she and Stieg "e-mailed a lot and talked on the phone." This report notes that Therese was a rebellious teenager, wearing black make-up, with black hair and heavy boots. She was anorectic and so very thin, but always wanted to help the weak. "I often interceded in fights. It didn't matter if those fighting were 7-feet guys. I was just angry and felt no fear," she says in a self-portrait reminiscent of Salander.

Others wonder how close Stieg's relationship really was to this niece in his faraway hometown. Skeptics would like to see the e-mail correspondence archive. Unfortunately, the e-mails appear to be gone, lost in a hard drive crash. There are those who even speculate that Joakim Larsson, Stieg's brother, may be promoting the idea of his daughter as inspiration for Lisbeth in order to help legitimize the role Swedish law has already conferred on him—and may someday confer on Therese—as legally recognized heir to Stieg Larsson's posthumous fortune.

Larsson gave exactly one interview to the media about his novels prior to his death. It was with Lasse Winkler, editor in chief of *Svensk Bokhandel,* the Swedish book trade magazine. Winkler recounted his experience in a 2010 article for the U.K. newspaper the *Telegraph*. According to Winkler, at some point in the early to mid 1990s, when Larsson was working at the news agency TT, he and his colleague and friend Kenneth Ahlborn were developing an article about the classic detective stories that were popular with young readers in Sweden in the 1950s, '60s, and '70s. Larsson is quoted as saying, "We were kidding around, talking about how you could write about those characters" who would now be much older. "That planted the seed, but nothing materialized back then." It was not until 2001 that Larsson stumbled upon the spark that would bring the Millennium trilogy into being. "I considered Pippi Longstocking," he said, referring to the most famous creation of the Swedish children's author Astrid Lindgren, a girl so strong she could carry a horse. "What would she be like today? What would she be like as an adult? What would you call a person like that, a sociopath? Hyperactive? Wrong. She simply sees society in a different light. I'll make her twenty-five years old and an outcast. She has no friends and is deficient in social skills. That was my original thought."

In Larsson's talk with Winkler about Lisbeth's archaeology, he did not mention Therese, at least not according to the published accounts. Nor did he mention Therese in any other correspondence that has yet come to light. Of course there could be many reasons why he might not have mentioned a young family member in public discussions. As with so much else in Stieg Larsson's fiction, we are left to guess at what the real facts are.

Ronald Niedermann's congenital analgesia: Niedermann is the evil giant who turns out to be Lisbeth's half-brother. (His character may well have been created by Larsson with the Swedish actor Dolph Lundgren in mind, since Lundgren's height and build is suggested by Niedermann's details, even though Lundgren has claimed he turned down offers to be cast in any of the films.) Niedermann is able to be a particularly good foot soldier for his father, the evil Zalachenko, because of the medical syndrome he suffers from, congenital analgesia. This is a real medical syndrome in which a person literally feels no pain, even from experiences that would be extraordinarily painful to the most stoic normal person. The real-life medical syndrome is much more of a problem than a blessing, since pain is, for most people, a valuable warning signal. If your finger is burning and you feel no pain, you don't instinctively pull it away. Although congenital analgesia is very rare, it is also very serious, especially in children, who haven't yet learned other ways of intuiting what stimuli or experiences might be destructive to their bodies. Unlike photographic memory (discussed earlier), researchers do believe that congenital analgesia is inherited. Zalachenko, Niedermann's father, shows signs of being able to endure a great deal of pain, but does not have his son's complete oblivion. It might be noted that imperviousness to pain is a not uncommon plot element in the science fiction stories Larsson read voraciously. A prime example is Andrew Miller's novel *Ingenious Pain* (1998).

Equations, mysteries, and Lisbeth's family relationships? Stieg Larsson liked facts. He particularly liked facts that most general readers were not likely to know, which would stimulate insights once focused on. In *Tattoo,* he opened each part of the book with statistics about violence and abuse of women. In *Hornet's Nest,* he opened each part with a mini-essay recording some obscure but fascinating histories of women warriors in different parts of the world. For *Fire,* in keeping with the subplot of Lisbeth Salander becoming fascinated with Fermat's Last Theorem, Larsson opened each part with a statement about different kinds of mathematical equations. These included statements about concepts in mathematics known as roots, solutions, absurdities, unknowns, and identity. For example:

> *A root of an equation is a number which substituted into the equation instead of an unknown converts the equation into an identity. The root is said to satisfy the equation. Solving an equation implies finding all of its roots. An equation that is always satisfied, no matter the choice of values for its unknowns is called an identity.*

Some critics have interpreted the mathematical concepts Larsson has selected—roots, solution, absurdities, unknowns, and identity—as each having relevance to Lisbeth's odyssey in the course of the book. The Web site Shmoop.com points out:

> Aren't the epigraphs a fancy way of saying that to solve an equation (or mystery) we need to discover what, or who, is "unknown" from the available possibilities? Ronald Niedermann, Salander's half brother, ends up being the "solution" to the mystery. He is both the killer of Dag, Mia, and Bjurman, and the link to Zala that helps Salander learn the "roots" of her "identity."

Until [near] the end of the novel, Niedermann is completely *"unknown"* to Blomkvist, Salander, and the police. At the end of the novel, although the readers know Niedermann is the killer, his *"identity"* as such is still *"unknown"* to the authorities, and to most of the characters. Hopefully, this will be rectified in the final book of the trilogy.

We should also comment briefly on the third epigraph, which discusses *"absurdities,"* equations with no *solution.* Think of the problems in the novel—violence against women, rape of women in the sex trade, abuse of children in psychiatric wards, and corrupt journalists and officials. Going with equation metaphor, to find the *"solution"* to these problems implies finding their *"roots."* This could mean asking the question, What is the *root* cause of these problems? Since it's impossible (arguably) to prove precisely what causes humans to mistreat one another in these ways, the question is *absurd.* The equation (the question, the mystery) becomes an absurdity. . . .

The girl with the golf club: Toward the end of *The Girl with the Dragon Tattoo,* when Lisbeth Salander is trying to free Blomkvist from the clutches of the horrific monster, Martin Vanger, she attacks Vanger with a golf club that she finds in his garage. In the Swedish movie version based on the book, she actually gives chase to Vanger and attacks his SUV with the golf club, breaking the windows. The movie was released in the U.S. in 2010, but it had already been shown in Europe throughout 2009. Did Elin Nordegren, the Swedish-born wife of Tiger Woods, see the Swedish version of the film before the fateful Thanksgiving evening in 2009 that ended with the use of a golf club to crack the window on Tiger's SUV, and marked the beginning of the unfolding of Tiger's marital infidelity story? Is this merely a coincidence or a case of life imitating art?

If you love your coffee like Lisbeth and Mikael: The Jura Impressa X7 Espresso Machine that Blomkvist finds on its own separate table in Lisbeth's luxury apartment at Fiskargatan 9 is a real top-of-the-line restaurant-style coffee machine for home use. Although Larsson noted the cost was 70,000 Swedish kronor (US$11,000) at the time he wrote *The Girl Who Played with Fire* (which was sometime around 2003–4), the current U.S. online discount price for this magical Swiss machine is "only" about $3,000.

The first best seller where the characters dine on burek: Although Sweden's own unique and un-exported Billy's Pan Pizza from 7-Eleven is a staple in the diets of both Blomkvist and Salander, Monica Figuerola seduces Blomkvist into going out for a quiet dinner featuring a different kind of stuffed dough: burek. In *The Girl Who Kicked the Hornet's Nest,* Figuerola and Blomkvist get to know each other over a restaurant dinner featuring burek, the meat-filled pastry common in Bosnia and Herzegovinia, as well as other areas of the eastern Mediterranean.

Stieg Larsson's ghost channels Franz Kafka's ghost: The novels of Stieg Larsson have been compared to those by many other writers. But in terms of life story, perhaps the best comparison is to Franz Kafka.

Kafka, of course, never saw real literary success in his lifetime. Like Stieg Larsson, the only fiction Kafka published while alive was a few short stories. Like Larsson, Kafka is best known for three novels that were published posthumously—*The Trial, The Castle,* and *Amerika.* While not exactly an integrated trilogy in the way Larsson's Millennium novels are, there is a certain philosophical and existential relationship among Kafka's three books. There is also a distinct Kafkaesque sensibility of the individual against the state that comes out in Larsson's work. Although there are other modern writers who became widely celebrated only after they died (the poets John Keats and Emily Dickinson, for example), Kafka and Larsson are probably the two best examples of novelists who achieved extraordinary success only after the world learned of their books posthumously. Kafka died at age forty-one from tuberculosis; Larsson died at fifty from a heart attack.

Kafka had instructed his friend and executor Max Brod to burn all his writings on his death in 1924. Brod never intended to honor this request (and argued later that Kafka knew he wouldn't burn them). Brod proceeded to publish one of the three Kafka novels each year for the three years 1925–27.

Kafka, like Larsson, never formally married. He was twice engaged to one woman, and he was living with another, Dora Diamant, at the time of his death. Unlike Larsson, and owing to the values of that time period (early twentieth century), in Kafka's case, there was never any question of whether the women he had lived with would have any say over his literary legacy or the financial value that ultimately came from Brod's publication of the work. Like Eva Gabrielsson, however, Diamant believed she knew much about the mind and heart of her lover. She kept the letters Kafka had written to her and many of his notebooks as well, although she did cooperate with Kafka's request made as he was dying to burn some of the material. Later, Brod insisted Diamant turn all of her Kafka papers over to him. She refused and retained her own extensive archive of Kafka's material. However, when the Gestapo raided the apartment where she was living in 1933, most (or all) of the remaining Kafka works disappeared. Ever since, there has been a hunt to find these missing papers, much as people are now wondering about Larsson's fourth and fifth novels and his notes for others.

Just as Larsson's death has triggered a Larsson-like real-life plot of Eva Gabrielsson fighting Larsson's father and brother for control of her lifetime partner's legacy, Kafka's posthumous story has been a tortured, nightmarish, surreal, and bureaucratic tale that appears to be torn out of the pages of *The Trial* or *The Castle*.

There are those who think Max Brod had a greater role than previously thought in the actual finishing, editing, and perhaps even basic writing of some of Kafka's novels, just as some people think Eva Gabrielsson had a significant role as Stieg Larsson's writing partner.

There is now a great debate in Kafka studies over whether Kafka was a Zionist or an anti-Zionist, just as there is debate about whether Larsson was a "feminist" writer determined to expose abuse against women, or whether his explicit sex scenes cross the line into exploitation of women and voyeurism.

Max Brod's secretary/lover Esther Hoffe took control of some of Brod's archive after his death. In 1988 she decided to auction the original manuscript for *The Trial*. The price turned out to be $2 million, and the buyer the German Literature Archive in Marburg. No doubt this German cultural institution was trying to demonstrate its passion for Kafka, a Jewish writer, as part of Germany's modern purging of its anti-Semitic past, but others found it horrifying that *The Trial* was not going to the library at the Hebrew University in Jerusalem where Brod intended it to reside, but rather to a German institution. Author Philip Roth characterized this outcome as "yet another lurid Kafkaesque irony" that was being "perpetrated on 20th-century Western culture," observing not only that Kafka was not German (although he wrote in German), but also that Kafka's three sisters perished in Nazi death camps.

In a brilliant piece for *New York Times Magazine* on the unquiet death of Franz Kafka, Elif Batuman brought the world up to date on the last several decades of court fights and acrimonious debates over the last writings of

Kafka, and the battles among various heirs and claimants to the right to manage his literary legacy. Although she never mentioned Stieg Larsson, all three of whose posthumously published books were on the best-seller list at the time of her article (September 26, 2010), the parallels are fascinating. Especially for those who are wondering when we might see the mysterious fourth and fifth Larsson novels, it might be useful to listen to Batuman's recounting of the 2010 scene she witnessed in a Tel Aviv courtroom, as the fate of a sealed archive of Kafka works was debated:

> Of five rows of wooden benches in the courtroom, the first three were occupied by more than a dozen lawyers: two lawyers for the National Library; a representative of the Israeli government office that is responsible for estate hearings; and five court-appointed executors: three representing Esther Hoffe's will (which the National Library [in Israel—ed.] considers irrelevant to the case) and two representing Brod's estate (which the sisters' attorneys consider essentially irrelevant to the case). The German Literature Archive in Marbach, which has supposedly offered an undisclosed sum for the papers (said to be worth millions), was also represented by Israeli counsel. Ruth's lawyer and Eva's three lawyers rounded out the crowd. It's impressive that the sisters had between them four lawyers, although, to put things in perspective, Josef K. [the central character of Kafka's novel, *The Trial*—ed.] at one point meets a defendant who has six. When he informs K. that he is negotiating with a seventh, K. asks why anyone should need so many lawyers. The defendant grimly replies, "I need them all."

Batuman goes on to chronicle all the varying interests represented by all those lawyers—Eva and Ruth, the two daughters of Esther Hoffe (who died in 2007 at the age of 101, triggering much of the current debate over the disposition of what had become, in effect, her property); the German archive, which was in correspondence with Esther Hoffe over acquisition of the remaining papers at the time of her death; the National Library in Israel, which believes it has a right to all the material under terms of Max Brod's will; and other interests.

Today, Eva Hoffe remains in control of the archive, but the court has ordered her to allow the Kafka material to be inventoried. As Batuman writes,

The bulk of the collection remained divided among an apartment on Spinoza Street in central Tel Aviv and 10 safe-deposit boxes in Tel Aviv and Zurich. It is unclear how much of Brod's estate is still housed in the Spinoza Street apartment, which is currently inhabited by Eva Hoffe and between 40 and 100 cats. Eva's neighbors, as well as members of the international scholarly community, have expressed concern regarding the effects of these cats on their surroundings. More than once, municipal authorities have removed some of the animals from the premises, but the missing cats always seem to be replaced.

In a scene with clear Larssonian overtones, Batuman describes the feelings of the sisters:

Eva and Ruth, who fled Nazi-occupied Prague as children, are elusive figures who keep out of the public eye. The fact that they are represented by separate counsel reflects Eva's greater investment in the case. While Ruth married and left home, Eva lived with their mother, and with the papers, for 40 years. Her attorney Oded Hacohen characterizes Eva's relationship to the manuscripts as "almost biological." "For her," he told me, "intruding on those safe-deposits is like a rape."

But the court has ordered an inventory and the safe deposit boxes have begun to be opened, yielding "a huge amount" of original Kafka material, including notebooks and the manuscript of a previously published short story. Nine decades after Kafka's death, and after the world was treated to Max Brod's initial publications of Kafka's novels, we have come a little closer to finding out what else he left behind.

Lisbeth Salander and Gabrielle Giffords: When Representative Gabrielle Giffords began to make her stunning recovery after the horrific assassination attempt in Tucson in early January 2011, Larsson readers may have been less surprised than others. They had made it through difficult scenes involving a bullet to the brain of Lisbeth Salander. They had read about Lisbeth's surgery, her survival against all odds, and the moments when she first opened her eyes, gained consciousness, and began to speak. *The Girl Who Kicked the Hornet's Nest,* published in the U.S. in mid 2010, was one of the biggest-selling holiday books in December of that year. Many readers had just recently read the description of Lisbeth's miraculous recovery when Representative Giffords began the amazing progress that characterized her recovery.

Cerebral Stieg: There's a lot of thinking going on in the Millennium novels. We encounter dozens of scenes where characters like Blomkvist, Berger, Bublanski, Figuerola, Salander, Modig, Edklinth, Armansky, and even the bad guys spend not just minutes thinking over a problem, but hours. They take a bath and think for so long the water grows cold. They close the door to their office and think for so long that everyone has left by the time they come out. They sit "as if paralyzed, thinking." They go for a long run in order to think through a problem. "She sat quietly for two hours, smoking one cigarette after another, thinking." Armansky spends the whole Easter weekend at his cabin, thinking. Lisbeth stares at her computer screen for eleven hours while an idea emerges in some "unexplored nook of her brain." The words "think," "thinking," and "thought" appear almost five hundred times in the three books.

The Millennium spirit(s): By Swedish standards, Blomkvist doesn't drink very much alcohol (and reportedly neither did Stieg Larsson). Blomkvist's beverage of choice is coffee (there are at least 240 cups of coffee mentioned in the three Millennium novels). However, Blomkvist is said to like strong to medium beer. He has a few bottles of vodka and single malt scotch in his liquor cabinet. (We understand Stieg Larsson also favored an occasional good quality single malt scotch.) Early in *Tattoo,* Blomkvist drinks vodka until two a.m. with the evil Martin Vanger—although he doesn't yet know Martin is evil. In fact, he thinks him a relatively amiable character as Vangers go, who loves cooking, vodka, and music. They talk, drink, and listen to the jazz classic *Night in Tunisia* (although Larsson doesn't tell us if it is the original Dizzy Gillespie version or one of the later versions by Art Blakey, Miles Davis, or Sarah Vaughan). Blomkvist stumbles home drunk after a pleasant evening.

Erika Berger, who also doesn't drink much, is seen in *Tattoo* drinking Aberlour, a rare and distinctive single malt made at a mystical Scotland location that was once the home to Druids and later to early Christian monks who used the spring waters that now go into the local whisky for baptisms.

In *Hornet's Nest,* Gullberg drinks miniature Glenfiddich bottles from the minibar. When Blomkvist decides to camp out in Lisbeth's penthouse apartment, he discovers a wine cellar with a single bottle—an unopened Quinta do Noval port from 1976 that sells for several hundred dollars a bottle today.

In the beginning of *Fire,* we see Lisbeth drinking rum and coke at Ella Carmichael's bar in Grenada. She also drinks the occasional local Carib beer. Most of the time she sits alone with her drink and reads her math texts, trying to solve Fermat's Last Theorem, although there was one night when Lisbeth got so drunk, Ella had to call the porter to take her back to her hotel room. Lisbeth is also said to favor the Irish whisky Tullamore Dew—a drink that does not require luxury budgets or tastes, although it has a premium single malt version. The official Web site for Tullamore Dew even sports a description of Stieg Larsson's books and a quote about Lisbeth from *Hornet's Nest:* "When she ordered whisky, she always chose Tullamore Dew."

Tullamore Dew comes up several times, including when Mikael, Erika, and Malin Eriksson join Dag Svensson and Mia Johansson for a dinner to discuss their collaboration for an upcoming Millennium-themed issue on sex trafficking, which is based in part on Johansson's research for her thesis, *From Russia with Love: Trafficking, Organized Crime, and Society's Response.* The dinner takes place in the apartment where Dag and Mia will later be murdered, in the double homicide for which Lisbeth will be framed. But on this occasion, there is a festive mood. Mia serves "the best sweet-and-sour chicken Blomkvist had ever tasted." Over dinner, they put away "two bottles of robust Spanish red," and then Mia offers Tullamore Dew with dessert.

At the very end of *Hornet's Nest,* Lisbeth is in Gibraltar, binge drinking Tullamore Dew and beer at Harry's Bar, two blocks from her hotel. At one point she decides to try something else and, after staring at the bottles to narrow down her selection, she asks Harry for a shot of Lagavulin, a good quality but not particularly extreme premium single malt scotch. (Lagavulin is produced on the island of Islay in an area that has a storied past going back at least eight hundred years.) After a small sip of Lagavulin, Lisbeth decides it is awful stuff. In fact, she considers the contents of her glass to be "her mortal enemy," and asks Harry for something that could not be used to "tar a boat." Harry gives her another Tullamore Dew. After seven Tullamore Dews, "Liz," as Harry calls her, falls off her bar stool and crashes to the ground. Harry tenderly helps her to the toilet whereupon she throws up. It is after she sobers up that she propositions the German businessman for a sexual encounter with no questions, no commitments, and no responsibilities—other than that he needs to use a condom.

Putting out the fire: "She listened to David Bowie singing 'putting out fire with gasoline.' She didn't know the name of the song, but she took the words as prophetic." This is how Stieg Larsson describes Lisbeth's experience after she gets into a stolen rental car and heads toward what will turn out to be her near-death experience at the hands of her maniacal, brutal father (Zalachenko or Zala) and half-brother (Niedermann) at the farmhouse in Gosseberga. The song is an allusion to the incident in Lisbeth's past that gives the English-language book its title, *The Girl Who Played with Fire.* The fire is both real and metaphorical, referring to Lisbeth's attempt at age twelve to burn her father to death by pouring gasoline on him and setting him on fire. She is also "playing with fire" in the sense that she is taking on her violent father, his criminal gang, and, as we will find out, secret conspirators within SAPO and in the upper echelons of the Swedish government.

To more prosaic matters of pop culture: the song with the lyrics about "putting out the fire with gasoline" is David Bowie's 1982 song generally known as "Cat People (Putting out the Fire)." Among the lyrics: "I've been putting out fire/With gasoline . . . These tears can never dry . . . You wouldn't believe what I've been through. . . ." The song, which seems to capture Lisbeth's spirit in many ways, was originally written for the 1982 erotic-horror movie *Cat People* and was used again by Quentin Tarantino in his 2009 film *Inglourious Basterds.*

Does Lisbeth have Asperger's syndrome? Blomkvist wonders to himself if Lisbeth has Asperger's syndrome in *Tattoo.* She seems to fit the criteria. But elsewhere in the trilogy, particularly in *Hornet's Nest,* as we read through all the efforts to trump up mental disorders against Lisbeth that will succeed in rendering her mentally incompetent and in need of guardianship, Larsson seems to be steering us away from any diagnosis at all. Although she seems to show classic signs of Asperger's syndrome, Larsson is also trying to tell us: look at the whole person, don't put labels on people, understand and be tolerant of the wide variety of personalities in our world, judge, if you judge at all, by what people do and how they live their lives, not by fear of nontraditional behaviors or differences in clothing, habits, or tattoos, nor by abstract diagnoses in a mental health book.

Larsson appears to raise the idea of Asperger's only to dismiss it. Yet we know from his correspondence while he was writing the trilogy that he intended to feature Lisbeth as a character with Asperger's syndrome and that he believed having such a lead character was a breakthrough thing to do in a crime novel.

Lisbeth's friendly brain surgeon, Dr. Jonasson, who removes the bullet from her brain in *Hornet's Nest,* argues with the evil Dr. Teleborian that Lisbeth is not a paranoid schizophrenic or a paranoid, delusional sociopath as Teleborian believes, but should be thought of with a much "simpler" diagnosis—Asperger's. In fact, there are many kinds of Asperger's on the spectrum of autism, and a variety of overlaps between Asperger's and other types of spectrum disorders. Most people with Asperger's are fairly ordinary people and are not necessarily either incredibly brilliant nor completely socially clueless. However, there is a not infrequent form of high-functioning Asperger's whose hallmarks include various kinds of specialized intelligence in a person who, despite their brilliance, simultaneously lacks the ability to read basic social cues and to conform to "normal" social standards and expectations. If you have ever known a person like this, you know that part of their repertoire of survival skills is an uncanny ability to get under your skin, into your thoughts, and win a place in your life, even though they are supremely difficult and hard to deal with. Lisbeth is just like that in the way she captures Blomkvist emotionally, to the point that he can't stop thinking about her, even though there is no rational explanation for why he would want to remain involved with her.

At exactly the moment that Larsson was finishing the trilogy and getting it ready for publication, the first literary novel to win critical acclaim featuring a character with Asperger's was published: *The Curious Incident of the Dog in the Night-Time,* by Mark Haddon. (Haddon has since said he is not an expert on Asperger's or other forms of autism and thinks that readers who want to learn about these syndromes should read books written by people who have experienced them.) Both the title of Haddon's book and much of the plot relates in various ways to Sherlock Holmes—with the not-so-subtle implication that Arthur Conan Doyle, in his presentation of Holmes's character, may have been suggesting that Holmes was afflicted by something like Asperger's, although it was not then a known diagnosis. In a recent BBC series that brings Sherlock Holmes to life as a twenty-first-century character in contemporary London, Sherlock clearly has Asperger's or something resembling it. Played by Benedict Cumberbatch, this brilliant new Sherlock displays amazing feats of intelligence and intuition (and we see special effects that simulate the neurons firing in his brain to arrive at his conclusions so quickly). But he is a terrible friend and an extremely difficult person to all around him. At one point he blurts out, "I'm not a psychopath, I'm a high-functioning sociopath!"

Recent films and TV shows that have tackled Asperger's syndrome and other types of autism include: *Adam* ("A story about two strangers. One a little stranger than the other." Adam is played by Hugh Dancy and portrays the life of a young man with Asperger's whose passions are astronomy and a girl who just moved in upstairs); *Mozart and the Whale* (a 2005 movie based on the true story of Jerry and Mary Newport, showing how two people with Asperger's met and how their relationship developed); and episodes of *Boston Legal* and *In Plain Sight.* Some people think the only explanation for Sheldon's behavior on the comedy *Big Bang Theory* is Asperger's syndrome.

In the Pippi Longstocking children's books, Pippi is such a wild character drawn so clearly from an imaginative fantasy world that it would be hard to make an argument or even a comment about her psychological or behavioral profile. But by the time Pippi was turned into a Swedish TV character in the 1960s, the TV show's creative team clearly intended to convey that Pippi has a "problem," however unnamed or undiagnosed that problem might be. In numerous episodes of the TV show, Pippi consciously expresses the self-knowledge that she is not good at interacting with people in social settings. Even when she steels herself to be on her best behavior, she can't do it and something always goes radically wrong. Commentaries on Larsson have stressed his own stated interest in exploring the grown-up Pippi, now in her twenties, through Lisbeth. The similarities are obvious. Pippi and Lisbeth not only share red hair, Lisbeth shares Pippi's mythical strength despite her small size, her independence, her wealth, and her freedom to define her own personal and moral standards. But Larsson may also have been thinking about the Pippi from Swedish TV, which he would have seen in his youth, who had more than a hint of some sort of Asperger's-like syndrome.

John-Henri Holmberg tells us, "My suspicion would be that Stieg initially had the idea of an Asperger heroine, but gradually reached the conclusion that Lisbeth would be a stronger character if allowed simply to be totally self-sufficient but with no 'mental problems.' This would make her into a heroine and a possible role model, not an 'unfortunate' towards whom at least Swedish readers would automatically feel pity. Stieg was no friend of pity. My guess instead is that he began writing the first novel more or less without plan, got drawn into it, went ahead full steam into book two, and somewhere in there started to consider this as a series of novels." According to Holmberg, thinking of the books as a series caused Larsson to rethink a number of his initial assumptions, including possibly about Lisbeth and Asperger's.

The Lisbeths of American pop culture: In 2010, while all three Stieg Larsson novels were on the best-seller list and all three Swedish versions of the movies had their first U.S. showings, at least three new American TV series, with certain resonances to *The Girl with the Dragon Tattoo,* had their debuts. *Outlaw,* starring Jimmy Smits as a voluntarily retired Supreme Court justice, featured a goth-dressing, computer-hacking, define-your-own-morals character named Lucinda. The *New York Post* described her as: "a young, mentally disturbed, leather-and-hot-pants-wearing rocker chick/private eye," and said the show itself should be called *Girl with the Dragon Tattoo, Too.* Around the same time, the J. J. Abrams–created *Undercovers* premiered, featuring an episode set in Stockholm and a scene where Samantha Bloom, played by Gugu Mbatha-Raw, was in bed reading *The Girl with the Dragon Tattoo.* A new reincarnation of *La Femme Nikita,* this time called just *Nikita,* also premiered in 2010. *Nikita* (which was not canceled after its first season, unlike *Outlaw* and *Undercovers*) features two different takes on martial-arts-fighting/cyber-hacking/techno-savvy bad girls—the actress Maggie Q as Nikita, an elegant, stylish interpretation of Lisbeth Salander, and her partner in seeking rough justice, Alex, played by Lyndsy Fonseca, who performs a younger, more streetwise spin on the same character.

Aside from the powerful pull of the Lisbeth character, we also see other themes from Larsson's work reflected in other pop culture formats. The relationship between the aging Boomer-generation male investigative reporter for a newspaper (i.e., Blomkvist) and the young, computer-savvy female (i.e., Salander) is one that a variety of other authors and filmmakers have been exploring. In his 2009 novel *The Scarecrow,* best-selling crime writer Michael Connelly mined the relationship between Jack McEvoy, a veteran print reporter looking into a curious murder, and Angela Cook, an up-and-coming ambitious reporter he is supposed to train as his replacement. Similar sparks fly between Russell Crowe and Rachel McAdams at a screen version of the *Washington Post* in the 2009 film *State of Play.* In both *Scarecrow* and *State of Play,* the creators are dealing with generational issues, gender issues, and the different worlds of gumshoe-based print journalism and Web-based research and blogging. Larsson deals with all the same issues in the trilogy.

Women warriors: In *Hornet's Nest,* Stieg Larsson introduces each part of the book with a glimpse of little-known historical facts about women warriors. He writes about Boudicca, the warrior queen of the Iceni tribe who led a major uprising against the Roman Empire's invasion of the British Isles in about 60 CE, offering up the detail that tourists can see a statue in Boudicca's honor near London's Westminster Bridge. Queen Victoria is said to have found Boudicca a fascinating historical character and role model. (A few critics have noted that the English-language text of *Hornet's Nest* refers to Boudicca as leading an "English revolt" against the Romans, when, of course, there was no England or English people in that time period. Larsson was not wrong; the Swedish text refers to her as a tribal leader. This is another of translation mistake.)

Larsson suggests Hollywood has been missing a good story by not making a movie about what he says were some six hundred American women who disguised themselves as men to fight in the Civil War. A novel about this, with which Stieg was almost certainly familiar, and which was published in Sweden in 1988, was Rita Mae Brown's *High Hearts* (1986), about Geneva Chatfield who enlists in the Confederate Army after Fort Sumter. He also calls the reader's attention to *Amazons of Black Sparta: The Women Warriors of Dahomey,* a book by Stanley B. Alpern, which provides a fascinating historical account of the role of African women in the palace guard and the fighting forces of the African kingdom of Dahomey in the eighteenth and nineteenth centuries. This title had been out of print for a decade, but Larsson's reference to it has no doubt given the publisher good reason to reissue a new paperback in 2011.

Interestingly, one woman warrior Larsson does not address is Sweden's own Queen Christina. Of course she was not actually a warrior, although her father was the greatest of Swedish warrior kings. Her great seventeenth-century accomplishment was bringing peace to a northern Europe wracked by wars for decades. She also tried to create a Swedish renaissance by inviting scholars and thinkers from throughout Europe to visit at her court, including the father of modern philosophy, Rene Descartes, who ended up dying shortly after his arrival in Stockholm after catching pneumonia.

Thesis/antithesis/synthesis: In the evolution of the relationship between Mikael and Lisbeth, Stieg Larsson ended each book with a different scene that could have been drawn out of the Marxist dialectic of history's progression. At the end of *Tattoo,* Lisbeth, who has developed an emotional attachment and a sexual relationship with Blomkvist, has made the very difficult decision to communicate her loving feelings to him. On her way to doing so, with one of the first ever holiday gifts she has ever bought for anyone in hand, Lisbeth sees Mikael with Erika Berger, laughing and kissing outside Kaffebar. Having never before had this kind of emotional attachment, she now finds herself with other never-before-experienced sensations of pain and jealousy. She wants to use the sharp edge of her gift for Mikael to "cleave Berger's head in two." She calms down and takes no action. But she has determined she will never allow Mikael into her life again. Act 1 of the Millennium trilogy ends with Lisbeth forcing the demon of her love for Mikael out of her heart, mind, and world.

Lisbeth manages to keep Mikael out of her life for almost all of *Fire,* despite the fact that he is trying mightily to communicate with her and to help her when she is framed for triple homicide. He has no idea that she saw him with Erika, or even that she would care, given her hard-hearted, steely emotional persona. He also cannot understand why she won't communicate with him. Several reviewers have commented on Larsson's ability to use thoughts, dialogue, and e-mail to keep the relationship between Mikael and Lisbeth going for most of *Fire.* Emblematic of the increasingly virtual world we all live in—and unlike Nick and Nora Charles in Dashiell Hammett's *The Thin Man,* which Larsson loved, or Watson and Holmes, or any other sleuthing pair—Lisbeth and Mikael have most of their "conversations" over e-mail. Yet at the very end of *Fire,* on literally the last page, Blomkvist chivalrously rescues her from certain death at the farmhouse in Gosseberga where Zalachenko and Niedermann have tried to kill her. His heads-up thinking (taping her brain and skull together with duct tape and calling the ambulance) will save her life. So act 2 ends with events having finally pulled Mikael and Lisbeth physically together again.

Their relationship will move through a high-speed roller coaster of dangers, deaths, conspiratorial cabals, and plot twists throughout *Hornet's Nest.* But in the end, Mikael will ring Lisbeth's doorbell, and she will let him in, with his bagels and espresso, and the promise that he will show her how to use her expensive Jura Impressa X7 espresso machine. So act 3 ends with resolution of a kind—they will be good friends. But it is not crystal clear that she no longer has "those kinds of feelings" for him, as she thinks to herself. Or whether the more important point is that, "standing on her doorstep, he was still fucking attractive. And he knew her secrets just as she knew all of his."

We won't know for sure what happens until we see the currently AWOL act 4 of the mysterious fourth book manuscript. But while the very last published line of the last book of the trilogy can be interpreted any way you want, the suggestion of future intimacy seems palpable: "She opened the door wide and let him into her life again."

THE MORAL GEOGRAPHY OF STIEG LARSSON: EXPERIENCING STOCKHOLM IN THE FOOTSTEPS OF MIKAEL BLOMKVIST AND LISBETH SALANDER

by Dan Burstein

I am waiting for my luggage in Stockholm's Arlanda airport on an early morning in November, eager to get into town and start the experiential part of research for this book. Accompanied by my wife Julie and my co-author Arne de Keijzer and his wife Helen, I intend to walk the streets Stieg Larsson walked for the twenty-five years he lived in Stockholm, particularly his beloved Södermalm where much of the action in the Millennium trilogy is set. Many noir genre crime writers bring their cities to life even as their characters deal in death. Raymond Chandler's Los Angeles or Sara Paretsky's Chicago come to mind. But the attention to detail in Larsson's fictional Stockholm is more like James Joyce's vision of Dublin in *Ulysses*. The city itself is one of the stars of the show. And everything said about the city has a moral, political, and character-oriented overtone.

Above the luggage carousel in Arlanda is a huge banner. Where many cities might be featuring news about a local trade show or music festival, Stockholm's baggage claim has a more urgent and important message: a hotline for women to call if they are victimized by sex traffickers. The information is in several languages, including Russian. It is an immediate reminder that the fictional sex trafficking of Zalachenko and Niedermann—the subplot that drives much of the action in Larsson's second and third novels in the trilogy, The *Girl Who Played with Fire* and *The Girl Who Kicked the Hornet's Nest*—is an unfortunate and ugly reality of today's Sweden, as it is in the world.

Luggage in hand, we move through an exit corridor featuring a portrait gallery of the most famous Swedes of modern times: Greta Garbo, Björn Borg . . . and Stieg Larsson. Just a few years ago, Larsson would have been unknown to arriving tourists. But now he is a giant Swedish celebrity and a major national export industry, well known to millions all over the world as a result of the posthumous publication of *The Girl with the Dragon Tattoo* and his other books (as well as the three Swedish films and soon to be three

Hollywood films based on them). Larsson's books are actually one of the reasons thousands of tourists now flock to Stockholm. Package tours bring groups from France, Italy, Spain, the U.K., and the United States to Sweden specifically to go on Millennium tours. The prime minister of Spain, fascinated with the Larsson novels, is said to have gone on the walking tour incognito, pretending to be an ordinary tourist so he could focus on the experience of the tour.

The City Museum of Stockholm, for many years a sleepy institution frequented primarily by groups of school classes and grandparents with their grandchildren, is now host to the official guided "Millennium" walking tour of Södermalm. The tour is currently offered in nine languages, with more being added each season.

We will go on the Millennium tour soon after our arrival. Any tour of a city is a lesson in geography. But this one is a window into Stieg Larsson's "moral geography." One of the first things the museum guide explains is that the majority of the "good" characters—Mikael Blomkvist, Lisbeth Salander, etc.—live or work in Södermalm. The offices of the fictional *Millennium* magazine are said to be on Götgatan in the heart of Södermalm, approximately where we find the real-life offices of Greenpeace today.

The evil characters generally inhabit other parts of Stockholm, such as Östermalm, known for the highest priced real estate and the wealthiest citizens in Stockholm. And, if Södermalm is good and Östermalm is evil, then Kungsholmen, which lies between them, is a middle ground from which new good characters can be discovered and developed. Monica Figuerola, who I expect would have become a recurring investigator and love interest in future Larsson books (with her well-described combination of Olympic athleticism, intellectual brilliance, strong moral sense, and comfortable belief in sex without commitment), keeps in shape by running along Kungsholmen's Norr Mälarstrand, facing Södermalm, but not quite in or of it. She is, after all, an agent of the state. Bloomkvist's location mirrors hers: his apartment literally faces Kungsholmen, with the courthouse and other state institutions in full view. Even after Blomkvist has bedded her, even after he has witnessed her dedication to the constitution and to clearing Salander of murder charges, he still has to open up his own mind to his natural skepticism of the powerful Swedish state bureaucracy across the water.

Larsson had deep affection for Södermalm, appreciating its working-class history and wanting his key characters to have their roots on this southerly "island" of Stockholm.

Södermalm was once an isolated place, its residents largely made up of fishermen who were socially exiled here in order to keep the stench of fish out of the city's finer precincts. The high bluffs that make Södermalm among the few areas of this seaport city much above sea level were considered a major barrier to the island's accessibility until industrial-strength elevators began running in the late nineteenth century. Isolated and different from the rest of Stockholm, Södermalm developed as a bit of a wild west, bohemian area of town—a kind of Greenwich Village of Stockholm. Even as recently as the 1970s and '80s, it was considered a "rough" area.

Several of the writers and thinkers we interviewed in the fashionable cafe of the Hotel Rival (a renovated 1937 art deco treasure, now owned by ABBA's Benny Andersson) recalled that in their youth, their families discouraged them from going to Söder, as the locals call it. When we had tea with Paolo Roberto here (Paolo being the real-life boxer and martial arts champion who became an important character in two of Larsson's novels—see his interview in this chapter), we found out that, although he was considered the third most dangerous man in Sweden in his youth, he is now a businessman promoting events, producing TV shows, and importing olive oil from Italy, all from an office in fashionable Söder.

Even though Södermalm has been gentrified and the real estate prices have shot up (a fact highlighted by Larsson several times in the novels), the area retains a neighborly feel and a more diverse personality than other parts of the city. Each shop reflects the unique taste of its owner. We step in to an art gallery showing visual work in postmodern colors and multimedia collages. Nearby is a shop selling teas of the world, next to one selling beautiful hand-knit baby items. We look at the avant-garde jewelry creations of Efva Attling, who married popular singer Eva Dahlgren (who hails from Stieg Larsson's hometown of Umeå) as soon as Sweden's marriage law changed to allow gay marriage.

Most guidebooks will direct you to Gamla Stan (Old Town) if you want a quaint experience. But Stieg Larsson loved Söder, which I suspect he found more authentic and less pretentious than the more touristic Gamla Stan. As a result of reader interest in his books, Söder has begun to close the gap with Old Town for attracting international tourists.

August Strindberg, a leading novelist, playwright, and essayist of the late nineteenth century, set his path-breaking 1879 novel, *Röda rummet (The Red Room)*, in Södermalm. The novel is a biting satire of bourgeois life in the Stockholm of Strindberg's day. Many of Larsson's themes and ideas, not to mention his geographic sense of place, echo Strindberg. In Strindberg, readers can find the birth of a modernist critique of corruption, bureaucracy, hypocrisy, false moralism, and the failures of politicians and journalists. Larsson's novels provide an update of Strindberg, at least on some points. If the two could time travel to a meeting with each other, however, they would undoubtedly argue over their view of women. Strindberg famously declared that, "Every healthy man is a woman hater." Larsson, whose Swedish title for *The Girl with the Dragon Tattoo* was *Men Who Hate Women,* saw himself as standing against the all-too-pervasive results of Strindberg's philosophy.

The opening of *The Red Room* is set in the Mosebacke area, which is also featured prominently in the Millennium novels. In Mosebacke Square, Lisbeth will walk past Nils Sjögren's statue, "The Sisters," multiple times. In the center of the square, this artwork depicts two naked women fused together. Sjögren sculpted it on commission from the city using a mix of classical techniques from Greek mythology and heaviness more typical of the Stalinist era in which he did much of his work. Does Lisbeth think about her twin sister Camilla when she walks past this sculpture? Or does she think about Miriam Wu? There is a theory that, although Sjögren called the work "Sisters," the two women are actually lesbian lovers and represent the spirit of two young Swedish "sisters" who drowned themselves in an apparent joint suicide in 1911.

One end of Mosebacke Square is dominated by the Södra Teatern, a theater that dates back to 1859. Today, it is often used for pop and rock concerts, from the Red Hot Chili Peppers to Zap Mama. Upstairs and toward the back of the theater is a bar that spills out in the summer time onto a beautiful beer garden with a spectacular view of the city. In the Södra bar, Annika Giannini (Blomkvist's sister who is serving as Lisbeth's lawyer) meets with Lisbeth after the victorious trial is over. She reminds her, among other things, of her responsibilities to her sister Camilla in estate matters resulting from her father's death. The Södra location was also where Stieg Larsson's wake was held in December 2004 after a public memorial meeting.

Södra Teatern and Mosebacke Square are just a few steps from the penthouse apartment at Fiskargatan 9 that Lisbeth Salander purchases with 25 million kronor from the vast fortune she has cyber-siphoned out of the accounts of the criminal Hans-Erik Wennerström.

Like most things in Larsson's work, setting a luxury apartment at Fiskargatan 9 is not the product of a random walk on the local map. And in selecting his buildings, addresses, and locations to feature, Larsson had extensive research help from his partner Eva Gabrielsson, who is not only an architect and urban planner, but also an expert on Per Olof Hallman, a major planning and design influence on early-twentieth-century Stockholm. Almost every

building, landmark, and street address is selected for its subtle layers of nu-
anced meaning, including allusions to politics, history, art, sociology, architecture, gender issues, and more.

Fiskargatan 9 turns out to be the former address of Percy Barnevik, once
CEO of the giant Swedish-Swiss conglomerate ABB. The obviously upscale
apartment building at that address, with its distinctive green roof, turret-
style architecture, and commanding views of all of Stockholm, is the ultimate symbol of Södermalm's gentrification, as well as the more freewheeling
moral order of modern times. When the building was first constructed, it
was known as the "scandal house," because it blocked the previously pan-
oramic, spectacular view of the Katarina church nearby.

Percy Barnevik was at the helm of ASEA and its successor company,
ABB, for seventeen years throughout much of the 1980s and '90s. During
his tenure, Barnevik was known as one of Europe's leading businessmen—a
European equivalent of GE's Jack Welch. But his record was later blemished
by the disclosure of the large bonus (estimated to be around $150 million) that
he received from the company at the time of his retirement, and the subsequent collapse, several years later, of ABB's stock price. (Jack Welch actually
faced similar problems on his retirement from GE, with the disclosure of
some of the perks he had received.) While not larger than the biggest American executive retirement packages, Barnevik's bonus scandalized Sweden,
especially because the company charged that he had taken more than the
board had originally contemplated paying out. Several years later Barnevik
reached an agreement to return a substantial portion of the money.

Larsson's point of mentioning Barnevik and the provenance of Lisbeth's
apartment is another manifestation of his class-conscious mentality. I can
almost hear him chuckling at the thought of setting the girl with the dragon
tattoo and goth wardrobe down in the very same digs where Percy Barnevik,
captain of Swedish industry, once lived.

Lisbeth tries to live incognito at Fiskargatan 9. The name on the door is not
Salander but V. Kulla, an allusion to Pippi Longstocking's fictional home, the
Villa Villekula. Indeed, another highlight of our visit to Stockholm would be
a pleasant cold fall day spent indoors at Stockholm's Junibacken, a museum
and children's center devoted to children's book author Astrid Lindgren, Pippi
Longstocking, and all the other characters she created. Located in Djurgården,
Junibacken was built with Lindgren's active involvement. (Lindgren died at 94
in 2002, so she was able to see Junibacken through its construction and opening in 1996.) Aside from demonstrating the positive side of Sweden's social
democratic, egalitarian culture—hundreds of children playing delightedly,

quietly, cooperatively with each other—the visit also allowed us to find Lindgren's books for boys, featuring Pippi's male counterpart, the boy detective Kalle Blomkvist (known in English as Bill Bergson). Kalle Blomkvist is, of course, the nickname that Mikael Blomkvist pretends to hate. But it is clear Larsson undoubtedly liked both Pippi Longstocking and Kalle Blomkvist as a child. Perhaps it resonated with his own rural upbringing in the first eight years of his life with his grandparents and all the adventures he had in the vast northern wilderness of Sweden.

"One of the most interesting things about the Bill Bergson books," says Pippi'sWorld.com, a website devoted to Lindgren's work, "is the way in which the setup of the surrounding environment has been created by Astrid Lindgren. The surroundings are always very Swedish, rural Swedish at that. . . . The houses are very Swedish, red in color with white borders. . . . One of the main points in which Bill Bergson stands apart from other child detectives is that some of the scenes here are really quite bleak. The crimes can get to be very dangerous, which is a very unique feature in children's detective literature." Although Pippi herself is still well known and much loved by American children, Kalle Blomkvist has disappeared and is mostly out of print in English today. But it was interesting to learn about Kalle Blomkvist and his obvious similarities with both Mikael Blomkvist and Stieg Larsson.

Moving from Lisbeth's apartment at Fiskargatan 9 to the apartment of Mikael Blomkvist at Bellmansgatan 1, we find there are many good Larssonian reasons for why Blomkvist lives at this specific address. For one thing, there is an actual person named Blomkvist (a not uncommon Swedish name) who lives nearby. We heard he has grown tired of Millennium tourists ringing his bell, however. What's more, the actual address in Stockholm houses a very charming and picturesque building, approached from a third-story bridge. It is the perfect setting for Blomkvist, and might have even made a great home for Stieg Larsson and Eva Gabrielsson had Larsson lived to see the royalties from his books. The real-life configuration of Bellmansgatan, which sits along a sharp altitudinal angle that makes this street look more likely to be in San Francisco than in Stockholm, allows Larsson to write one of the most brilliant scenes in *Hornet's Nest* where everyone is watching everyone else and no one can be sure who the good guys and the bad guys are. There are enough watchers and watchers watching the watchers that Monica Figuerola wonders if a spy convention has been convened on Bellmansgatan.

But follow the place names and you will gain new levels of insight into how Larsson's mind worked. Bellmansgatan is named for Carl Michael Bellman, a Swedish poet and composer from the eighteenth century. Bellman is a central figure in the Swedish song tradition. Many of his songs allude to bars, restaurants, and other spots well known in the Södermalm of Bellman's day, just as Larsson's novels allude to more contemporary locations.

Unique in his time period, Bellman wrote odes to drunkenness and sexual pleasure. He emphasized the everyday reality of the common person and argued for living life in the moment—a radical idea in that era. He also played around with many different forms and genres, much as Larsson utilizes a wide variety of crime and thriller genres in his writing. It would not have been lost on Larsson, the Nazi hunter and antifascist, that Karl Liebknecht, a German communist and early denouncer of Hitler, loved Bellman's songs and even translated some of them into German.

Larsson, with his puckish sense of humor, may also have been alluding to "Bellman jokes," a form of Swedish children's jokes that rely on Bellman being perceived as a wild and crazy character.

Södermalm is home to many fine restaurants, but, in keeping with Stieg Larsson's relatively proletarian tastes, we find Blomkvist and Salander mainly catching fast food on the run. They both have an apparent passion for Billy's Pan Pizza, which is mentioned seven times in *Fire* and at least once in each book. (Lisbeth "ate a meal consisting of a Billy's Pan Pizza, which she heated in the microwave, and a sliced apple.") Having read about this unique Swedish delicacy in Larsson's novels, I imagined that my research trip to Stockholm might lead me to become an importer of Billy's Pan Pizzas to the U.S., where advance inquiry told me that the product has never been distributed. I bought a Billy's Pan Pizza at the 7-Eleven on Götgatan, which is where Mikael and Lisbeth frequently get their supplies of cigarettes, fast food, and other necessities. Back at the hotel, I heated it up in the microwave. But I was seriously disappointed in the taste and texture.

Ironically, as I was buying my Billy's, I noticed Swedish tabloid headlines in the 7-Eleven featuring stories about Noomi Rapace (the brilliant actress who played Lisbeth in the Swedish films) and her husband heading toward splitsville. They would officially divorce a month later in December 2010. Photos of Noomi as Lisbeth were staring out at me, much the way Lisbeth sees a bad photo of herself splashed across the tabloids along with giant headlines accusing her of triple homicide.

(Note to history buffs: Lisbeth's wardrobe, tattoos, hairdos, and makeup are described by Larsson as "goth"—a word we use in English without a second thought to describe this subculture that appeared in the U.S. and Europe in the 1980s and '90s. However, the historic Goths—the ones who attacked the Roman Empire—had their origins in Baltic lands that may have reached as far north as modern Stockholm. Götgatan, where *Millennium*'s office is said to be located and the 7-Eleven vends its fast food, means "street of the Goths" in Swedish.)

Considering Larsson's anti-Nazi stance, it is not surprising that Jewish characters figure far more prominently in his novels than in the actual population of Stockholm, which is thought to be around ten thousand. Jan Bublanski, the thoughtful, determined police inspector who ends up doing a good job on the Salander case despite all the obstacles put in his way, is Jewish and (sometimes) attends services at Adat Jisrael on St. Paulsgatan. This temple is perhaps the most nondescript I have ever seen anywhere in the world. From the outside, it looks like a mundane apartment building. Had our guide not pointed it out, we could have missed it. In Norrmalm, the Great Synagogue of Stockholm is as attractive and imposing a building as Adat Jisrael is low-key. But even this outward-facing symbol of Jewish life in Sweden must surround itself with security gates in an era of neo-Nazi threats.

Bublanski has a secret meeting with Dragan Armansky at Adat Jisrael. Armansky, a character who pops up just when he is needed in Larsson's novels to help solve problems (a modern-day Gandalf from *Lord of the Rings* in my opinion), has a complex ethnic background, Serbian and Croatian, Jewish and Muslim. Larsson makes efforts throughout his Stockholm-based books to introduce diverse and unusual characters that reflect the new Sweden of the last several decades, which is no longer the blond, blue-eyed stereotype, but one that has taken on a new international persona for the twenty-first century.

Larsson's novels reflect a keen interest in the geography of islands. He clearly likes their separation, their inaccessibility, and the watery boundaries that define them. In *Tattoo,* Larsson creates a fictional island, Hedeby, where the Vanger family lives. It is cut off from the mainland for a period of time on a September day in 1966, owing to an accident on the bridge, and it is at this moment that Harriet Vanger disappears, creating the basic mystery of the book.

In *Fire,* Lisbeth undertakes extensive travels. But Larsson mentions only a handful of specific places she visits. Three of them are islands or coastal port cities that begin with G: Grenada, Genoa, and Gibraltar. If we follow the clues Stieg Larsson left with his friend John-Henri Holmberg (see the "Mystery of the Fourth Book" in chapter 9), we understand that the unfinished novel was likely to be set on the huge and extremely remote island of Canada's Northwest Territories—Banks Island, which is ten degrees—about 700 miles—farther north than even Stieg Larsson's hometown of Umeå.

Although not technically meeting the true definition of an island, Södermalm is popularly thought of as one of Stockholm's fourteen islands.
This is Stieg Larsson's ultimate personal island, a place where he knew virtually every block and every building, where he had drunk coffee in every
coffee bar, and where he chose to set the characters and much of the action
of the Millennium trilogy. Here the conspiracies unfold, the murders take
place, and Salander and Blomkvist, aided by Erika and the staff of *Millennium,* Bublanski, Modig, Figuerola, Armansky, Miriam, Paolo Roberto, and
the rest, eventually figure it all out.

In Södermalm, Lisbeth and Mikael achieve vengeance and justice and
find answers and truth. Some of the good triumphs over "all the evil." And
they are now ready to launch their next adventure together on the next
geographic and moral island they find themselves on . . . in the fourth book
we are all waiting for.

ABBA, IKEA, VOLVO . . . AND LARSSON
an interview with Ambassador Matthew Barzun

Matthew Barzun is the United States ambassador to Sweden. Considering the cultural impact of Larsson's vision of Sweden on readers all over the world, we asked the ambassador about the effects of the books on foreigners' perceptions of Sweden.

Given how many Americans have read Stieg Larsson's novels, do you think they have actually had an impact on the way Americans perceive and think about Sweden?
Absolutely—especially when you consider the influence of the films in addition to the books. Americans of course already have lots of associations with Sweden through the familiar litany of famous brands: ABBA, IKEA, Volvo, Saab, Ericsson, etc. But the novels allow them to identify with well-developed characters, and that helps people get beyond generalizations. One question I got from a few people when I was back in the USA for the holidays was, "Do they really drink that much coffee?" My answer: "Yes."

Have you read the Larsson novels yourself?
I loved reading them all. I doubt that the first book would have sold so well in America if its title had been directly translated into English as *Men Who Hate Women*. We Americans are used to titles that are about the hero, not the villain.

What is your view of the situation for women in Sweden?
Sweden is rightly proud of its progress in the area of women serving in Parliament and also within the government ministries. When I talk to Swedish colleagues and friends, people often mention how more progress needs to be made in the business world at the board level and in senior management. That is an area where progress has been made in America, although more needs to be achieved there, too. In my agency, the Department of State, we're proud that three of the last four U.S. secretaries of state have been women. You could say this issue is in my DNA as my great (times four)

grandmother, Lucretia Mott, was a well-known leader in women's rights in America. She chaired the Seneca Falls convention in 1848, which was a seminal moment for women's rights in America.

Do you see parallels in the other issues Sweden is now grappling with—immigration, for example?
I think immigration is indeed an issue that is a hot topic of debate back home and in Sweden. I can speak to America more than Sweden, and I agree with President Obama who says that America is a nation of laws and a nation of immigrants—we must continue to be both and find balance. Sweden's history is different, of course, so there are no easy parallels, but seeking balance in a manner befitting a great nation will be key for both countries.

TEA WITH THE ONE-TIME "THIRD MOST DANGEROUS MAN IN SWEDEN"
an interview with Paolo Roberto

In The Girl Who Played with Fire, *the second volume of Larsson's Millennium trilogy, there is a long and fascinating cameo appearance made by the boxer Paolo Roberto, who comes to Miriam Wu's rescue after Miriam has been kidnapped by the "giant" who feels no pain, Niedermann. Paolo Roberto's fight with Niedermann is one of the great action scenes of the book, which was reprised dramatically in the Swedish film version.*

Roberto is one of the rare real-life characters who appear under their real name in Larsson's fiction. Most of Larsson's characters are either invented or composites of people Larsson knew or knew of; others are only loosely based on real-life people. But even though Larsson did not know Roberto personally, he knew he wanted to use him as a character in the book. Indeed, in the weeks after Larsson had sold the novels to his Swedish publisher and before his death, he e-mailed his editors to tell them that he would need to get in touch with Paolo Roberto, not wanting to use his name without ever having even spoken to him.

Paolo Roberto is a man of many roles and experiences. He first came to prominence as a young, tough gang leader in his teenage years. But he discovered martial arts and was able to channel his fighter personality into becoming a martial arts champion as well as a pro boxing champion. A Swedish cult film was made about his early life. He was Swedish national kickboxing champion, Nordic Tae Kwan Do champion, and held several world welterweight boxing titles. Since his retirement from competition, Roberto has emerged as a successful entrepreneur. He was active in the campaigns to relegalize previously banned pro boxing in Sweden and then to expand the number of rounds a fight can go from four to six. He ran for political office as a Social Democrat (although he has since moved in other political directions) and he now imports high-quality/low-production olive oil and writes about food and cooking.

Stieg Larsson died before he had the chance to make contact with Paolo Roberto. We sought out the charming, charismatic ex-boxer for an afternoon's discussion of his unusual experience of discovering himself as a character in three of the world's best-selling books.

You are one of a handful of real-life people that Stieg Larsson used by name in his novels. Tell us about the experience of finding yourself as a character in a best-selling novel?
It was a really strange experience to find myself in Stieg Larsson's book. I did not know about him, but he knew about me and I guess he decided I would be a good character to put in his book. One day I got a call from Norstedts, the publisher. They said, "We're sending you a manuscript of a book written by Stieg Larsson, who has since died. He put you in his book as a character and we want you to take a look at it. If you want to change something you can." Actually, I didn't change anything. But it was really, really strange reading this story that had me as a character. It was like Stieg Larsson had somehow gotten inside my head and knew the things I might think or say or do. Here I am reading the book and I am almost saying out loud, "Don't die Paolo," as the character that is supposed to be me gets beat up very badly.

Why do you think he picked you to be a fairly important character in the story?
When I was a teenager I was known for being a bad guy. I was good at being bad. I was a gang leader and I was ranked one of the three most dangerous men in Sweden. If I had not discovered martial arts, I don't know what would have happened to me. I have been a boxing and martial arts champion, a TV show host, and I've been in films and written five cookbooks. But probably the thing I am most famous for is how much pain I could take as a boxer. In my 1999 WBC world title fight with Javier Castillejo, my nose, jaw, and ribs were all broken, but I never went down. I was mad when they stopped the fight.

My guess is that being a guy who came out of the gangs and the streets to become a champion athlete appealed to Larsson. And he probably also liked the idea that I could take a lot of abuse without going down.

Recently, I met Eva Gabrielsson, Larsson's widow, on the set of a TV show that is very well known in Sweden. I asked her, "Why me?" and she said, "We needed that person and it was you."

Did you really say you have written five cookbooks?
If you had told me when I was seventeen and a gang leader that I would be writing cookbooks at forty, I would have kicked your ass. But when my

wife became pregnant with our first child, I started worrying about whether our children would lose touch with my Italian roots. So I started to write down all these fantastic stories I remembered my aunt telling me as a child when she was cooking. I found this was a really good thing to do for my own family, and the books became popular, so I did more of them. So far, I have published five books.

What do you think of the substantive political and social issues Larsson wrote about—and what's going on in Sweden today? For example, what do you think about the fact that this extreme right party, the so-called Sweden Democrats, have gained twenty seats in Parliament?

The fact that the Sweden Democrats have gained strength is very threatening to Sweden's self-image. They are pretty strong in places like Malmö. They attract young men without an education. And because the rest of Swedish society won't talk openly about the problems we have with immigration for fear of being called racist, these more extreme people get the opportunity to capitalize on common concerns and fears about immigrants, many of whom are out of work and on welfare. The government has to create an environment friendly enough to business so that business will begin to hire more immigrants and they will start to have good jobs, pay taxes, and become more a part of Swedish society. I am not against taxes, but taxes are still too high. I think the economy is on the right track now. Sweden is the strongest economy in Europe. But it could still be stronger, and bring more of the unemployed into the workforce, if taxes were reduced further.

You are in your forties now . . . and you are still very fit. Any health tips besides your family's olive oil?

Green tea is very good for you. And running is the best exercise.

STIEG LARSSON: TIMELINE OF A LIFE
by Julie O'Connor

1954:	August 15: Born Karl Stig-Erland Larsson in Skelleftehamn, 475 miles north of Stockholm to unwed teenage parents Vivianne Boström and Erland Larsson.
1955:	Stieg's parents move to Stockholm and he is left to be raised by his maternal grandparents in Bjursele. He will see his biological parents only occasionally (for holidays, etc.) over the next nine years.
1956:	Parents move to Umeå, seventy-five miles south of where Stieg is living. Vivianne works in a dress shop; Erland works as a window dresser and a graphic designer.
1957:	Stieg's brother Joakim is born but lives with his parents.
1958:	March: Stieg's parents marry.
1962:	December 20: Severin Boström dies of a heart attack at fifty-six. Stieg was deeply shaped by his beloved grandfather, a staunch antifascist and union activist.
1963:	June: Stieg and his grandmother move in with his parents and brother in Umeå, after he finishes second grade.
1966:	In a notebook, Stieg handwrites a story set in America.
	As a birthday gift, Stieg's parents give him a Facit typewriter and a telescope.
1967:	Father rents a basement room in the building next door for Stieg so he can use his noisy typewriter without disturbing others. "After that we never saw him," said his father. "He would come up just to eat and talk politics."

1968:   Grandmother Tekla dies of heart attack at fifty-seven.

The fundamental belief in equal rights and justice was instilled in Stieg by his grandparents. He absorbed his grandfather's stories of Swedish internment camps where thousands who were critical of Hitler and the Nazis were locked up. His maternal grandfather was a traditional Soviet-style Communist.

1969:   No later than this May Day, and possibly earlier, Stieg and his family march in two different parades: he as a staunch opponent of the Vietnam War, and his parents as supporters of the Social Democrats, whose prime minister had not yet fully broken with U.S. policy on Vietnam.

Massive popular protests take place in Sweden, with hundreds of thousands of people protesting the Vietnam War. The key organizers in Umeå are the Maoist groups, and Larsson begins working with them while still keeping to his own political path.

Summer: Stieg reportedly sees teenage boys rape a girl at a campsite in Umeå. He does not intervene. Later he contacts the girl and tries to apologize, but she says she could never forgive him. It is a painful memory that some see as having an impact on his entire life and of course on the creation of Lisbeth Salander as a fictional character.

1970:   March: Stieg begins writing for publication in the Umeå DX club's mimeographed magazine.

Around his sixteenth birthday, Stieg moves out of his parents' apartment.

Begins two-year vocational school program.

1971:   Submits two works to the science fiction magazine *Jules Verne* that are not published. Almost forty years later, in June 2010, the stories surface in an archive donated to the Swedish National Library.

Hitchhikes on a truck to Stockholm in attempt to go to Algeria but is mugged and forced to return home.

1972:   Begins research on racism and political extremism for a
             school project.

             Becomes active in Swedish sf (science fiction) fandom. Rune
             Forsgren and Stieg start their first fanzine, *Sfären*.

             Stieg is rejected by the Stockholm School of Journalism.

             Autumn: Meets aspiring architect Eva Gabrielsson at an anti–
             Vietnam War movement event in Umeå; they would become
             lifelong partners, collaborators, and companions.

             Stieg enters normal gymnasium school program for the next
             three years.

             Attends his first science fiction convention, SF•72, in Stock-
             holm. He would continue to write for and publish sf fanzines
             throughout the '70s. He edits and writes for *Sfären* and *Fi-
             jagh!* until 1978.

             Meets John-Henri Holmberg and they remain friends until
             Larsson's death.

             Works as an apprentice locksmith, newspaper delivery man,
             and dishwasher.

1973:   Stieg enters a short story competition run by the sf fanzine
             Cosmos Bulletin. In February 1974 he learns he has won the
             competition.

1974:   He and Eva start living together as a couple. Stieg joins a
             Trotskyist Party and begins contributing to their magazines.
             He also begins to use "Stieg" instead of his birth name,
             "Stig." However, his 1975 *Fijagh!* cover drawing he signs Sev-
             erin, after his grandfather.

1975–1976:   Stieg completes about a year of compulsory national military
             service. Smuggles Trotskyite magazine *Röd Soldat* [*Red Sol-
             dier*] into the barracks.

1977:   February 9, on the eve of a secret trip to Africa, Stieg creates
             two documents "to be opened after my death": a love letter
             to Eva and a "will" leaving his minimal assets to an Umeå
             Trotskyist group. From February to July, probably at the

behest of the "4th International" (a Trotskyist group), he brings aid of some type to the Eritrean rebels. A nearly fatal kidney infection and malaria force his return to Sweden.

Summer: Eva moves to Stockholm to attend architecture school; in August Stieg follows. Later, they move into a culturally diverse neighborhood of Rinkeby, where they will live for the next twelve years.

Starts a two-year stint at the Post Office in Stockholm while seeking writing opportunities.

1978–1980:   Stieg and Eva edit or contribute to several fanzines, including *Fanac, Science Fiction Forum, Feminac,* and *The Magic Fan.* He also becomes a board member of the biggest sf fan club, Scandinavian Science Fiction Association, 1978–1979. He is its president in 1980.

1979:   Recruited to work at the Stockholm-based News Agency Tidningarnas Telegrambyrå (TT) as a graphic news artist. Over two decades he writes many feature articles. Twice a year he reviews the top works of crime fiction.

Eva translates Philip K. Dick's sf novel *The Man in the High Castle* from English into Swedish.

1981:   Stieg and Eva spend summer vacation in Grenada. Later Stieg writes about the Grenada revolution in *Internationalen,* a Trotskyist publication, and together they start the "Free Grenada" bulletin, published until 1985.

1982:   Stieg begins his series of contributions to the British antifascist magazine *Searchlight,* which continue until his death more than twenty years later.

1983:   Stieg joins, is active in, and contributes magazine articles for an organization called Stop Racism, which is a precursor to and evolves into *Expo.*

1986:   February 28, Olof Palme assassinated in Stockholm—seminal event in modern Swedish history.

1987:   Stieg determines he no longer wishes to defend foreign socialist regimes of dubious democratic content and leaves the Trotskyist Socialist Party (former Communist Workers' Union).

1991:   Spring: Stieg publishes his first book *Extremhögern* (*The Extreme Right*), in collaboration with Anna-Lena Lodenius. (Lodenius reports that Stieg talked about writing detective novels even then.)

Stieg's mother, Vivianne Boström, dies of a heart attack at fifty-six.

The shooting of eleven people, and death of one of them, between August 1991 and January 1992 by the "Laser Killer," racist John Ausonius, in Stockholm, highlights growing trend of hate crimes and violence against immigrants.

1992:   February: Stieg Larsson calls Kurdo Baksi without knowing him to discuss the immigrants' strike Baksi is organizing and to encourage him to broaden it to include all people. They meet nine months later. Over the next few years they will collaborate on articles and publications, including incorporating *Expo* as an insert into Baksi's publication for a period of time.

Eva Gabrielsson's mother dies.

1993:   White Aryan Resistance magazine publishes Stieg's photograph and address, suggests he should be eliminated as an "enemy of the white race." Publisher sentenced to four months' imprisonment.

1995:   Eight people killed by neo-Nazi activity in Sweden.

Stieg and other journalists and concerned citizens come together to launch Expo Foundation "to study and survey antidemocratic, right-wing extremist and racist tendencies." First issue of *Expo* is published.

The first *Expo* office is in a basement on Lundagatan, in the Södermalm district. In the Millennium novels, Lisbeth Salander is said to have grown up in an apartment building on this street.

1996:   May: Attack on the premises of *Expo*'s printer leaves every window smashed. Also, retail stores that sell *Expo* are vandalized. The two leading Swedish afternoon newspapers come together to defend *Expo* by publishing the next *Expo* issue as an insert on June 10 in their own editions, in an act of solidarity.

Robert Aschberg calls *Expo* to ask how he can help. He contributes money but doesn't meet Stieg for months. Later, he becomes publisher and a member of the board. In 2004, he will open the door at Norstedts to get Stieg's novels published.

1997:   Stieg is still working at TT and ever more intensely on *Expo* as well. In his spare time, Stieg writes "a short story about a man who receives an anonymous bunch of flowers every year on his birthday," which eventually becomes the opening of *The Girl with the Dragon Tattoo*.

1998:   Due to economic problems, *Expo* ceases as an independent publication. Stieg becomes editor in chief, but the magazine is published for the next five years as part of Kurdo Baksi's magazine *SvartVitt* (*Black/White*). Stieg remains chief editor of *Expo* magazine and president of the foundation until his death in 2004.

1999:   Björn Söderberg, an antifascist trade union leader, is killed by neo-Nazis. Police find information about Stieg and Eva in one of the murder suspect's homes. A fellow investigative journalist had a bomb placed under his car, shattering his spine. Stieg and Eva are given police protection.

Stieg takes voluntary retirement from TT.

2000:   Stieg publishes *Överleva Deadline: Handbok för Mordhotade Journalister* (*Surviving Deadline: A Handbook for Threatened Journalists*) for the National Union of Journalists.

2001:   Stieg publishes a book about the Sweden Democrats, an extreme-right-wing party, co-written with Mikael Ekman. He warns that they could win seats in Parliament, which they since have done.

2002:   On summer holiday with Eva, Stieg begins writing what becomes the Millennium trilogy.

2003:   April: *Expo* again begins independent quarterly publication. *SvartVitt* stops publication after five years.

Summer: Stieg submits his novel to Piratförlaget, a Swedish publishing house. They never opened the envelope. Eva hand redelivers the manuscript after getting verbal assurances that they will consider it. They nevertheless reject it, unopened, with a form letter.

Foreign Minister Anna Lindh, a leading female political figure, is murdered on September 11.

2004: April: Stieg submits the books to Norstedts and is immediately offered a three-book deal. Having already submitted two, he delivers the third a few months later.

Stieg writes a provocative piece on violence against women in *The Honor Killing Debate*, a book of essays he edits with Cecilia Englund.

November 9: Stieg suffers a heart attack after arriving at the *Expo* office. He is rushed to the hospital and after an hour-long revival process, he is declared dead at 4:22 p.m.

December 10: Funeral and memorial service at Forest Cemetery, Stockholm. Later there is a public memorial meeting to honor Stieg at the Worker's Educational Association (ABF) Hall and a final gathering for friends at Södra Teatern.

2005: January: Nortstedts tells Eva that Stieg's request the year before to have the paperwork drawn up that would pass royalties on to a joint company Steig and Eva had planned to set up had not yet been done.

Eva receives a brown envelope from the Swedish government informing her that Larsson's entire estate, including half their apartment and the rights to his books, belong to Larsson's father and brother. She inherits nothing.

It becomes clear Stieg has died without a written will and Swedish estate law does not recognize common law marriage. Therefore his father and brother, not his lifetime partner, receive the inheritance.

August: Publication of Larsson's *Män som hatar kvinnor* (*Men Who Hate Women*) in Sweden. Later, the U.K. publisher will rename the book *The Girl with the Dragon Tattoo*.

Numerous issues begin to arise between Eva and the Larsson family. It's not clear exactly what is fact and rumor, but among the reports: Eva asks Larsson family if she can handle Stieg's literary legacy, supervise the quality of the translations, have literary and creative control of the work in exchange for a percentage of the royalties. They refuse. One of the most shocking stories is recounted in Eva Gabrielsson's memoir, where, as Eva tells it, Stieg's brother, Joakim, suggested that "I marry Erland, because that way this whole story of splitting the inheritance would no longer be a problem." After that, she does not speak to them again. The Larssons reportedly offer Eva $2.6 million to drop her pursuit of her rights and stop talking about all the issues; she refuses. Later reports have the Larssons offering to trade Eva their half of the apartment for the manuscript still on Stieg's computer. Eva declines.

2006:   Stieg is posthumously awarded the prestigious Glass Key Award for the best Nordic crime novel of the year.

May: Book number two, *Flickan som lekte med elden* or *The Girl Who Played with Fire,* is published in Sweden and earns the Best Novel of the Year Award by the Swedish Crime Fiction Academy. The three books, as well as the three Swedish films, will go on to win numerous awards all over Europe, Scandinavia, and the USA.

2007:   May: Book three, *Luftslottet som sprängdes* or *The Girl Who Kicked the Hornet's Nest*, is published in Sweden. In 2008, it also wins the Glass Key Award for best Nordic crime novel of the year.

The books are huge hits in Sweden when Sonny Mehta (publisher of U.S.-based Knopf/Random House) is handed a rough translation of the first novel at the 2007 Frankfurt Book Fair.

Autumn: The Larssons allow Eva to keep Stieg's half of her apartment.

2008:   January: U.K. publication of *The Girl with the Dragon Tattoo*.

May: Stieg's unwitnessed "will," dated 1977, which bequeathed his financial assets to the Communist Workers' Union (Socialist Party) in Umeå, is deemed not legally binding.

September: *The Girl with the Dragon Tattoo* is published in the U.S.

2009: February: The film version of *The Girl with the Dragon Tattoo* is released in Sweden and becomes a major hit.

April 22: Jan Moberg, a Norwegian former newspaper executive, launches a Web site to raise funds in support of Eva Gabrielsson's cause: supporteva.com.

May: First annual Stieg Larsson prize of 200,000 kronor (about US$32,000) for a person or organization that acts in the spirit of Stieg's journalism is awarded to Daniel Poohl, editor in chief of *Expo*. The award is established by Norstedts Publishing House together with Erland and Joakim Larsson.

July: The U.S. edition of *The Girl Who Played with Fire* is published.

2010: March 20–April 24: The broadcast of the Millennium films as a Swedish six-part TV series is a huge hit. Over the course of the year, all three films will be distributed in the U.S. and do strong box office by the standards of foreign films.

May: *The Girl Who Kicked the Hornet's Nest* published in U.S. by Knopf Doubleday. David Fincher begins developing the Hollywood version of *The Girl with the Dragon Tattoo*.

July: Larsson, already dominating the *New York Times* bestseller list for *Tattoo* and *Fire,* becomes the first author to sell over a million Kindle e-books through Amazon.com.

Stieg Larsson's Millennium trilogy is increasingly recognized as the dominant global publishing phenomenon of the current era, with total book sales exceeding 45 million copies by the end of 2010 and still going strong. Over 15 million copies have been sold in the U.S., or roughly the equivalent of recent works by John Grisham, Dan Brown, Stephenie Meyer, and Stephen King combined.

September: The Sweden Democrats, one of the right-wing groups Larsson had warned about before his death, win twenty seats in the Parliament.

December 4: World premiere of a stage production of Stieg's first novel at the Nørrebro theater in Copenhagen. Eva Gabrielsson is actively involved in the production.

2011:   January 14: Eva Gabrielsson announces she is ready to complete writing the fourth book based on the partial manuscript Stieg left behind. The title is to be *God's Vengeance*.

January 19: *Millénium, Stieg et Moi* (Eva Gabrielsson's memoir) is published by Actes Sud in French, as well as in a Swedish edition. U.S. publication is planned for later in 2011 as *"There Are Things I Want You to Know" About Stieg Larsson and Me* by Seven Stories Press.

January 20: The number of Stieg Larsson books sold worldwide reaches 50 million. U.S. sales alone are 14 million, of which 2.5 million are e-books.

January, February, March: A swirl of publicity concerning Eva Gabrielsson's memoir and the response to it by the Larsson family reignites the long-simmering debates of the prior six years over Eva's lack of recognition as an heir, her fear of a "Stieg Larsson industry," Stieg's relationships with his father and brother, and, most especially, the mystery manuscript for the fourth book, and future outlines and plots for what are said to be up to ten books.

May: *The Tattooed Girl: The Enigma of Stieg Larsson and the Secrets Behind the Most Compelling Thrillers of Our Time* by Dan Burstein, Arne de Keijzer, and John-Henri Holmberg published by St. Martin's in North America and publishers all over the world.

October: Planned publication of *En annan sida av Stieg Larsson* (*Another Side of Stieg Larsson*), a collection of his *Expo* writings on feminism, racism, rightwing extremism, and other matters, edited by current *Expo* editor Daniel Poohl.

December: Planned release of the American film version of *The Girl with the Dragon Tattoo,* starring Daniel Craig as Blomkvist and Rooney Mara as Lisbeth.

Acknowledgments

From Dan Burstein and Arne de Keijzer

First, a few important words about our co-editor and co-author, John-Henri Holmberg. John-Henri knew Stieg Larsson through a thirty-two-year friendship that lasted from Larsson's teenage years to his untimely death in 2004. John-Henri was able to bring to this book the insights and personal touches that result from that background. He also has deep experience as a publisher, translator, and editor, as well as being a reviewer and commentator on crime fiction, science fiction, and many other subjects, and is a member of the Swedish Crime Writers' Academy. He introduced us to many of Stieg Larsson's friends and colleagues, and to the rising stars in Swedish crime fiction today. He added immense value to this volume every step of the way.

We also wish to note that, like a good Swedish shrimp sandwich, John-Henri has provided much of the thought-provoking filling for this book, as evident from his many bylines. However, we have provided the bread and assorted side dishes. The selection and editing of the totality of this material is, in the end, our responsibility, not his.

Marc Resnick, our editor at St. Martin's, was an enthusiastic supporter of this book from the first moment he heard about it. We deeply appreciate the warm welcome and support we have been accorded throughout the St. Martin's organization. Many thanks to Marc and his assistant, Sarah Lumnah, for their help in producing this book quickly and efficiently.

Our agent, Danny Baror, once again outdid himself. He has taken our books to almost as many global markets as *The Girl with the Dragon Tattoo* has reached. We also deeply appreciate the support of Danny's next-generation partner at Baror International, Heather Baror-Shapiro.

A special thanks to our contributing editors Paul Berger, Paul De Angelis, and Lou Aronica for helping us through challenging deadlines and massive amounts of material. Brian Weiss and Hannah de Keijzer brought their considerable editorial talents to the book as well. Shirley Reiss was kind enough to rush to a Paris bookstore to buy Eva Gabrielsson's book the day it came out and provide us with a translated synopsis within days.

The production of the graphics in this book was accomplished under the creative eye of Julie O'Connor, who also took the photos of Stockholm that appear in this book and will appear in electronic slideshows on the Web in the future. Paul Pugliese did a masterful job creating the map of Söder-malm.

We benefited greatly from the insights of a wide variety of commentators and experts, both in the U.S. and Sweden, as well as interviews and essays that include the ideas of numerous people with special insights into Stieg Larsson and his books. We are grateful to: Karin Alfredsson, Alexander and Alexandra Ahndoril, Stephen Armstrong, Robert Aschberg, Ambassador Matthew Barzun, Andrew Brown, Craig Buck, Sarah Cleasson, Åsa Danielsson, Mikael Ekman, Jordan Foster, Judy Friedberg, MeraLee Goldman, Adam Guha, Icke and Lotta Hamilton, Börge Hellström, Christopher Hitchens, Laura Gordon Kutnick, Kasja Lindhof, Mian Lodalen, Anna-Lena Lodenius, Carl Loof, Per Loof, Ian MacDougall, Christopher Marcus, Jenny McPhee, Laura Miller, Daniel Poohl, Brooks Riley, Paolo Roberto, Anders Roslund, Melissa Silverstein, Lizzie Skurnick, Veronica von Schenck, Steve Smith, Katarina Wennstam, and David Wilk.

The Secrets books have turned out over the last seven years to be a cottage industry of our own family cottages. Our families, immediate and extended, have rallied around us, not only to support us in the strenuous work of doing a book like this, but with important research, interpretations of the Larsson books, interview questions, photographs, correspondence, and new thoughts about politics, philosophy, literature, morality, character, reactions to the Swedish films, and every aspect of our odyssey into the world of Sweden, Stieg, and Salander. This is a constantly engaging, enriching, and refreshing process that makes every page of the book better than it would be otherwise. With gratitude, thanks, and love, we appreciate all the contributions of Julie, Helen, Hannah, and David.

Personal Acknowledgments from John-Henri Holmberg

For helping out with memories, views, opinions, suggestions, and material, my thanks above all to Bim Clinell and Jacques de Laval, and also to Lena Jonsson, Mats Dannewitz Linder, Maria Neij, Roger Sjölander, Lasse Winkler, and those others who know I owe them. For endless and enriching discussions, suggestions, and opinions, my thanks to Evastina, and for standing my work habits, again thanks to her as well as to Daniel and Laura.

Contributors

Dan Burstein is the co-author and co-editor of the Secrets series, which was launched in 2004 with the global blockbuster, *Secrets of the Code: The Unauthorized Guide to the Mysteries Behind The Da Vinci Code.* Seven Secrets titles have been published in the last seven years, with more than four million books now in print in over thirty languages. The Secrets books have appeared on more than a dozen best-seller lists all over the world. Three documentary films have been made based on Secrets titles.

Burstein is a prominent venture capitalist who has been an investor in innovative companies since his first experiences in Silicon Valley in the 1980s. He is a Managing Partner of Millennium Technology Value Partners, a New York–based family of venture capital and private equity funds that is known for its leadership in providing alternative liquidity to leading technology companies, some of which include Facebook, Chegg, Twitter, Tellme Networks, Zappos, ArcSight, Airvana, Wayport, eHarmony, Green Dot, NetSpend, RigNet, and Epocrates, among many others. Prior to Millennium, Burstein served as Senior Advisor for more than a decade at The Blackstone Group.

Dan Burstein is also an award-winning journalist and author of numerous books on global economics, politics, technology, and culture. His first best seller (*Yen!*) focused on the rise of Japanese financial power in the late 1980s, was a best seller in more than twenty countries, and achieved recognition as the no. 1 business book in Japan in 1989. His 1995 book *Road Warriors* was one of the first to analyze the impact of the Internet and digital technology on business and society. In 2005, Burstein's book *Blog!* was the first in-depth analysis of the emergence of new social media in the first decade of the twenty-first century. *Big Dragon,* written with Arne de Keijzer in 1998, outlined a long-term view of China's role in the twenty-first century that has proven generally accurate in its forecasts for China's growth and development. Burstein's leading-edge journalism in the 1980s and '90s was recognized with Sigma Delta Chi and Overseas Press Club awards. He has appeared on talk shows that span the gamut from *Oprah* to *Charlie Rose,* with dozens of appearances on CNN, MSNBC, and CNBC.

Burstein's Millennium venture capital firm has nothing to do with the fictional *Millennium* magazine described in Stieg Larsson's novels. The similarity of the names is purely coincidental.

Arne de Keijzer is co-creator, with Dan Burstein, of the Secrets series. Over his writing career, de Keijzer has contributed to a wide variety of publications and authored books on topics ranging from international business to new technologies. For over two decades he was directly involved with the development of cultural, educational, and business exchanges with China, which led him to form his own business consultancy in the China trade. During that period de Keijzer also wrote the world's no. 1 best-selling *China Guidebook* (eight editions) and two editions of *China: Business Strategies for the '90s*. He turned to writing full-time in the mid 1990s and, together with Dan Burstein, wrote *Big Dragon,* an innovative look at China's economic and political future and its impact on the world. The team subsequently formed Squibnocket Partners LLC, a creative content development company whose first book was *The Best Things Ever Said About the Rise, Fall, and Future of the Internet Economy* (2001).

John-Henri Holmberg is a Swedish writer, critic, translator, and editor who first met Stieg Larsson at a Swedish science fiction convention in 1972 when Larsson was only seventeen. They would remain friends until Larsson's death thirty-two years later. Larsson showed Holmberg all three of the Millennium novels in manuscript form and discussed publishing strategies with him. Just before his death, Larsson also discussed with Holmberg key details from the planned fourth Millennium book.

As a translator, Holmberg has worked on some two hundred books, among them many by Stephen King and Lemony Snicket, as well as works by notables such as Vladimir Nabokov, Dick Francis, Robert A. Heinlein, Dean Koontz, Armistead Maupin, Mickey Spillane, and Donald E. Westlake. As a critic, his reviews of crime fiction have appeared regularly in one of Sweden's largest newspapers, *Sydsvenska Dagbladet,* for the past fifteen years. This body of work won him the prestigious Broberg Excellence in Criticism Award, as well as election to the Swedish Academy of Crime Fiction. Among his books are critical overviews of science fiction literature, fantasy literature, and psychological thrillers; he has contributed to the National Encyclopedia of Sweden, to international encyclopedias of science fiction and fantasy, and to many other standard works. Holmberg has also been active in publishing, working as an editor for a series of Swedish publishers. He was editorial director for fiction at Bra Böcker Publishing Group.

An avid science fiction reader since age six, Holmberg has been active in Swedish and international sf fandom for many years. He has published 212 fanzines; is a past chairman of the Scandinavian Science Fiction Society; has received the international Big Heart Award; and has been selected Guest of Honor by six science fiction conventions, among them the 2011 European SF Convention.

Alexander and Alexandra Ahndoril are a married couple who author their crime novels under the penname Lars Kepler. Their collaborative crime novels, *The Hypnotist* (2009) and *The Paganini Contract* (2010), were both best sellers in Sweden. In their individual work, Alexander is a novelist and playwright with nine highly regarded novels and some twenty plays to his credit; Alexandra is a critic, writing in Sweden's largest daily newspaper, *Dagens Nyheter,* and has published three meticulously researched novels based on historical characters: astronomer Tycho Brahe, Saint Bridget of Sweden, and the socialist activist August Palm.

Karin Alfredsson is an award-winning Swedish print and television journalist and thriller writer with extensive experience in international development issues. She has worked for *OmVärlden,* the magazine of the Swedish Agency for International Development Co-operation, and has also been a news editor and managing editor for several programs on SVT (Swedish Television), as well as a visiting professor of journalism at Umeå University. Her first book was the literary documentary *Beauty, Blessing and Hope*, for which she was awarded the Swedish Crime Academy's Debutant Award in 2006. Since then she has published three crime fiction novels featuring the Swedish doctor Ellen Elg, each of them set in a different part of the world.

Stephen Armstrong is a freelance journalist who writes for the *Sunday Times* (London), *The Guardian,* the *New Statesman, GQ,* and *Esquire,* and presents an occasional documentary on Radio 4. His first book was *The White Island,* a history of Ibiza.

Robert Aschberg is one of Sweden's most well-known and respected journalists and TV hosts. He is also the publisher of the magazine Stieg Larsson founded, *Expo,* and serves on its board. Aschberg was among the most forceful voices encouraging Stieg Larsson to find a publisher for his then-unpublished Millennium trilogy. Aschberg began his career as a reporter and columnist with Sweden's largest afternoon newspaper, *Expressen*. Later, he moved to TV3, where he has hosted a number of popular, often controversial shows, including the investigative hidden camera program *Insider*, which ran for thirteen seasons and twice won the prestigious *Aftonbladet* TV Award for the best program on social issues. He is one of the founders of the international independent TV production company Strix.

Matthew Winthrop Barzun is the U.S. ambassador to Sweden. He was among the early executives of CNET, the technology news site, and is also known for his grassroots fundraising work for Barack Obama's 2008 presidential campaign. He is a descendent of John Winthrop, the first governor of Massachusetts, as well as a descendent of Lucretia Mott, the nineteenth-century proponent of women's rights. His grandfather is the French-born American cultural historian and former Columbia University professor Jacques Barzun.

Paul Berger is the co-author/contributing editor of eight books, including four previous Secrets titles. His recent book, *As I Saw It: The Inside Story of the Golden Years of Television*, is an "as told to" memoir written with former CBS vice president Michael H. Dann. Paul's articles have appeared in *The New York Times*, *The (London) Times*, *The Washington Post*, and Wired.com, among others. He lives in New York.

Andrew Brown is a journalist and writer who is editor of the Belief section of *The Guardian*. He has won prizes for religious journalism and written well-received science books (*The Darwin Wars* and *In the Beginning Was the Worm*). He lived in Sweden from 1977 to 1984 and his book on that time, *Fishing in Utopia*, won the 2009 Orwell Prize for political writing.

Craig Faustus Buck is a print journalist, nonfiction book author, writer-producer of dramatic television shows, movies, and miniseries, and a feature film writer. He has written extensively on the issues that inform his first novel, *Go Down Hard*. His first assignment, for *The Staten Island Advance*, became a three-part investigative series about child abuse that resulted in a restructuring of New York City's child services. His short film *Overnight Sensation*, nominated for an Oscar in 1984, was about emotional abuse in marriage. His first book, *Betrayal of Innocence: Incest and Its Devastation* (co-authored with Dr. Susan Forward), was among the first lay books to explore the subject of incest. His second book, *Toxic Parents,* a no. 1 *New York Times* best seller, explored how adults can overcome self-destructive behavior driven by childhood trauma. He is currently in preproduction on a feature film he wrote and is also co-producing called *Selling Drugs for Gandhi* and is working on his second novel.

Paul De Angelis served more than three decades in the book publishing business as editor, editorial director, or editor in chief of such publishing companies as St. Martin's Press, E.P. Dutton, and Kodansha America. After becoming an independent editor in 1996, he founded Paul De Angelis Book Development, which assists authors, agents, publishers, and organizations in turning ideas and manuscripts into books. Since 1997 Paul has edited, contributed to, and co-published the quarterly guide to the Rhinebeck-Red Hook-Hudson area of the mid-Hudson Valley, *AboutTown.* In the past few years his main writing and research interest has been American culture and politics in its intersection with the wider world.

Mikael Ekman is the co-author of two books about the Sweden Democrats, a Swedish extreme right-wing party, including one with Stieg Larsson in 2001: *Sverigedemokraterna: den nationella rörelsen (Sweden Democrats: The National Movement).* For the last fifteen years he has worked for the Expo Foundation on a voluntary basis, researching right-wing extremism. He has also produced talk shows, the Swedish version of *Most Wanted,* and was executive producer for *Survivor* in Denmark, Norway, and Holland.

Jordan Foster is a freelance writer living in Portland, Oregon. He is a frequent contributor to *Publishers Weekly,* the industry trade publication.

MeraLee Goldman is the former mayor of Beverly Hills, California, and that city's cultural ambassador.

Christopher Hitchens is an internationally recognized critic, journalist, author, and speaker. An outspoken atheist and controversial pundit, Hitchens has written for *The Nation, Slate, The Atlantic Monthly, Vanity Fair, The Wall Street Journal,* and many other publications. Hitchens's television appearances run the gamut from *Hardball with Chris Matthews* to *Real Time with Bill Maher* to *The Daily Show with Jon Stewart.* His books include *Hitch-22: A Memoir* and *God Is Not Great: How Religion Poisons Everything,* both *New York Times* best sellers.

Laura Gordon Kutnick received her B.A. *magna cum laude* in comparative literature from Dartmouth College before pursuing film studies in France and earning a master's degree from the University of Pennsylvania. After working on several award-winning documentaries, she transitioned to raising a family and directing the Kutnick Foundation, which supports social justice and seeks a cure for Lyme disease.

Mian Lodalen is a feminist, gay rights activist, and prolific columnist, essayist, and author. Her first novel, *Smulklubbens skamlösa systrar* (*The Shameless Sisters of the Crumbs Club,* 2003), told the story of a journalist trying to find true love in Stockholm. Her latest, *Tiger,* portrays the sexual awakening of a teenage girl in a strongly religious community.

Anna-Lena Lodenius collaborated with Stieg Larsson on a path-breaking book about the extreme right, bringing her own research and experience to complement his. The result was the co-authored *Extremhögern,* published in 1991.

Carl Loof is a native of Sweden but grew up in London and southern Florida. He is a graduate of the University of Chicago and writes on a broad range of topics, splitting his time between Washington and Paris in hopes of encouraging transatlantic conversations on contemporary social and political issues.

Ian MacDougall has written for *n+1* and *The Guardian,* among other publications. Until recently, he lived in Norway, where he was a reporter in the Oslo bureau of The Associated Press. He has read the Millennium trilogy in Swedish as well as English.

Jenny McPhee is the American author of the novels *A Man of No Moon, No Ordinary Matter,* and *The Center of Things,* a *New York Times* Notable Book, as well as the co-author with her sisters Martha and Laura of *Girls: Ordinary Girls and Their Extraordinary Pursuits.* Her short stories and articles have appeared in *Bookslut, Bookforum, Brooklyn Review, Glamour, The New York Times Book Review, The New York Times Magazine,* and elsewhere.

Laura Miller is a senior writer at Salon.com, which she co-founded in 1995. She is a frequent contributor to the *New York Times Book Review,* where she wrote the Last Word column for two years. Her work has also appeared in

The New Yorker, the *Los Angeles Times, The Wall Street Journal,* and many other publications. She is the author of *The Magician's Book: A Skeptic's Adventures in Narnia* (2008) and the editor of *The Salon.com Reader's Guide to Contemporary Authors* (2000).

Julie O'Connor is the photo editor of this book and contributed significantly to the research and interviewing process. She also compiled the Stieg Larsson timeline that appears in chapter 11. She is an award-winning fine art photographer and photojournalist known for her "Doors of Tibet" series and is author of the book *Doors of Weston: 300 Years of Passageways in a Connecticut Town.* Her work can be seen at www.JulieOConnor.com.

Daniel Poohl is the editor in chief and CEO of *Expo,* the anti-right-wing magazine co-founded by Stieg Larsson. Poohl is also head of the Expo Foundation, formed to study antidemocratic, extreme right-wing trends in society and share that knowledge through lectures, seminars, and publications. In addition to subscriptions, lectures, and advertisements, Expo has received funding from the Swedish government, private donors, and, most recently, a grant from Erland and Joakim Larsson, Stieg's father and brother.

Brooks Riley is a former senior editor of *Film Comment* magazine and a critic for WNYC-TV. She has written for *The New York Times, The Village Voice, The Boston Phoenix, Opera News,* and *The Washington Post.* She also worked for Jean-Luc Goddard and as producer at Francis Ford Coppola's Zoetrope Studios. She was an executive producer on a number of films, including *Mee-shee the Water Giant, Puckoon,* and *Fuhrer Ex.* Recently, she has directed and edited nine opera productions for television and DVD, including Wagner's *Ring of the Nibelung* for the Deutsches Nationaltheater in Weimar.

Paolo Roberto, a real-life former champion boxer who figures prominently in *The Girl Who Played with Fire* and elsewhere in the Larsson oeuvre, was a dangerous gang leader in his youth. He was saved from a life of crime by developing an interest first in martial arts and then in boxing. Roberto was Swedish national kickboxing champion, Nordic Tae Kwan Do champion, and held several world welterweight boxing titles. These days, he promotes boxing and martial arts events and hosts a Swedish version of *Survivor.* He also imports olive oil from Italy and has written five books about food and cooking.

Anders Roslund and Börge Hellström are the authors of five international best-selling crime thrillers, including the current U.S. best seller *Three Seconds*. Several of their books are being made into movies. Roslund worked for years as a television news reporter and news director specializing in criminal and social issues. His investigative reporting into right-wing organizations in the 1990s led to multiple death threats. Hellström is a singer, guitar player, and the founder of a noted rehabilitation and crime prevention organization called KRIS (Criminals Return Into Society). A reformed criminal himself, he devotes much of his nonwriting time to counseling young lawbreakers and drug addicts.

Melissa Silverstein is a writer, blogger, and marketing consultant focused on women in social media. She is founder and editor of Women & Hollywood, the respected Web site for issues related to women and film as well as other areas of pop culture (blogs.indiewire.com/womenandhollywood). She is the producer and co-founder of the Athena Film Festival at Barnard College in New York, a celebration of women and leadership.

Lizzie Skurnick is a teen lit columnist for Jezebel.com and the author of ten teen books in the Sweet Valley High, Love Stories, and Alias series. Her literary blog, Old Hag (www.theoldhag.com), is a *Forbes* Best of the Web pick. Skurnick is on the board of the National Book Critics Circle and has written on books and culture extensively for the *New York Times Book Review*, *Times Sunday Styles*, the *Los Angeles Times*, NPR.org, *The Washington Post*, and many other publications.

Veronica von Schenck was a computer gamer who became an editor of computer magazines and editor in chief of the event magazine *Allt om Stockholm*. She published her first crime novel, *Änglalik* (a pun that means both *Like an Angel* and *Corpse of an Angel*) in 2008. Her second novel, *Kretsen* (*The Circle*), followed in 2009, and she is currently finishing her third. Her novels feature Althea Molin, a woman of mixed Swedish-Korean parentage raised in the U.S. but living in Stockholm, with profiler experience from the New York Police Department.

Katarina Wennstam, an award-winning crime journalist and nonfiction writer on violence against women, is also a best-selling author of crime fiction. Her Swedish-language books *The Girl and Guilt: A Book on How Society*

Views Rape and *A Real Rapist* won numerous awards. In 2007, Wennstam published her first of three thematically related novels on men's violence against women: *Smuts* (*Dirt*). Her most recent book is *Alfahannen* (*The Alpha Male*, 2010).